DEFINING ISLAM

Critical Categories in the Study of Religion

Series Editor: Russell T. McCutcheon, Associate Professor, Department of Religious Studies, University of Alabama

Critical Categories in the Study of Religion aims to present the pivotal articles that best represent the most important trends in how scholars have gone about the task of describing, interpreting, and explaining the place of religion in human life. The series focuses on the development of categories and the terminology of scholarship that make possible knowledge about human beliefs, behaviors, and institutions. Each volume in the series is intended as both an introductory survey of the issues that surround the use of various key terms as well as an opportunity for a thorough retooling of the concept under study, making clear to readers that the cognitive categories of scholarship are themselves historical artefacts that change over time.

Published:

Syncretism in Religion
A Reader
Edited by Anita M. Leopold and Jeppe Sinding Jensen

Ritual and Religious Belief
A Reader
Edited by Graham Harvey

Defining Hinduism
A Reader
Edited by J.E. Llewellyn

Religion and Cognition
A Reader
Edited by D. Jason Slone

Mircea Eliade
A Critical Reader
Edited by Bryan Rennie

Forthcoming:

Myths and Mythologies
A Reader
Edited by Jeppe Sinding Jensen

Defining Buddhisms
A Reader
Edited by Karen Derris and Natalie Gummer

Readings in the Theory of Religion
Map, Text, Body
Edited by Scott S. Elliott and Matthew Waggoner

Defining Religion
A Reader
Edited by Tim Murphy

Religious Experience
A Reader
Edited by Russell T. McCutcheon

Defining Judaism
A Reader
Edited by Martin S. Jaffee

What is Religious Studies?
A Reader in Disciplinary Formation
Edited by Steven J. Sutcliffe

DEFINING ISLAM

A READER

Edited by

Andrew Rippin

Routledge
Taylor & Francis Group

LONDON AND NEW YORK

First published 2007 by Equinox, an imprint of Acumen

Published 2014 by Routledge
2 Park Square, Milton Park, Abingdon, Oxon OX14 4RN
711 Third Avenue, New York, NY 10017, USA

Routledge is an imprint of the Taylor & Francis Group, an informa business

Notices
Practitioners and researchers must always rely on their own experience and knowledge in evaluating and using any information, methods, compounds, or experiments described herein. In using such information or methods they should be mindful of their own safety and the safety of others, including parties for whom they have a professional responsibility.

To the fullest extent of the law, neither the Publisher nor the authors, contributors, or editors, assume any liability for any injury and/or damage to persons or property as a matter of products liability, negligence or otherwise, or from any use or operation of any methods, products, instructions, or ideas contained in the material herein.

British Library Cataloguing-in-Publication Data
A catalogue record for this book is available from the British Library.

Library of Congress Cataloging-in-Publication Data
Defining Islam : a reader / edited by Andrew Rippin.
      p. cm. — (Critical categories in the study of religion)
   Includes bibliographical references and index.
   ISBN 1-84553-061-6 (hb) —
   ISBN 1-84553-060-8 (pb) 1.
   Islam—Essence, genius, nature. 2. Islam—21st century. 3.
   Islam—Doctrines. I. Rippin, Andrew, 1950-
BP165.D35 2007
297—dc22
2006023173

ISBN-13   978-1-84553-061-7   (hbk)
               978-1-84553-060-0   (pbk)

Typeset by S.J.I. Services, New Delhi

CONTENTS

Contents

Contents

PREFACE

Producing an edited volume such as this demands that some level of editorial uniformity be imposed upon a diversity of publication styles. I have attempted to provide a uniform but simplified transliteration system throughout the book, regardless of the original text. Only in this way is it possible to provide a meaningful index to the work; some inconsistencies do remain where I have judged them to be inconsequential for the reader but yet appropriate to preserving the integrity of each author's original text. Diacritics have been eliminated, although the distinction between *'ayn* and *hamza* has been maintained. References have been changed to in-text format such that in many cases the footnote numbers no longer correspond to the originals. The phrasing of the language of the essays has been maintained despite the antiquated nature of the wording in some instances and the non-inclusive language of some others.

I would like to thank Mona Sedky Goode of Victoria for her assistance with many aspects of this project—matters of proofreading, translation and source verification; her help and enthusiasm has been greatly appreciated.

Andrew Rippin
Victoria, BC, June 2006

SOURCES

PART I

Abu Hanifa, "The Epistle of Abu Hanifa to ʿUthman al-Batti." Translated from *Kitab al-ʿAlim waʾl-Mutaʿallim riwaya Abi Muqatil ʿan Abi Hanifa*, 34–36. Cairo: Matbaʿat al-Anwar, 1948. The text has previously been translated by John Alden Williams in his edited volume *Islam*, 162–64. New York: Washington Square Press, 1963; this translation is indebted to that version.

Muhammad ibn ʿAbd al-Wahhab, "Ten Things That Nullify One's Islam." Translated from Ibn ʿAbd al-Wahhab, *Muʾallafat al-Shaykh al-Imam Muhammad ibn ʿAbd al-Wahhab*, V, 212–14. Riyad 1398 A.H.; an English translation of a somewhat different version of the text may be found at http://islamicweb.com/beliefs/creed/what_negates_ Islam.htm [May 27, 2006].

Ibn Baz, "Ten Things That Nullify One's Islam: *Fatwa* on *Shirk*." Translated from the Arabic text at http://www.khayma.com/hazem/naqd.html [May 27, 2006]. An "official" but incomplete translation is available at http://www.fatwa-online.com under "Fatwa Categories - Creed - Shirk" [May 27, 2006] or directly at http://www.fatwa-online.com/fataawa/creed/shirk/9991120_1.htm [May 27, 2006].

Sayyid Qutb, "The Formation of Muslim Society and its Characteristics." Translated from Sayyid Qutb, *Maʿalim fiʾl-Tariq*, 61–73. Damascus: Dar Dimashq liʾl-

xi

Tiba'a wa'l-Nashr, ca. 1960; this translation is indebted to an English version of this text under the title *Milestones* which is widely available on the Internet.

M. R. Bawa Muhaiyaddeen, "The Spread of Islam." Material used with the permission of The Bawa Muhaiyaddeen Fellowship Press from M. R. Bawa Muhaiyaddeen, *Islam and World Peace: Explanation of a Sufi*, 86–96. Philadelphia: The Fellowship Press, 1987.

PART II

Ronald A. Lukens-Bull, "Between Text and Practice: Considerations in the Anthropological Study of Islam." First published in *Marburg Journal of Religion* 4/2 (December 1999): 1–21. © Ronald A. Lukens-Bull 1999 and used by permission of the author.

Dale F. Eickelman, "The Study of Islam in Local Contexts." *Contributions to Asian Studies* 17 (1982): 1–16. Reprinted by permission of Brill Academic Publishers, Leiden.

Abdul Hamid M. el-Zein, "Beyond Ideology and Theology: The Search for the Anthropology of Islam." Reprinted, with permission, from the *Annual Review of Anthropology* 6 (1977): 227–54. © 1977 by Annual Reviews www.annualreviews.org.

Clifford Geertz, "Two Countries, Two Cultures." In his *Islam Observed: Religious Development in Morocco and Indonesia*, 1–5, 7–9, 11–22. New Haven: Yale University Press, 1968. Reprinted by permission of Yale University Press. © 1968 by Yale University Press.

William R. Roff, "Islamic Movements: One or Many?" In *Islam and the Political Economy of Meaning: Comparative Studies of Muslim Discourse*, ed. William R. Roff, 31–52. London: Croom Helm; Berkeley CA: University of California Press for Social Science Research Council (NY) 1987. Reprinted by permission of Taylor and Francis, Andover UK.

Barbara D. Metcalf, "Islam in Contemporary Southeast Asia: History, Community, Morality." In *Islam in an Era of Nation-States: Politics and Religious Renewal in Muslim Southeast Asia*, ed. Robert W. Hefner and Patricia Horvatch, 309–20. Honolulu: University of Hawai'i Press, 1997. Reprinted by permission of the University of Hawai'i Press. © University of Hawai'i Press 1997.

Armando Salvatore, "Beyond Orientalism? Max Weber and the Displacements of 'Essentialism' in the Study of Islam." *Arabica* 43 (1996): 412–33. Reprinted by permission of Brill Academic Publishers, Leiden.

PART III

Duncan Black Macdonald, "The Muslim East as It Presents Itself." In his *Aspects of Islam* 19–45 ("Lecture 1"). New York: Macmillan, 1911.

Wilfred Cantwell Smith, "The Special Case of Islam." In his *The Meaning and End of Religion*, 75–81, 94–99; originally published New York, 1964. Fortress Press edition © 1991. Used by permission of Augsburg Fortress.

Charles Le Gai Eaton, "Religion is a Different Matter." Reprinted by permission from *Islam and the Destiny of Man*, by Charles Le Gai Eaton, 1–6, the State University of New York Press © 1985, State University of New York. All rights reserved. Text taken from *Islam and the Destiny of Man* (2nd edn) by Gai Eaton. © Islamic Texts Society 1994, reproduced here by permission of the publishers.

Jacques Waardenburg, "Official, Popular, and Normative Religion in Islam." In his *Islam: Historical, Social, and Political Perspectives*, 85–106. Berlin: de Gruyter, 2002. Reprinted by permission of Walter de Gruyter GMBH & Co KG, Berlin.

Norman Calder, "The Limits of Islamic Orthodoxy." In *Intellectual Traditions in Islam*, ed. Farhad Daftary, 66–86. London: I. B. Taurus, 2000. Reprinted by permission of I. B. Taurus, London.

Abdulkader I. Tayob, "Defining Islam in the Throes of Modernity." *Studies in Contemporary Islam* 1/2 (1999): 1–15. Reprinted by permission of the journal editor and the author.

Mohammed Arkoun, "Islam, Europe, the West: Meanings-at-Stake and the Will-to-Power." In *Islam and Modernity: Muslim Intellectuals Respond*, ed. John Cooper, Ronald Nettler, and Mohamed Mahmoud, 172–89. London: I. B. Taurus, 1998. Reprinted by permission of I. B. Taurus, London.

PART IV

Gustave E. von Grunebaum, "The Problem: Unity in Diversity." In *Unity and Variety in Muslim Civilization*, ed. Gustave E. von Grunebaum, 17–37. Chicago and London: University of Chicago Press, 1955. Copyright © 1955 by Robert Redfield and reprinted by permission of the University of Chicago Press.

Marshall G. S. Hodgson, "The Dialectics of a Cultural Tradition." In his *The Venture of Islam: Conscience and History in a World Civilization*, vol. I, 79–99. Chicago: University of Chicago Press, 1974. © 1974 by the University of

PART V

INTRODUCTION

As the world has been rocked by the emergence of self-proclaimed warriors on behalf of Islam, an issue, long of interest to scholars in the disciplines associated with Islamic studies, has emerged as particularly crucial. One does not have to look far to find statements issued by people as diverse as George Bush and Prince Charles, as well as media spokespeople "on behalf of Islam," proclaiming that actions of bombing, hijacking, assassination, and all sorts of arbitrary violence perpetrated by actors who proclaim "*Allahu akbar*" before their actions, are "not Islam." "Islam" in such a phrase frequently becomes defined by an implicit set of negatives and vaguely by the invocation of fundamental principles of human social justice which do not, in fact, serve to distinguish one mode of self-identification from another. The issue that lingers, of course, and that cries out for definition, is what do we mean by "Islam"? It may seem to many modern Muslims that the question has a simple answer and it is only those who refuse to "surrender" to its imperative, as the word *islam* in its root meaning suggests, who have any problem understanding the idea. Such a response clearly lies behind the frequent media statements that we encounter which allow the simplistic declaration of what Islam stands for. Yet the reality is that Muslims have debated this issue of identity since the earliest formation of the community, as indeed other religious traditions have similarly done. Those debates, the focal point of the first part of this Reader dealing with theology, set the stage for both the ideological and theological discussions which go on today and many of the scholarly reflections which comprise the main substance of this Reader. The goal of this book is, after all

1

is said and done, to bring into focus the nature of the "critical category"—in this case, "Islam"—that functions as a definition of the entire discipline of Islamic studies (itself only a discipline in the sense of an academic institutional category; rather, it is a conglomeration of methodologies, each of which bring its own set of assumptions to this definitional category) as well as a category within the multi-disciplinary framework of religious studies specifically. Indeed, understanding whether we are talking about a "religion" (whatever that concept might mean) or a "civilization" (weighted down in a notion of history) or a "culture" (evaluated in terms of its material accomplishments) or a "people" (in an anthropological sense) is a difficult and multi-layered matter of significant complexity.[1]

The structure of this Reader suggests that the question of what Islam is became a topic of reflection first within a theological (or religio-juristic more precisely, perhaps) setting. There was a group of people who called themselves "Muslims" and who understood themselves to be adhering to a certain group of practices and basic assumptions about the nature of existence ("beliefs") in common. But the fact of "difference"—with those "outside" who did not call themselves Muslims and with those "inside" who shared some of the same assumptions but not all of them—conjured forth attempts to define membership. This was an effort that was undertaken for very practical reasons. What self-respecting father would want his daughter marrying in violation of Muslim law, for example? The status of one's son-in-law is important (as is the source of one's food, it may be added), given the plain sense of the Qur'anic passage in chapter 5, verse 5:

> This day the good things have been made lawful to you; the food of those who were given the book [the Jews and the Christians] is lawful to you, and your food is lawful to them; and so are the believing women who are chaste, and the chaste women of those who were given the book before you, provided you have given them their dowries and take them in marriage, not in lewdness, nor as mistresses. If anyone disbelieves the faith (*iman*), his work shall be of no avail to him and in the hereafter he will be among the losers.

For the Muslim community, reflecting upon its own origins, the death of Muhammad and the end of his prophetic utterances stand as foundational events causing a shift in the understanding of authority in the community. Membership in the community became a matter of the acceptance of the various theories of authority which emerged in the wake of those formative circumstances. Muhammad is pictured as a single and sole source of authority within the world, a revelation from God in himself; he was a prophet and a statesman, able to wield power in the world to the glory of God. In his aftermath, being a Muslim was no longer a matter of following the authority of Muhammad in his person but rather paying obeisance to those who claimed to be representing him and his decisions. Discussed through the paradigmatic event of the struggles between the early caliphs, 'Uthman and 'Ali, over their moral right to rule and the implications of the assassination of the two of them, the question became reduced to a simple one: do one's actions affect one's status as a Muslim? Did 'Uthman's actions as ruler make him a non-Muslim and thus ineligible to lead the community? Does failure to live up to the law of Islam indicate that one has moved outside the fold of the Muslim community?

Historically, for most Muslims, the response was a pragmatic one. If a person claims to be a Muslim, then that person must be treated as a Muslim. Only God truly knows the status in faith of the individual, and thus, on a legal plane, the individual's rights and privileges of membership in the community of Islam must be honoured. Most discussions revolve around how to understand the Muslim who sinned. Is such a person "less" of a Muslim, as some suggested, or is such a person to be declared a "hypocrite" as others suggested; or, is it a matter that only has implications after death as reflected in the level of reward and punishment in the hereafter? The trends within these theological debates may be separated into four major streams.[2]

A group known as the Murji'a adopted a position dedicated to preserving the communal status quo and this is reflected in "The Epistle of Abu Hanifa to 'Uthman al-Batti." Ascribed to the early jurist and theologian Abu Hanifa (d. 767), the text is one of the earliest reflections upon the meaning of being Muslim. For Abu Hanifa, even if people do not follow the outward precepts of Islam, they must still be accepted as Muslims if they claim to be Muslims; only God truly knows their religious state. A profession of faith along with an inward assent to Islam was all that was required to confirm community membership; faith (*iman*) is "of the heart and of the tongue." This position is supported in Abu Hanifa's text by the notion that God, in the Qur'an, used the word "believers" to refer to those who had confessed their faith (and that alone) historically prior to the revelation of the ritual duties of Islam. Good works will be rewarded primarily in the hereafter. In the here and now, any increase in faith as manifested in pious works is really only an increase in conviction on the part of the individual. This doctrine was successful in history primarily because it eased conversion into Islam.

Other Muslims, however, felt that such a position did not provide the moral motivation that believers needed, although the same basic point found in the thought of the Murji'a was held in common. Some thus argued that there are degrees of "being Muslim." Works do count towards one's status in the community, although one can still be a believer and commit sin. There are, therefore, degrees of faith. This position is found as the fundamental thread in the later books of *hadith* (and thus the position is often referred to as that of the "traditionists") and it became the position associated with the theological school of al-Ash'ari which dominated classical Islam.

Yet another position in the overall debate became attached to those known as the Qadariyya. As with the Murji'a, a person who professes faith in Islam is considered a member of the community. However, those who can be observed not to be following the requirements of Islam are to be considered neither believers nor unbelievers, but somewhere in between; they are hypocrites. In practical terms, then, the only difference this makes is that it is, in fact, possible to have an opinion about the status of a believer's adherence to Islam.

However, another group took an activist position which proved disruptive to the early Muslim community. The legacy of the movement and the theological position lingers until today. The group is known as the Kharijites; in their most extreme form, they claim that all those who fall short of the total adherence to the Islamic precepts are unbelievers. Any of those who might happen to slip are thus deemed targets for an Islamic *jihad* against all non-believers; membership in the community, at the very least, provides protection from such attacks. The duty of rebellion against what might be declared an illegitimate government is seen as an absolute.[3]

This activist position has its connection to various manifestations of Islam in the modern world as displayed in the texts ascribed to Muhammad ibn ʿAbd al-Wahhab, Ibn Baz and Sayyid Qutb. The document entitled "Ten Things That Nullify One's Islam" is a popular one today, spread across the Internet in various forms. It appears to have originated with Ibn ʿAbd al-Wahhab (d. 1792) who was a prolific writer and the founder-figurehead of the Wahhabi movement, the underlying ideology of modern Saudi Arabia and of significance around the world today. The tract sets out, in point form, the limits to what a Muslim may believe or do and still maintain membership in the community. For modern readers, an update of that document was composed by the Saudi chief *mufti* Shaykh ʿAbd al-ʿAziz ibn ʿAbd Allah ibn Baz (d. 1999). When viewed within the context of Muslim discussions of defining community membership, this document shows evolution of those discussions through time and how the standards of membership become adapted to the situation of the writer; in doing so, the documents reflect the perceptions of the social and political pressures of the day. A comparison of the versions of the text from Muhammad ibn ʿAbd al-Wahhab and Ibn Baz illustrates this point quite clearly. The internal dangers facing Islam in the view of Ibn ʿAbd al-Wahhab in the eighteenth century are supplemented significantly by Ibn Baz in the late twentieth century by the threat of the West.[4]

Sayyid Qutb (d. 1966) is considered the intellectual spokesperson for contemporary Islamist movements. His vision of the submergence of Islam within the culture of *jahiliyya*—the antithesis of Islam that Muhammad had encountered at his time and which continues until today—such that existence itself has lost all value and can only be saved by a strict adherence to the world-view of Islam, led by a vanguard of devotees who will struggle against the powers of evil that manifest themselves in the governments of the so-called Muslim world, finds its most strident and mature formation in his essay "The Formation of Muslim Society and its Characteristics"; this comes from his most famous and most activist-oriented book entitled *Milestones*. As will be seen in the course of this Reader, this "totalizing" approach to Islam that Qutb sees as key—Islam must dominate all of life—is a theme that, ironically perhaps, has its resonances in the debates of scholars that make up the rest of this Reader. The scholarly (and often critiqued) tendency to speak of Islam as a single, overarching entity meshes with this Islamist perspective, adding a clear and controversial, if unintended, ideological angle to many academic discussions.

By no means do all modern Muslims accept such a bleak and destructive picture of the world. "The Spread of Islam," by M. R. Bawa Muhaiyaddeen, is written from a Sufi perspective with a particular goal in mind: that of proclaiming the unity of Islam which is taken to command that everyone should separate themselves from those thoughts, intentions, and actions that separate them from others. Religious intolerance and religious differences are declared at odds with the responsibility to follow the guidance of Muhammad. The individual must follow that guidance on the individual level and only then can the campaigning to correct the world take place. Religion in general and Islam specifically, in this view, become internal matters with the focus on the individual as the grounding of a "lived relationship" with the divine. The language is a familiar one, used in many religious traditions, but is one that potentially reduces the external indicators of membership to a bare minimum. It is a solution that was suitable for a context of living in a society which maintained a theoretical unitary sense of identity (e.g., the mediaeval Islamic empire) and is one that is amenable to the situation of a global civilization in which the individual is asserted over the identifiable elements of the collective such as many people experience today.

* * *

The contemporary study of Islam within the context of the discipline of religious studies does its work within the milieu of these competing conceptions that have been and are enunciated within the community. This is, of course, no different from the situation in Christianity, for example, where the universalistic vision of some people conflicts with the strident exclusivist notions of others. Scholars have been able to take advantage of the multiple methods of the discipline of religious studies to investigate the ways in which Muslims have and do conceptualize themselves as a group. Theology has thus been supplemented in scholarly discussions by anthropology, history, phenomenology and cultural studies, as the various sections of this Reader suggest.

Such reflections have taken the issue of defining membership in the community well beyond the theological attempts to set limits to the conception of the community. The problem, recognized early on within the study of any group of people who identify their membership in any given way, is that of competing visions: how do we, or even can we, reconcile internally contested claims of membership? Anthropologists have spent a good deal of energy debating the topic.

An introduction to the variety of anthropological (and social scientific in general) approaches, Ronald A. Lukens-Bull, "Between Text and Practice: Considerations in the Anthropological Study of Islam," considers the general question of what is being (or should be) studied when an anthropologist indicates that "Islam" is the focus of interest. The topic may be approached through consideration of, for example, local practices, written texts and/or standards of practice. The essay reviews the major trends in the anthropological study of Islam and suggests some directions for future study. Lukens-Bull puts forth the core matter from the perspective of the anthropologist directly: are what we call beliefs in local spirits, worshipping at saints' shrines and local festivals "Islamic"? The problem is not one unique to the study of Islam by any means but arises in the context of reflection upon any tradition that forms itself around an unchanging textual basis. In the Islamic context, however, the discussion has taken on distinctly ideological implications since it is a topic much discussed outside the scholarly world among those who stake a claim at being able to determine membership in the community and declaring such practices to be "un-Islamic." Various trends in the academic study of Islam have thus emerged to try to deal with the situation: some speak of the "great and little traditions"; others deny that a concept "Islam" exists at all; others look to insiders to define the range of "Islam"; others hold to a concept of a historical principle that organizes social life; others speak of a "discursive tradition." In another approach to providing an overview of the issues, Dale F. Eickelman in "The Study of Islam in Local Contexts" pays special attention to issues related to social class and ideology as they affect local practices and beliefs. Eickelman emphasizes the need to move beyond very specific time and place studies while also avoiding the essentialist, non-sociological views of earlier scholars.

The ideas and summaries put forth in the chapters by Lukens-Bull and Eickelman are expanded upon and illustrated by the detailed examples of studies provided in the following chapters in this part of the Reader. Abdul Hamid M. el-Zein's oft-cited article, "Beyond Ideology and Theology: The Search for the Anthropology of Islam," argues for the multiplicity of "*islam*s," each with its own legitimacy and none with a claim to primacy (as opposed to older essentialist theories). Religion itself is an "arbitrary category" and "Islam" has no function as a category of analysis. Meanwhile, Clifford Geertz's "Two Countries, Two Cultures" is a classic study from his book *Islam Observed* in which he tries to see what it is that would allow us to talk of an Indonesian Islam and a Moroccan Islam as having a similar set of symbols (a "family resemblance") yet being radically different in overall social context. Rituals and beliefs through a discursive tradition become key to this central definition of Islam but are also to be seen within their historical development. William R. Roff, "Islamic Movements: One or Many?" elaborates a version of this point of view by seeing Islam as a constraining prescription conveyed through the Qur'an and the *sunna*, with its manifestation varying through time and place. Social constraints are created through the discursive tradition of education and debate. There are, Roff suggests, many *islam*s with many differences between them but all having a "shared repertory of principles of individual and collective action" which can be called Islam. Barbara Metcalf's "Islam in Contemporary Southeast Asia: History, Community, Morality" looks at how the discourse of Islam finds its place in the modern nation-state, creating the marker of being a citizen or an identifiable group within a state. Metcalf underlines the very modern character of the emerging definitions of Muslim self-understanding and sees the sense of Islam emerging in that commonality of discourse across states that the modern situation has both created and facilitates.

Armando Salvatore, "Beyond Orientalism? Max Weber and the Displacements of 'Essentialism' in the Study of Islam," puts much of this discussion into historical perspective by examining the search for "Islam" as a readily identifiable entity reducible to certain essential characteristics. Salvatore points out that this essentializing tendency towards Islam has its counterpart in the creation of a notion of the "West" as a critical part of the emergence of ideas of modernity. Max Weber's attempts to understand European development through a contrastive exercise with Islam provides an often unacknowledged basis for later studies of Islam as, Salvatore argues, they became displayed in especially American "Area Studies" and modernization theory.[5]

* * *

The attention that social scientists pay to the role of Islam in social and political formation and the discursive element of Islam in an individual's construction of daily reality is clear. But another approach to the entire question comes from what we might describe as the religious approach: using a concept of "religion," Islam can be described as a category within that overall classification.

Duncan Black Macdonald's "The Muslim East as It Presents Itself" is an older essay, written at a time when the nature of the assumed audience of a scholar's work was much different from what it is today; in that regard, it is a good illustration of what is meant by the work of missionizing Orientalists. However, the essay does provide an attempt to grapple sympathetically with the definition of Islam as it is encountered by somebody self-consciously coming from a Christian perspective: the outsider–insider dichotomy that underlies the religious approach. The commonality of faith is emphasized and the need to overcome misinformation—which can stem from outsiders as well as Muslims themselves—is seen to be essential. That sense of sympathetic approach to Muslims and Islam is at the core of Wilfred Cantwell Smith, "The Special Case of Islam," from his *The Meaning and End of Religion*, a work that has stood as the foundation of the discipline of religious studies from its formation; only in recent decades has its stance been subject to robust interrogation for its avoidance of the fundamental critical questions concerning the concept of religion itself and the assumptions within that sympathetic approach. Smith focuses on the idea that Islam is a concept which is defined by the community itself, in that same sense of assertiveness that Macdonald comments upon—something that Smith traces to a process of internal community reification. Described as a "coherent and closed system," Smith's Islam is the textually based religion defined by its legal structures but it is also one that is subject to historical variation through the process of interpretation.

The special status of religion as requiring that sympathy that is core to writers such as Madonald and Smith is made explicit in Charles Le Gai Eaton, "Religion is a Different Matter." Eaton poses the question of what happens when one does not write about Islam from an insider's perspective: the "whole structure falls apart" for such a person if the central tenet of belief is not acknowledged. The life of a Muslim cannot "make sense" if the totality of the orientation towards belief is not experienced as the key to Islam. Writing from a self-asserted position of an "insider," Eaton defines Islam as a unity in diversity, focussed around a sacred community of people devoted to the confession of faith in God. He recognizes, however, that differences of opinion on many matters render any simple definition problematic.

The sense in which these approaches are not sufficiently expansive, being as they are focused on textual and elitist traditions of beliefs, is certainly a critique that has been adopted within religious studies, as it has in anthropology. The idea of "popular" versus "official" religions, attached to notions of social status and control of information, especially in the pre-literate, pre-printing press periods of existence, provides one solution to the lack of definitional certainty that underlies many of the discussions of Islam as a "religion" in moving away from a picture dominated by the elitist sense. If we declare certain practices to be "popular" (meaning usually without official sanction) then that can clarify definitional boundaries while asserting the existence of a "core" about which we can talk quite plainly. Such is what Jacques Waardenburg in his "Official, Popular, and Normative Religion in Islam" discusses.

Waardenburg tackles the popularly repeated notion that Islam has no central authority by which to define itself, a position which implicitly postulates a definition of religion that sees itself as an institution somehow apart from, and separate from, other elements of the society. He suggests that the position internal to the community associated with Ibn Taymiyya and lasting down until today in Islamist circles, as pointed out above, postulates a core of Islam and then sees some items that are practised by Muslims as "foreign" accretions. This is a moral position, of course: that is, it is those behaviours with which one disagrees that are declared foundationless and an "abomination," such decisions being supported through a process of judicial reflection upon the Qur'an and the *sunna*. Such a position is, of course, precisely what scholars have also adopted. While they have not accepted the moral evaluation of thinkers such as Ibn Taymiyya they have, in fact, accepted it implicitly by imposing moral criteria of what defines (appropriate) religious behaviour without questioning the status of that category. For example, Waardenburg notes the often-perceived "decline" of popular Islam in modern times which implicitly associates "popular" with "irrational." But other ways of categorizing popular Islam may be postulated as well: that which is fostered by those outside "recognized religious leadership" and that which provides emotional support at times of stress. This bifurcation of categories emerges because, as is always observed, there is no central authority by which Islam can be defined and controlled. Adherence to the Qur'an and the *sunna* becomes the fundamental characteristic and, as such, a class of people charged with the responsibility for administering that law and defining doctrine emerges, often with strong connections to the state-governing apparatus which provides employment for the learned classes.

Waardenburg also adds that a concept of normative Islam—taken to mean a collection of "norms" which govern life, that being the *shari'a*—can be (and often is) distant from Islam as it is practised. With no central authority there is no means of enforcing this collection of norms; yet, especially through the vehicle of language (the use of the Arabic script for many languages but also the administrative use of Arabic throughout the empire) and other factors such as a geographical definitional limitation, there has emerged a uniformity that might not otherwise have been expected.

Norman Calder speaks of "The Limits of Islamic Orthodoxy" in an innovative and controversial way. He posits that membership in Islam was, and can be, defined by adherence to a set of beliefs constrained within certain internally agreed-upon boundaries, and that the differences in practice were insignificant: Islam is an orthodoxy and not an orthopraxy, to invert what has become a popularly accepted characterization. Calder argues, picking up on a thought that is familiar from the earliest discussions about membership in the community, that acts have classically not been taken into account by Muslims in determining the status of the individual as eligible for eternal existence in paradise. It is not the neglect of acts that puts one outside the fold of Islam; only the outright denial of the incumbency of an act renders such a judgement. Calder argues that Islam is a religion of community within salvation history which encapsulates itself within a set of literary genres in which scholars reflect upon the experience of the community and use the existence of alternative traditions as a foil for definition of orthodoxy.

The idea that there might be a difference between Muslim practice and "Islam"— that is, one should not take what Muslims do as a definition of Islam—is the basis of the earliest discussions about membership but also provides the starting point and context for contemporary reflection. The question is critical today, as Abdulkader Tayob points out in "Defining Islam in the Throes of Modernity," because the contemporary quest to find the value in religion has driven the question of what the core values are which must be maintained in order to continue to hold that Islam has value in the modern context. That Islam is a meaningful category of discussion is recognized at least at the symbolic and social level of daily life; but the modern context renders some attempts problematic. The challenge of secularism, the dismissal of the transcendental, and the triumph of the rational all combine to undermine Islam as a viable world-view; responses to this are illustrated by modern thinkers such as Fazlur Rahman, Isma'il al Faruqi and Seyyed Hossein Nasr, all of whom argue for a way to preserve the relevance of Islam, when defined in a certain way. All positions lead to an "intense debate" on the "true and authentic meaning of Islam."

As discussed briefly in Tayob's overview, Mohammed Arkoun provides another example of how to grapple with the question when he expounds on the three words that form the basis of the beginning of his title, "Islam, Europe, the West: Meanings-at-Stake and the Will-to-Power." Arkoun refers to these as "spheres of production of contemporary history" that have become mired in ideological interpretation. New terminology is introduced: "Islam-as-fact" isolates the use by the state of religion for legitimation, a process long seen in the Muslim world, and one separate from what Arkoun calls the "Qur'an-as-fact" which sets the epistemological basis of Muslim existence.

* * *

The historical question of what we mean by Islam has become another hotly debated topic and even the subject of some popular exposés conducted in the mainstream media as a result of what has become called the work of "revisionist" historians. The genealogy of these ideas are mired in a debate tinged with an ideological and polemical character. The earliest Christian writers, after all, liked to picture Islam not as revelation but as a derivative (via Satan) of Christianity or, even worse, Judaism. Islamic identity, therefore, was something created wilfully on the basis of something else and only emerged after a period of time. The association of these polemical ideas with later scholarly notions developed by people such as Joseph Schacht and especially John Wansbrough has been quite strong among those who wish to discredit scholarly insights into Islam and who are apologists for Islam (and, in one of those perversions of scholarship, has also found favour with certain anti-Muslim groups who wish to continue the tone and attitudes of mediaeval polemic). In focusing on law, Joseph Schacht argued for the late emergence of a firm sense of what today would be deemed (by normative Islam) to make Islamic law "Muslim": the authority of the Muhammad. Arguing on the basis of the theoretical elaborations of the sources of the law in al-Shafi'i, Schacht saw such a position—deemed to be a defining characteristic of what "Islam" is—as only emerging after about two centuries of debate. Wansbrough took the position further: the first three centuries of "Islam" could not be recovered from history because they had been absorbed by a retrospective projection of Islamic identity that emerged well into the 'Abbasid period. Even the Qur'an, the text that historians had always assumed to be contemporaneous with Muhammad, emerged in the third Muslim century at best. The pivotal elements of normative Muslim identity, therefore, were late to emerge and what we now call Islam did not exist prior to that point. Wansbrough certainly acknowledged that elements of the Qur'an (and other such central elements of Muslim identity) existed before this time (he even suggests that some are pre-Muhammadan); the question really comes down to our central one of definition: What is this thing we call Islam, whose definition of it shall we use and what evidence of it do we need to assert its existence? These are general historiographical questions which, while currently controversial in the context of the study of the emergence of Islam, underlie every reflection upon the subject of academic research we call Islamic studies.[6]

Gustave von Grunebaum's "The Problem: Unity in Diversity" brings the view of the historian and literary scholar to bear on the question of the relationship between Muslim civilization and Islamicized local cultures, and whether the two elements are separable. Von Grunebaum points out how, throughout history, Muslim writers have characterized groups of Muslims living in other countries. But such an analysis does not often go beyond the anecdotal and von Grunebaum sets out schemes by which the universal culture of Islam adjusts to local cultures, using typically Islamic tools (and language), such as appealing to consensus. In the end, the overriding factor is postulated to reside in the individual and his or her willingness to identify with the overarching vision of Islam (and the relationship to God) without concern for variation from that perceived (and accepted) norm.

Marshall Hodgson's "The Dialectics of a Cultural Tradition," from his *The Venture of Islam*, puts forth the notion (despite the title of the book) that we need a new range of vocabulary to clarify the matter: thus he coined (and the words continue to have some success in the discipline) the idea of the Islamicate world—a civilizational concept that conveys the notion of a "high culture" that brings unity to the diversity of culture which can be declared separate from the ideas of religion in the concept known as Islam. Hodgson's notable achievement is to bring a broader perspective to the study of history than the "standard" focus on the Arab world. The move away from "Arabism" and textual analysis and putting the Islamic world within the context of world history are clearly his motivating drivers: but the question of what can serve to define the area and the concept being discussed remains. The ever-changing and ever-disputed nature of Islam is such, according to Hodgson, that any sense of unity that does emerge cannot be traced to an "attribute of Islam as such." The unity emerges in the patterns of relationships that developed through history between the Islamic tradition and different cultural settings: it cannot be reduced to the ultimate commitments of the religion but conveys far more in terms of social patterns in the broadest sense.

The separation between religion and civilization in the manner proposed by Hodgson comes in for analysis in Bryan Turner, "Conscience in the Construction of Religion: A Critique of Marshall G. S. Hodgson's *The Venture of Islam*." Turner points to Hodgson's definition of religion as a personal, private, inner activity and questions whether it is conceptually viable to separate this from a "sociological explicable phenomenon" and thus concludes that a postulated distinction between Islam and an Islamicate civilization is untenable.

Meanwhile, Richard Bulliet's focus on "Conversion as a Social Process," approaches the question of membership through attention to what he calls "social conversion" as it plays out in the context of community. Religious leaders and their offices, legal structures, language, and personal names all mark aspects of this process. Conversion also involves, Bulliet points out, the unlikelihood of lowering of social status of the individual: Islam was the religion of the empire and Arab became synonymous with Muslim. For those whose status under the Arabs was not high, even if they did convert, the option, he argues, must have been worse. Observing the emergence of a religious community in this manner brings out what might be argued to be the key elements in community definition and can be viewed as a historical process, affording us a dynamic picture of the emergence of the Muslim community.

* * *

Discussions about Islam are not all carried on in scholarly treatises. The role of the popular media has drawn a good deal of attention in reinforcing categories that are based not on scholarly critical reflection but upon the acceptance of media images; such images are ultimately expressions of power, often overtly political or ideological. Perhaps no name is associated more in the popular mind with the question of the definition of Islam than Edward Said, whose *Orientalism* argued that the impositions of conceptualizations of Islam were tools in the hands of colonialist powers to control and to manage the "Other" they encountered in their empires. Said saw this happening not only in the work of the Orientalists, but, as he explores in "Islam and the West," in the image of Islam portrayed in the Euro-American media. The images associated with Islam among the general populace are argued to reveal more about the West than they do about Islam. The oil crisis and the Iranian revolution in the 1970s marked the emergence of what had always been perceived in Europe to be a latent power which had, until that time, been controlled by being encapsulated in an association with the demonic and the immoral.

Said's "Islam and the West" originates in his book entitled *Covering Islam: How the Media and the Experts Determine How We See the Rest of the World.* The essay examines the reflections of scholarly analyses for the way that they become embedded in the popular press especially. Scholars become mouth pieces for policy makers; scholars are frequently informed by the media on information about circumstances in distant places; and forming the full circle, the media drives policy makers in their decisions by influencing public opinion. The notion that Islam is to be feared, that Islam is a fervent and growing religion, that Israel is the only Middle Eastern home of democracy are all familiar themes of attention to the Islamic world in the popular imagination, themes which Said draws out for analysis of their implications.[7]

An informed reflection on some of Said's points from the point of view of a journalist is to be found in Edward Mortimer, "Islam and the Western Journalist." Edward Mortimer is a foreign specialist and editorial writer for *The Times* of London. The journalist becomes an "expert" but only on the basis of a rapid assimilation of information said to represent the truth as ascertained through personal experience. Mortimer points out that academics do not always get their story straight either. But the generalizations about Islam as a religion like any other religion have been, for journalists as for others, facile ways of dealing with the complexities of the world. Mortimer gets at the core issue that demonstrates the relevance of all the modern discussions that are the focus of this reader: the problem is the common "assumption that Muslims are different and that their behavior can *only* be explained in terms of Islam." Social, political and economic factors cannot be explained away through blithe assertions of religious commitment. That is a lesson that applies not only to journalists but to all those who grapple with the complexities of the world around us.

* * *

Islam, then, as a critical category in the study of religion, has been extensively debated. The question of what it is remains a highly controversial one for those who choose to identify themselves as members of the community, especially today when the notion of "Islamic" terrorists is so much a part of the contemporary world-view in many countries. The question is most pressing, perhaps, for those who do not wish to have their identity merged with people who advocate violence in support of religion and who wish to impose laws deemed to offend modern sensibilities; for them, the issue of how to define Islam constitutes the major task of re-visioning an orientation to the world that is understood to still have relevance for individuals today. That task is approached from every angle and by every means, with popular preachers and refined intellectual academics trying to convince others of the need to preserve Islam while defining it in a range of ideas that will not be the source of tension when put in conjunction with contemporary moral, ethical, political, economic, and social principles.

For academics, the study of Islam is a microcosm of the discussions that are protracted within the disciplines that make up religious studies. Just what is it we are studying? What assumed categories of thought are being used to approach the topic? How do we reconcile what we are told about the religion by insiders with what we might observe as historians or sociologists? While many scholars consider Islamic studies to be rather a backwater in the discipline of religious studies when it comes to explicit treatments of methodology—perhaps partially due to the attention that its methods and perspectives have drawn from people such as Edward Said—the evidence of this Reader is that the basic issues are subject to lively debate and are such that the fundamental questions cannot but be a significant factor in every scholar's consideration of their endeavours. We may not be any closer to an answer to the question but we certainly do have something to contribute both to public understanding of the debates in Islam and to the discussions in religious studies regarding the hows, whys and whats of our study.

Notes

1. A number of works have appeared recently that are relevant to this general topic of the definition of Islam. For an in-depth analysis, see, for example, Daniel Varisco, *Islam*

Obscured: The Rhetoric of Anthropological Representation (New York: Palgrave Macmillan, 2005).

2. The following summary of the positions of the early theological schools is based upon material in my *Muslims: Their Religious Beliefs and Practices*, 3rd ed. (London: Routledge, 2005), chapter 5.

3. The question of the duty that Muslims have to try to stop other people from doing wrong is extensively and compellingly treated in Michael Cook, *Commanding Right and Forbidding Wrong in Islamic Thought* (Cambridge: Cambridge University Press, 2000).

4. I have analysed these documents in Andrew Rippin, "Islam and the Politics of Violence: Defining the Muslim Community," in *The Twenty-first Century Confronts its Gods: Globalization, Technology and War*, ed. David Hawkin (Albany, NY: SUNY Press, 2004), 129–40. I am indebted to Rosalind Gwynne of the University of Tennessee for providing me with a copy of the text by Ibn 'Abd al-Wahhab translated here; Dr. Gwynne's online article "Al-Qa'ida and al-Qur'an: The 'Tafsir' of Usamah bin Ladin," available at http://web.utk.edu/~warda/bin_ladin_and_quran.htm first piqued my interest in this document. A revised version of this paper has now been published: Rosalind W. Gwynne, "Usama bin Ladin, the Qur'an and Jihad," *Religion* 36 (2004): 61–90.

5. Salvatore's ideas and approach to political Islam are developed further and in a broader context in his *Islam and the Political Discourse of Modernity* (Reading: Ithaca Press, 1997).

6. An overview of the historiographical issues with some excellent analysis of the issues raised is to be found in Chase F. Robinson, "Reconstructing Early Islam: Truth and Consequences," in *Method and Theory in the Study of Islamic Origins*, ed. Herbert Berg (Leiden: Brill, 2003), 101–34. His call is to "abandon 'Islam' as a term of historical explanation" (134).

7. Said's influence on the study of religion has become a field of study on its own. A sense of the issues at stake can be gathered from Mathieu E. Courville, "The Secular Masks of Religion: A (Re)constructive Critique of W.D. Hart's *Edward Said and the Religious Effects of Culture*," *Studies in Religion/Sciences Religieuses* 34 (2005): 233–49; the point is made in this article of Said's appreciation of the work of Marshall Hodgson as a part of a solution towards understanding religion and its place in secularism.

PART I

THEOLOGY

THE EPISTLE OF ABU HANIFA TO ʿUTHMAN AL-BATTI

Abu Hanifa

This epistle is sent from Abu Hanifa to ʿUthman al-Batti. Peace be on you. I extol God, of whom there is no other god than Him, to you. I counsel you in the fear and obedience of God; God suffices as reckoner and compensator. Your epistle has reached me and I have understood your advice in it. You say that you were moved to write it by what I had written to preserve you in good actions and to provide you with good advice. You mention that it has reached you that I belong to the Murjiʾa, and that I claim that a believer may err, and that this distresses you, and that there is really no excuse among the people of God for a thing which keeps one apart from God; that there is nothing by which one may be guided in what people create and innovate; that moral commands are only in found in what the Qurʾan states and in what Muhammad preached and his Companions agreed upon until the people became divided; and that anything beyond this is human innovation and human creation.

You must understand what I am writing to you. Keep your thoughts to yourself and fear Satan entering upon you; God preserve us both in obedience to Him—we ask the assistance of His mercy for us both.

I can tell you that the people were idolaters before God, most high, sent Muhammad. Then He sent Muhammad to call them to Islam, and he called them to testify that there is no god but God alone who has no partner, and to profess what he brought them from God. Whoever entered Islam was a believer, freed of idolatry, and his possessions and blood inviolate, while he was entitled to the rights of a Muslim and the protection of Muslims. Whoever neglected Islam when called to it became an infidel, free of faith, his possessions and blood lawful to Muslims, from whom nothing could be accepted except his entry into Islam or his death, except for the People of the Book whom God explicitly exempted, who paid tribute-money.

Then the laws were revealed after this for people who had believed, and adoption of the laws became a work of faith. Thus God says in Qur'an 2/25 (etc.), "Those who believe and do good works," and in Qur'an 2/62 (etc.), "He who believes in God and does good works," and similar expressions in the Qur'an. Therefore an absence of works does not result in a loss of belief, and belief may be attained without any acts. If an absence of works involved a loss of belief, one would be taken by the absence of works from the name of faith and its continuance, just as people who lose belief move as a result from the name of faith and its continuance and truth, and revert to their former state of idolatry. One of the ways by which this may be known is the disagreement between act and belief. People do not disagree in belief and do not excel each other, but they excel each other in acts and their laws differ as well; yet the religion of the people of heaven and the religion of the prophets does not differ. Thus God says in Qur'an 12/13, "We have laid down for you as religion what was prescribed for Noah, and what We have revealed to you, and what We prescribed for Abraham, and Moses, and Jesus."

Know that guidance in belief in God and His prophet is not like guidance in what is legislated as to acts. Why does this disturb you? You call a man a true believer for what he believes, and God calls him so in His book; and you call a man ignorant for what he does not know of the laws. He needs only to learn that of which he is ignorant. Is one who errs in knowledge of God and His prophets the same as one who errs about what people learn when they are already true believers?

God has said in His teaching about the law in Qur'an 4/176, "God explains it to you for you may err. And God is the Knower of all things." And He says in Qur'an 2/282, "If one of you errs, then another one of you will remember" and in Qur'an 26/20, "I [Moses] did it then, when I was of those who err," that is, among the ignorant. The proof from the book of God and the *sunna* for believing this is something so apparent and obvious that it does not pose a problem for someone like you. Do you not say "a wicked believer," "a sinful believer," "a trespassing believer," "an uncouth believer," "a cruel believer"? Can one be rightly guided in wickedness or error as he is rightly guided in faith? Can one be led astray from the truth while committing error?

Consider the speech of the sons of Jacob to our prophet, their father, in Qur'an 12/95, "Indeed, you are in your old error." Do you think they meant, "You are in your old disbelief"? God forbid that you, who are learned in the Qur'an, should understand it so!

Ten Things That Nullify One's Islam

Muhammad ibn 'Abd al-Wahhab

Know that the greatest matters which nullify your Islam are ten:

1. Ascribing partners (*shirk*) in the worship of the one God who has no partners. The indication of that is in His saying in Qur'an 4/116, "God does not forgive setting up partners with Him but He forgives whom He pleases for sins other than that." This includes slaughtering animals in the name of someone other than God, as in slaughtering the name of the *jinn* or graves.

2. Setting up intermediaries between oneself and God, making supplication to them, or asking their intercession with God is unbelief by the consensus of the community.

3. Anyone who does not consider the polytheists to be unbelievers, or who has doubts concerning their unbelief, or considers their way to be correct, is an unbeliever by consensus.

4. Anyone who believes any guidance to be more perfect that the prophet's, or a decision other than his to be better, is an unbeliever. This is like those who prefer the rule of evil (*taghut*) to his rule.

5. Anyone who hates any part of what the messenger of God has brought, even though he may act in accordance with it, is an unbeliever by consensus. The indication of this is that God has said in Qur'an 47/9, "This is because they hate what God has sent down, so He has made their deeds fruitless."

6. Anyone who ridicules any aspect of the religion of God, or any of its rewards or punishments, is an unbeliever. The indication of that is in the saying of God,

most high, in Qur'an 9/65–6, "Say: Was it God, and His signs and His Messenger that you were mocking? Make no excuse; you have disbelieved after you had believed."

7. The practice of magic. Included in this, for example, causing alienation or attraction [between people]. Doing such things or getting pleasure from them is unbelief. God, most high, said in Qur'an 2/102, "But neither of these two [angels, Harut and Marut] taught anyone magic until they had said, Indeed, we are a trial; then do not disbelieve."

8. Supporting and aiding polytheists against the Muslims. The indication of that is the saying of God, most high, in Qur'an 5/51, "Whoever among you who takes them as allies is surely one of them. Truly, God does not guide the wrongdoers."

9. Anyone who believes that some people are not required to follow Muhammad is an unbeliever and that leaving its *shariʿa* is possible just as al-Khidr left the *shariʿa* of Moses, is an unbeliever.

10. To turn completely away from the religion of God neither learning its precepts nor acting upon it. The indication of that is the saying of God in Qur'an 32/22, "And who does greater wrong than he who is reminded of the revelations of his Lord and turns aside there from. Truly, We shall exact retribution from the guilty."

In all of these errors, it makes no difference whether such violations are committed as a joke, in seriousness or out of fear, except when done under compulsion. All of these are the most severe perils and the worst things that can occur. Every Muslim must be one on their guard against them and fear them for the sake of his soul. We seek refuge in God from such deeds as entail His wrath and severe punishment. May the prayers of God be upon Muhammad.

Fatwa on *Shirk* – Ibn Baz

There are a number of things which, if Muslims succumb to them, will nullify their faith and remove them from Islam. Unfortunately, many people are ignorant of these things, even though it is incumbent on all Muslims to know them and teach them to those who are ignorant of them. Those who persist in these things while having knowledge and certainty of them and knowing the soundness of these things according to the Qur'an and the *sunna* are indeed seized by unbelief. On the day of resurrection they will not be included among the Muslims; may God forbid such a thing!

These things are as follows:

1. Associating partners with God in worship. "Truly, whosoever sets up partners with God, paradise is forbidden to him and the fire will be his abode. There are no helpers for the wrongdoers" (Qur'an 5/72). Calling upon the dead, asking their help, or offering them gifts or sacrifices are included in this.

2. Setting up intermediaries or intercessors between oneself and God, making supplication to them, and asking for their intercession is certainly unbelief. God, most high, says in Qur'an 39/43–4, "Have they taken others as intercessors besides God? Say: Is that so, even if they have no power over anything and know nothing? Say: To God belongs all intercession!" He also says in Qur'an 2/48, "Fear the day when people will not help one another at all, nor will intercession be accepted from them," and He says in Qur'an 6/94, "Indeed, you have come to Us alone just as We created you for the first time. You have left behind you all that We bestowed on you. We do not see your intercessors, whom you claimed to be partners, with you."

3. Not declaring the polytheists to be unbelievers (among the Jews and the Christians and so forth [see Qur'an 98/1]), or having doubts concerning their unbelief, or considering their way to be correct, or saying that it is possible that they will enter paradise, is unbelief. This is due to the inconsistency of such claims with the clear sense of the text of the Qur'an about the unbelief of all those who do not enter Islam after the prophethood of Muhammad. Confirming this is the statement of God, most high, in Qur'an 4/150–1, "Those who disbelieve in God and His messengers and want to make a distinction between God and His messengers and say, 'We believe in some and disbelieve in others,' wanting to find a way between them, they are the true unbelievers." It is clear from this verse that God is saying that whoever disbelieves in one prophet while believing in all the other prophets is most certainly an unbeliever. This applies to the Jews and the Christians because of their disbelief in the prophethood of Muhammad (and the disbelief of the Jews in Jesus as well). Confirming this is the statement of Muhammad, "By He who has the soul of Muhammad before Him, whoever is from the community of the Jews or the Christians and hears about me, but does not affirm his belief in that with which I have been sent and dies in this state [of disbelief], will be one of the companions of the fire [of hell]" (transmitted by Muslim and Ahmad [ibn Hanbal]). Additionally, the Christians of today are divided into two groups. First are the Jacobites (the Catholics and the Protestants) who believe that God has three parts, the Messiah being one of them. The following verse (Qur'an 5/73) indicates their unbelief: "Those who say that God is the third of three and not that there is no god other than the one God, disbelieve." The other group is the Nestorians (the Orthodox) who believe that the Messiah is fully divine. Their unbelief is indicated by the following verse (Qur'an 5/72): "Those who say that the messiah, the son of Mary, is God, disbelieve." Qur'an 5/17 also confirms this. As for the Jews, they were unbelievers during the time of Jesus. "When Jesus came to know of their disbelief, he said, 'Who will be my helpers towards God?' The disciples said, 'We are the helpers of God. We believe in God and we bear witness that we have submitted [become Muslims]'" (Qur'an 3/52). Similar is the statement of God, most high, in Qur'an 2/40–1, "O children of Israel, remember My blessing which I bestowed on you.

Fulfil your covenant and I will fulfil My covenant. I alone should you fear. Believe in what has been sent down confirming what you have and do not be the first to disbelieve in it."

4. Anyone who holds that there is guidance better, more perfect or more complete than that of the Prophet is an unbeliever. This includes those who hold that Islam obligates one to give into or blend in with communism, capitalism, populism or even democracy. Islam is a complete and perfect religion. "Today I have perfected your religion for you, completed My grace on you, and approved Islam as a religion for you" (Qur'an 5/3). It is a religion that has nothing extra in it. "Whoever introduces something into this matter that was previously not there is an apostate" (transmitted by al-Bukhari, Muslim, Abu Dawud, Ibn Maja and Ahmad). It is perfect for all times and places.

    As for these ways, they are the product of the thought of the unbelievers such as Marx or George Washington. God rules over and has power over any of their systems of thought. This includes whoever holds that the Islamic system is not suitable for the twentieth century or that it is the cause of the backwardness of the Muslims, or that secular laws are better that those of Islam, or that it is necessary that Islam be limited to a relationship between the individual and their Lord that does not enter into the affairs of life in the hereafter, or that stoning of an adulterer or cutting off of the hand of the thief or the execution of an apostate is not suitable for this day and age. All this is unbelief.

5. Anyone who hates any part of the *sunna* of the prophet Muhammad, "This is because they hate what God has sent down, so he has made their deeds fruitless" (Qur'an 47/9).

6. Anyone who ridicules God or his prophet, any aspect of the laws of Islam (including trimming beards, wearing full-length clothes, wearing the *burqa*, protecting women from exposure to other men, purity practices, and using a *siwak* as a toothbrush), or those who uphold the traditions of Islam and their practices. This is total unbelief.

    The indication of this is, "Should you ask them, they would say, 'We were only talking idly and playing.' Say: Was it God, and His signs and His messenger that you were mocking? Make no excuse; you have disbelieved after you had believed" (Qur'an 9/65–6). It makes no difference if this is done jokingly or seriously, just as is made clear in this verse. Either way it is unbelief.

7. The practice of magic, according to the interpretation of Qur'an 2/102 ("But neither of these two [angels, Harut and Marut] taught anyone [magic] till they had said, Indeed, we are a trial; then do not disbelieve"). Magic includes soothsayers, those who claim to have knowledge of the unseen, reading tea leaves. Muhammad said, "Whoever goes to a soothsayer and believes what he says has disbelieved in what has been sent down to Muhammad" (transmitted by Ahmad, al-Tirmidhi, Abu Dawud, Ibn Maja and al-Hakim). Also included are using astrology, making horoscopes, or trusting blue amulets which the ignorant

believe will bring protection from evil. This is unbelief. Those who do not believe its influence is absolutely forbidden are likewise in error.

8. Supporting and aiding polytheists against the Muslims. God says in Qur'an
    5/51, "Whoever among you who takes them as allies is surely one of them."
9. Believing that some people are permitted to deviate from the religion of Islam is
    disbelief. "And whoever seeks a religion other than Islam, it will not be accepted
    of him, and in the hereafter he will be from among the losers" (Qur'an 3/85).
10. Turning completely away from the religion of God, not following its precepts
    nor acting upon it. God says in Qur'an 32/22, "And who does greater wrong
    than he who is reminded of the revelations of his Lord and turns aside there
    from. Truly, We shall exact retribution from the guilty."

3

The Formation of Muslim Society and its Characteristics

Sayyid Qutb

The Islamic message brought by the prophet of God, Muhammad, was the last link in the long chain of messages calling for the submission to God by the noble prophets. Throughout human history, this message has remained singular in its focus: that people should recognize that their true Sustainer and Lord is one God; that they should submit to Him alone, and that the lordship of created beings be destroyed. Except for a few people here and there in history, humanity as a whole has never denied the existence of God and His sovereignty over the universe; however, they were mistaken in the true understanding of their God, by associating other gods with Him in their belief and worship, or in obeisance and adherence. Both of these aspects are *shirk* in the sense that they take human beings away from the religion of God which was brought by the prophets, a religion which people gradually forgot with the passage of time, slipping into the state of *jahiliyya* from which they had been previously delivered. They found themselves in the state of *shirk*, either in their belief and worship or in their submission to the authority of others, and sometimes in both.

This is the nature of the call to God throughout human history, a call to Islam, a submission to the worship of God, and a liberation from servitude to other human beings, being the worship of God who has one nature—the liberation from the clutches of human lordship and human laws, value systems and traditions to God's sovereignty and authority over all spheres of life. Thus Islam came to Muhammad—as it came to earlier prophets—to lead people back to recognize God's dominion over the entire universe, humans being just a small part of it. And so it is necessary that the authority that orders people's lives is the same authority that orders His manifestation. People should not deviate by method, authority or plan from the method, authority and plan by which the universe is organized. Indeed, it is that authority which administers that part of their existence inherently. People are governed by the natural laws which come from God that rule over their creation and growth, the conditions of health and disease, life and death, as they are governed by these laws in their social life and even in the effects of their voluntary actions. They cannot change the *sunna* of God in all these matters, nor can they change the *sunna* of God in the laws prevailing in the universe. It is therefore desirable that people should follow Islam in those aspects of life in which they are given choices and should make the divine law the arbiter in all matters of life so that there may be harmony between the voluntary and involuntary aspects of life, and between humans and the rest of the universe.

Jahiliyya, on the other hand, consists of one person's lordship over another, and in this respect it is against the system of the universe and brings the involuntary aspect of human life into conflict with its voluntary aspect. Such was the *jahiliyya* which confronted all the prophets of God, including the last prophet, in their call toward submission to One God. This *jahiliyya* is not an abstract theory; in fact, under certain circumstances it has no theory at all! Yet, it always takes the form of a social movement which is subject to its own leadership, its own concepts and values, and its own traditions, habits and feelings. It is an organized society and its members share a close cooperation, interaction, integration and loyalty between each other, and it is always prepared, consciously or unconsciously, to defend its existence. It crushes all elements which threaten it in any way.

Because the *jahiliyya* does not represent a theory but a social movement in this fashion, any attempt to abolish this *jahiliyya* and bring people back to God once again cannot be undertaken in a theoretical manner. *Jahiliyya* controls the mundane world, and for its support there is a living and active organization. In this situation, mere theoretical efforts to fight it cannot even be equal, much less superior, to it. When the purpose is to abolish the existing system and to replace it with a new system which in its character, principles and all its general and particular aspects is different from the controlling *jahili* system, then it stands to reason that this new system should also come into the battlefield as an organized movement and a viable group. It should come into the battlefield with a determination that its strategy, its social organization, and the relationship between its individuals should be firmer and more powerful than the existing *jahili* system.

The theoretical foundation of Islam in every period of history has been to witness that "There is no god but God" (*la ilaha illa Allah*), which means to bear witness that the only true god is God, that He is the sustainer, that He is the ruler of the universe, and that He is the real sovereign; to believe in Him in one's heart, to worship Him in one's religious practice, and follow His laws in one's life. Without this complete acceptance of *la ilaha illa Allah*, which differentiates those who say they are Muslim from non-Muslims, there cannot be any practical significance to this utterance, nor will it have any weight according to Islamic law.

From a theoretical standpoint this means that human life should be devoted entirely to God; people should not decide any affairs on their own but must refer to God's injunctions concerning them and follow them. God's guidance is only known through only one source, that is, through the messenger of God. This is attested to, in the second part of the Islamic creed, the first pillar of Islam, *shahada anna Muhammad rasul Allah*, "a testament that Muhammad is the messenger of God."

This is the theoretical foundation that represents Islam and upon which it is based. It forms a complete methodology for life when it is applied to all aspects of life; with it a Muslim can confront every personal and collective facet of life within and without the domain of Islam, in his relationships to the Muslim community and the relationship of the Muslim community to other communities.

But, as we have said, Islam cannot be represented by an abstract theory, believed in by believers and adhered to in worship, its believers remaining in this manner within the actual existing structure of collective *jahili* movements. For the presence of the believers in such circumstances—irrespective of their numbers—cannot lead to an actual existence of Islam, because these individual "theoretical Muslims" who are present within the structures of a *jahili* society will be, necessarily, obliged to acquiesce to the demands of that society. They will be motivated, acquiescent or resentfully—with awareness or unconsciously—to satisfy the essential needs of such a society and insure its continued existence, and they will defend its integrity as an entity and repulse those factors that threaten its existence and integrity. That is because such a *jahili* society carries out such tasks by means of all of its members regardless of their willingness or not. In other words, the individual "theoretical Muslims" continue in actuality to strengthen *jahili* society that they are working "theoretically" to remove, and they will continue as living cells of this entity to nourish it, giving it existence and growth, and they will give it of their abilities, skills and activities that it will live and strengthen. This will be the result rather than their activities being directed to surpassing this *jahili* society to set up an Islamic society.

It is therefore necessary that Islam's theoretical foundation of belief materialize in the form of an organized and active group from the very beginning. It is necessary that this group separate itself from the *jahili* society, becoming independent and distinct from the active and organized *jahili* society whose aim is to block Islam. The center of this new group should be a new leadership; leadership, which first came in the person of the Prophet and in those after him, was delegated to those who strove for bringing people back to God's sovereignty, His authority and His laws. A person who bears witness that there is no god but God and that Muhammad is God's messenger should cut off his relationship of loyalty from the *jahili* society, which he has forsaken, and from *jahili* leadership, whether it be in the guise of priests, magicians or astrologers, or in the form of political, social or economic leadership, as was the case of the

Quraysh in the time of the Prophet. He will have to give his complete loyalty to the new Islamic movement and to the Muslim leadership.

This decisive step must be taken at the very moment a person enunciates *la ilaha illa Allah, Muhammad rasul Allah* when first converting to Islam, because Muslim society cannot come into existence without this. It cannot come into existence simply as a creed in the hearts of individual Muslims, however numerous they may be, unless they become an active, harmonious and cooperative group, distinct by itself, whose different elements, like the limbs of a human body, work together for its formation, its strengthening, its expansion, and for its defense against all those elements which attack its system. They must strive under a leadership which is independent of the *jahili* leadership, organizes its various efforts into one harmonious purpose, prepares for the strengthening and widening of their Islamic character, and directs them to abolish the influences of their opponent, the *jahili* life.

Islam was founded in this manner. It was founded on a creed which, although concise, included the whole of life. This creed immediately brought into action a viable and dynamic group of people who became independent and separate from the *jahili* society, immediately challenging it; it never came as an abstract theory devoid of practical existence. And therefore, Islam can appear again in this manner. There is no other way for the revival of Islam in the shade of *jahiliyya*, in whatever age or country it appears, except by following its natural character and developing it into a movement and an organic system.

When Islam, according to the method described above, starts a Muslim community on this basis, forms it into an active group, and makes this faith the sole basis for the relationship between the individuals of this group, its ultimate aim is to awaken the humanity of people, to develop it, to make it powerful and strong, and to make it the most dominant factor among all the aspects found in a person's being. It seeks to implement this purpose through its teachings, its rules, its laws and injunctions.

Some human characteristics are common with those of animals, even with those of inorganic matter. This has misled the exponents of "scientific *jahiliyya*" to consider humans to be nothing more than animals, or even than inorganic matter! But in spite of the characteristics which humans share with animals and inorganic matter, humans possess certain other characteristics which distinguish them and make them a unique creation. Even the exponents of "scientific *jahiliyya*" were forced to admit this, the evidence of observational facts choking them; even then, their admission of this fact is neither sincere nor unequivocal.

In this respect the service rendered by Islam's pure way of life has produced concrete and valuable results. Islam based its society on the collectivity of belief alone, instead of the base collectivities of race and color, language and country, or regional and national interests. Instead of stressing those traits which are common to both humans and animals, Islam promoted human qualities, nurtured them and made them the dominant factor. Among the concrete and brilliant results of this attitude was that Islamic society became an open and all-inclusive community in which people of various races, nations, languages and colors were members, there remaining no trace of those base animalistic traits. The rivers of higher talents and various abilities of all races of humanity flowed into this vast ocean and mixed in it. Their intermingling gave rise to a high level of civilization in a very short span of time, dazzling the whole world and compounding the essences of all the human capabilities, ideas and wisdom of that period, in spite of the fact in those times travel was difficult and the means of communication were slow.

In this great Islamic society Arabs, Persians, Syrians, Egyptians, Moroccans, Turks, Chinese, Indians, Romans, Greeks, Indonesians, and Africans were gathered together—in short, peoples of all nations and all races. Their various characteristics were united, and with mutual cooperation, harmony and unity, they took part in the construction of the Islamic community and Islamic culture. This marvelous civilization was not an Arabic civilization, not even for a single day; it was purely an Islamic civilization. It was never a nationality but always a community of belief.

Thus Muslims all came together on an equal footing in the relationship of love, with their senses set upon a single goal; thus they used their best abilities, developed the qualities of their race to the fullest, and brought the essence of their personal, national and historical experiences for the development of this one community, to which they all belonged on an equal footing and in which their common bond was through their relationship to their Sustainer. In this community their humanity developed without any hindrance. These are characteristics which were never achieved by any other group of people in the entire history of humanity!

The most distinguished and best known society in ancient history is considered to be the Roman empire. Peoples of various races, languages and temperaments came together in this society, but all this was not based on human relationships nor was any sublime faith the uniting factor among them; rather, their society was ordered on a class system, the class of nobles and the class of slaves, throughout the empire. Moreover, the Roman people—in general—held the leadership, and the other races were considered its subjects. Hence this society could not achieve that height which was achieved by the Islamic society and did not bring those blessings which were brought by the Islamic society.

Various societies have also appeared in modern times, for example, the British empire, which is similar to the Roman society to which it was an heir. It is based on national usurpation, in which the British nation has the leadership and exploits those colonies annexed by the empire. The same is true of other European empires. The Spanish and Portuguese empires in their times, and the French empire, all are equal in respect to oppression and exploitation. Communism also wanted to establish a new type of society, demolishing the walls of race and color, nation and geographical region; however, it is not based on humanitarianism but on a class system. Thus communist society is like Roman society with a reversal of emphasis; there, nobles had distinction, while here, the proletariat has distinction. The underlying emotion of this class is hatred and envy of other classes! Such a selfish and vengeful society cannot but excite base emotions in its members. The very basis of it is founded in promoting, developing and strengthening animalistic characteristics. Thus, in its view, the most fundamental needs of a human being are those which are common with the animals, that is, food, shelter and sex. From its point of view, the whole of human history is nothing but a struggle for food!

Islam, then, is the only divine way of life which brings out the noblest human characteristics, developing and using them for the construction of human society. Islam has remained unique in this respect to this day. Those who deviate from this system and want some other system, whether it be based on nationalism, color and race, class struggle, or similar corrupt theories, are truly enemies of humanity! They do not want people to develop those noble characteristics which have been given to them by their Creator nor do they wish to see a human society benefit from the harmonious blending of all those capabilities, experiences and characteristics which have been developed among the various races of humanity.

God Most High says about such people:

Say: Shall We tell you who will be the greatest losers in their deeds? Those whose efforts have been wasted in the present life while they were thinking that they were doing good deeds. Those are the ones who disbelieve in the signs of their Lord and in the encounter with Him. Their works are in vain and on the Day of Resurrection We shall not assign to them any value. That is their payment—Hell—for their disbelief and taking My signs and My messengers in mockery. (Qur'an 18/103–6)

God Almighty speaks the truth.

4

The Spread of Islam

M. R. Bawa Muhaiyaddeen

I seek refuge in Allah from the evils of the accursed satan. In the name of Allah, Most Merciful, Most Compassionate.

May all the peace, the beneficence, and the blessings of God be upon you.

My brothers and sisters in Islam who are true believers, I give you my greetings. May the peace of Allah be upon you.

It has been 1,408 years since the congregation called Islam emerged from among the children of Adam. Allah, all glory and exaltedness be His, perfected the state of true Islam with the coming of the Final Prophet, Muhammad, His Chosen Messenger. Through the Angel Gabriel, Allah sent the Holy Qur'an as revelations to His Prophet. In turn, Muhammad explained the five principles of Islam to the great holy men of divine wisdom, to the saints, to the archangels, and to all mankind.

But Islam is not just 1,408 years old. Islam is truth. It is Allah's radiant light, His qualities and actions, His attributes, and His compassion. It is perfect purity. Allah placed this purity within man when He created Adam. Islam, therefore, existed even before the creation of man. It existed in the world of the pure souls. This has been revealed in the traditional stories of Islam.

Truth is one and Islam is one. It shows no preference for any particular religion, sect, race, or tribe. It sees no differences between black, white, red, and yellow. It does not distinguish between people from China and people from Africa, America, Europe, Australia, Asia, Russia, or any country in the world. It does not even show differences between those in the realm of the primal beginning and those in the hereafter.

The word Islam has only one meaning: the unity and peacefulness of truth. That truth is Allah. He rules all the universes with His truth and peacefulness and with absolute faith, certitude, and determination. Islam is comprised of His three thousand gracious qualities and attributes, His unity, tranquility, and virtuous conduct, His equality, and His compassion. They are His wealth. To attain that wealth we recite the *kalima*, "There is nothing other than You, O God. Only You are Allah." God is the One to whom we pray. He is the truth which we must accept in this world and in the hereafter.

My brothers who are true believers must realize this. Islam must realize this. There should be no divisions among those who, with perfect faith, have accepted the truth of Allah and affirmed the *kalima*. All those who worship Him and pray to Him should pray in unity. All must unite as one in times of sorrow and in times of joy, in death and in life. To be in Islam means to be united as one congregation in all three realms: in the primal beginning, in this world, and even in the hereafter. It means to see Him face to face, worshiping Him, and greeting Him with peace in our hearts.

Here and in the hereafter, we must embrace all those who with absolute faith accept Allah in their hearts. We must pray to Allah in a state of unity, peacefulness, and truth, and then give greetings of peace to each brother. Standing face to face, our eyes looking directly into our brother's eyes, our hands clasping his hands, and our hearts embracing his heart with love, we must say, "May the peace of God be upon you."

This is the unity and beauty of Islam, the beauty that Muhammad brought to the people. Wherever we go, our hearts must be in that state. Our prayers must be one—pointed, directed toward the same place, toward Allah, the One who is truth. If we can recite the praises of Allah and the Prophet, then look each other in the eye, give peaceful greetings, and embrace each other—if we can achieve that oneness of the heart with all lives, then we will be true believers.

As brothers in Islam, we must open our hearts and look within. Without jealousy, envy, deceit, or trickery, without divisiveness or discrimination, we must turn our hearts to the straight path and glorify Allah. Accepting the truth and abiding by it, we must establish that truth in the right manner, with love, forbearance, and equality. This is the state of *Iman-Islam*, which the Prophet explained 1,408 years ago. This is what is spoken of in the Qur'an.

My brothers, before the time of Prophet Muhammad, there were many, many divisions and sects among the people of Mecca. They worshiped three hundred and sixty different idols, which they housed in the Ka'ba. They performed mantras, magic, and miracles. Although so many prophets had come to the world, including Adam, Noah, Abraham, Ishmael, Moses, and many others, Mecca was still a place of idol worship. Those who lived at this time are commonly referred to as the ignorant ones. Even after Muhammad came and taught the *kalima*, most of the people in both Mecca and Medina still had no faith and rejected his teachings. They were referred to as unbelievers.

But did Islam reject the people of Mecca and Medina? No. It was not the purpose of the Prophet to divide or to create enmity. Islam tells us not to discard the unbelievers or those who are ignorant, but rather to transform them. Once they acquire faith and their hearts are filled with light, once they perform their prayers to Allah alone, they too will be in Islam.

All those in Islam must reflect on this today. If we consider the way in which the Prophet transformed the people of Mecca and Medina, can we not follow that same process now, in the rest of the world? Islam is compassion, tolerance, forbearance, and the gracious qualities of Allah. It should not create barriers or divide people; it should show them the way and invite them into itself. That was the way of Muhammad and the way of the earlier prophets.

Just as the Prophet transformed the unbelievers into Islam through his love and his gracious qualities, each one of you must turn those evil qualities within yourself into good qualities. You must develop inner patience, contentment, trust in Allah, and praise of Allah. Only then can you truly be a follower of Islam.

It is these good qualities and good thoughts that can attract and capture the hearts of others. It is love that can open and reveal a person's innermost heart to himself. Once his heart is opened, absolute faith can bring him to a state of steadfastness. Then that person is ready to go in search of the truth, and when he finds the truth, he will find Allah, who is that truth. And once he finds the justice and the peacefulness of Allah, he too will be able to dispense justice and peacefulness throughout the world. In this state, he will glorify Allah, the Protector, the Most Compassionate. Such a man will embrace and comfort others with his life, his heart, and his body. This is how the individual, the world, and Allah's kingdom of justice can be ruled by the qualities which emerge from within the heart of one who has absolute faith, certitude, and determination.

You should not call anyone an unbeliever. When your love goes out and embraces the hearts of others, when truth enters their hearts and perfect faith conquers them, at that moment, at the very instant that faith appears in their hearts, they are in Islam, are they not? They have turned around and hoisted the flag of Islam, have they not? At that moment, those whom you once called unbelievers are changed. They accept Allah as the truth and now they worship only Him. Only the grace called faith can overcome and conquer the unbelievers.

Faith alone can capture another heart. Faith alone can rule the world. The qualities of Allah that exist within the heart of one with determined faith must reach out, enter the heart of another, and give him comfort and peace. It is seeing Allah's compassion, His equality, His tranquility, His integrity, His honesty, and the manner in which He embraces and protects all lives with equal justice which can bring a person to the state of harmony and compel him to bow in unity. It is these qualities that can conquer people and nations. They begin by capturing the hearts of a few, then they reach out to all those in the village, then the city, and eventually these qualities reach out to the entire population of the country.

Through Allah, faith can conquer the primal beginning, this world, the hereafter, and all of everything. This is the proof that Allah alone rules His kingdom. This is how true Islam spreads, not by going to war to conquer other lands. If we can complete the war within ourselves against our own bad qualities, then our faith will be able to conquer other hearts and other countries.

To be in Islam is to act with virtue, modesty, compassion, peacefulness, forbearance, Allah's three thousand gracious attributes, His unity, His tranquility, and His equality. Islam embraces all equally in both joy and sorrow. If one is hungry, all are hungry. If one is sad, all are sad. If one is happy, all are happy.

In this state of Islam, if we have a quarrel with somebody after the afternoon prayer, we must make peace, and embrace each other by the time of the early evening prayer. Any evil influences created must be thrown away before the next time of prayer. We must ask God for forgiveness for the faults we committed and strive for repentance. For what is happening now, during this very breath, we must glorify His name. And we must surrender to God the next breath, the next time of prayer to come. Whether or not we are alive in the next moment is Allah's will. May His will be fulfilled. If we have this faith with perfect certitude, if we have this intention with every breath, if we can acquire His qualities and His actions, then that is the state of Islam lived by true believers.

Whatever suffering each one of us faces, we must have patience. If we undergo even greater suffering, we must have contentment. If we undergo still greater difficulty we must surrender it to God. And when our suffering extends yet further, beyond our endurance, we can do nothing but praise Him. This is Islam—to praise Allah for whatever happens.

To worry about what has happened before or what is to come later is not Islam. If one constantly worries about what has gone by, his heart will be filled with grief and darkness. Grief and darkness are not Islam. Envy, jealousy, and treachery are not Islam. For what has gone by, all we can do is ask for forgiveness and strive for repentance and then complete whatever needs to be done now. This is the correct state of Islam, the state that a man who is a true believer must attain.

If our hearts attain this state of clarity, we will never see differences anywhere. If His qualities develop in us, we will never show discrimination toward anyone. Allah does not see any differences. Truth sees no differences. The prayer that accepts Allah as the only One worthy of worship sees no divisions. His equality and His peacefulness do not see any differences. Islam brings that equality and that peacefulness to every heart. It demonstrates unity and compassion to every heart.

Just getting together and talking about these things is not the true voice of Islam. Islam is not idle talk. In order to give voice to Islam, we must bring these words into our hearts, make them steadfast within us, and then act accordingly. We must praise Allah saying, "All praise is to You," greet His prophets, saying, "God bless them and grant them peace," and greet those who have faith, saying, "May the peace of God be upon you." That is the true voice of Islam. Coming together to glorify Allah alone is Islam.

We must bring God's qualities into action within us. This is the command of Allah, shown to us by every prophet He sent, from Adam to Prophet Muhammad. If every one of us can establish this state, if we can exhibit and prove this within our own hearts, we will be true believers. May we who have the determined faith of true believers think deeply about this. May every heart reflect on this. The kings who are true believers, the elders who are true believers, the rulers, the learned ones, the teachers, and those with the wealth of Allah—all those who are true believers—must reflect upon this. Our entire generation must reflect upon this.

We must understand the words of Allah, the words of the Prophet, and the treasure of grace buried within the Qur'an. We must embrace that treasure to our own hearts before we can explain it to the hearts of others and help them to accept it. The Qur'an is our treasury, the wealth of Islam, from which everything comes. Even though we may be poor in this world, we can earn the wealth of God in the hereafter. The wealth of this world will be left behind, but the wealth of His qualities, His actions, and the divine knowledge of His grace will be with us forever. Those who have made their hearts the repository of this wealth of Allah's grace and have acquired that divine knowledge and put it into practice are the ones who can truly be called the wealthy ones in the hereafter.

May this beneficence which Allah has given fill the hearts of everyone around us, in all three realms of the primal beginning, this world, and the hereafter. May their hearts be filled with the wealth of grace-awakened wisdom, the wealth of prayer and worship, and the wealth of justice. And may we make our hearts the repository of Allah's wealth and share it with the hearts of our brothers and sisters. May we strive hard to help them fill their hearts with divine knowledge and faith, so that they will be the wealthy ones in the hereafter. May all attain peace within their hearts. May we make every effort to do this. In our prayer, in our congregations, in the mosques, in our jobs, in our worldly life, in death and in life, in sorrow and in joy—may we strive for only this wealth, this unity, this grace.

My very precious brothers who have opened out the umbrella of grace called Islam, unfurled the flag of perfect faith, and walked on the good path, with awareness in our hearts, let us establish this state of unity called Islam and lead our lives in that unity. Amen.

Certain words may have been repeated here, but they contain meanings which must be said over and over and over again until they are understood. They have been repeated so that we will gain more and more understanding each time we read them. Therefore, please forgive the repetition. Please forgive us in the name of Allah and Muhammad. These are the words that came to our heart. Please do not reject them.

If there is any fault, please forgive me in the name of Allah and His Messenger. I give peaceful greetings to all of you.

May all the peace, the beneficence, and the blessings of God be upon you. Amen. May Allah guide us on the path of equality and peacefulness. May He strengthen our faith, take us on the straight path, and accept us. Amen.

Part II

Social Sciences

5

Between Text and Practice: Considerations in the Anthropological Study of Islam

Ronald A. Lukens-Bull

1. Introduction

Recently, a colleague who is a sociologist and a Muslim commented on another paper of mine and complained that I did not adequately address the "fact" that the practices that I described were not really Islam but only traditions that had been Islamized. He quickly pointed to the work of Hobsbawm and Ranger (1983) to support his claim that I was only dealing with invented traditions. As an anthropologist, of course, I was familiar with what is now a cliché in anthropology, traditions are invented. In this paper, I do not revisit the question of the invention of *islam*s, or local Islamic traditions, or even the invention of "universal Islam." Rather, this paper will reflect on the invention of "scientific," specifically anthropological, traditions in the study of Islam.

The anthropological study of Islam is one that has been plagued by problems of definition. What exactly are we studying? Local practices, universal texts and standards of practice, or something else entirely? At heart is how anthropologists define Islam. This paper reviews the major trends in the anthropological study of Islam and then suggests plausible theoretical directions for the future.

2. "Orientalism" and the Study of Islam

The question "What is Islam?" is shaped in each scholar's mind by what Talal Asad calls the scholar's "narrative relation" to the tradition. Asad further argues that this relation is shaped by one's view of the tradition. Whether one supports, opposes, or views as neutral a particular tradition shapes how one will study and write about it (Asad 1986, 17). Pierre Bourdieu agrees that "the anthropologist's particular relation to the object of his study contains the making of a theoretical distortion ..." (1977, 1). Edward Said's criticisms of Orientalism demonstrate how the relationship between the scholar and the subject shapes the scholarship. Said states that Orientalism is a body of theory about the "Orient" and about Islam based on power differentials between the European scholars and their subjects (Said 1978, 31–34).

Robert Fernea and James Malarkey write that early European impressions of the Arab world were colored by the historical opposition between Islam and Christianity (1975, 184). While Islam is monotheistic, differences between it and Christianity were emphasized in European discourse. In the Victorian era, the Arab world was not only a political and religious threat, but was also seen as a force of desecration and eroticism (Fernea and Malarkey 1975, 185). Said states that Islam became a symbol of terror, devastation, and all that was hated by Europe (1978, 59–60). This view of Islam served to legitimize colonial policies (Hussain, Olson, and Qureshi 1984, 1).

In the strictest sense, nineteenth-century Orientalism, as an academic discipline, was the study of the languages, texts, and culture histories of Islamic societies (Fernea and Malarkey 1975, 183). Part of the recent criticism of nineteenth-century Orientalism is based on the rather distant relationship scholars had with Islamic peoples. However, Lane, Westermarck, and Snouck Hurgronje wrote descriptive ethnographies of Islamic societies which, in many cases, are unsurpassed. Their writings remain important sources of comparative data.

While Lane, Westermarck, and Snouck Hurgronje had a more direct relationship with their subjects than did many other nineteenth-century scholars of Islam, their work does not escape completely from Said's criticism. For example, Snouck Hurgronje's work was directly related to the colonial administration of Islam in the Netherlands East Indies. Edward Lane went to Egypt to study Arabic at Al-Azhar, a school famous for its training of *'ulama'* from around the world. Lane's "narrative relation" to mystical and popular Islam is shaped by his exposure to *shari'a*-centric Islam. Lane divides religious behaviors and beliefs into those which he sees as truly Islamic and those which he sees as superstition. Lane places Sufism, saint-cults, and *jinn* within the category of superstition (1860, 222–46) and reserves religion for more respectable practices. While Lane pre-dates Robert Redfield by nearly one hundred years, there is a clear sense of great and little traditions in his writings.

The critics of Orientalism do not advocate rejecting all the works produced by Orientalism and even recognize contributions made by various Orientalists. For example, H.A.R. Gibb, the Dutch Islamist, has been praised by some Muslims both for his rediscovery of 'lost' material and for his sympathetic studies of Ibn Khaldun and Salah Ad-Din (Hussain, Olson, and Qureshi 1984, 3–4; Faruqi 1984, 177, 180, 183). However, Ziya-ul-Hasan Faruqi argues, even Gibb was subject to anti-Islamic biases including the belief that the Qur'an owes its origins to Judaeo-Christian traditions, the refusal to see any spiritual dimension in either the early or later parts of Muhammad's life, and the failure to comprehend the Islamic concept of prophethood. Faruqi concludes that if such a unanimously revered scholar was subject to such biases, then what can be expected of lesser scholars (1984, 189).

Said makes the distinction between *manifest* and *latent* Orientalism (Said 1978, 206). *Manifest* Orientalism is that of scholars (for example, the works of Gibb, Lane, and Westermarck), which grew and changed, and perhaps now is extinct. *Latent* Orientalism is part of folk theory[1] and, as such, it is more likely to persist "in the face of formal ... training" (Kempton 1987, 223). Said salutes Clifford Geertz's work as breaking from Orientalism because Geertz's primary allegiance was to the discipline of anthropology (1978, 326). However, Said overlooks the impact of latent Orientalism in Geertz's work. Some of the nineteenth-century knowledge about the "Orient" trickled down to the popular level and now functions as folk theories about Islam. These folk theories, particularly the "enemy other" view of Islam, finds their way into the works of various modern scholars including Geertz. In Java studies, for example, the above mentioned folk theories of Islam manifest themselves as a tendency to distrust, dislike, and downplay Islam (e.g. Kahin 1952; Geertz 1960; Anderson 1972; Helman 1989).

One possible way to conceptualize Islam involves explicit comparisons between Christianity and Islam. Each of these religious traditions is conceived of as a different historical configuration of power and belief, with Christianity located primarily in Europe, and Islam located primarily in the Middle East. Asad suggests that such a conceptualization is a central part of Orientalism, but it has also become an implicit part of much of contemporary anthropology (1986, 3).

The critics of Orientalism remind us that cultural analyses are shaped by culture-bound assumptions. A non-Muslim will always approach the study of Islam with non-Muslim assumptions about the nature of the world, religion, and human nature. The question becomes whether a non-Muslim can study Islam without being subject to the criticism of being an Orientalist. At least to some of the more extreme critics, it seems as if any critical analysis of Islam or an Islamic society is "Orientalism." I assert that such a position is mistaken. It suggests that only Muslims can study Islam and have intelligent, insightful things to say about it. While an insider's view contributes much to our understanding of any social situation, sometimes insiders have too much at stake to draw a clear picture. With any religion, an adherent studying the tradition has a theological position at stake.

3. Diversity of Tradition

Part of the answer to the anthropologist's question "What is Islam?" is conditioned by what she may or may not include in her definition of Islam. For instance, are local spirit beliefs, saint's shrines, and festivals Islamic? To deal with these issues more effectively it is necessary to take a step back from Islam. The problems encountered by anthropologists studying Islamic societies are also faced by anthropologists studying other monotheistic societies. John Bowen argues that the main impediment to the anthropological study of monotheisms is that these religions do not fit well in the normal ethnographic model. The texts and rituals common to a monotheism transcend any particular locale. These texts and rituals take the believer, and should take the ethnographer, outside the village to a "worldwide confessional community" (Bowen 1993a, 185). He argues that these rituals and texts, "encode a sameness, a conformity, a remove from cultural specificity and social structure" (1993a, 185). These are family resemblances among all expressions of a single world religion. However, within this range of family resemblance, there is also a great deal of diversity. I will now turn to an exploration of the various theoretical means of dealing with this diversity.

Great and Little Traditions

An influential model for anthropological studies of world religions was proposed by Robert Redfield. He suggested that all world religions, and some local religions (i.e. Mayan religion) could be divided into a "great tradition" and "little tradition" (1956). The great tradition, the orthodox form of the cultural/religious center, is that of the urban elite. It is the religion of the reflective few and is cultivated in schools and temples and is "consciously cultivated and handed down" (1956, 70). Great traditions have also been called "textual traditions," "orthodoxy," "philosophical religions," "high traditions," and "universal traditions." The little tradition is the heterodox form of the cultural/religious periphery. The little tradition incorporates many elements of local tradition and practice. The little tradition is the religion as it is practiced in daily life by ordinary people (in Redfield's assessment, the largely unreflective many). The little tradition is taken for granted and is not subject to a great deal of scrutiny, refinement, or improvement (1956, 70). Little traditions are also referred to by the terms "local tradition," "low tradition," and "popular religion."

The great-and-little-traditions model was part of Redfield's view of peasant societies as half-societies with half-cultures. Redfield taught us that peasant communities could not be studied as if they were isolated from any outside influence; they are, almost by definition, part of a wider civilization which draws its subsistence from the fruits of their labor (1956, 68–69). He suggests that the relationship between the peasant sector and other sectors (trade, nobility/administration, religious elite) is reflected in the shape of their religious beliefs.

The great-and-little-traditions dichotomy arose out of the attempt to understand the social organization of tradition. Richard Antoun states that "the social organization of tradition" is an absolutely necessary process in all complex societies. It is the process by which various religious hierarchies are established between the folk and the elite via cultural brokers which serve as intermediaries between the folk and the elite (Antoun 1989, 31). These hierarchies shape the form that religious practices take by imposing communicative constraints (Hefner 1987, 74). Hence, it is necessary to know the specific relationships between adherents of great and little traditions in each local setting. Redfield concurs that while anthropology may be primarily interested in the local practice of religion, it cannot ignore the interaction between these two aspects of tradition (1956, 86, 98).

The question to be explored is *how* the two aspects are interconnected. Implicit is the notion that in order for any great tradition to spread and be commonly practiced it must have mass appeal, that is to say, it must become a little tradition. On the other hand, the communication between great and little traditions is not just one way. McKim Marriott has suggested that universalization and parochialization are two ways in which the little and great traditions interact. Universalization is the process by which a local tradition is transformed into a great tradition or part of a great tradition. In Hinduism, Marriott suggests, the goddess Laksmi of Hindu orthodoxy is derived from local village goddesses (as cited in Redfield 1956, 94–96). As a further example, the Old Testament ethics rose from the little tradition of a tribal people. Parochialization is the process by which some element of the great tradition is learned and then shaped to become part of local religious practice (Redfield 1956, 96). Parochialization, or contextualization, involves the "translation" of symbols by means of drawing out certain aspects of the world religion and expressing it in terms meaningful to the local culture.

Redfield affirms that the two traditions are interdependent by stating, "Great and little tradition can be thought of as two currents of thought and action, distinguishable, yet ever flowing into and out of each other" (1956, 72). The influences on the little tradition may have never been present in a particular village, and may have originated far away in both space and time, and yet they shape the little tradition (1956, 70).

The very fact that Islam started in Arabia and then spread around the world suggests the process of universalization. In contemporary Islam, certain nearly universal practices, such as the *jilbab* (a women's garment covering the head and extending to the wrists and ankles, but not veiling the face) have their origins in Arab cultural practices and not in the teachings of Muhammad. However, the *jilbab*, the veil, and other *shari'a*-based practices become symbols of orthodox Islam and, in some settings, ethnic markers (Ewing 1988, 2).

Redfield suggests that the relationship between the great and the little tradition can be marked by deprecation or adjustment. In the case of the deprecation, the religious elite may view the religion of the common folk as superstition. In the case of adjustment, the teachers of the tradition may recognize popular tradition as the religion of those who do not fully understand the truths of the faith; hence they tolerate practices that would otherwise be considered heretical (Redfield 1956, 84). In this instance, Redfield states, the teachers interpret doctrine in such a way as to provide a sanction for local beliefs and practice within orthodoxy (Redfield 1956, 84).

Critique of "Great and Little Traditions"

Asad suggests that one problem that must be solved by an anthropology of Islam is the conceptual organization of the diversity in Islam (1986, 5). The great/little tradition division was one way to solve the problem of diversity. However, the division has been widely criticized. Bowen states that the dichotomy was attractive for anthropologists because it allowed them to study what they were used to studying, villages, and left to Orientalists the problem of understanding the texts (1993a, 185). Bowen states that anthropologists and other scholars concerned with local forms of culture looked for the rites, myths, or ideas that made the group they were studying distinctive rather than those they shared with other Muslims (1993b, 4). Dale Eickelman suggests that when scholars mention great and little traditions they tend merely to juxtapose them and not explore their complex interrelationships (1982, 2). The distinction between great and little tradition also leads to a division of labor between those who are interested in local forms of a religious tradition and those who are interested in religious texts (Bowen 1993b, 4). This, however, leads to an overly narrow view of the tradition. In Islam, the universal aspects of tradition are sometimes thought of as the core of Islam. This has "lent a normative and cultural priority to the Middle East vis-à-vis the rest of the Muslim world" (Bowen 1993b, 6).

A further problem with the model, according to Talal Asad, is that it leads anthropologists to assert that "neither form of Islam has a claim to being regarded as 'more real' than the other" (Asad 1986, 6). Asad seems to take a theological position about the "corrupted" nature of local Islam, and seems to suggest that the great tradition is indeed more real than the little tradition.

Abdul Hamid el-Zein criticizes academicians who, like Asad, make theological assertions. He argues "both theology and anthropology claim a higher degree of reflection than folk expressions of Islam" (1977, 243). Therefore, both regard local Islam as "less ordered, less objective, and somehow less complete versions of the religious experience" (1977, 243). Anthropologists often regard local variants of Islam as a diluted form corrupted by magic and superstition. El-Zein argues that this view of local "islams" implies that a "pure and well-defined essence of Islam" exists, even if it cannot be readily found (el-Zein 1977, 243). Theologians construct what Gellner (1981, 5) sees as a traditional division between folk Islam and scholarly Islam (el-Zein 1977, 241). Further, theologians view Islam as an "isolable and bounded domain of meaningful phenomena" which by its very nature is distinct from other cultural forms (1977, 241).

El-Zein argues that the dichotomy of folk Islam (little tradition) versus elite Islam (great tradition) is infertile and fruitless. This dichotomy is part of an Islamic elite's attempt to dominate the discourse about what constitutes real religion (el-Zein 1977, 252). He argues that various theological and anthropological interpretations of the meaning of Islam are dependent upon assumptions which define and limit what can be properly considered "religious" and "Islamic." These assumptions distinguish a "folk from an elite, and a real from a false Islam" (el-Zein 1977, 249). El-Zein suggests that it is ironic that anthropology studies folk Islam while using the principles of elite Islam (el-Zein 1977, 246).

Antoun suggests that el-Zein's criticisms overlook the fact that Redfield dealt with a two-way flow of cultural materials. He states,

> Redfield assumed that great traditions were built up out of little ones and Marriott and Singer, among others, have documented instances of such a process in the study of Hindu society and culture in India (1989, 43).

Antoun argues that the dichotomization of tradition is not inherently infertile. However, what is infertile and even dangerous is the assignment, by the anthropologist, of the superiority of the great tradition over the little tradition (Antoun 1989, 43). Asad is wrong in wanting anthropologists to declare which form of Islam is "more real." I contend that the ultimate "truth" of a theological claim is beyond the jurisdiction of anthropology.

Ignaz Goldziher suggested as early as 1910 that it was a mistake to see Islam as a monolithic whole (1981 [1910], 4). Goldziher demonstrated the dynamics of diversity evident in Islam from early in its history to the time of his writing (ca. 1910). The diversity in Islam is far more than the split between Shi'i and Sunni. The world-wide Islamic community, even within each major section, is typified by cultural diversity (Davies 1988, 63). Neither great nor little traditions are unified wholes. Even the little tradition of a single village is not unified (Antoun 1989, 39). There is individual interpretation in theology and practice involved at both levels.

4. Diversity and Discourse

If, as much contemporary scholarship suggests, we cannot use the distinction between great and little traditions, we must find some other way to deal with the diversity in Islam. Talal Asad suggests that there are three common anthropological solutions to this problem. The first suggests that there is "no such theoretical object as Islam" and therefore there is no need to deal with the diversity between Muslim societies. The second uses Islam as a label for a "heterogeneous collection of items, each of which has been designated Islamic by informants." The third holds that Islam is a "distinctive historical totality which organizes various aspects of social life" (1986, 1). In about a paragraph each, Asad hastily disposes of the first two approaches. He examines at length the third approach but concludes that it is not acceptable. He offers the notion of Islam as a discursive tradition as an alternative approach. I will explore all three approaches, the first two at greater length than Asad himself, concluding that there is some value in the first two approaches which Asad overlooked. Also, there are some problems with the third approach which Asad overlooked.

According to Asad, the approach that suggests there is no such theoretical object as Islam is typified by Abdul Hamid el-Zein's article "Beyond Ideology and Theology: The Search for the Anthropology of Islam" (1977). This approach, according to Asad, holds that there "are diverse forms of Islam, each equally real" (1986, 2). What el-Zein contributed to the scholarly discourse about Islam was an alternative to essentialist approaches to Islam. El-Zein suggested that the term *Islam* be replaced by *islams* (1977, 227–54). Dale Eickelman states that this approach emphasizes the multiplicity of Islamic expressions and does not privilege one expression over another (1987, 19). Embedded in el-Zein's article is a rebuttal to Asad's criticism. El-Zein criticizes any anthropological work which takes a theological, or quasi-theological, position in regard to local traditions. Asad's repeated assertion that anthropology must be able to determine which forms of Islam are most real falls into this category of theologically inclined anthropology.

Ironically, a version of the "no such thing as Islam" approach is seen in Middle East studies, where some anthropologists assume Islam to be non-problematic and static; hence they have no need to deal with the diversity in Islam. The assumption is that if a scholar has a basic understanding of Islam, there is no need to explore the local Islam. Hence, these scholars tend to discuss all culture as local. For example, Abu-Lughod's book *Veiled Sentiments: Honor and Poetry in a Bedouin Society* (1986) has few references to Islam and does not deal with Islam in any significant way. Elsewhere, Abu-Lughod states that it is mistaken to see all practices and discourses in the Arab world as related to an Islamic tradition (1989, 294). While she is correct, an over-zealous application of this position would suggest that it is possible to study an Islamic society without considering the nature of Islam within that local context. Asad accuses Michael Gilsenan of the shortcomings of the second approach by stating,

> The idea [Gilsenan] adopts from other anthropologists—that Islam is simply what Muslim everywhere say it is—will not do, if only because there are everywhere Muslims who say that what other people take to be Islam is not really Islam at all (1986, 2).

Asad sells short Gilsenan's work (1982). Far from seeing Islam as whatever Muslims in an area say is Islam, Gilsenan explores the complexities of Islam. He looks at how certain central features (*baraka*, *'ulama'*, etc.) vary throughout the Arab world. Gilsenan states,

> What Islam means for Muslims in the modern world is now an issue for debate and action in the context of the politics of nation states, the struggle for energy supplies, superpower rivalry, and dependency. What is the *umma*, the Islamic

community, and how and where is *ijma*, or consensus to be formed? What is Islamic government and in what forms and institutions must it be embodied? (1982, 14–15).

Gilsenan sees the definition of social elements as Islamic or non-Islamic as part of a political process. He describes an overall process whereby,

certain classes and groups that are politically and economically dominant in society legitimize a form of religion that increasingly relates to a specifically class view of how Islam is to be defined, practiced, studied, taught, and authorized. This will be the "real" and legitimate Islam ... (1982, 211).

Abu-Lughod defends Gilsenan's work because of his view of the social forces in Islam and because of his "fundamental respect for the ordinary people through whom he comes to recognize Islam ..." (1989, 295).

Asad states that Ernest Gellner's *Muslim Society* (1981) is the most ambitious attempt to describe Islam as "distinctive historical totality which organizes various aspects of social life" (1986, 1). Gellner opens his book by saying,

Islam is the blueprint of a social order. It holds that a set of rules exists, eternal, divinely ordained, and independent of the will of men, which defines the proper ordering of society (1981, 1).

Gellner continues to state that while Judaism and Christianity are also social blueprints, they are less so than Islam. He attributes this to the fact that Islam, unlike Christianity and Judaism, quickly became the religion of the political elite (1981, 2). However, even since Christianity became accepted by the Roman Emperors politics became and continues to be intimately related with Christianity. One need look no further than Liberation Theology in Latin America, or the Moral Majority in the United States to see contemporary examples of such a connection (Asad 1986, 3).

Many anthropological studies of Islam echo Gellner's sociological focus. In a way, the ideological aspects of Islam are assumed to be so similar to Christianity that it is thought that they have little impact on life in a Muslim society. Gellner bases his model on the interactions between towns and tribal peoples in Arab Middle East-North Africa (Asad 1986, 5). This clearly overlooks the impact of Islam in Southeast Asia, sub-Saharan Africa, and other non-Arab Islamic areas. One consequence of such an approach is to assert that those who do not follow the cultural practices of Arabs are somehow not good Muslims. This is the position of some contemporary Muslim reformists; again anthropology takes a theological position.

Gellner uses David Hume's notions of "flux and reflux" of polytheism and monotheism to argue that a natural part of the human experience is the cyclical movement from polytheism to monotheism and back again. None of this movement, both to and away from monotheism, is based on rational motivation. Gellner argues that a return to polytheism is marked by God sharing the stage with other important figures. Hence, paganism has its heroes, Catholicism its saints, and Islam its dervishes (Gellner

1981, 9–11). He avers that popular Islam, with its saints, tombs, and mystics, is polytheism, an argument with which many fundamentalist Muslims would be quick to agree.

Although Asad sees too little value in approaches to Islam other than his own, his definition of Islam as discursive tradition is useful. The approaches which Asad hastily rejects contribute two important reminders. The first suggests that it is a mistake to study an Islamic study with a monolithic, essentialist conception of Islam; there may be as many forms of Islam as there are Muslims. The second suggests that it is crucial that we accept the self-identification of Muslims. If someone calls himself a Muslim and identifies certain practices as Islamic, as scholars, we must begin by accepting that statement as true and then examine how these practices differ from those of other Muslims. The question to be explored is why there are differences between various groups which identify themselves as Muslims. This is where Asad's notion of Islam as a discursive tradition is most useful. As a discursive tradition, Islam is constantly being reshaped to fit with an ever-changing world.

Asad asserts that anthropologists of Islam, most notably Geertz and Gellner, have ignored the role of indigenous discourses in the tradition (1986, 8, 9). Asad counters Eickelman's suggestion that there is a need for a middle ground between Islam's great and little traditions (1982) by suggesting that instead of the right level of analysis, an anthropology of Islam needs the right concepts. He suggests that "a discursive tradition" is such a concept (1986, 14). It is in discourse, and not in social structure, or political style, that one finds the unifying principles of Islam (Asad 1986, 11). The discursive nature of Islam means that everywhere Islam is concerned with deciding what is allowable (*halal*) and what is not (*haram*) (Davies 1988, 62). Asad states that anthropological studies of Islam should start from the same assumption Muslims do, that Islam is a discursive tradition that "includes and relates itself to the founding texts of the *Qur'an* and the *Hadith*" (1986, 14).

Asad defines a discursive tradition as a discourse which seeks to instruct practitioners about the correct form and purpose of a given practice. Further, it seeks conceptually to link a past and a future through a present. However, Asad asserts, not all that Muslims say and do is included in an Islamic discursive tradition (Asad 1986, 14–15).

So far the discussion about discourse has skirted around the central question of the content and intent of Islamic discourse. Roff states that Islamic discourse often concerns a dialectic between the ideal and the actual (1988, 26). It is often about how to live as Muslims in a less than ideal world. This often includes questions about the place of *shari'a* and how to balance indigenous practices with it. These are questions about what is permissible and what is not, which are central to much of Islamic discourse.

Islam is far from unique as a discursive tradition. The world's other two major monotheisms (Christianity and Judaism) are also discursive traditions (Bowen 1993b). In fact, all world religions and major ideologies (i.e. Marxism) could be considered discursive traditions. However, in its concern with determining the forbidden (*haram*) and the permissible (*halal*), and in allowing whatever is not forbidden as permissible Islam seems unique.

Asad criticizes other anthropologists for not looking at indigenous discourses; on the other hand, however, his depiction of Islamic discourse focuses too much on the Qur'an and *hadith*. Asad rejects Gilsenan's view of the discursive (or debated) nature of Islam as being too far removed from the Qur'an and *hadith*. While these texts certainly play a role in Islamic discourses (both local and inter-local), other texts (those of various Islamic thinkers, both contemporary and past), local concerns, and local practices also play into this discourse.

Asad provides a necessary corrective to the non-literate approach anthropologists tend to take toward religion. Abu-Lughod states that anthropologists have tended toward non-literacy in their approach to religion, much like most of the people they have studied. By this she means that anthropologists have tended not to have access to the archives and texts which would illuminate the behavior they are seeing. While Abu-Lughod salutes this "healthy bias toward looking for religion in what people say and do," she recognizes the need for anthropologists to explore texts (1989, 297). Indeed, even very prominent ethnographers have made analytical errors because of a lack of knowledge of Islamic texts (e.g. Geertz 1960; 1968).

Most discussions about Islamic texts and their relationship to local *islam*s seems to suggest a unified position of the texts vis-à-vis popular practice. However, as Messick points out, Islamic texts are polyvocal (1988, 637). There are contradictory *hadith*, and lesser texts are much more prone to sharp disagreement on a range of theological and legal questions. Islamic discourse is not just between texts and practice but also between different practices.

Bowen states that in Islamic discourse there is a tension between the local situation and the universal aspects of Islam that is central in the lives of many Muslims (1993b, 7). He states that a new generation of scholars has begun to pay attention to this tension. The point of departure for these scholars has been "the social life of religious discourse: how written text and oral traditions are produced, read, and reread" (Bowen 1993b, 7). Bowen states that looking at Islam in terms of distinct local "*islams*" runs the risk of obscuring "both the historic connections across different Muslim societies and many Muslims' strong sense of an external, normative reference point for their ideas and practices" (1993b, 7). Whereas Asad wishes to center the discourse around the Qur'an and *hadith*, Bowen, and others, suggest that both other religious texts and other "foundations of Islamic knowledge" such as oral traditions and systems of cosmological speculation become part of the discourse (1993b, 10; Abu-Lughod 1989, 297).

If we are to approach Islam as a discursive tradition we must take the self-identification of Muslims seriously. Although Roff wishes to take seriously what Muslims say, he defines "Muslim" narrowly as one who accepts the *shari'a* (Islamic law) (1987b, 31). Although Roff claims to reject essentialist views of Islam (1987a, 1), he privileges *shari'a* and hence forwards an essentialist view which could easily ignore the discourse of those who are Muslims but do not necessarily follow *shari'a*. In both Persia and Java, there are stories about a Sufi saint[2] who proclaimed that the *shari'a* was only for common people who need the guidance to know right and wrong but could be ignored by advanced mystics. The saint was condemned not for the belief, but for discussing it publicly and hence potentially confusing people (Woodward 1989, 192).

Mark Woodward's definitions of the components of Islamic discourse shed light on the nature of the discourse. The universalist Islam with which local islams interact is far more than the Qur'an and *hadith*. It includes rituals such as the *hajj*, the *salat*, *'id al-adha*, *'id al-fitr*, and the fast of Ramadan among others. However, local islams do not enter into discourse with the entire universalist corpus of Islam. Received Islam is what Woodward calls that portion of universalist Islam present in specific local contexts. Finally, local islams are those rituals and texts, both oral and written, that are not known outside of a specific local context. These local rituals and texts arise from the interaction of local culture and received Islam (Woodward 1988, 87–88). Further, local islams can interact with each other (Woodward 1988, 65).

Richard Antoun suggests five perspectives which are useful for understanding the discursive nature of traditions. The first perspective is that of the beliefs or texts themselves and "involves sorting out the elements in the text, noting the mix of little and great tradition elements." In Antoun's case, he examines a set of sermons. It could also include school curriculum, myths, folktales, and explanations of ritual practices (Antoun 1989, 5). The second perspective is that of the linker and interpreter (e.g. preacher). Linkers and interpreters, or cultural brokers, must be part of the community to which they wish to convey the tradition if they are to be effective (Antoun 1989, 656). The third perspective is that of a cognitive system. The fourth is that of social structure. The final perspective is that of the common folk (1989, 5).

One place of interaction between the textual traditions and local concerns in this discourse is the Friday sermon (Antoun 1989, xiii). Antoun describes the *khutba*, or Friday congregational sermon, as "a formal oral presentation delivered and subdivided according to set rules and interspersed with well-known prayer formulas, Quranic verses, and Traditions of the Prophet." But more than that, "it is an opportunity for the preacher to articulate the formal religious message of Islam with the needs of the community, its problems and its weltanschauung" (1989, xiii).

Islamic education is another locus of this discourse. Soebardi and Woodcroft-Lee point out the role of *pesantren* (residential Islamic schools) in the spread of Islam in the rural areas in Java (1982). Johns states that many of the concerns in the Islamic literature of Southeast Asia seem to concern the pastoral needs of the communities for whom the authors were writing (1975). A religious teacher draws from the texts and traditions for the spiritual benefit of his followers. Specific needs and concerns are addressed, and the shape of local concerns will influence the concerns of the religious instruction and secondary texts. This specifically local instruction would be repeated by teachers in an educational chain.

Islamic discourse has long included trans-national communication. For several centuries, ideas have circulated around the Islamic world via traveling scholars. First Mecca and then Cairo emerged as centers of Islamic learning where students from the Ivory Coast to Mindanao would come to study (Roff 1987b, 36). When they would go home the former students would attract students of their own, spreading the ideas they learned in these learning centers. Not all the teachers in these centers of learning are Arabs. For example, during the nineteenth century several prominent scholars in Mecca were from the Malay Archipelago (Snouck Hurgronje 1931, 276–9; Dhofier 1982, 89). Furthermore, texts are commonly circulated between various Islamic societies (e.g. Johns 1965). Roff cites a 1937 case in Kelantan, Malaya, regarding the polluting nature of dog saliva which brought *'ulama'* from other places (Roff 1988, 29).

The question remains, what are the criteria for selecting what is included in the discourse and what is not? Asad says a practice is Islamic if "it is authorized by the discursive tradition of Islam, and is so taught to Muslims—whether by an *'alim*, a *khatib*, a Sufi *shaykh*, or an untutored parent" (Asad 1986, 15). What Asad would and would not include is unclear. Woodward states that the criteria for determining whether something is Islamic should not focus on *shari'a*-centric conceptions of piety. The criteria must consider "the degree to which core symbols, beliefs, and modes of religious action are derived from interpretation of Muslim texts and tradition" (1988, 62).

The concepts of *sunna* and *ijma'* contribute much to a theory of a discursive Islam. A most basic definition of *sunna* is the codified traditions (Gellner 1981, 63). The establishment of *sunna* requires scholarly consensus (*ijma'*). In arriving at *ijma'* there may be room for *ijtihad* (interpretation). To what degree could *sunna* be seen as continually evolving? As Islam spread, to what degree was *sunna* redefined by local scholars?

Davies answers the above questions by suggesting the procedure of *fiqh* (jurisprudence) developed in order to understand how to apply Islam to cultural settings other than Arabia (Davies 1988, 63). In this process, the scholars' decisions about what is *halal* (permitted) and what is *haram* (forbidden) shaped the *sunna* of Islam. She states,

> The examination of *al-urf*, customary usage and practice, subject to the categories of *halal* and *haram*, was one way customs were validated and entered into the cultural body of Islam. All that was not expressly prohibited was permitted according to the framework, and since the Prophet himself had cautioned against burdensome restrictions affirming local custom was therefore in keeping with the conceptual framework (Davies 1988, 62).

This process of incorporating customary practices into Islam is based on public interest and utility (Davies 1988, 62). Hence, if a local practice did not interfere with the goals of Islam, it was embraced and transformed into an Islamic practice. However, the meaning of *ijma'* shifted from a general consensus to a consensus of the scholarly elite (Messick 1988, 645). This shift suggests that any notion of a discursive tradition based on *ijma'* excludes popular voices as part of the discourse.

5. Critique of the Discourse Approach

While the idea of discursive traditions seems fresh, it is not clear how new this approach really is. Firstly, Marshall Hodgson suggested such an approach in the 1950s and 1960s (Eickelman 1987, 18). Secondly, although Redfield's paradigm was indeed overly mechanistic, it did call for the study of the interaction of great and little traditions. The idea of "discursive traditions" is the Redfield paradigm dressed in contemporary jargon. Redfield was right; practitioners of a little tradition do tend to have a sense of a wider tradition. What the concept of discursive traditions contributes is not a totally new paradigm, but the introduction of individual discussants. The great-and-little-traditions dichotomy, like much theoretical work of the 1950s, was overly functionalistic in its orientation. The discursive tradition approach can overcome this peril, but it too must tread carefully to avoid it.

To fully understand the significance of Islam as a discursive tradition we must understand the nature of social discourse. Discourse can be defined as the social process of constructing shared meaning. This process is necessarily social, although it may not require actors to interact on a face-to-face basis; discourse can be conducted through texts. Discourse is historically situated; an instance of the discourse necessarily involves the history of it. Discourse is political; the power relations between individuals, or groups of individuals, shape the nature of the discourse: what is said, how it is said, and the nature of the response it invokes.

Asad states that orthodoxy is not just a body of opinion but is rather a relationship of power (Asad 1986, 15). Therefore, the task of an anthropology of Islam is to understand the historical production and maintenance of specific discursive traditions. It will also be concerned with both the transformation of discursive traditions and "the efforts of practitioners to achieve coherence" (Asad 1986, 17). The concern with the social organization of tradition found in the Redfield paradigm suggests the role of power in the discursive nature of any tradition. Although Redfield, and those who use his paradigm, are not explicitly concerned with the power relations, the very fact that great traditions are seen as those of the urban elite and that little traditions are those of the masses suggests the inherent power imbalance in the relationship between great and little traditions.

Ewing states that, in the history of Islam, the periods of greatest discourse about the nature of Islam and society have occurred in periods of political upheaval and change (1988, 6). For example, because of the threat to Islamic identity posed by British rule in India, the question of what behaviors were acceptable for Muslims was thrust into the forefront. Practices which previously had been non-problematic were deemed un-Islamic in order better to define Islamic ethnic identity (1988, 15, 17). Much of the debate and controversy in Islamic societies about how to be a good Muslim is about defining the relationship of the Islamic community with sometimes secular national governments.

We would be mistaken if we assumed that only things Islamic entered into Islamic discourse. The process of determining *halal* and *haram* allows local cultural features to enter into the discourse. However, what if there was a great tradition already in a region when it was Islamicized? Redfield suggests, in regards to Latin America, that to consider Orthodox Catholicism as the great tradition and folk Catholicism as the little tradition is to commit a sin of omission. Folk Catholicism needs to be understood as a little tradition that draws on at least two great traditions: Roman Catholicism and the great traditions of aboriginal America (Mayan, Incan, Aztecan) (1956, 78). Similar circumstances exist in some Islamic countries. For example, before Java was Islamicized the kingdoms of Java were Hindu-Buddhist (Saivite) in their orientation. An argument could be made that the little traditions of Java draw upon both the great traditions of Islam and the great traditions of the peculiar form of Hindu-Buddhism that was known only in Java. For example, an important Sufi concept is the distinction between external (*zahir*) and internal (*batin*). Judith Becker argues that in the pre-Islamic Javanese Hindu-Buddhism very similar distinctions existed (1993, 35). In establishing *zahir*[3] and *batin* as important to Javanese Islam, the discourse involved two great traditions. Because this particular doctrine was not forbidden (*haram*) it was permissible (*halal*). Further, this doctrine had strong congruencies with Islamic mysticism, and hence was probably embraced as a bridge between the message and the Javanese populace.

Not only may Islamic discourse include local traditions and other great traditions, but it may also include concerns about modernization, development, and nationalism. As each Muslim society deals with placing local concerns within Islamic discourse, the problems of modernization, development, and relationships with national governments become part of the Islamic discourse. Clifford Geertz sees scripturalism as attempting to deal with the problems of modernization within an Islamic framework (1968, 62). Various Islamic groups have also asked what are the proper Islamic forms of development. The arguments often concern social justice, democracy, and participatory development, all of which have been justified and understood in Islamic terms (Lukens-Bull 1996; Yatin 1987, 167).

If we are to understand Islam as a somehow connected discursive tradition and not a myriad of discursive local traditions, we need to understand what links various local "islams" together. What is similar in the various local practices; what is different and why? To do this we need to develop a comparative study of local "islams." Although anthropologists base their careers on the intensive study of one society (ethnography), they also are concerned, at some level, with a comparative venture (ethnology). An ethnology of Islam is needed.

A good ethnological comparison of two Islamic societies, although lacking in the ethnography of each case, is Clifford Geertz's *Islam Observed* (1968) which compares Moroccan Islam and Javanese Islam. Strikingly, it remains the only monograph of its kind. While both Moroccan and Javanese Islam drew upon the same general set of symbols, the end result in each society was radically different because of the social climate in which they each evolved (1968, 20). Islam and the social climate in each location interacted in both particularizing and generalizing ways. Geertz argues that the universality of a great tradition comes from its "ability to engage a widening set of individual, even idiosyncratic, conceptions of life and yet somehow sustain and elaborate them all" (1968, 14).

The particularizing forces of Islam attempted to accommodate what Geertz considers a universal, standardized, unchangeable, and well-integrated system of rituals and beliefs to a local moral and metaphysical landscape. The generalizing forces attempted to deal with this flexibility and maintain not only the identity of Islam as religion in general but also "the particular directives communicated by God to mankind through the preemptory prophecies of Muhammad" (1968, 15). Islamic societies can be compared with each other in terms of Wittgenstein's notion of family resemblances (Geertz 1968, 66).

It is interesting to note that, for Geertz, it is the earlier, mystical, forms of Islam that are more susceptible to particularization than are the scripturalist, or fundamentalist, forms of Islam. Although each society has Sufi saint cults, the exact nature of these cults is different. Further, a saint or an Islamic culture hero from one of these societies would be neither saintly or heroic in the other. On the other hand, according to Geertz, scripturalism looks pretty much the same regardless of the setting. This overlooks two facts. First, a great deal of communication has always been common in the Islamic world; philosophical texts have long been circulated. While the particular myths and parables used to communicate mystical ideas vary, the basic ideas, or at least the broad set of ideas drawn upon, are the same. Second, while fundamentalists do say and do some things that may not seem out of place among fundamentalists in another country, they also have very local concerns. To draw a methodological distinction between mystical and normative Islam, as Geertz does, is a mistake.

At this point, it is useful to review a few case studies to see some of the various aspects which comprise the Islamic discursive tradition. Roff describes a debate which took place in Kelantan, Malaya, in 1937 over the relative cleanliness of dogs. The Raja Kelantan, the heir apparent and younger brother of the Sultan of Kelantan, kept a dog. His sister objected to the dog, stating that, according to the *shari'a*, dogs are polluting. The Raja Kelantan sought the legal opinion of a scholar (*'alim*) who had recently returned from Mecca. The matter quickly became one of public concern, and eventually a public council of debate (*majilis muzakara*) was convened. Scholars were brought in from Singapore and elsewhere if they were educated in Islamic learning centers outside of Malaya. The debate was about much more than the purity of dogs; it was about the basis of Islamic authority in a changing world (Roff 1988, 29).

Elsewhere, I have discussed the Indonesian Islamic discourse about development (Lukens-Bull 1996). A new sort of Islamic scholar has recently emerged in Indonesia. This new breed of scholars have western education in addition to, or even instead of, traditional Islamic education (Dhofier 1992, 26). Their role in the Indonesian Islamic community is not yet clearly defined. They are learned and respected men, but they are not traditional *'ulama'*. Within the Indonesian Islamic discourse about development, they are trying to define three things: (1) their role within the Indonesian Islamic community, (2) their role in national politics, and (3) the role of Islam in the Republic of Indonesia. One way in which Muslim intellectuals define these things is through a careful selection of the symbols, models, and metaphors used to discuss development. Different groups select different Islamic symbols to emphasize (Lukens-Bull 1996).

Sandria Freitag has discussed how in North India, certain aspects of Islamic life such as prayer, the mosque, the Qur'an, and the *shari'a* were isolated and became a "shorthand" to represent the entirety of Islamic life (1988, 144). An important basis of this discourse was a long-held division between the *ashraf* (elite) and low "caste" Muslims. She states that the elite had long enjoyed a superior social position and many claimed *sharif* status. The elite emphasized education, literary and artistic accomplishment, the study of Islamic law, and Muslim reformist activities. Freitag argues that although this elite way of life was shared with non-Muslims as well, those who embraced it thought of it as Islamic (1988, 144). In the wake of the political changes accompanying British rule, this version of Islam gradually became the only acceptable "orthodoxy." The less *shari'a*-centric practices of the non-elite Muslims was abandoned as not sufficiently distinctive vis-à-vis their Hindu neighbors.

The three cases above barely begin to cover the degree of diversity in Islamic discourse. However, they point to the central role of elites in many local Islamic discourses. In a sense, without the elite there would not have been these cases. In Kelantan, the debate started as a palace dispute. It quickly involved questions of authority based on Islamic training. In contemporary Indonesia, Muslim intellectuals are part of a small circle of people directly involved in the discourse about the nature of society. Their legitimacy is based on a predominantly Western education and a degree of public piety. In North India, the practices of the elite became the standards for all Muslims. These cases also demonstrate the importance of ethnology in anthropological studies of Islam.

6. Conclusion

This paper has reviewed various concerns facing anthropologists of world religions. It has focused on the specific problems faced by anthropologists of Islam. The primary problem is that of defining what is meant (to the anthropologist) by the term "Islam."

The theoretical question "What is Islam?" and the theological question "What is Islam?" are not the same. The theoretical question must be addressed and wrestled with by every ethnographer of an Islamic society. The theoretical question is what must be included, and what can be excluded, in our analyses of things Islamic. The theoretical problem is that of level of analysis. The theological question addresses the ontological status of things and seeks the foundations of faith within the tradition. These two questions, while dealing with similar cultural forms, are fundamentally different. However, because the forms and the discourses about them overlap there is a danger that these questions become conflated.

With the above caveat in mind, I would like to suggest that an anthropological definition of Islam begin at the same point that a Muslim definition of Islam does. This is not an unusual proposition; many have proposed such a starting point. However, I would like to start with the Islamic definition of "Islam" as submission to God. All Muslims will agree with this definition. Where they differ is in defining how one should go about submitting to God. A comparative study of the different conceptions of how to submit to God (that is, how to be a Muslim) should be the central task of an anthropology of Islam.

This task, as I have described it, puts the anthropologist in a strange, and sometimes uncomfortable, subject position. Frequently, I find myself in situations like the one I described at the top of this essay. I am alternately a perverter of truth, the preserver and defender of minority views, and the scientific observer of what Muslims actually do. The last role is the one I was trained to play, and I know it well. The other two are thrust upon me by some of my interlocutors. It is not only Orthoprax Muslims that see ethnographic studies of Muslims as missing the mark. As detailed above, many Western scholars, even anthropologists, wish to essentialize Islam. For them, there needs to be a real, true Islam with which local practice can be compared. This approach certainly simplifies research because it allows anthropologists to get a firm grasp on a complicated and shifting part of the lives of the people they study. There is a tradition in anthropology called "salvage ethnography" in which the anthropologist records and preserves the "way things were." This tradition means that there is a tendency for ethnographic studies of local practice to be seen as the defense of minority views. Given the realities of research and writing, I cannot retreat to safety of white towers and claim to be "only an observer of what is"; I must carefully balance all three subject positions as I strive to discover "What is Islam?"

Notes

1. A folk theory: "(1) is based on everyday experience; (2) varies among individuals, although important elements are shared; and (3) is inconsistent with principles of institutionalized [theories]" (Kempton 1987, 223).

2. In Java, the saint is identified as Seh Siti Jenar and in Persia, the saint is identified as al-Hallaj.

3. While this paper has followed the standard Arabic transliteration of this term as *zahir*, the standard transliteration for the Javanese loan word is *lahir*.

References

Abu-Lughod, Lila. 1986. *Veiled Sentiments: Honor and Poetry in a Bedouin Society*. Berkeley, CA: University of California Press.

—1989. "Zones of Theory in the Anthropology of the Arab World." *Annual Review in Anthropology* 18: 267–306.

Anderson, Benedict. 1972. "The Idea of Power in Javanese Culture." In *Culture and Politics in Indonesia*, ed. Claire Holt, 1–70. Ithaca, NY: Cornell University Press.

Antoun, Richard T. 1989. *Muslim Preacher in the Modern World*. Princeton, NJ: Princeton University Press.

Asad, Talal. 1986. *The Idea of an Anthropology of Islam*. Washington, DC: Georgetown University Center for Contemporary Arab Studies.

Becker, Judith. 1993. *Gamelan Stories: Tantrism, Islam, and Aesthetics in Central Java*. Tempe: Monographs in Southeast Asian Studies, Program for Southeast Asian Studies, Arizona State University.

Berger, Peter, and Thomas Luckmann. 1967. *The Social Construction of Reality: A Treatise in the Sociology of Knowledge*. Garden City, NY: Anchor Books/Doubleday.

Bourdieu, Pierre. 1977. *Outline of a Theory of Practice*. Trans. Richard Nice. New York: Cambridge University Press.

Bowen, John R. 1993a. "Discursive Monotheisms." *American Ethnologist* 20/1: 185–90.

—1993b. *Muslims through Discourse: Religion and Ritual in Gayo Society*. Princeton, NJ: Princeton University Press.

Davies, Merryl Wyn. 1988. *Knowing One Another: Shaping an Islamic Anthropology*. New York: Mansell Pub.

Dhofier, Zamakhsyari. 1982. *Tradisi Pesantren: Studi ten tang Pandangan Hidup Kyai*. Jakarta: LP3ES.

—1992. "The Intellectualization of Islamic Studies in Indonesia." *Indonesia Circle* 58: 19–31.

Eickelman, Dale F. 1982. "The Study of Islam in Local Contexts." *Contributions to Asian Studies* 17: 1–18.

—1987. "Changing Interpretations of Islamic Movements." In *Islam and the Political Economy of Meaning,* ed. William R. Roff, 13–30. London: Croom Helm.

el-Zein, Abdul Hamid. 1974. *The Sacred Meadows: A Structural Analysis of Religious Symbolism in an East African Town*. Evanston, IL: Northwest University Press.

—1977. "Beyond Ideology and Theology: The Search for the Anthropology of Islam." *Annual Review of Anthropology* 6: 227–54.

Ewing, Katherine P. 1988. "Introduction: Ambiguity and Shari'at—A Perspective on the Problem of Moral Principles in Tension." In *Shari'at and Ambiguity in South Asian Islam*, ed. Katherine P. Ewing, 1–22. Berkeley, CA: University of California Press.

Faruqi, Ziya-ul-Hasan. 1984. "Sir Hamilton Alexander Roskeen Gibb." In *Orientalism, Islam, and Islamists*, ed. Asaf Hussain, Robert Olson, and Jamil Qureshi, 177–98. Battleboro, VT: Amana Books.

Fernea, Robert, and James Malarkey. 1975. "Anthropology of the Middle East and North Africa: A Critical Assessment." *Annual Review of Anthropology* 4: 183–206.

Freitag, Sandria. 1988. "Ambiguous Public Arenas and Coherent Personal Practice: Kanpur Muslims 1913–1931." In *Shari'at and Ambiguity in South Asian Islam*, ed. Katherine P. Ewing, 143–63. Berkeley, CA: University of California Press.

Geertz, Clifford. 1960. *Religion of Java*. Chicago: University of Chicago Press.

—1968. *Islam Observed: Religious Development in Morocco and Indonesia*. New Haven: Yale University Press.

Gellner, Ernest. 1981. *Muslim Society*. Cambridge: Cambridge University Press.

Gibb, Hamilton A. R., and Harold Bowen. 1958. *Islamic Society and the West*. Vol. 1, two parts. London: Oxford University Press.

Gilsenan, M. 1982. *Recognizing Islam*. London: Croom Helm.

Goldziher, Ignaz. 1981. *Introduction to Islamic Theology and Law*. Princeton, NJ: Princeton University Press [1910].

Hefner, Robert. 1987. "The Political Economy of Islamic Conversion in Modern East Java." In *Islam and the Political Economy of Meaning*, ed. William R. Roff, 53–78. London: Croom Helm.

Helman, Sarit. 1989. "The Javanese Conception of Order and its Relationship to Millenarian Motifs and Imagery." In *Order and Transcendence: The Role of Utopias and the Dynamic of Civilizations*, ed. Adam Seligman, 126–38. Leiden: E.J. Brill.

Hobsbawm, Eric, and Terrance Ranger, eds. 1983. *The Invention of Tradition*. Cambridge: Cambridge University Press.

Hodgson, Marshall G. S. 1974. *The Venture of Islam: Conscience and History in a World Civilization*. Chicago: University of Chicago Press.

Hussain, Asaf, Robert Olson, and Jamil Qureshi. 1984. "Introduction." In *Orientalism, Islam, and Islamists*, ed. Asaf Hussain, Robert Olson and Jamil Qureshi, 1–4. Battleboro, VT: Amana Books.

Johns, Anthony. 1965. *The Gift Addressed to the Spirit of the Prophet*. Canberra: Australian National University.

—1975. "Islam in Southeast Asia: Reflections and New Directions." *Indonesia* 19: 33–55.

Kahin, George McTurnan. 1952. *Nationalism and Revolution in Indonesia*. Ithaca, NY: Cornell University Press.

Kempton, Willet. 1987. "Two Theories of Home Heat Control." In *Cultural Models in Language and Thought,* ed. Dorothy Holland and Naomi Quinn, 222–42. New York: Cambridge University Press.

Lane, Edward William. 1860. *Manners and Customs of the Modern Egyptians*. London: John Murray.

Lukens-Bull, Ronald A. 1996. "Metaphorical Aspects of Indonesian Islamic Discourse about Development." In *Intellectual Development in Indonesian Islam*. Chapter 8. Tempe: ASU Program for Southeast Asian Studies Monograph Series.

Messick, Brinkley. 1988. "Kissing Hands and Knees: Hegemony and Hierarchy in Shari'a Discourse." *Law and Society Review* 22/4: 637–59.

Redfield, Robert. 1956. *Peasant Society and Culture*. Chicago: University of Chicago Press.

Roff, William R. 1987a. "Editor's Introduction." In *Islam and the Political Economy of Meaning*, ed. William R. Roff, 1–10. London: Croom Helm.

—1987b. "Islamic Movements: One or Many?" In *Islam and the Political Economy of Meaning*, ed. William R. Roff, 31–52. London: Croom Helm.

—1988. "Whence Cometh the Law? Dog Saliva in Kelantan, 1937." In *Shari'at and Ambiguity in South Asian Islam*, ed. Katherine P. Ewing, 25–42. Berkeley, CA: University of California Press.

Said, Edward. 1978. *Orientalism*. New York: Random House.

Snouck Hurgronje, Christiaan. 1906. *The Achenese*, trans. from the Dutch by R. J. Wilkinson. Leiden: E. J. Brill.

—1931. *Mekka in the Latter Part of the 19th Century*. Leiden: E. J. Brill.

Soebardi, S., and C. P. Woodcroft-Lee. 1982. "Islam in Indonesia." In *The Crescent in the East: Islam in Asia Major,* ed. Ralph Israeli, 180–210. Atlantic Highlands, NJ: Humanities Press.

Woodward, Mark. 1988. "The Slametan: Textual Knowledge and Ritual Performance in Central Javanese Islam." *History of Religions* 28/1: 54–89.

—1989. *Islam in Java: Normative Piety and Mysticism in the Sultanate of Yogyakarta*. Tucson: University of Arizona Press.

Yatin, Jean-Claude. 1987. "Seduction and Sedition: Islamic Polemical Discourses in the Maghreb." In *Islam and the Political Economy of Meaning*, ed. William R. Roff, 160–79. London: Croom Helm.

6

THE STUDY OF ISLAM IN LOCAL CONTEXTS*

Dale F. Eickelman

A text is imbedded in specific historical time .... To read fully is to restore all that one can of the immediacies of value and intent in which speech actually occurs.

George Steiner, *After Babel*, 24

The study of a world religion in local contexts implies what from some perspectives is obvious—any religion's ideology and practice are elaborated, understood and subsequently reproduced in particular places and at particular moments. Even eternal truths are necessarily revealed in a specific language and setting; for the instance at hand "in Arabic, that ye may be understood."[1] The notion of locality as represented here is now at least in principle a familiar part of the intellectual landscape of social historians and social anthropologists concerned with the study of Islam. Yet, like any complex notion, it has diverse ramifications and has developed in manifold, sometimes even incongruous ways. One scholar has recently gone so far as to suggest that the term *Islam* be replaced by *islams*, thus emphasizing the multiplicity of Islamic expression and asserting that in all historical and cultural contexts the *islams* of elite and non-elite, literate and illiterate, and theologians and peasants, are all equally valid expressions of fundamental, "unconscious" Islamic principles. The *islams* approach, inspired as a reaction both to the orientalist search for an ahistorical Islamic "essence" and to the somewhat parallel venture of neo-*tawhidi* or unitarian Muslim fundamentalists who regard their interpretations of Islam as definitive, ironically and unintentionally provides a conceptual end product which likewise reduces Islamic tradition to a single, essentialist set of principles (el-Zein 1974, 172).[2] It also disregards the fact that most Muslims quite consciously hold that their religion possesses central, normative tenets and that these tenets are essential to an understanding of Islamic belief and practice.

The main challenge for the study of Islam in local contexts is to describe and analyze how the universalistic principles of Islam have been realized in various social and historical contexts without representing Islam as a seamless essence on the one hand or as a plastic congeries of beliefs and practices on the other. This essay seeks to assess major recent trends in the study of Islam in local contexts and suggests new directions for further research on the basis of recent scholarship.

Beginnings

The notion of local as recently developed is considerably more complex than earlier sharp distinctions between, for instance, the concept of "great" and "little" (or "folk") traditions introduced by anthropologists and historians in the late 1940s as a means of better describing large-scale civilizations such as those of China, India, and Islam. As initially employed, this conceptual distinction was a useful way of indicating the possible relationships between religious traditions as known through the texts and exegeses of literati on the one hand and religious expressions and interpretations in village or folk contexts on the other. Unlike the earlier doctrine of "survivals," which presumed that folk traditions were somehow vestiges of earlier civilizations and less permeable than "high culture" to change, the notion of great/little traditions made no gratuitous assumptions concerning the historical precedent of some civilizational elements over others. As the notion of great/little traditions first began to develop, it enabled scholars working primarily with texts and those working in "field" settings to see the complementarity of their interests and to reassess their working notions of text and context. Yet as ordinarily reported, these various forms of religious expression were often merely juxtaposed and were not used as a base for the analysis of their complex interrelationships. Some anthropologists and historians, for instance, derived notions of normative or "orthodox" Islam from the tenets of orientalist scholars and wrote of observed village practices or local documents as "deviant," or accepted without question similar interpretations by Muslim scholars. The notion of "local" in such instances carried the misleading implication of something provincial, or an inferior and imperfect realization of "genuine" or "high" culture religious belief and practice, as opposed to popular and "vulgar" ones.[3]

One of the more influential Islamic historians of the 1950s and 1960s to incorporate the notion of great and little traditions in an integral way into his own work was the late Marshall Hodgson. His explicit concern was with "high" culture in the "primary milieu of Islam," which to him was constantly renewed and transformed by the dialogues of successive generations of "piety minded Muslims" with the formative ideals of their civilization. Hodgson acknowledged that the traditions of "peasants or even non-lettered peoples" share substantially the same dynamics of change, but he explicitly left aside any detailed description of such changes or how they may have been interrelated to those of the "high" culture (Hodgson 1974, 80). As Edmund Burke III subsequently argued, Hodgson's notion of the dialogue of successive generations of "piety minded Muslims" with Islam's formative ideals comes close to an essentialist vision of Islam which minimizes some aspects of historical context and which Hodgson himself deplored in the work of other scholars (Burke 1979, 261–2). Nonetheless, Hodgson constructed a history of Islamic civilization that unlike many others was not unduly centered upon the Arab Middle East and that depicted in detail the changing forms and contexts in which Islamic ideals were expressed. Moreover, the recognition at least in principle of such transformations occurring among peasants and the non-lettered was a major step in advance of many other historians of Islamic civilization.

If the problem of Islamic historians as exemplified by Hodgson has been how to relate the vicissitudes of high culture to the rest of society, anthropology's basic conceptual problem has been how to apply what ethnographers have learned from the study of religious practice in small-scale groups or communities to larger entities such as Islamic faith or civilization. Because the published work of Clifford Geertz now spans more than two decades and has had a pervasive influence on scholars of many disciplines, it provides the best point of departure for tracing shifts in how anthropologists have sought to contribute to the study of Islam. Three of his principal studies are considered here.[4]

Although Geertz modestly asserts that his principal goal in *The Religion of Java* (1960) is primarily descriptive, his text contains a set of theoretical assumptions concerning how to represent adequately the culture of a complex religious tradition not limited to a single regional or national setting (Geertz 1960, 7). Javanese religious beliefs and practices are divided into three principal "orientations" or "cultural types." The *abangan* is "broadly related to the peasant element of the population"; the *santri* stresses the "purer" Islamic aspects of Javanese syncretism and is "generally related to the trading element"; and the Hinduist *prijaji* tradition is related principally to the "bureaucratic" element of the population (Geertz 1960, 4, 5–6, 234). Geertz argues that these three "subtraditions" are refractions of an underlying cultural unity, so that for instance the *prijaji* and *abangan* cultural orientations are "in part but genteel and vulgar versions of one another" (Geertz 1960, 234).

The "in part" caution in the last citation and the use in other contexts of qualifications such as "generally" and "broadly" in relating religious subtraditions to particular social categories suggest Geertz's awareness of the difficulties involved in adequately representing the subtraditional "strands" of Javanese religious belief in the context of cultural theory as it had developed through the 1950s. The title of the book itself, as opposed to alternative possibilities such as *Islam in Java* or some sort of parallel to Bellah's *Tokugawa Religion*, represents an implicit choice in how to depict Islam in a Javanese setting. When Geertz writes, perhaps ironically, that the holiday of *rijaja* is "a kind of master symbol for Javanese culture, as perhaps Christmas is for ours," and that if one understood "everything" concerning *rijaja*, "a simple impossibility— one could say one understood the Javanese," he appears to suggest reservations concerning the usefulness of the holistic notion of culture as a guide to ethnographic reporting, at least in complex cultural settings (Geertz 1960, 379).

Islam Observed (1968) makes two major conceptual contributions through its detailed comparison of religious belief and practice in two geographically antipodal Islamic settings. First, in discussing what analytic notions such as "mysticism" can mean in particular settings, Geertz suggests a strategy of comparison based upon "family resemblances" rather than upon typological classifications which presume in advance the essential features of phenomena being compared. The result is to depict in concrete instances how Islam can remain catholic to "an extraordinary variety of mentalities ... and still remain a specific and persuasive force with a shape and identity of its own" (Geertz 1968, 15, 23–4). Second, Geertz seeks to convey the historical context in which the dominant "classical" styles of Islam in Indonesia and Morocco developed and reached their full form, thus setting his work apart from cultural studies that attenuate historical concerns. As a consequence even Edward Said exempts Geertz from the condemnatory strictures which he applies to most other scholars and characterizes him as a scholar "whose interest in Islam is discrete and concrete enough to be animated by the specific societies and problems he studies" (Said 1978, 326).

"Suq" (1979), although not intended principally as a discussion of religion, complements Geertz's earlier studies on Islam by describing in intricate and convincing detail the relationship between the institutional framework of the bazaar economy of Sefrou, Morocco, and local religious institutions. These were the religious lodges (*zawiya*s) in which most urban traders and artisans participated, and the system of pious endowments (*hubus*; *waqf*) which were controlled in practice by the local trading community that in turn benefited most from it. This was in part because the commercial properties rented by pious endowments were generally offered below market value, thus serving as an indirect subsidy to the bazaar sector of the economy (Geertz 1979, 140–50). In "Suq" more than in Geertz's earlier studies, the practical articulation of religious ideologies and institutions with specific social classes and groups is made explicit. If in the *Religion of Java* religious "subtraditions" were "broadly" and "generally" correlated with particular social categories without any elaborate discussion, in "Suq" these interrelations are, in my judgment, more precisely documented.

Yet a paradox emerges from the ethnographic analysis in "Suq" which is also present to some degree in the earlier studies mentioned here. Geertz describes the shifting political and economic contexts in which Sefrau's bazaar economy has existed as meticulously as oral history and written sources allow. Despite the major political and economic changes that have occurred since 1900, he argues that the "cultural framework" for economic transactions "has altered but in detail" (Geertz 1979, 139). Geertz carefully specifies that it is the cultural framework for economic transactions in the bazaar and, by implication anyway, not the "total" cultural framework that has hardly altered over the last eighty years. Yet in *Islam Observed* the argument is similarly weighted toward an elucidation of the more constant classical religious "themes" and "styles."

To my knowledge, Geertz's most thorough discussion of religious change occurs in a 1972 article, based upon a 1971 return visit to Java and Bali, which serves as a temporal extension and reconsideration of his earlier *Religion in Java* (Geertz 1972). In this article, which provides an explicit discussion of the 1965 coup and subsequent massacres, Geertz suggests that the most salient religious development has been the "hesitant" emergence of "something rather like a denominational pattern of religious organization or affiliation," toward a "more openly pluralistic system," if not always a tolerant one, composed of Islam, *kebatinan* (Javanese mysticism), Christianity, and Bali-Hinduism, in which there is a growing recognition that the Muslim community, "properly understood" (i.e., composed of exemplary purists), is a minority community in Java (Geertz 1972, 70–1). In spite of this growth of denominationalism, there is paradoxically—Geertz's term—a "convergence in religious content" as each denomination is becoming Indonesianized by "a turn toward a more experiential sort of faith, and especially toward mysticism," a trend which "has been a central characteristic of Javanese religiosity for centuries" and which constitutes an "underlying—*the* underlying—theme of Javanese ... religiosity: personal, inward, transcendental experience—a direct, personal confrontation with the numinous" (Geertz 1972, 72–3).[5] If cultural frameworks alter so little despite major political and economic shifts—the "great transformations" described by Marc Bloch in depicting the emergence of feudal society in Europe, Max Weber in analyzing the "iron cage" of modern industrial and bureaucratic society, or perhaps Clifford Geertz in discussing religious change in twentieth-century Java—then a much more explicit theoretical discussion is needed of what is it in the nature of "cultural frameworks" that seemingly allow them to be transmitted and reproduced over time with relatively little change.

Class and the Social Reproduction of Religious Forms

In recent years there has been a shift in studies of culture or systems of meaning toward discerning how they are transmitted and reproduced, and how they shape and in turn are shaped by configurations of power and economic relations among groups and classes in different societies. Much more than in earlier studies, there is an effort to articulate specific economic, political and historical contexts with patterns of religious faith and experience. For some scholars, the writings of Max Weber have provided a useful point of departure in understanding changes in religious ideologies and institutional forms. Michael Gilsenan, for instance, used Weber's ideal typical notions of authority as a means of explaining why one Egyptian brotherhood was able to expand and maintain its membership at a time when other brotherhoods experienced apparently irreversible declines. Gilsenan suggested that the brotherhood, by adapting the patterns of bureaucratic authority characteristic, for instance, of the government office for which the order's founder worked, managed to solve leadership and organizational problems that plagued other brotherhoods. At the same time the brotherhood's emulation of "modern" organizational forms enhanced its status in the eyes of members and potential recruits (Gilsenan 1973, 188–207).[6]

Studies that depict the debate in specific cultural contexts over *what* is Islam and *who* opts for particular interpretations of Islam are especially valuable for comprehending changes in how Islam is locally understood, even when such studies are not explicitly informed by theoretical problems. One of the most outstanding of such studies is the work of Ali Merad on the reform movement in Algeria (Merad 1967). He argues that reformist ideologies in the period from 1925 to 1940 essentially were educated urban interpretations of an "intelligible and simple" Islam made against the backdrop in Algeria of prevalent and nearly all-pervasive maraboutic interpretations of Islam tied to specific tribal and rural contexts. Unlike Hodgson, who merely assumes that both "high culture" and folk versions of Islam undergo change and renewal, Merad shows the intimate and necessary interrelationship between the religious understandings of the reformist elite and those of ordinary tribesmen and peasants. Although the conscious goal of reformist leaders was to reconstitute a more purist version of Islam in Algeria, Merad suggests that an indirect consequence of reformism was to popularize a "rationalist" conception of Islam which set religious doctrines and practice apart from other aspects of social life (Merad 1967, 437–9).[7] Similar linkages between elite and popular interpretations of Islam and their relations to social classes and status have been explored in other regions as well.[8]

A recent anthropological study that particularly seeks to explore the relation between religious ideology and class is Clive Kessler, *Islam and Politics in a Malay State* (1978). Kessler claims that he has methodologically tried to steer a dialectical middle passage between what he calls "idealist phenomenology," in which cultural symbols are analyzed and elaborated without significant reference to "nonideational elements," citing Clifford Geertz as an example, and an equally unsatisfactory "hard 'objectivism' that reduces all cultural phenomena to some underlying material or quantifiable base" (Kessler 1978, 20). The only effective means of eliciting what Kessler precisely implies by his dialectical middle course is to follow his basic argument in detail.

Essentially he seeks to analyze the factors which contributed to the success in Kelantan of the Pan-Malayan Islamic Party (PMIP) from 1959 to 1969 in attracting a majority of peasants' votes. Some prior analysts attributed the PMIP success simply to the "exploitation of religious sentiments for political objectives" or to "illicitly invoked religious slogans" that assume the existence of "irrational" religious sentiments. To demonstrate the weakness of such assumptions, Kessler elaborately describes the historical and social contexts in which the PMIP operated and what were the dominant religious sentiments in Kelantan at various times (Kessler 1978, 32–3, 35).

For Weber, Islam is one of the few major world religions with an "essentially political character" (Weber 1963, 263). Kessler argues that the nature of Islam's political character has not been clearly understood. Despite the claims of some Muslims that Islam possesses a "perfect social theory," he argues that this theory is "sociologically deficient" because it primarily concerns individual ethics and ignores the presence of groups and classes. Its focus is upon how to motivate individuals, "initially governed by base and personal interests," by higher moral principles which enable them to transcend narrow self-interest. Even in "classical" Muslim society, the "idealistic, ethical, and individualistic" Islamic vision of a just society remained unrealized, so that there is almost inevitably "a tension between the social experience a believer seeks to apprehend and the terms his religion furnishes for its apprehension" (Kessler 1978, 210–13).

Throughout his text Kessler rapidly shifts from writing about Islam to discussing Kelantanese Islam—an adjectivalized term used by him to emphasize the elaboration in a regional context of elite and popular notions of belief and practice. In this context the Islamic vision of a moral, ideal society is sustained principally if sporadically through the major collective rituals of Islam. Occasions such as the fast of Ramadan, which is shared equally by all Muslims and thus symbolizes the ideals of equality, harmony and disinterested motivation of all believers, enables them temporarily to discard all other social distinctions. It is a period in which the *akal* (reason [Arabic *'aql*]) of each believer informs him with the discipline necessary to overcome *nafsu* (passion and self-interest) and live a fuller life as a Muslim. Kelantanese Islam thus enables peasants "to fashion social action, and thus experience themselves, in a manner consonant not so much with formal and explicit Islamic social theory as with its implicit but often problematic terms" (Kessler 1978, 208).

To explain how the PMIP became popularly identified with the Islamic vision of Kelantanese peasants, Kessler provides a convincing social history of the interrelationships between landownership, religion, and political action, and especially the various divisions which occurred among the traditional ruling elite. Although opposition political parties promised the peasant electorate that they would undertake concrete measures to improve peasant life if granted support, most nonetheless voted for the PMIP despite its lack of a practical platform to improve the lot of the peasants. The PMIP won peasant support because it articulated the Islamic vision of the just society, "consisting of individuals motivated by principle rather than immediate self-interest." Kessler argues that like fasting and the pilgrimage, elections entailed for most peasants a suspension of the normal social order. By claiming to be "implementing Islam," the PMIP identified itself with the exercise of *akal* and other Islamic ideals. By attacking the claims of the PMIP and asking peasants to consider their material conditions, the opposition became popularly associated with self-interest (*nafsu*) and against Islam. Since in making these judgments Kelantanese peasants were acting in terms which they generated themselves rather than those which others imposed upon them, an adequate explanation of the PMIP successes and the significance of "idealized

Islamic notions of personal identity and social existence" long remained inaccessible to outsiders (Kessler 1978, 232–4).

Kessler's elegantly argued explanation of PMIP success inadvertently indicates how difficult it is to steer a middle course between presenting a political economy of the contexts in which religious beliefs and practices are developed and maintained, and describing how such beliefs serve (to paraphrase Kessler) as an idiom for apprehending social experience and shaping social action. The political economy component of Kessler's argument, detailing patterns of change in trade and landownership and their impact upon the Kelantanese elite and peasant society, is excellently presented, built as it is upon his own research and complementary monographs by social historians concerning the development of Malay nationalism and the growth of the Malay intelligentsia during the colonial period.[9]

Yet Kessler's account of how peasants actually apprehend their religion is largely inferential. In Chapter 11, "Religious Ideas and Social Reality," he uses extracts from the speeches of several political leaders and quotations from James Siegel's excellent presentation of key elements (including *akal* and *nafsu*) in the world-view of Atjehnese Muslims (Siegel 1969). Only once does Kessler quote the remarks of a "devout Kelantanese woman, a teacher of religion to small children," concerning the Ramadan fast (Kessler 1978, 218–19). No direct citations are provided for the key to Kessler's argument, that elections were seen by peasants as an act of collective self-denial and egalitarian self-assertion similar to the pilgrimage and the fast. Just as Talal Asad, in discussing Marxist studies of seventh-century Arabia, warns against deducing the "primary motive" of a religious ideology from its major political consequences or reducing "the complex implications of religious texts ... to simple political meanings" (Asad 1980, 460), there is the inverse difficulty exemplified by Kessler of inferring, albeit plausibly, the contours of the relation between popular religious ideologies and politics from patterns of achieved political action alone. Moreover, Kessler treats peasant religiosity as relatively fixed. His detailed account of historical changes in landownership, economic conditions and political movements is not matched by an equal (although admittedly more difficult) attempt to suggest what were the major transformations in peasant religiosity, or if there were none, to explain why the Islamically-based peasant conceptions of a general order of existence—to adopt part of Geertz's (1973, 90) characterization of religion—were relatively impermeable to the growing impoverishment of peasants. Despite these reservations, Kessler's rather crude characterization of his study as an analytical articulation of "material" and "ideal" factors does not do justice to the much more intricate and rewarding case study which he presents.

"Great" Transformations and Styles of Religiosity

The implications of major changes in political and economic forms and in the intellectual "technology" of how ideas get reproduced and disseminated are just beginning to be explored in the context of Islamic studies and in all probability will have a major impact upon the direction of research over the next few years. Changes in basic patterns of thought and religiosity are often self-evident only in retrospect. Marc Bloch, writing of the "great transformation" of the emergence of feudalism in Europe, wrote that "these generations of men had no conscious desire to create new social forms, nor were they aware of doing so. Instinctively each strove to turn to account the resources provided by the existing social structure and if, unconsciously, something new was eventually created, it was in the process of trying to adapt the old" (Bloch 1964, 148). An example of the sort of "great" transformation under discussion here is Jack Goody's discussion of the impact of literacy upon historically known and contemporary societies and the sociocultural consequences of the introduction of such a new intellectual technology (Goody 1977). What concerns us most here is the impact of such major innovations upon religious belief and experience, an important component of how individuals think about their social and spiritual universe and manage to act within it. As Marilyn Waldman has pointed out, Goody relegates his discussion of the implications of the more nuanced problem of restricted versus generalized literacy to the last ten pages of his most recent book, although her own essay concisely suggests how forms of literacy have influenced the formation of early Islamic tradition (Waldman 1985). In a recent study of Islamic higher education in early twentieth-century Morocco, my own point of departure has been the sociology of Pierre Bourdieu. I have sought to depict how the collapse of traditional institutions of learning and the rise to prominence of other educational forms has begun to bring about shifts in what Moroccans consider to be religious knowledge and its appropriate carriers at both the popular level and that of religious specialists (Eickelman 1978, 510–12).

One of the most important efforts to assess the impact of technological and economic changes upon religious styles and movements is a recent work by Serif Mardin on the Turkish fundamentalist Saïd Nursi (1873–1960), the Bediüzzaman ("Nonpareil of the Times") and founder of the Nur movement (Mardin 1981). The Nur movement first took shape in western Turkey in the 1920s, and between 1950 and 1975 became international in scope. It developed in the context of Republican Turkey and its leaders gradually learned to work with "modern" ideas and materials. That it became international was in part due to the efforts of a talented translator based in California, and to the fact that the content of its message attracted a "new world clientele" experiencing "the spiritual crisis which accompanied modernization" (Mardin 1981, I, 3–4). The movement has no formal organizational structure, thus meeting the challenge of "modernization" in a way almost antithetical to the Egyptian brotherhood studied by Gilsenan. Nor does it have clear boundaries of membership; anyone who joins in its task of disseminating the truth of the Qur'an is a disciple. In terms of the content of Saïd Nursi's message, Mardin sees him

> as using both the Koran and the residues of Anatolian mysticism as a transformational medium which allows him to ... establish contact with popular religion, draw followers of folk Islam in the direction of a belief focused on the unicity of God, shift the dead weight of traditional Islamic orthodoxy and join the stream of an understanding of the laws of nature as they appear in Western European modern thought (Mardin 1981, IV, 9).

Saïd Nursi was aware that he was conveying Islamic doctrine with new emphases, particularly upon the dynamic quality of the Qur'anic message and its relation to science and the modern world. Mardin is aware of the difficulties of linking explicit ideologies to particular social groups and classes, but indicated that when Saïd Nursi's message was first disseminated in western Turkey (to which he was exiled in the 1920s by the Republican government), it appealed primarily to "the important contingent of small town dwellers with some education but an inconsistent status—part modern, part traditional," thus presumably receptive to new forms of religious discourse (Mardin 1981, I, 31).

So far this skeletal representation of Mardin's argument suggests that it contains the elements of a fascinating yet theoretically conventional study of an Islamic movement, although even in these terms it is rare that the thinking of a single religious leader is so effectively placed in a socio-historical context. What makes Mardin's study almost unique is his complementary concern with explaining the appeal of Saïd Nursi's message in terms of the "communications revolution" that began to be felt in Turkey by the late nineteenth century and of course elsewhere in the world. Patterns of governmental organization and authority changed radically, as well as the forms in which knowledge and information were construed and communicated. Even when persons in authority thought they were using new technologies to preserve the old, new elements and patterns of thought and authority were introduced with the telegraph, newspapers, magazines and an expanded (even if not mass) educational system. Newspapers and magazines, for instance, "replaced expostulation [with] arguments which were addressed to the presumed shared rationality of the readers" (Mardin 1981, I, 13).

This great transformation in modes of communication implicitly affected notions of what was considered to be religious knowledge and discipline as well. Through the nineteenth century, the accepted popular and elite notion of religious knowledge was that it was acquired under the guidance of an acknowledged master, without whom religious insight could not be achieved. This mode of communication also implied new forms of social control introduced with the impact of modernization. In the Nur movement the "message" of the founder—his opinions on religious subjects and his commentaries on the Qur'an (in Turkish, in itself a major innovation)—was more important than his person or personal ties to him. This aspect of the Nur movement is remarkably different from the practices of almost all other Sufi movements. The form of Saïd Nursi's message was thus characterized by "the written text replacing the instructions of the charismatic leader and the attempt to make the central truths of the Koran intelligible to a wide audience" (Mardin 1981, I, 19).

Even if the shift in the technology of intellectual reproduction is not consciously recognized or is even substantially denied, it has had a major impact upon belief and practice throughout the Islamic world. The analysis offered by Mardin offers a necessary link between the microsociological analysis of ideologies, their carriers and their contexts, and the worldwide economic and technological transformations that often have unanticipated implications for religious belief and practice as well as for other aspects of social life.

Conclusion: New Directions

There are several implications to the emerging trends in the study of Islam in local contexts depicted above. When studies of local interpretations of Islam were guided by the assumptions of the great/little tradition dichotomy, religious beliefs and practices frequently were not specifically related to classes or groups within a given society. Nor was much attention given to how such beliefs and practices changed as they pass from one social group or class to another. When adapted to new settings, class or status groups, religious ideologies often have implications far removed from those that were consciously intended by their original carriers. To understand such transformations, concern with the internal differentiation of belief and practice within "local" societies is essential. Moreover, any discussion of class necessitates wider notions of political and economic context than have frequently been utilized in past studies of Islam. Kessler's extensive analysis of regional political and economic transformations is an example of the wider scope required by such studies.

Another good example is Michael Fischer's ethnographic discussion of the interlocking patterns of friendship, discipleship and intermarriage of Shi'i *'ulama'* in Qum and their relation to *madrasa* education and the style of religious discourse conveyed by it. The core of Fischer's discussion of these themes is set against the backdrop of a fairly general account of the historical development of Shi'i ideology and religious leadership and the political context in which they have developed. A limited geographical locale is no longer a prerequisite of a study of Islam in a local context; specific categories of religious specialists, as in Fischer's case, can be just as "local." Similarly, Nazih Ayubi's recent account of the characteristic ideological orientations and backgrounds of participants in Egyptian neofundamentalist movements—he indicates that they are often educated (but significantly not in formal institutions of religious studies, which have a very different clientele), middle class and urban—require as sufficient contextual backdrop Egyptian society as a whole (Fischer 1980, 61–135; Ayubi 1980).[10]

What the studies of Kessler, Fischer, Ayubi and others mentioned earlier all have in common is a notion of context wider than earlier anthropological concerns with specific village locales and more narrow than the Islam of all times and places sometimes invoked by scholars and believers with non-sociological views of religious experience. The "middle ground" between these two extremes appears to be the most productive for comprehending world religious traditions. Exploration of this middle ground also facilitates an understanding of how the universalistic elements of Islam are practically communicated and of how modes of communication affect religious "universals." Among crucial topics that have not been sufficiently studied are (1) the pilgrimage to Mecca as a vehicle for disseminating or reformulating popular interpretations of Islam (prior studies have concentrated principally upon the *hajj* as a means of confirming social status or as a religious *rite de passage*), (2) the impact of Saudi efforts to fund younger religious teachers from throughout the Islamic world for studies in revitalized (and sect-free) institutions of higher learning in Saudi Arabia, (3) the use of oil revenues to enhance religious movements or institutions in less wealthy Islamic states, and (4) the study of dispersed, transregional "minority" Islamic groups such as the Isma'ilis.

A second major implication of the newer approaches to the study of Islam in local contexts is to reopen in a more constructive way the old debate among Islamic scholars as to what constitutes "normative" beliefs in Islam. In the past, discussion of the notion of normative Islam was often devoid of specific social and political contexts. When in the 1950s the late Gustave E. von Grunebaum considered the various ways in which great and little traditions could relate to one another, one possibility he considered was that the great tradition constituted the norm, the little traditions actual practice (von Grunebaum 1955, 30). Norms must be carried and at times be imposed by some persons over others; they do not simply exist. The "great transformation" brought about by new forms of communication raise salient questions concerning who accords legitimacy to various "normative" interpretations of Islam. Ayubi makes it clear that Egyptian fundamentalists rarely seek support or approbation from the traditionally educated religious elite or their supporters. Their point of reference is a "new," educated and urbanized audience with rather different religious expectations. The studies by Mardin on Bediüzzaman and by myself on the demise of Islamic mosque-university education in Morocco also suggest the importance of fundamental shifts in the intellectual technology used in transmitting and legitimating religious knowledge and authority. Colonel Qadhdhafi's *Green Book*, which at least in the English edition advertises that it provides the "ultimate solution" to world problems, nowhere specifically uses the term *Islam* although it can be argued that it is implicitly informed by an appeal to Islamic beliefs and principles (Qadhdhafi n.d.).[11] The low esteem of the author of the *Green Book* for the traditional interpreters and arbitors of Islamic tradition could not be more clear.

If current debates over what are "correct" or "normative" interpretations of Islam are particularly intense, they are hardly unique to the present or to the recent past.

Now that the first rush of studies on clergy–state relations in Iran has peaked, more historically reflective analyses suggest that there has not been any single "golden age" in which a particular form or doctrinal interpretation of such relations has prevailed, and that the content of what is regarded as normative as well as *whose* norms prevailed in practice has continuously undergone major shifts.[12] What is "traditional" in Islam is necessarily subject to ongoing debate and interpretation, so that the "problem" sometimes raised by scholars in the past of how Islam is accommodated to local and regional realities is somewhat misconstrued. The crucial issue is to elicit the implicit and explicit criteria as to why one interpretation of Islam is considered more normative than others at particular times and places, thus integrally relating ideologies to both their carriers and contexts. So one returns to the necessity of not taking meanings for granted. Even in Qur'anic recitation, which many Muslims regard as the essence of immutable communication, what is communicated is subject necessarily to considerable variation despite the best conscious efforts of reciters. As Richard Martin has written: "In order to know *what* the Koran means we have to ask *how* it means in Muslim culture. To answer this question we need to identify the various contexts—the textual, ritual, social and cosmological spaces—it occupies in Muslim culture" (Martin 1980b; also Martin 1980a). What is recited is central and significant, but inseparable from an account of how the recitation occurs and in what particular context. Without all these elements present, it is difficult to understand what is meant. A recitation of the Qur'an in seventh-century Arabia can take on a very different meaning than its recitation in twentieth-century Afghanistan. Whether the meaning at issue is a Qur'anic recitation or the wider expressions of religiosity, the renewed study of Islam in local contexts involves greater attention to how religious tradition and religious organization specifically shape and in turn are shaped by the wider political and economic contexts in which they occur.

Notes

* I wish to thank Karen I. Blu, Richard C. Martin, William R. Rolf and Kenneth Sandbank for their constructive comments on an earlier version of this paper.

1. Sura 12, verse 2; trans. Pickthall 1953, 174.
2. See also el-Zein 1977. I owe the phrase "neo-*tawhidi*" to John Voll.
3. For example, see Barclay 1964, 136–210, who uses "genuine" in this sense, and Rahman 1979, 153, who labels the leaders of popular religious orders as "charlatans" and "spiritual delinquents" because of their deviance from his own notion of accepted Islamic tradition. Although the polymath Gustave E. von Grunebaum also tended to juxtapose great and little traditions, the richness of his examples served as a stimulus to critical thought. See, for example, von Grunebaum 1955; Martin discusses von Grunebaum's concept of culture in Martin 1981.
4. These are Geertz 1960; Geertz 1968; and Geertz 1979, 123–313. For an assessment of the anthropological contribution to the study of Islam in the Middle East, see Eickelman 1981,

201–60. Significant studies by anthropologists and others dealing with Islam in other regions but not discussed in this essay for reasons of space are Lewis 1980; O'Brien 1971; Paden 1973; Ahmed 1976 (and subsequent works now in preparation); Eaton 1978; Roff 1974. A particularly important recent collection of essays that indicates the state of the art is the special issue of *Annales* 35, nos. 3–4 (May–August 1980), "Recherches sur l'Islam: Histoire et Anthropologie."

5. For an early discussion (originally published in 1957) of the problem of change in religious identity and faith, see also Geertz 1973, 142–69. Geertz's approach to "thick description" has recently been attacked by Fischer 1980, 266, as "trivial" because Geertz presumably "turns away from [an account of] the larger historical and sociological contexts." This notion is echoed in Kessler 1978, 20, who asserts that Geertz disregards his own warning (in Geertz 1973, 30) that cultural analysis should not "lose touch" with the political, economic and stratificatory "hard surfaces of life." In my judgment, Geertz recognizes and at times vividly describes these larger contexts and harder surfaces, but has deliberately chosen to clarify problems of cultural meanings, providing only historical and contextual detail appropriate to further their comprehension, than to represent details of political economy reasonably accessible in other works. Hence the question is *how* such larger contexts are invoked in ethnographic and social historical accounts, not whether they are. Thus in Kessler's monograph, discussed in detail later in this essay, his excellent account of the "harder surfaces" is complemented by a largely inferential one of popular religious beliefs which takes for granted many of those aspects of systems of meaning that Geertz, despite an occasionally over-luxuriant prose, seeks with some success to elucidate. Perhaps Kessler should be criticized for neglecting what he might call the "softer" surfaces of life, surfaces which however are crucial for understanding how persons in a given society perceive their opportunities and alternatives.

6. Another study that uses a Weberian framework (but one divergent from that employed by Gilsenan) is Eickelman 1976. See also Eickelman 1977.

7. For another discussion of the implications of Merad's work, see Gellner 1981, 149–73. The entire collection of essays in this volume constitute essential reading. In some regions of Algeria the reform movement appears to have been so firmly set in the milieu of maraboutic practices that reformist leaders often came from the same local maraboutic families that dominated other forms of religious expression and practice. See Colonna 1977.

8. See Eickelman 1978, and 1976, 211–37, for an account of historical shifts in popular religious assumptions; also Ahmed 1979.

9. Particularly the studies of Roff 1967 and the various contributors to Roff 1974.

10. On Egypt, see also the factually interesting but analytically thin study Ibrahim 1980; on Iran a useful complement to Fischer is Akhavi 1980.

11. In the Arabic version the term *din* (religion) is used throughout the text.

12. See Arjomand 1979 and 1981; Keddie 1980, 531; and Floor 1980, 501–24.

References

Ahmed, Akbar S. 1976. *Millennium and Charisma among Pathans*. Boston, MA: Routledge & Kegan Paul.

Ahmed, Rafiuddin. 1979. "Islamization in Nineteenth Century Bengal." In *Contributions to South Asian Studies*, I, ed. Krishna Gopal, 88–119. Delhi: Oxford University Press.

Akhavi, Shahrough. 1980. *Religion and Politics in Contemporary Iran.* Albany, NY: State University of New York Press.

Arjomand, Said Amir. 1979. "Religion, Political Action and Legitimate Domination in Shi'ite Iran: Fourteenth to Eighteenth Centuries A.D." *Archives Européenes de Sociologie* 20: 59–109.

—1981. "The Shi'ite Hierocracy and the State in Pre-Modern Iran: 1785–1890." *Archives Européenes de Sociologie* 22: 40–78.

Asad, Talal. 1980. "Ideology, Class and the Origin of the Islamic State." *Economy and Society* 9: 450-73.

Ayubi, Nazih N. M. 1980. "The Political Revival of Islam: The Case of Egypt." *International Journal of Middle East Studies* 12: 481–99.

Barclay, Harold B. 1964. *Buurri al Lamaab: A Suburban Village in the Sudan.* Ithaca, NY: Cornell University Press.

Bloch, Marc. 1964. *Feudal Society.* Trans. L. A. Manyon. Chicago, IL: University of Chicago Press.

Burke, Edmund, III. 1979. "Islamic History as World History: Marshall Hodgson, 'The Venture of Islam'." *International Journal of Middle East Studies* 10: 241–64.

Colonna, Fanny. 1977. "L'Islah en milieu paysan: le cas de l'Aurès 1936–1938." *Revue algérienne des sciences juridiques, économiques et politiques* 14: 277–88.

Eaton, Richard Maxwell. 1978. *Sufis of Bijapur, 1300–1700.* Princeton, NJ: Princeton University Press.

Eickelman, Dale F. 1976. *Moroccan Islam: Tradition and Society in a Pilgrimage Center.* Austin, TX: University of Texas Press.

—1977. "Ideological Change and Regional Cults: Maraboutism and Ties of 'Closeness' in Western Morocco." In *Regional Cults,* ed. Richard P. Werbner, 3–28. New York and London: Academic Press.

—1978. "The Art of Memory: Islamic Education and Its Social Reproduction." *Comparative Studies in Society and History* 20: 485–516.

—1981. *The Middle East: An Anthropological Approach.* Englewood Cliffs, NJ: Prentice-Hall.

el-Zein, Abdul Hamid M. 1974. *The Sacred Meadows: A Structural Analysis of Religious Symbolism in an East African Town.* Evanston, IL: Northwestern University Press.

—1977. "Beyond Ideology and Theology: The Search for the Anthropology of Islam." *Annual Review of Anthropology* 6: 227–54.

Fischer, Michael M. J. 1980. *Iran: From Religious Dispute to Revolution.* Cambridge: Harvard University Press.

Floor, William M. 1980. "The Revolutionary Character of the Iranian Ulama: Wishful Thinking or Reality?" *International Journal of Middle East Studies* 12: 501–24.

Geertz, Clifford. 1960. *The Religion of Java.* New York: The Free Press of Glencoe.

—1968. *Islam Observed: Religious Development in Morocco and Indonesia.* New Haven: Yale University Press.

—1972. "Religious Change and Social Order in Soeharto's Indonesia." *Asia* (New York) 27 (Autumn): 62–84.

—1973. *The Interpretation of Cultures.* New York: Basic Books.

—1979. "Suq: The Bazaar Economy in Sefrou." In *Meaning and Order in Moroccan Society,* ed. Clifford Geertz, Hildred Geertz and Lawrence Rosen, 123–313. New York: Cambridge University Press.

Gellner, Ernest. 1981. *Muslim Society*. Cambridge and New York: Cambridge University Press.

Gilsenan, Michael. 1973. *Saint and Sufi in Modern Egypt*. Oxford: Clarendon Press.

Goody, Jack. 1977. *The Domestication of the Savage Mind*. Cambridge and New York: Cambridge University Press.

Hodgson, Marshall G. S. 1974. *The Venture of Islam*. 3 vols. Chicago: University of Chicago Press.

Ibrahim, Saad Eddin. 1980. "Anatomy of Egypt's Militant Islamic Groups: Methodological Note and Preliminary Findings." *International Journal of Middle East Studies* 12: 423–53.

Keddie, Nikki R. 1980. "Iran: Change in Islam; Islam and Change." *International Journal of Middle East Studies* 11: 527–42.

Kessler, Clive S. 1978. *Islam and Politics in a Malay State: Kelantan 1838–1969*. Ithaca, NY: Cornell University Press.

Lewis, I. M. ed. 1980. *Islam in Tropical Africa*. 2nd ed. Bloomington, IN: Indiana University Press for the International African Institute.

Mardin, Serif. 1981. "Bediüzzaman Saïd Nursi: Preliminary Approaches to the Biography of a Turkish Muslim Fundamentalist Thinker." Manuscript. Cited by permission.

Martin, Richard C. 1980a. "Structural Analysis and the Qur'an: Newer Approaches to the Study of Islamic Texts." *Journal of the American Academy of Religion* 47: 665–83.

—1980b. "Understanding the Koran in Text and Context." Unpublished manuscript in the author's possession.

—1981. "Geertz and the Study of Islam: An Evaluation." Paper presented to the American Academy of Religion, San Francisco, Dec. 19–22.

Merad, Ali. 1967. *Le Réformisme musulmane en Algerie de 1925 à 1940*. Paris and The Hague: Mouton & Co.

O'Brien, D. B. Cruise. 1971. *The Mourides of Senegal*. Oxford: Clarendon Press.

Paden, John N. 1973. *Religion and Political Culture in Kana*. Berkeley and Los Angeles: University of California Press.

Pickthall, Mohammed Marmaduke, trans. 1953. *The Meaning of the Glorious Koran*. New York: Mentor Books.

Qadhdhafi, Muammar al-. n.d. *The Green Book*. Tripoli: Public Establishment for Publishing, Advertising and Distribution.

Rahman, Fazlur. 1979. *Islam*. 2nd ed. Chicago: University of Chicago Press.

Roff, William R. 1967. *The Origins of Malay Nationalism*. New Haven: Yale University Press.

Roff, William R., ed. 1974. *Kelantan: Religion, Society and Politics in a Malay State*. Kuala Lumpur: Oxford University Press.

Said, Edward W. 1978. *Orientalism*. New York: Pantheon Books.

Siegel, James. 1969. *The Rope of God*. Berkeley and Los Angeles: University of California Press.

Steiner, George. 1975. *After Babel: Aspects of Language and Translation*. Oxford and New York: Oxford University Press.

Von Grunebaum, Gustave E. 1955. "The Problem of Unity in Diversity." In *Unity and Variety in Muslim Civilization*, ed. G. E. von Grunebaum, 17–37. Chicago, IL: University of Chicago Press.

Waldman, Marilyn R. 1985. "Primitive Mind/Modern Mind: New Approaches to an Old Problem Applied to Religion." In *Approaches to Islam in the History of Religions,* ed. Richard C. Martin, 91–105. Tucson, AZ: University of Arizona Press.

Weber, Max. 1963. *The Sociology of Religion*. Trans. Ephraim Fishcoff. Boston, MA: Beacon Press.

Beyond Ideology and Theology:
The Search for the Anthropology of Islam

Abdul Hamid M. el-Zein

In the course of our intellectual history, Islam came to be understood as a unified religious tradition and, in common with other institutional religions, taken as a guide to its own understanding (Levy 1957). The concept of Islam thus defined the nature of the subject matter and its appropriate modes of interpretation or explanation, but discoveries emergent within this framework have begun to contradict these premises.

In order to reveal the significance and complexity of this problem, this review first examines two apparently opposed positions on Islam: the "anthropological" and the "theological." These perspectives emerge from different assumptions concerning the nature of Man, God, and the World; use different languages of analysis; and produce different descriptions of religious life. Five anthropological studies are taken here to represent the internal variation within the anthropological perspective, while a general commentary suffices to describe the more standardized theological paradigm. Of course, the works discussed here do not exhaust the relevant studies of Islam, but they exemplify certain major approaches well enough to allow discussion of the interaction of theoretical views and ethnographic description. In all approaches, the meaning of religion as a universal form of human experience and of Islam as a particular instance is presupposed, invariable, and incontestable. Consequently, all claim to uncover a universal essence, the real Islam. Ironically, the diversity of experience and understanding revealed in these studies challenges the often subtle premise of the unity of religious meaning. It then becomes possible to ask if a single true Islam exists at all.

By virtue of its scope and sophistication, the work of Clifford Geertz offers a suitable point from which to begin the investigation. Although he proceeds by assuming a single form of religious experience and a unity of meaning within Islamic tradition, Geertz simultaneously accentuates the diversity in the actual content of religious experience as lived in the everyday world. Although they are intricately imbedded in his most recent study on Islam (Geertz 1968), the theoretical notions which permit the eventual integration of this diversity are never systematically stated or elaborated. These crucial assumptions emerge clearly only through reconstructing implicit relationships between statements presented in other works.

For Geertz, human phenomena are simultaneously organic, psychological, social, and cultural. Certain universal problems and qualities of being human arise from the reality of man's biological condition and in necessary social and psychological processes. Yet, when grasped by man's immediate consciousness, these existential problems and conditions appear plastic and elusive. It is through the dimension of culture, which is man's unique capacity, that these problems and processes are given meaning, organized and controlled (Geertz 1964, 52–63; 1965, 51; 1966, 5; 1968, 100; 1973, 5). These four dimensions of human reality are mutually determinative, and therefore must ultimately be integrated within a single analytic framework. But because culture particularly is the means of interpretation of all experience, it becomes the central concept in Geertz's understanding of human existence. Culture lends both order and significance to man's direct and matter-of-fact apprehension of the reality of nature and existence. In this sense, culture does not refer to a set of institutions, traditions, or customs, but involves the conceptualization of life: an intersubjective process of the interpretation of immediate experience (Geertz 1968, 93–94).

The cultural processes of giving meaning to the world are rooted in the human capacity for symbolic thought. All men impose thought or meaning upon the objects of their experience (events, images, sounds, gestures, sensations) which, when defined, become attached to symbols or the material vehicles of meaning (Geertz 1966, 5). In turn, meaning arranges these objects in intelligible forms. This expressive capacity results in the creation of cultural systems understood as patterns of symbols which must possess a certain degree of coherence in order to establish for man the structure of his own existence (Geertz 1973, 17).

For Geertz, symbols and the meanings they carry are culturally defined and socially shared. An individual is born into an already meaningful world. He inherits cultural interpretations from his predecessors, shares them with his contemporaries, and passes them on to the following generations. Therefore, symbolic thought is always social, intersubjective, and public. It cannot escape into a mysterious and inaccessible domain of private subjective meaning.

So while man creates his own symbols, these symbols define for him the nature of his own reality. For Geertz, the analysis of culture consists of the study of these social, intersubjective, and culturally relative worlds. It is a positive science in the sense that it deals with symbols as empirical expressions of thought. And it is cast in phenomenological terms: his intention is to develop "a method of describing and analyzing the meaningful structure of experience ... in a word, a scientific phenomenology of culture" (Geertz 1966, 7). The emphasis of this approach is on "meaning." Because it is impossible to discover directly the ontological status of events, actions, institutions, or objects, the problem lies in grasping their meaning when brought to consciousness.

The formation of different forms of cultural systems corresponds to certain levels of the organization of thought. Geertz refers informally to the variety of possible cultural systems throughout his studies: religion, art, common sense, philosophy, history, science, aesthetics, ideology (Geertz 1964, 62; 1968, 94). In his study of Islam, common sense, religion, and science become the most essential symbolic forms in his analysis.

Common sense constitutes a primary dimension through which man gives meaning to his immediate experience (Geertz 1975a). Common sense is not the mere matter-of-fact apprehension of reality but the judgments, assessments, or colloquial wisdom which structure a practical reality. This set of shared notions is not the outcome of deliberations or reflection, but emerges in the experiential engagement' with reality. Common-sense notions involve such basic aspects of survival that they are invariably taken for granted.

However, the relation between common-sense notions, matter-of-fact reality, and human creativity is never stable. The nature of man's engagement with the world changes through time with increasing awareness and differs from place to place. Therefore, common-sense notions differ and change accordingly—or when common sense simply fails to account for experience, its authority dwindles, and religion as a higher and more general interpretive order emerges (Geertz 1968, 94–95). Religion, in Geertz's view, offers a wider interpretation of the world and serves as a correction of common sense. In this sense, religion and common sense enter into a continued dialectic and must be studied as reciprocal traits of man's experiential reality.

Geertz refers to religion as the synthesis of two dimensions of human experience: "world view" and "ethos." In any culture, the collective notions, images, and concepts of the world view establish the essential reality of nature, self, and society. They define the sheer actuality of existence (Geertz 1957, 421; 1968, 97). Ethos constitutes the evaluative aspect of existence; it expresses the desired character, tone, style, and quality of social and cultural life. It concerns the way in which things are properly done (Geertz 1968, 97–98). Ethos and world view, or values and the general order of existence, continually reaffirm each other. Their interrelationship is powerfully and concretely expressed in the form of sacred symbols which not only objectify but condense multiple rays of the universe of meaning and focus them in tangible and perceptible forms. Any culture will require only a limited number of synthesizing symbols due to their immense power to enforce this integration of fact and value (Geertz 1957, 421–22).

Systems of religious symbols continually respond to the inevitable force of historical change. Geertz regards history as the continual process of formation and sedimentation of meaning. No laws or processes of history exist but the creation of meaning which, because meaning is intersubjective, constitutes a process of social transformation as well. To arrive at any general explanation, history is studied in reverse for there are no predictive and necessary sequences of meaning. Yet, in spite of his rejection of grand-scale historical necessity, Geertz does impose the constraint of the concept of tradition. For most civilizations, the structure of possibilities of change is set in formative years (Geertz 1968, 11). Thus, traditions, such as Islam, emerge with the continuity of culturally shared meanings.

Yet, the concept of history in Geertz's work contains an internal tension. On the one hand, historical change is the necessary field for man's continual creation of meaning through which he realizes himself as a human and cultural being. On the other hand, change is continually denied by man, whose very creation of symbols reflects the intention to fix and stabilize meanings in objectified forms. Religion reflects this struggle. In situations of extreme change such as foreign intrusion or conquest, religious symbols and beliefs may weaken in the face of upheaval and contradiction in previously coincident social conditions. Yet, it is equally possible that by virtue of the commitment of faith, these symbols may persist by denying other forms of experience such as moral, aesthetic, scientific, or even practical considerations. In this sense, faith is the true counterpart of change. While belief may stabilize reality momentarily and partially, faith attempts to fix it absolutely.

It is through yet another mode of experience, science, that these other cultural systems may be understood. Because science is itself a cultural system, it too becomes a process of interpretation. Yet, it constitutes a privileged mode of understanding in the sense that it grasps the reality of the entire process of human existence, unlike common sense and religion which remain limited to particular forms of experience. As a scientist, the anthropologist must not merely observe and report, he must interpret the native's interpretation of reality, or give a "thick" description (Geertz 1973). This thick description is achieved when the scientific imagination succeeds in suspending its own cultural attitudes in order to comprehend the essential nature of human experience. Scientific explanation in Geertz's view is a matter of discovering the intricacies of expression. To explain is to reorganize and clarify the complexity of meaning by revealing its order in symbolic forms (Geertz 1965, 47; 1973, 16).

The scientific understanding of religious experience is perhaps the most difficult. These moments of subjective spiritual experience demand complete involvement, and therefore are never directly communicated between subjects. Rather, the immediate religious experience usually becomes translated into common-sense terms. But science, as a privileged mode of interpretation, recognizes and accounts for this process of "secondary revision" and is capable of an indirect understanding of religious symbols. Furthermore, this very rephrasing into common sense reveals to the scientific mind the relevance of religion to social action.

In *Islam Observed* (Geertz 1968), it is this scientific phenomenology of culture which Geertz applies to the analysis of the diverse cultural expressions of Islam in Morocco and Indonesia. Geertz examines the interrelationship of sacred symbols with world view, ethos, faith, common sense, and social context which constitutes the total religious experience. The precise contents of the religious system and the social order vary through time and from culture to culture. In this study, the detailed and intricate variations in the meaning of the religious experience result from both the pressure of history and the already-given distinctions in cultural or social traditions. However, the complex diversity of meaning which emerges from the comparison of Indonesian and Moroccan Islam is always intended to reveal similarities at a higher analytic level which embrace the diverse processes of formation and transformation of cultural expressions or styles of a core tradition.

The first factor of variation is simply the accidental sequence of historical events. In Morocco, Islam was introduced as early as the seventh century by Arabic warriors who espoused the loosely defined concepts of a newly established religious community. The Indonesians, however, received a far more developed and well-ordered Islamic doctrine from traders who arrived in the fourteenth century. During these initial periods when Islam first put its roots into foreign lands, certain conditions in each society set the limits within which Islamic meaning might develop and change (Geertz 1968, 11). These constraints created the boundaries of possible variation which are the basis of the development of distinct "traditions" of meaning. Perhaps the most significant constraint in Geertz's analysis is the nature of the social order into which religious symbols and ideas must naturally fit in order to seem authentic (Geertz 1968, 20).

In the case of Morocco, the relevant social context consisted of an unstable pattern of settlement and continuous feuding. Religious symbols both defined and interpreted this social reality. In coincidence with a fragmented social structure, Moroccan Islam lacked a religious order or hierarchy which would determine who could and could not aspire to leadership and sainthood. Instead, personal charisma, which any man might possess regardless of social or religious status, became the sole criterion of authority and power. The symbol of authority, the saint, took on the image of the warrior zealously enforcing his own doctrine, continually striving to enhance his charisma by producing miracles, and demanding the blind obedience of as many followers as possible.

The Indonesian setting differed entirely. The population was quietly settled in towns or outlying agricultural villages, and their social relations were built upon a sense of order and cooperation. Their version of Islam involved a strict, hierarchical order of graded spirituality and corresponding rules determining who was to attain the highest stages. The saint became a symbol of self-contained order, inward reflection, and self-reform. His power lay not in the brute force of his authority but in the rewards of internal insight through years of meditation.

Geertz sees these saints as metaphors or cultural constructions in which society objectifies its values, norms, ideals, and notions defining significant actions. Each embraces and condenses thousands of meanings and is able to create a symbolic unity between otherwise discordant elements (Geertz 1964, 58–59). Through the selection and comparison of these key synthesizing symbols, and through the investigation of particular historical and social dimensions of their expression, Geertz builds up the diverse patterns of existential meaning in these local *islam*s. With precision, he locates the uniqueness which distinguishes one culture's experience of Islam from another's. While the saints of Morocco and the saints of Indonesia might play a similar role as condensing metaphors, their meanings will never be the same.

Despite his emphasis on the particularity and historicity of these religious experiences, Geertz continues to refer to them collectively as "Islamic" and to speak of "Islamic consciousness" and "Islamic reform." The unity which he thus imputes to the religious phenomena emerges as a consequence of his presupposed notions of human existence. For Geertz, human reality at its most fundamental level is unified. It involves the universal conditions of being. For all men, the lived-in world is an experienced world constituted through symbolically expressed meanings which are intersubjectively or socially shared. Geertz establishes not only the reality of shared experience but also the forms in which it is expressed. His work on Islam emphasizes the primacy of common sense, religion, and science. Although they vary according to the content of particular cultural expressions, the forms themselves and their interrelationships remain fixed and universal. The dynamics of these forms and the expression of their content yield the dimension of existence called history; and the continuity of meaning in time and space leads to the formation of historical traditions of meaning.

Thus all expressions of Islam find unity of meaning through two dimensions of these universal conditions: first as expressions of a particular form of experience, religion, with certain defined characteristics such as the integration of world view and ethos; and second as an historically continuous tradition of meaning in which the original expression and all those following it in time and space do not exist as complete distinct realities but as delicately related developments of an initial symbolic base linked by the social process of shared meaning. Islam is seen in terms of Wittgenstein's notion of family resemblances. Striking similarities seem to appear over many generations, yet a careful look shows that no one characteristic is held in common. Rather, features overlap and crisscross. There is less order than in a trend within a single tradition. Continuities arise in oblique connections and glancing contrasts (Geertz 1975b). This unity of Islam established at the level of his philosophical premises allows Geertz to speak legitimately of an "Islamic" consciousness at the level of actual experience as well. Each individual experience contains the universal characteristics assigned to the religious form of experience and those particular shared meanings which recall an entire tradition of Islam.

It is this notion that the diverse expressions of Islam may be unified at the level of a universal meaning of human reality that links Geertz with otherwise opposed anthropological analyses. Crapanzano (1973) in discussing the Hamadsha sect in Moroccan Islam addresses culture not as the intersubjective interpretation of experience but as the expression of a Freudian unconscious. From this psychological perspective all the consciously known and accepted meanings which make up culture become arbitrary and illusory. Their only reality lies in the fact that they repress and socially control the universal instincts and conflicts of the psyche. Therefore, Islam taken as a cultural and, in this case, religious expression constitutes an historical representation of these underlying tensions. At the level of conscious meaning, the diverse expressions of Islam are not considered as different cultural realities but as historically related ideologies or illusions built upon a single reality. This absolute truth which unifies all Islam, and all religion in general, lies in the unconscious and in the universal conditions of the human psyche.

Crapanzano's analysis focuses on a single Islamic order in Morocco, the *Hamadsha*. He intends to reveal how their expression of Islam is constructed in a way which resolves certain universal psychic conflicts manifest in the interrelationship of their social structure, values, and role expectations. The followers of the *Hamadsha* consist mainly of Arabs. In their traditional family structure, males claim complete authority while women remain passive and submissive. However, the Arab father requests this same feminine submission from his sons, who wish to satisfy their father by complying with these demands and at the same time aspire to the ideal dominant behavior of the male. So the tension becomes apparent. A son is raised as a female and expected to behave as a male. If he realizes his male ideal, then he loses it by defying his father. In Crapanzano's view, these conflicts which arise from sexual instincts rooted in the Freudian psyche create the need for release achieved through the *Hamadsha*'s religious expression.

Both legend and ritual are interpreted in order to uncover these hidden psychic meanings. The Hamadsha myths of the two dominant saints, Sidi ʿAli bin Hamdush and Sidi Ahmed Dghughi recreate the contradiction of dominance and submission, male and female. The saint's relationship mimics the bond between father and son. Sidi ʿAli takes an active, dominant role, while Sidi Ahmed affirms his manhood through passive submission to the orders of the other. The true meaning of rituals lies in the mediation of these conflicts. In the ritual of the *hadra*, the she-demon ʿAʾisha functions as an externalized superego who enforces the position of the feminized male and at the same time reinforces his manhood. In this way she assists male participants in passing through the psychological trauma of the feminine role in order to recognize their ideal.

The above interpretations rest totally on two premises, one theoretical and the other ethnographic. First, Crapanzano assumes the Freudian hypothesis of the sexual tensions of the psyche. And secondly, he attributes a simplistic and clear-cut opposition of dominance and submission to the relationship between the Arab male and female which then confirms his theoretical position. Like Freud, Crapanzano forces extreme limitations on his material through seeking a single predetermined meaning. Because all consciously expressed cultural meanings are condemned as pure illusion, they must be reduced to the same underlying hidden reality. His Freudian assumptions restrict the universe of meaning to a limited and totally fixed vocabulary of symbols— the instincts—which determine the experience of all human beings regardless of their cultural background.

For this reason, Crapanzano's analysis never requires an interpretation of the many versions of the Hamadsha myths. He need examine only one, for all will ultimately reveal the same human truth. Yet, these variations present significant questions. In one legend, Sidi 'Ali dies before Sidi Ahmed brings back the she-demon, and in another he dies after Sidi Ahmed returns. Such slight differences in the sequence of events may entail interpretations of the relationship of the saints or of the power of the she-demon which do not conform to the interpretation of reality given by Crapanzano.

However, from the perspective of the Freudian paradigm adopted by Crapanzano, these variations in cultural meaning add no new knowledge to the understanding of human experiences. Diverse cultural expressions do not distinguish different human realities, but merely provide an imaginary mode by which man escapes a single and universal reality: the unresolvable situation, the traumatic archaic experience where desires can neither be suppressed nor satisfied. So all apparently unique and diverse institutions, thoughts, and events merely repeat what man has always done before, and their variation through time or history is reduced to an endless sequence of recreations with no accidents and no surprises.

Reading Freud in this way gives the analyst the privileged power of seeing through illusion to a hidden reality. As Ricoeur puts it, "this can be understood as reduction pure and simple" (1974, 192). However, Freud might be read in a different way—for instance, as Ricoeur reads him. Interpretation does not have to return to a single meaning. For if it is accepted that a symbol has one meaning, then all varying meanings at the level of consciousness are distortions hiding the real meaning which is secret, which cannot be grasped by those who actually live these meanings but only through the insight of the analyst. But if the symbol is left open, its real meaning is no longer a secret but an enigma to be restored by continual interpretation. Without these cultural interpretations the fixed content of the psyche is mute, and the symbolic relations are not yet in existence (Ricoeur 1970, 91–98). Meaning then is not to be interpreted once, and correctly, but continually reinterpreted, as in Geertz's position, in order to reveal the significance of human life.

It is clear that Crapanzano's paradigm includes, beside the location of meaning in the primordial experience, definite assumptions about man, consciousness, and history. Man is imprisoned in a world which he did not create, and all his efforts to escape from it are doomed. In this view, history and change are mere illusions. Conscious meaning, or culture, which includes the religious expression of Islam, is a mechanism to cover and avoid the essential reality of the primordial experience (Rieff 1951, 114–31).

This pessimistic view of life, history, and consciousness can be contrasted with the human reality addressed by Geertz. For Geertz, man's dialectical relation with the world transforms—through reflection and intention—the given, meaningless perceptions into a meaningfully lived human world. The mode of reflection and its intensity varies from the passive reflection on the socially given world to an active and critical reflection in which the world is not taken for granted but questioned, reinterpreted, and sometimes uprooted. But this critical and doubtful mood does not eliminate meaning or consciousness; rather, it expands both. There are no limits to man's abilities and creativity; progress itself is one of these meaningful concepts created by man in the course of his own history.

However, it is essential for man, in order to continue to produce meaning, to reflect upon his taken-for-granted reality, to modify it, transform it, and even deny it. In order to do this, he must view reality not as fixed and finished but as open to novel and new articulations. Social systems which hinder this openness will end in fossilizing man, history, and consciousness. Geertz alludes to the force of such restrictions when he describes stability in the Islamic societies which he studied: it will be a long time before someone in Morocco or Indonesia might declare that God is dead. In both societies, systems of meaning are socially and religiously imposed upon the members of the society to an extent which prohibits them from questioning or criticizing their reality.

Due to more frequent and more politically significant encounters with Western ideology and science, however, certain Islamic societies have begun to reflect critically upon the religious assumptions at the base of their understanding of the world. The two monographs to be considered now both deal with the impact of social change on religious structure and with the changing shape of traditional society as a whole. Bujra's (1971) contribution deals with the politics of social stratification in the southern Arabian town of Hureidah (in Hadramut). Gilsenan's (1973) monograph investigates the formation of a mystical order and its relation to social and political change in twentieth-century Egypt. Both analyze the response of religious systems to the dwindling of the social arrangements which once supported them. Although the ecology, social structure, and even the history of Islam in these two societies are different, both were characterized by well-defined, stable, and closed systems of traditional religious symbols and meanings which social upheaval now challenges.

In the case of Southern Arabia, it is the *Sadah*, or descendents of the Prophet Muhammad, who traditionally stand as the religious elite. The *Sadah* define themselves as a group according to their genealogical descent from the Prophet. Through claiming a necessary correspondence between religious knowledge and the concept of privileged descent, they possess the authority both to create the content of religious ideology and to enforce this ideology among the people.

According to the *Sadah*, descent from the Prophet passes on to them a superior knowledge with which they create the content of a system of religious symbols. They believe that their Islam is not a mere interpretation of the Qur'an or sacred tradition of the Prophet but rather that it is the real Islam inherited from their ancestor, Muhammad. They claim to be not only the mediators between man and God but the direct representation of God's reality on earth, restoring order to the world and defining the meaning of both nature and ordinary man according to the Word of God. Access to this knowledge is further controlled in a closed system of religious education. Although theoretically such training is open to all social groups by tradition, it is available only to the *Sadah* or to those whom they consider capable of religious knowledge, the *Mashaikh*.

The *Sadah* then enforce their own dominating position and perpetuate the religious ideology which they have constructed by means of certain social and political controls over the other groups within their society, and they legitimize these powers in terms of religious authority. They arbitrate continuous tribal feuds and establish sanctuary towns in which tribes may meet peacefully. In this way they also protect the rest of the population—the peasants and artisans known as *Masakin* (the poor) and *Du'fa* (the weak)—from the tribesmen's attacks. Although the *Sadah* are a unified group by virtue of the sacred symbol of descent, they have dispersed and settled over a large area in order to set up an extensive network of political relations with the many different tribes and segments of the *Masakin* stratum. They further infiltrate and control the other social groups through religious justification of the *Kafa'a* marriage system which allows marriage only within the same social group or with women of a lower social stratum, in which case the children take the status of their father. No woman, however, may marry into a lower social group and diminish the social status of her children. By following this system, the *Sadah* create the delicate balance of being able to establish the controls of kinship within all social groups of lower birth and yet maintain their own higher status by claiming the children from such marriages as their own. By means of these controls based ultimately on religious ideology, the *Sadah* accumulated political power, social prestige, and economic superiority.

In a society constructed in this fashion, social change is completely curbed by the religious elite. If mobility is possible at all, it is downward and not upward (Bujra 1971, 112). Bujra finds only two courses of potential change within this framework: first, the migration of the lower status groups to areas with a different social system and associated opportunities, and secondly, political intervention. Neither has totally erased the pre-established hierarchy, however; migrants often arrive in towns where the *Sadah* also settle and maintain economic advantages due to reputation. And although the British occupation disarmed and pacified the tribesmen, thus depriving the *Sadah* of a source of political power, the *Sadah* still dominate economic relations. Bujra assumes that real change will come only when this economic infrastructure is transformed by whatever means possible.

In his study, Bujra understands Islam as a set of ideas created by an elite and accepted by the masses, which enables its producers to enforce and manipulate social, economic, and political hierarchies. Islam is thus reduced to an instrumental ideology. According to his own understanding, Bujra interprets religious symbols as conscious means of achieving political and economic goals. The masses' reverence of the *Sadah* becomes a sign of submission which perpetuates the superior position of the *Sadah*. And the *Kafa'a* marriage rules are understood only as a mechanism which allows the *Sadah* to marry into all groups and prohibits other groups from exercising the same right. Bujra, like Crapanzano, closes the system of meaning and interpretation. Crapanzano uses the idiom of the unconscious; Bujra uses the idiom of politics and domination. Bujra, who questions the significance of religious phenomena in the creation of a meaningful world in favor of a social and economic explanation of changing historical conditions, ends by interpreting the position of the *Sadah* and the meaning of their religious symbols within an analytic frame of reference which is imposed upon their cultural system rather than cast in the system's own terms.

To some extent, Gilsenan's analysis (1973) of an expression of Islam in a changing society avoids this problem. He studies the emergence of a saint and his vision of God and human existence during a period of social upheaval in Egypt. He defines the saint as a charismatic leader, who, as Weber would have it, has a unique and personal power to shape the meaning of existence during a time of social crisis and to convince a group of people to commit themselves to his vision. Weber emphasizes, although Gilsenan does not, the revolutionary nature of the charismatic leadership and belief which "revolutionizes men 'from within' and shapes material and social conditions according to its revolutionary will" (Weber 1968, 1116). Charisma starts as a conflict with the rational-legal norms: "Hence, its attitude is revolutionary and transvalues everything: it makes a sovereign break with the traditional or rational norms: 'It has been written, but I say unto you'" (Weber 1968, 1115). The system of meaning which the charismatic leader creates must be clothed in novel, personal, and emotional insights which continuously capture the imagination of the believers and convince them to follow him without question. The essence of charisma arises in its spontaneity and dies as soon as it becomes routinized and depersonalized. Therefore, in its pure form, charisma opposes bureaucracy which represents formal, impersonal, and fixed systems of rules and meanings.

Gilsenan's analysis of the saint as a charismatic leader is more in line with the interpretation of Weber associated with Edward Shils, who emphasizes the extraordinary quality of charisma but then links it with established orders of society (Bensman and Givant 1975, 570–614). The saint described by Gilsenan did not contest the existing social order. Instead, he appears to be a leader with a personal vision, arising at a time of crisis, and trying to establish a mystical order according to the organizational requirements created by the government. He intended social readjustment rather than revolution.

In Egypt, at the time of the appearance of the Saint Sidi Salama al-Radi (1867–1927), the British occupation and the influence of technological and economic success in Western societies disrupted traditional values, social structure, and religious order, particularly the significance of mystical orders shattered in the face of the rising importance of secular means of achievement. The *'ulama'*, the religious elite whose authority rested upon legalistic and formal theological interpretations of the Qur'an, joined with the government in an effort to revive the image of Islam by purifying its concepts and formalizing its structure. Therefore, by official decision in 1903, the mystical orders were organized as a bureaucratic system. However, in spite of this, their inherently fluid notions of affiliation allowed continuous changes in membership and segmentation of the orders themselves. The political disfavor which this incurred, combined with competition from secular education, political parties, and social clubs, brought the entire rationale of mystical orders and knowledge into question.

The Saint Sidi Salama al-Radi intended to reestablish the preeminence of mysticism through the creation of a new order which would satisfy the needs of the rising middle class and offer the working class a personal expression of religion. He possessed the traditional mystic criterion of leadership: he received the teachings of an already established line of religious leaders, and claimed the gift of supernatural power of God. In this sense, the Egyptian saint strikes a compromise between the miraculous charisma which Geertz finds in Morocco and the genealogically based charisma of the *Sadah*. His power is determined both by revelation and by a sacred lineage of teachers. Yet, in this period of rapid modernization, the legitimization of sainthood also required formal theological knowledge. Although in the past mysticism was ambivalent concerning the worth of studying theology, it now claimed to include it. Thus, Sidi Salama al-Radi incorporated miraculously the currently valued tenets of formal theology into a mystical tradition in which knowledge comes directly from God.

The order he established, the Hamidiya Shadhiliya, was based upon a corpus of laws which he decreed in order to define a strict hierarchy of roles and functions. Each member was responsible to the saint or to his representative. The actions of the members had to be watched carefully, and the branches of the order were to be inspected from time to time to secure their obedience of the laws. A sacred oath, the *'ahd*, that enforced an irrevocable and life-long commitment to the order was required. A structure of the saint's religious innovations then fell directly into the existing pattern of the formal bureaucratic rigidity that mysticism claimed to challenge.

Perhaps the most puzzling aspect of Gilsenan's analysis is the use of the framework of charisma to elucidate the sociological power of this saint. If the investigation is pursued, the mystic appears to lack the requirements of the concept. First, the saint was originally a member of the Qawigjiya-Shadhiliya order, and from that group he drew the followers who constituted the core of his new order (Mustafa 1974). Therefore, he did not found the order through the power of his personal charisma, but through systematic recruitment from members of a group already socially and politically predisposed to commitment. Secondly, the history of the Shadhiliya order in Egypt reveals a traditional compatibility between theological concepts and mystical knowledge (al-Shayal 1965, 162–90). Sidi Salama's efforts to integrate theological formulations with mysticism were more a rephrasing of the content of an established pattern rather than a personal and revolutionary synthesis in line with Weber's definition of the charismatic leader.

And finally, the bureaucratic structure of the new order directly contradicts the nature of change which occurs through charisma. The saint, through his laws and through the sacred oath, abolished the vital process of continual reinterpretation that characterizes a charismatic message. Even Gilsenan admits that, according to sociological criteria, the charisma of the saint failed to capture the nature, direction, and intensity of change in the social and political life of Egypt at that time. Instead his visions and organizations portrayed a static world which conformed to the traditional concept of formally structured religion.

Now the question of the proper role of religion in social processes arises. Unlike Bujra, who reduces religion and Islam to a political ideology which is used to manipulate a socioeconomic base, Gilsenan explores the power of religious meaning, through charisma, to create and define the nature and historical sense of social life. In this way, he brings out the cultural significance of religion which Geertz also has emphasized. Yet, as in Bujra's analysis, religion at base remains an ideological system designed to cover and justify a social reality. For Bujra, religion manipulates a social world; for Gilsenan, it merely defines and orders it. In the end, the role of the charismatic saint and of religion in general was to satisfy certain social and political conditions. The degree to which these demands were met determined the success of the saint and the legitimacy of the religious system. If religious means had failed to cope with changing social relations and attitudes, other institutions would have arisen as alternative solutions. So for both Bujra and Gilsenan the process of social change proceeds along a single path. And Islam constitutes a temporary ideological obstacle which will eventually be superseded by a more modern and rational form of society.

According to both Gilsenan and Bujra, religion constrains and stabilizes its social base. Islamic societies would have remained locked into a traditional form, determined by the rigidity of their religious world view, had it not been for the external forces of change arising through contact with the West. And even at that, the expressions of Islam in both Southern Arabia and in Egypt perpetrated their significance either by completely resisting change in other dimensions of society, as in the instance of the *Sadah*, or by readjustment to new social and political conditions with the foundation of a bureaucratic mystic order. In neither case did religion itself become an innovative force.

It is Eickelman's contribution to contest this notion of religion's inherently static form (1976). He makes history the dominant theoretical perspective which views social reality and all cultural or symbolic systems, including religion, as in a continuous state of change. He criticizes other models of change as mere comparisons of two static states, the before and the after, without accounting for the social processes which make the transition possible. Certainly Gilsenan and Bujra fall into this category. They compare traditional and stable Islamic societies with new social forms conceived as the after-effects of Western influence. Yet, they ignore the immanent dialectic within each society which constitutes the basis of that change.

In order to reveal the complexity of these processes, Eickelman insists that social reality must be analyzed in both its synchronic and diachronic dimensions. A diachronic view of society over time preserves a sense of the uniqueness and particularity of its characteristics; a synchronic study uncovers the interrelationships among its elements that hold at one point in time but which, by virtue of a necessary incongruity between the symbolic and the social, inevitably lead to change. Thus these two points of view become complementary rather than contradictory as in many other anthropological approaches (Sahay 1972, 153–64). In this respect, Eickelman claims to follow in the footsteps of Max Weber. He tries to refute those who find a basic conflict between Weber's sociological and historical analyses (Bendix 1945–46, 518–26).

In Weber's own work, the immediately given reality is an essentially undefined, chaotic, and irrational stream of experience (Burger 1976, 77–93). Man selects and imposes meaning on certain aspects of life which then constitute his actual historical and social world. The range of possible meanings which he may choose to impose remains inexhaustible. Therefore, the creation of historical relevancies is also unlimited and "in flux, ever subject to change in the dimly seen future of human culture" (Weber 1949, 111). In order to grasp and organize the concrete social and historical phenomena defined by the subjective meanings held by the actors themselves, the sociologist uses the concept of the ideal type which simplifies the complexity of the historical data by typification of subjective meaning. The ideal type itself is formed by the selection and exaggeration of one or several viewpoints. It is a thought-picture designed by the analyst. "In its conceptual purity, this mental construct cannot be found empirically anywhere in reality. It is a utopia" (Weber 1949, 90). History and sociology then are combined in the sense that phenomena which conceptually change through time, or diachronically, are the source of the synchronic idealization of sociological understanding.

Eickelman's analysis of Maraboutism in Morocco reinterprets rather than reproduces these Weberian concepts. If he were to build his model on perpetual change in the strict Weberian sense, then the meanings, interests, and relevancies of the matter he studies must change. However, he states that "From an analysis of Maraboutism in its contemporary context and an attempt to comprehend the fundamental assumptions which Moroccans now make about social reality, one develops a sense of expectation of what is crucial and often absent in evidence concerning earlier periods" (Eickelman 1976, 63). This implies the use of the present to reconstruct the past, which in turn suggests a continuity of values and interests which violate Weber's notion of historical change. Eickelman further remarks that after considerable immersion in the contemporary aspects of Maraboutism, "it became clear that something was missing, that what I saw were fragments of a pattern of beliefs, once solid, that was beginning to crumble" (Eickelman 1976, 64). Again, a stable social and religious reality takes shape. Here the present is not conceived as a particular historical reality in its own right. Instead it is evaluated as incomplete against a reconstructed or presumed past totality.

Eickelman treats history as a real sequence of empirical events. He reconstructs historical facts according to documents, French travelogues, and observations of the present. These events are linked by an inherent continuum of meaning, values, and interests which reach from some point in the past into the present. This extension of historical meaning implies stability rather than change. The Moroccan cultural systems are not open to continual and unlimited variation but constrained by boundaries inherent in the notion of historical continuity.

If change takes place, it is within this bounded reality. For Eickelman the force of change in any society lies in the lack of fit between social conduct and symbolic systems which express the culturally defined universe of meaning. He feels that a tendency exists in anthropological analyses to place these two dimensions in perfect correspondence. Either the social structure is considered the essentially stable domain and the symbolic system becomes its reflection, or vice versa. In these cases, the problem of historical change is avoided. However, an interaction occurs between these two systems which indicates that they remain distinct and out of balance. This asymmetric relationship can be seen when the individual, Eickelman's basic unit of analysis, manipulates symbols in order to realize his social goals and interests, justify or acquire a social position, or accumulate power. Eickelman refers to the means of manipulation as ideologies which mediate the opposition of the symbolic and the social. Ideologies themselves must be conceived as social activities maintained through various forms of expression, including ritual action. In the process of expression and manipulation, ideologies change over time. In turn, they reshape and redefine the social order. Yet, because ideology continually varies according to its historical moment of use, a social structure can never be in complete coincidence with its ideological counterpart.

All expressions of religion—in this case Islam—are dealt with in terms of the notion of "ideology" defined as an essentially instrumental and pragmatic function. Religious ideology works at two social levels: the explicit ideology articulated by intellectuals and the religious elite, and implicit ideology which consists of local and popular interpretations of religious tradition. Although they do share certain elements in common, these two dimensions continually come into conflict. With respect to a particular version of Moroccan Islam, Maraboutism, the local interpretations that Eickelman investigates are the outcome of a world view resting on five key concepts: God's will, reason, propriety, obligation, and compulsion. Although these concepts are not related to each other in any permanent pattern, they all serve to render social action both meaningful and coherent. For instance, God's will is considered to be the cause of all that happens in the world. Men of reason must continually modify their own course of action to accommodate that will (Eickelman 1976, 126) in order to maximize their chances of worldly success. Those who are closer to God, as the Marabouts who are saints, will be able to decipher the acts of God and claim a privileged access to this knowledge. Therefore, "closeness" to a saint becomes the ideology used by the people to realize and justify any form of social gain.

The saint, at least for those who follow him, defines the initially unordered stream of reality by imposing meaning and coherence on the lived world. The vision of the world which he perpetuates is one of a fixed and universal reality where "everything is written from the eternity." Change becomes an illusion for the Marabout. Within this system, a player may gain or lose, reach the status of saint or be disgraced as a sinner. But in spite of these possibilities, he must remain within a total framework of the universe which he cannot change.

In order to analyze this religious ideology, Eickelman has placed it within the explanatory framework of history. However, on two accounts the very content of his study raises certain questions concerning the nature of this theoretical perspective. First, although history, and consequently all religion and Islam, are said to involve continual change, their study is based upon assumptions which claim to be universal and invariable; the fact of history itself does not change. And while the content of actual religious symbols may vary, religion is always defined as an ideology and ideology is defined as instrumental. The significance of all cultural expressions of Islam can then be interpreted in terms of these premises. It appears that in order to analyze change, the concept of change itself must be fossilized by presuppositions which define its nature and subject matter in order to make the recognition and description of any significant historical moment possible. Religion as an ideology of God's will as understood by the Moroccans dissolves history with the premise of eternity. The opposite notion, the validity of history, for Eickelman is perhaps ideology as well. A certain paradox then emerges. The study of religion as ideology must be conducted from another ideological position (Lapidus 1974, 287–99).

Not only Eickelman's work but all anthropological monographs reviewed here begin from certain fundamental, theoretical premises concerning the nature of human reality, conscious or unconscious experience, history, and religion. Each set of interdependent assumptions implies a corresponding mode of interpretation which will reveal the real meaning of the diverse cultural expressions of Islam. Yet, in spite of their differences, all positions approach Islam as an isolable and bounded domain of meaningful phenomena inherently distinct both from other cultural forms such as social relations or economic systems and from other religions. Within the domain of Islam, they also construct an internal dichotomy between local or folk Islam and the Islam of the elite, or 'ulama'. However, the criteria of distinction differ in order to serve each view of reality, history, and meaning.

For Geertz, different societies transform Islam to fit their own unique historical experience, and therefore at the local level there exist as many meanings and expressions of Islam as historical contexts. However, the elite, the *'ulama'*, separate themselves from the local interpretations or the specifications of particular historical embodiments of Islam. They reflect upon the sacred tradition with its unique experience in order to grasp the eternal essence of Islam. Yet, their superior position, by definition one of separation from popular knowledge, makes it impossible for them to relate this universalism to the level of common experience. The Islam of the *'ulama'* is highly abstract, formal, and legalistic. Theology in this sense is more reflective than popular systems of religious meaning. At the same time it is less ritualistic and less bound to common-sense experience and social action.

The mode of expression differs as well. Most folk interpretations of Islam dwell upon the meaning of natural phenomena conceived as the reflection of God and the authority of the saints. The power of these religious elements does not reside in their physical manifestation. The saint, for instance, is not the white-washed shrine or the person buried inside, but the system of meanings which differs from one society to another according to historical tradition and current circumstances. The theological versions deny the authority of these symbols. Their notion of Islam centers upon the reading of the Qur'an and the prophetic traditions which yield meanings intended to transcend any particular cultural idiom. Formal religious education becomes a process of repetition in which meanings are already defined and stabilized in the pretense of universality (Ibn Khaldun 1967). These unchanging formulations of the essence of Islam and the folk concepts which change continually according to social usage in any particular circumstance exist simultaneously in all Islamic societies.

The anthropologist taking a phenomenological approach focuses on the daily lived experience of the local Islams and leaves the study of theological interpretation to the Islamists. Therefore, he faces the problem of grasping meanings which are fluid and indeterminant. He must stabilize these meanings in order to understand them and communicate them to others. Symbols then become finite and well-bounded containers of thought, and at the moment of analysis the continuous production of meaning is stopped. Meaning becomes static through its objectification in the symbol (Waardenburg 1974, 267–85). In order to isolate these objectifications of subjective meaning, the analyst must regard the symbol itself as an objective reality which he can describe without the influence of his own symbolic patterns. Science then requires a disinterest and detachment, a certain neutrality common to the scientific community. Although the scientist's understanding is still a mode of interpretation which can only guess at the meaning of another's experience rather than enter it directly, it retains its superior validity by recognizing the process and structure of interpretation itself.

This notion of science contains certain internal contradictions. Science is considered a mode of interpretation and reflection on experience just as any other cultural form; therefore, the suspension of cultural attitudes can never be complete—the criteria of true objectivity must be a higher cultural form of experience. Furthermore, in the scientific process of reflection, not only experience but the conscious subjects as well must become objects of reflection. In this way the very creators of symbols under study become passive carriers of meaning, while the scientific and supposedly disinterested consciousness takes over the active role.

The phenomenological position implies a certain hierarchy of experience based on the degree and intensity of different forms of reflection. The greater the reflection on experience, the greater the order in the systems of meaning. And objective understanding lies in the recognition of the order of the complexity of meaning. The local *islams* involve accepted, taken-for-granted experiences, and little directed reflectivity. Theological Islam entails more reflectivity and a more ordered system of meanings. Finally, history, because it specifically requires reflection on the past, and science, in this case anthropological reflection on human experience, become the privileged mode of understanding due to their awareness of the nature of the processes of human experience. Yet, within the total hierarchy, both theology and anthropology claim a higher degree of reflection than folk expressions of Islam. Therefore, they both regard these expressions as less ordered, less objective, and somehow less complete versions of the religious experience. Each, however, looks upon this diversity of experience in different ways. Theologians condemn it in order to enforce their view of the eternal meaning of Islam; anthropologists regard the various expressions as diluted forms, distorted by magic and superstition, and thus indirectly imply the existence of a pure and well-defined essence of Islam. Crapanzano, however, finds a different reality at the core of Islam. Instead of defining religious expression as an experiential form, he reduces it to the internal dynamics of the Freudian psyche. All religions, and thus all *islams*, become symbolic devices for the sublimation and expression of instinctual conflicts. Within this framework, both the Islam of the elite and the Islam of the folk serve the same existential function. However, the Islam of the *'ulama'* provides the incontestable and formal explications, the norms of religious meaning, while folk expressions such as the Hamadsha act as particular therapeutic versions of real Islam which must disguise and legitimate their deviations from the "norm" by expressing certain elements of mythology and ritual in terms of formal Islam.

Therefore, the distinction between these two dimensions of Islam is based on the content of their expressions. Yet, if both contents ultimately play the same role with regard to the reality of unconscious conflicts, if both attempt to normalize and socialize an otherwise neurotic tendency, then what exactly are the criteria used to distinguish the normal from abnormal or deviant content? According to Crapanzano's own premises, the content of both forms of Islam should be considered normal sublimations of abnormal tensions. This leads to the question of why the particularity of the Hamadsha order must be analyzed as "deviance." Crapanzano might have viewed the religious experience as a set of relations between the natural necessities imposed on man, his conflicting instincts, and the ideals developed on the superego. The uniqueness of any expression would be the result of the particular synthesis of these elements. But Crapanzano limits the real meaning of Islam both by reducing the function of religion to mediate conflicts of the unconscious psyche and by delineating an absolute standard of normal Islam. Indirectly, he rigidifies not only Islam, but the culture in which it exists and the symbols which express it. Moroccan society is portrayed in this paradigm as static and uninventive, constrained within a predetermined universe of meaning.

Like Crapanzano, Bujra regards the institutional expression of religious meaning as ideological illusion. The cause of its existence lies not in the tensions inherent in the human psyche but in conflicts rooted in the economic structure of society which embodies all essential human needs and values. Religion functions as the conscious reflection of social tension which results from material inequality and oppression. In the conservative and hierarchical society of Southern Arabia, the accepted form of Islam rationalizes and perpetuates the economic and political authority of the *Sadah*. Here it is an ideology of domination. So religious meaning is not an experiential form as for Geertz, or a mask of the Freudian psyche, but the mode of legitimization of an existing social structure. Religious symbols are social signs which may be manipulated for purposes of power and therefore directly expressed in actual behavior. They are produced by the *Sadah* but passively taken for granted by the rest of the population who must accept the religious along with other forms of social control.

The distinction between elite and local Islam which must correspond with the notion of the meaning of religion takes a new turn. For Bujra, the elite version of the *'ulama'* or *Sadah* does not constitute a privileged form of religious awareness as it does for Geertz, who insists that it is more reflective, or for Crapanzano, who refers to it as more "normal" than the local *islam*s. Rather, he views the *'ulama'*'s Islam as merely another distorted ideology designed for the purposes of the manipulation of secular, social power, as are all other local expressions of Islam such as that of the *Sadah*. Both local and elite *islam*s are compared to an ideal Islam which expresses the true and eternal principles of God found in the Qur'an and in the tradition of the Prophet which establish the reality of human freedom, equality, and justice. The problem becomes the recognition and actualization of this ideal Islam. Bujra optimistically predicts that the conflicts apparent in the current social order signal the inevitability of struggle and change towards this goal. Yet, only the reorganization of the economic base will allow the complete overthrow of false ideology and realization of true Islam.

Gilsenan, in his analysis, reveals a distinction between elite and local Islam based not on opposition and domination, as in Bujra's definition of the role of the *Sadah*, but on complementarity. The formal and systematized laws of the *'ulama'* differed in both content and style from the more mystical interpretation of the people. Yet, both were traditionally opposed to the overriding authority of the ruling class. While the *'ulama'* were considered a social minority with little claim to actual political power, the mystic orders (because they defined the popular notions and values of Islam) were capable of organizing a mass rebellion in response to any governmental threat. So in order to buttress their social power, the *'ulama'* allied with the mystics. Even if these two approaches to Islam did not directly support each other's system of beliefs, they at least became non-contradictory. Both forms of Islam defined for society a stable and eternal vision of the world according to the all-pervasive order and meaning of God's will.

The breakdown of these two systems of belief came with the influence of Western technology, ideas, and values. The consequent drive for modernization allowed a situation in which the structure of secular bureaucracy, now considered to be the truly rational social order, challenged the traditional order built upon notions of a hierarchy designed by God which was inherent in all societies. Due to its own principles of formal and rigid order, the *'ulama'* adjusted easily to the incoming social bureaucracy. However, they claimed the authority to redefine the spiritual premises on which that rational bureaucratic logic was based. Thus formal Islam is consonant with the new social order.

Along with the bureaucratic trend of modernization, the influence of other new systems of social relevance such as trade unions, political parties, and secular education caused the mystical orders, as well as the *'ulama'*, to reevaluate their own concepts of meaning and order. The saint who was the center of Gilsenan's analysis attempted to show both the *'ulama'* and secular forces that these rational principles could be gained only through mystical experience. Yet, his own solution, to formalize and bureaucratize the mystical order, contradicted his intention to reinstate the authority of the immediate spiritual encounter. According to Gilsenan's own criteria, the saint is considered a failure. He could not adjust the preexisting structure of mysticism to the changing social order. For Gilsenan, religion is idle; it does not define true reality, but functions instead to support the pregiven reality of the social order. Both the elite and local version of Islam are ideologies, not of an ideal Islam as in Bujra's case, but of the rational order of secular society. Therefore, there exist two systems of meaning, the religious system and social reality. If the two systems correspond, the society remains stable; if they do not, the ideological system of religion yields to fundamental social conditions. The conflict is essential for it constitutes society's drive to modernize itself. It leads to the creation of historical consciousness, rationality, and individualism. From this perspective, the rational order of modern bureaucracy, competition, and secular life will eventually destroy and leave behind those other systems of meaning which cannot adjust to it. If in traditional society Islam defines the meaning and order of social reality, in modern society, the actual empirical conditions of social life determine the meaning of Islam.

This relation between Islam and social change forms the core of Eickelman's study of Maraboutism. He too distinguishes the elite Islam from its local expressions according to his own notion of the formation of ideological systems. In contrast to Gilsenan, Eickelman believes that any social structure, even in so-called "traditional" and conservative ones, never remains stationary but changes at each moment. This change results from the lack of fit between social conduct and symbolic systems. Their dialectical interaction produces ideological systems as a means of social manipulation manifest in actual social activities defined by specific historical contexts. In this framework, the Islam of the *'ulama'* is considered an "explicit" ideology transcending the influence of culturally relative values and beliefs and therefore may legitimately be referred to as "religion." Local versions of Islam, however, are understood as "implicit" ideologies as they adhere to and are intertwined with common-sense notions, the untutored and accepted assumptions concerning the nature of reality specific to each social group. These interpretations then vary according to cultural background and historical moment. Systems of religious meaning thus retain their social and historical particularity. Because they never rise to a level of cross-cultural application, like the Islam of the elite which gives them the status of true ideology, local Islam is always a very culturally specific set of beliefs, rather than a fixed and wholly coherent institutionalized religion.

Both forms of Islam coexist in a state of tension. The elite continually contest the local traditions of Islam. People acknowledge the general concepts dictated by the *'ulama'*, but they choose to live according to more particularistic notions of Islam, which conform with the patterns of their daily experience.

This particular anthropological distinction appears to reinforce the *'ulama'*'s claim to a superior religious position by treating the elite version as "religion," and reducing other interpretations to implicit ideology. These distinctions between elite and popular Islam are obviously derived from the fundamental assumptions defining each anthropological paradigm. Although all positions argue the objectivity and universality of their own premises, the mere fact of a multiplicity of possible meanings at the fundamental level of the nature of Man, God, and the World challenges the notion of a single, absolute reality. Rather than being accepted as given truths, these anthropological premises might be treated as anthropologists themselves treat the tenets of Islam: as diverse, culturally relative expressions of a tradition—in this case, a "scientific" one. If versions of Islam must be called ideology, then perhaps these various anthropologies demand the same understanding (Fernea and Malarkey 1975, 183–206). It is hardly a new insight that scholars' own cultural ideas and values have molded the analysis of Islam. Even Weber, as Bryan Turner (Turner 1974, 34) suggests, made "all the usual nineteenth century references to Mohammed's sexuality as an important factor in the shaping of the Qur'an and Muslim-teaching of family and marriage."

Recognition of the imposition of premises alien to the subject matter itself in-volves a reevaluation of the authority of scientific understanding. From this perspec-tive, changes in the definition of the function or essence of Islam do not result from the accumulation of knowledge, but from the changing attitudes to religion in the West (Waardenburg 1973). The notion of the "disinterested observer" is, in fact, impregnated with the values of a scientific community. The self-declared superiority of such communities and their isolation from the common-sense world promotes the development of a common reality, language, and system of values and interests labeled "scientific" and "objective." The criteria of certain knowledge pertinent to this shared vision of the world delineate and define the theoretical approach and subject matter of studies (Feyerabend 1975, 18–19).

In terms of this supposedly scientific distinction between folk and elite Islam, anthropology studies the former, yet its principles of analysis resemble the latter.

Like science, theological positions which are referred to as elite Islam, regardless of how anthropologists define them in their different paradigms, assume the same detached attitude. In both science and theology, understanding the real meaning of religious phenomena comes only through a presumed separation from common subjective assumptions and from immediate involvement with the object of study. Both positions agree on the existence of a "folk" Islam as opposed to a formal Islam which, in order to be known, demands a greater degree of reflection and systematization of principles than found in popular expressions of belief. Anthropology and theology differ merely in the particular aspects of these local interpretations selected for analysis.

However, the authority claimed by theological Islam is contested by the recognition that in any given cultural system, a folk theology may be found which rivals formal theology in its degree of abstraction, systematization, and cosmological implication. It is even possible to argue that this folk Islam constitutes the real Islam and that the traditions of the *'ulama'* developed historically out of already established principles of the nature of spiritual reality entwined with the life of the Islamic community (el-Zein 1974). In fact, these opposing theologies are complementary. Because each form both defines and necessitates the other, the problem of determining a real as opposed to an ideological Islam becomes an illusion.

On the most general level of abstraction, folk theology involves reflection on principles of ultimate reality, nature, God, man, and history which are formally expressed in traditional literature, folk tales, heroic stories, proverbs, and poetry. For instance, in the tale of Seif bin dhi Yazan, the reality of the world according to Islamic principles and the existence of the Prophet was known before the actual historical birth of Muhammad and his articulation of that doctrine. Therefore, in the folk conception, counter to the view of historians and Islamicists, direct reflection upon the order of the world, rather than the actual statements of the Prophet and Qur'an, leads the mind to the origin of that order.

The order of both the natural and human world rests upon a hierarchical principle which arranges each thing or person continually in an ascending order: fire to water; the segments of a tribe, to the tribal section, to the tribe as a whole. Ibn Khaldun, better known in the West than any of the numerous folk writers on genealogy, pharmacology, folk tales, myths, etc., elegantly describes this cosmological progression: "Each one of the elements is prepared to be transformed into the next higher or lower one, and sometimes is transformed. The higher one is always lower than the one preceding it" (Ibn Khaldun 1967, 194). At the end this order arrives at the World of Spirituality which both creates and maintains these connections. Arabic, the sacred language taught to Adam by God, expresses this eternal structure and all names reveal the original nature of things, *tabi'a* or *fitra*. The entire world becomes an open text where God reveals his language and his will. The Qur'an too is read and interpreted within this paradigm.

Ideally, the human mind must submit itself to this natural logic. However, because man deviates from this density by imposing false and alien concepts upon the world, mind and nature are not initially in correspondence. The role of the Prophet and the saints is to bring these two dimensions together (Hindam 1939, 6–15). Yet, this tension persists and manifests itself in the events of human existence called history. In this sense, the study of history becomes a moral science in which explication of the ethical meaning of the world points out the mistakes and achievements of man in relation to the ideal of perfect existence. History shows that although Adam attained complete knowledge, the passage of time brought about the misinterpretation and degeneration of his heritage. Mohammed and the first Islamic community which he established regained all that the descendents of Adam had lost. Now man must continually attempt to re-enact this fixed moment in time. So history in this paradigm never refers to the everchanging creation of new meanings of human life but to the struggle to recapture and immobilize an eternal experience.

While nature is continuous and ordered, history remains discontinuous and chaotic. In folk theology, the remembrance of the Prophet, the actions of the saints and all rituals attempt to transform the discontinuities of history into the natural order by processes of ritual repetition which stops the passage of time.

Historically, in the Western sense, an institutionalized form of theology developed in reaction to Greek philosophy and Aristotelian logic which challenged the notion of the complete omnipotence of God. Internal dialogues between the conflicting positions resulted also in the establishment of the actual discipline of theology which countered the principles of rationality with the ultimate authority of the Qur'an (van Ess 1975).

While in the folk tradition the order of nature and the Qur'an were regarded as metaphors, the strict and formal theological interpretation gave complete authority to the sacred book to define the order of the world (Abu Zahra 1970a, 76–105).

This total focus on the sacred text led to the development of a strong formalism and traditionalism, a common language and the construction of a bounded universe of meaning (Makdisi 1971). The Qur'an and prophetic tradition prescribed an absolute reality expressed in a privileged language in which true meaning exists. There arose an interpretive tradition for understanding the different usages of the terms of the Qur'an and the distinctions between clear and equivocal verses (*mutashabihat*). This led to the development of the science of elucidation, *'ilm al-bayan*, designed to deal with the analysis of metaphor (*majaz*) and metonymy (*kinaya*) as found in sacred texts (Tabanah 1962, 18–23). The construction of such devices is now thought to be governed simply by the relation of implication, whether the meaning of one word implies or is implied by another (Nasif 1965, 184–98). These styles, used by God to express the final truth, allow the known to clarify and elucidate the unknown, and preserve both the known and unknown as real (Abu Zahra 1970b, 251–412).

Therefore folk theology and formal theology developed from the same principle: that both nature and the Qur'an reflect the order and truth of God. Yet, the two paradigms choose opposite priorities. While one locates meaning in nature and includes the Qur'an within that general order, the other finds truth first in the Qur'an and then extends that reality to the interpretation of the rest of nature. Their essential complementarity stems from a relation of mutual completion. Both seek to maintain the unity of God and the world, but both recognize processes which destroy that unity. Each position attempts to combat the other's point of dissolution. Formal theology begins from the unity of time and the word and combats the inevitable multiplicity of meaning in space—the fragmentation of local tradition (Braune 1971, 37–51). Folk theology begins from the acceptance of unity and order in space and combats the multiplicity of meaning created by the passage of time. Thus both attempt to contain the flux of experience: formal theology seeks to control space by fixing time, and the other to control time by fixing space.

In the end, there are no inherent differences in the content of either folk or formal theology to suggest that one is more objective, reflective, or systematic than the other. If Islamicists and theologians privilege the formal discipline, they do so only upon preconceived criteria of validity linked to their concept of truth. They claim an objectivity based upon systematic analysis of the Qur'an which is said to embody absolute truth. And they must therefore deny the legitimacy of an objectivity which bypasses the sacred text in favor of a direct insight into the order of the world. Actually, both forms of theology may be described as intricate systems of cosmological principles. They are complementary and equally "real." They differ only as modes of expression: one exists as an institution and the other as literature.

What unifies both expressions of theology with anthropology is the structure of their means of understanding Islam. All begin from positive assumptions concerning the nature of man, God, history, consciousness, and meaning. Their interpretations of the meaning of Islam depend themselves upon already presupposed and fixed meanings which determine the universality of Islam, define and limit properly "religious" and "Islamic" phenomena, and distinguish a folk from an elite, and a real from a false Islam. Only the specific content varies. Geertz begins from the reality of experience, Crapanzano from the psychic, Bujra and Gilsenan from the structure and function of social relations, Eickelman from a notion of history, and the theologies from God, nature, and the Qur'an.

Criteria of validity differ as well. The anthropological positions claim to be more objective than both the folk and the theological traditions. With respect to the folk expressions of Islam, they assume their scientific analyses to be more reflective and systematic. And although theology is recognized as highly reflective, it is not critical and therefore remains subordinate to the authority of anthropology which, being scientific, is critical as well. Anthropological analyses then establish their validity not only on the necessity of particular assumptions concerning the nature of reality but also on the epistemological criteria of scientific rationality. Theology, to the contrary, establishes truth on the incontestable basis of faith. So at the level of the content and form of knowledge, faith is opposed to science; theology and anthropology deny each other's capacity to grasp the final truth. Yet, from the perspective of the structure of knowledge, their opposition is only apparent, for they both begin from and impose preconceived and positive meanings which necessarily frame their understanding of other experiences of Islam. Another form of contradiction emerges from this summary. All analyses are built upon the assumption of a single, absolute reality and seek to discover this reality in Islam. Yet, when reviewed collectively, these studies reveal the incredible diversity of possible definitions and descriptions of Islam. This diversity is not due merely to differences in analytic perspective. Each paradigm, regardless of the nature of its premises, recognizes the uniqueness of religious expression at the level of the material it must analyze. Geertz works with different cultural and historical interpretations of experience; Crapanzano investigates the particularity of the Hamadsha's adjustment to their social relations; Bujra, Gilsenan and Eickelman deal with the inevitability of historical change in the expression of Islam. And all approaches, including the theological, stress a distinction in the content of elite and folk Islam. Finally, the significance of the initial problem becomes clear. In the midst of this diversity of meaning, is there a single, real Islam?

Both the anthropological and theological approaches outlined here assume that there is a reality of Islam which may be derived from principles of an encompassing universal reality of the nature of man or God. The importance of diversity is then overridden at the level of both the religious and the total human experience which take on absolute, fixed, and positive meanings. Because they begin from such assumptions, actual interpretations of any particular cultural situation, symbol, or passage of the Qur'an will reflect pre-given meaning in two ways. First, although particular content may vary, it must always contain the characteristic of meaning specific to a form of experience. For Geertz, the symbol of the saint in Morocco implies charisma and authority, while the Javanese is defined as meditative and withdrawn. However, according to his own paradigm, both symbols condense and synthesize world view and ethos. For Crapanzano, the different myths, legends, rituals, and orders of Islam all essentially serve to express psychobiological drives.

Therefore, the bounds and limits of such premises give each symbol, action or institution certain inherent and fixed characteristics. Further, even the culturally and historically relative dimensions of meaning which are said to change, change only in accordance with unchanging criteria of meaningfulness. For example, Eickelman is able to anticipate changes in ideological meaning only due to the continuous, perpetual state of imbalance in the relationship between the social and symbolic systems. So while diversity and fluidity of meaning are recognized at the level of actual cultural expression, synthesis is still the final purpose of analysis. When the essential and real principle governing this diversity is revealed, a web of frozen points of meaning is thrown over the subject's fluid meanings. It is impossible with such a rigid framework to suggest that each expression of Islam creates its own real world of meaning.

As the previously discussed positions would all agree, man does order his world through systems of meaning. Anthropologically, the problem now is to find a means of understanding that order which reaches the desired level of universality without diluting or destroying the significance of this diversity and the richness of meaning in human experience. The nature of the problem is exemplified in the various treatments of the Islamic saint. In the work considered here, the saint is alternatively viewed as a metaphor, a political man, an economic man, a survival, a fragment of ideology, or even an incoherence simply to be discarded. One thing emerges from the diversity of interpretation: each treated the saint as a thing and artificially added to it different dimensions of meaning which varied according to the investigator's interest. Each investigator selects from the multitude of possibly identifiable features and functions of the saint, one or two of which are deemed distinctive and which, in the subsequent analysis, are taken as the saint. Analysis based on such highly selective reading of ethnographic data artificially collapses the complexity of the "saint" to a single dimension, leaving unexplained many possible questions about the undeniable multiplicity of the cultural construct "saint."

Much of the behavior associated with the saint and his worshipers, along with the range of meaning signifiable through the saint, may appear to be spurious, idiosyncratic, and irrelevant. At the tomb of Egypt's most important saint, for example, Gilsenan observed what appeared to be wildly inappropriate behavior amongst the worshipers. Singing, dancing, shouting, joking, even cursing, accompanied the ritual of worship on the Saint's Day—behavior unexplainable either as piety of believers or as the intelligible actions of politically and/or economically rational actors. Indeed, the actions and modes described seem defiling in this religious context. It is not only in this Egyptian case where "defilement" makes an incongruous appearance. Westermarck observed an equally puzzling development in Morocco (Westermark 1968, 177–78), where the tomb of the saint was periodically ritually smeared with blood, a consciously recognized mark of defilement. I observed similar procedures in Nubia and in the East African town of Lamu, where visitors to the saint's tomb smear the blood of sacrificed animals on the tomb walls. The analyst confronted with such material must either demonstrate its rational "fit" with what he has identified as the real significance of the saint, expand his definition of the "saint" to accommodate dimensions of meaning beyond simple political or economic manipulation or metaphoric condensation or, as too often happens, he may find these data irrational and/or irrelevant accompaniments to the "essential" nature of the saint. It would seem most desirable to reexamine our original positive notion of "saint."

Elsewhere I have shown that the saint may be profitably viewed as a symbol, not in the sense of being a vehicle for meaning, but as a relational construct in which the dimension of purity/impurity, defilement and sacralization are articulated with a broad and variable range of content, including political, economic, and otherwise pragmatic aspects of life (el-Zein 1974). The saint thus symbolically embodies fundamental properties of a system of classification in the matrix of which all institutions (politics, economics, etc.) and institutionally related behavior (manipulation of power, disposition of resources, etc.) are necessarily framed. The precise opposition embodied by the saint at this level may, of course, vary from place to place, just as the content apprehended therein varies. But it is only by going beyond institutions and functions, actors, and positive meanings to the relatively simpler complexity of categorical opposition that the richness of the saint or any other "religious symbol" emerges along with its position in the logic of culture.

The positions reviewed here all accept in some way the principle of objectivity based on a separation of realities in which the subject occupies the privileged position of being able to encompass within his consciousness the reality of the object. The object in each case is a thing or set of things whose order or ultimate meaning is to be discovered through techniques which identify systematic *connections* between *things*. The things may be symbols constructed as vehicles for otherwise disembodied but contained "meanings," institutions, domains, or any other entities whose existence as entities is unquestioned. That is, we have been treating analyses of Islam which accept as fundamental the existence of "Islam," "religion," "economy," "politics," and even "saints," whose relation to each other within a given culture may vary, but whose existential "truth" is not subject to question. The goal of such analysis then becomes one of finding the "essence" of things at hand and the kind of connection which seems best to explain how these things work in a "cultural system." The exact kind of relation (conceived as a connection) which emerges as dominant varies with the nature of things studied.

Thus for Geertz, symbols condense and convey meaning, while for Crapanzano they create and sustain an illusory relationship between history, culture, and the psyche. Bujra, Gilsenan, and Eickelman are concerned with demonstrating the role of "Islam" in directing the behaviorally realized interaction between political and economic institutions and in mediating the disjuncture between the reality of history and the deceit of ideology.

But what if each analysis of Islam treated here were to begin from the assumption that "Islam," "economy," "history," "religion" and so on do not exist as things or entities with meaning inherent in them, but rather as articulations of structural relations, and are the outcome of these relations and not simply a set of positive terms from which we start our studies? In this case, we have to start from the "native's" model of "Islam" and analyze the relations which produce its meaning. Beginning from this assumption, the system can be entered and explored in depth from any point, for there are no absolute discontinuities anywhere within it—there are no autonomous entities and each point within the system is ultimately accessible from every other point. In this view there can be no fixed and wholly isolable function of meaning attributed to any basic unit of analysis, be it symbol, institution, or process, which does not impose an artificial order on the system from outside. That is, the orders of the system and the nature of its entities are the same—the logic of the system is the content of the system in the sense that each term, each entity within the system, is the result of structural relations between others, and so on, neither beginning nor ending in any fixed, absolute point. The logic of such a system, the logic of culture, is immanent within the content and does not exist without it. But while the "content" might differ from one culture to another, the logic embedded in these various contents are the same. In this sense, both the anthropologist and the native share a logic which is beyond their conscious control. It is a logic which is embedded in both nature and culture, and which can be uncovered through the intricate analysis of content. Here the problem of objectivity which haunted all the studies discussed above disappears, and since it was a problem created by a notion of the transcendence of consciousness and subjectivity of the investigator, it will vanish as a phantom, leaving in its place a logic which is shared by both the subject and the object. Islam as an expression of this logic can exist only as a facet within a fluid yet coherent system; it cannot be viewed as an available entity for cultural systems to select and put to various uses. "Islam," without referring it to the facets of a system of which it is part, does not exist. Put another way, the utility of the concept "Islam" as a predefined religion with its supreme "truth" is extremely limited in anthropological analysis. Even the dichotomy of folk Islam/elite Islam is infertile and fruitless. As I have tried to show, the apparent dichotomy can be analytically reduced to the logic governing it.

The works we have discussed here seemed not to offer a means for uncovering the logic of culture or the principles which are immanent in culture and which order and articulate the thoughts and actions of culture bearers. In this sense we have not yet been led to the structure of "Islam," nor can we be, for it is a contradiction in terms to speak of the systemic "fit"—the structure—of an autonomous entity. The fact of structure can never be shown in an isolated state and is reached only by unfolding patterns of both actual and potential diversity of cultural content. In its totality, this variability reveals the absence of any positive, universal content. Working from this perspective, from which meaning is strictly relational, the analyst cannot select relevant material according to some standard of truth, but must consider systems in their entirety. In this way, the multiplicity of cultural meanings is explored and developed. There are no privileged expressions of truth. "Objectivity" must be bound to the shared structures of both the analyst and the subject regardless of the content of their respective cultural systems.

This logic of relations implies that neither Islam nor the notion of religion exists as a fixed and autonomous form referring to positive content which can be reduced to universal and unchanging characteristics. Religion becomes an arbitrary category which as a unified and bounded form has no necessary existence. "Islam" as an analytical category dissolves as well.

Acknowledgements

I wish to thank Miss Sara Spang, who more than anyone else labored with the argument and style of this article. Charles Myers was also present throughout its preparation, and his suggestions were very valuable. My discussions with my wife concerning a religion in which we grew up were more enlightening than ever.

References

Abu Zahra, Muhammad. 1970a. *Usul al-Fiqh*. Cairo: Dar al-Fikr al-'Arabi.

—1970b. *Al-Qur'an, al-mu'jiza al-kubra*. Cairo: Dar al-Fikr al-'Arabi.

Bendix, R. 1945–46. "Max Weber's Interpretation of Conduct and History." *American Journal of Sociology* 51: 518–26.

Bensman, J., and Givant, M. 1975. "Charisma and Modernity: The Use and Abuse of a Concept." *Social Research* 42: 570–614.

Braune, W. 1971. "Historical Consciousness in Islam." In *Theology and Law in Islam*, ed. G. E. von Grunebaum, 37–51. Weisbaden: Harrassowitz.

Burger, Thomas. 1976. *Max Weber's Theory of Concept Formation: History, Laws, and Ideal Types*. Durham, NC: Duke University Press.

Bujra, Abdallah S. 1971. *The Politics of Stratification: A Study of Political Change in a South Arabian Town*. Oxford: Clarendon.

Crapanzano, Vincent. 1973. *The Hamadsha: A Study in Moroccan Ethnopsychiatry*. Berkeley, CA: University of California Press.

Eickelman, Dale F. 1976. *Moroccan Islam*. Austin, TX: University of Texas Press.

el-Zein, Abdul Hamid. 1974. *The Sacred Meadows*. Evanston, IL: Northwestern University Press.

Fernea, R., and Malarkey, J. 1975. "Anthropology of the Middle East and North Africa: A Critical Assessment." *Annual Review of Anthropology* 4: 183–206.

Feyerabend, Paul. 1975. *Against Method: Outline of an Anarchistic Theory of Knowledge*. London: NLB.

Geertz, Clifford. 1957. "Ethos, World View and the Analysis of Sacred Symbols." *Antioch Review* 17: 421–37.

—1964. "Ideology as a Cultural System." In *Ideology and Discontent*, ed. D. E. Apter, 47–76. New York: Free Press.

—1965. "The Impact of the Concept of Culture on the Concept of Man." In *New Views of the Nature of Man*, ed. J. Platt, 93–118. Chicago, IL: University of Chicago Press; reprinted in C. Geertz (1973) *The Interpretation of Cultures: Selected Essays*, 33–54. New York: Basic Books.

—1966. *Person, Time and Conduct in Bali: An Essay in Cultural Analysis*. New Haven, CT: Yale University Press.

—1968. *Islam Observed: Religious Development in Morocco and Indonesia*. New Haven: Yale University Press.

—1973. *The Interpretation of Cultures: Selected Essays*. New York: Basic Books.

—1975a. "Common-sense as a cultural system." *Antioch Review* 33: 5–26.

—1975b. "Mysteries of Islam." *New York Review of Books* 22/20: 18–26.

Gilsenan, Michael. 1973. *Saint and Sufi in Modern Egypt: An Essay in the Sociology of Religion*. Oxford: Clarendon.

Hindam, A. A. 1939. *Hidayat al Qasidin*. Cairo: Dar al-Anwar.

Ibn Khaldun. 1967. *The Muqaddimah*. 2nd ed. Trans. F. Rosenthal. Princeton, NJ: Princeton University Press.

Lapidus, Ira. 1974. "Notes and Comments." *Humanoria Islamica* 2: 287–99.

Levy, Reuben. 1957. *The Social Structure of Islam*. 2nd ed. Cambridge: Cambridge University Press.

Makdisi, G. 1971. "Law and Traditionalism in the Institutions of Learning in Medieval Islam." In *Theology and Law in Islam*, ed. G. E. von Grunebaum, 75–88. Weisbaden: Harrassowitz.

Mustafa, F. A. 1974. *The Social Structure of the Shadhilya Order in Egypt*. MA thesis. University Alexandria, Egypt.

Nasif, M. 1965. *Nazariyat al-Ma'na fi'l-Naqd al-'Arabi*. Cairo: Dar al-Qalam.

Ricoeur, Paul. 1970. *Freud and Philosophy: An Essay in Interpretation*. New Haven, CT: Yale University Press.

— 1974. *The Conflict of Interpretations: Essays in Hermeneutics*. Evanston, IL: Northwestern University Press.

Rieff, P. 1951. "The Meaning of History and Religion in Freud's Thought." *Journal of Religion* 31: 114–31.

Sahay, Arun. 1972. *Sociological Analysis*. London: Routledge & Kegan Paul.

al-Shayal, J. 1965. *'Alam al-Askandriya*. Cairo: Dar al-Ma'arif.

Tabana, Badawi Ahmad. 1962. *al-Bayan al-'Arabi*. 3rd ed. Cairo: Egyptian Anglo Press.

Turner, Bryan. 1974. *Weber and Islam*. London: Routledge & Kegan Paul.

Van Ess, J. 1975. "The Beginning of Islamic Theology." In *The Cultural Context of Medieval Learning,* ed. J. E. Murdoch and E. D. Sylla, 87–111. Dordrecht: Reidel.

Waardenburg, Jacques. 1973. *L'Islam dans le miroir de l'occident*. The Hague and Paris: Mouton.

—1974. "Islam Studies as a Symbol and Signification System." *Humanoria Islamica* 2: 267–85.

Weber, Max. 1949. *The Methodology of the Social Sciences*. Trans. and ed. E. A. Shils and H. A. Finch. Glencoe: Free Press.

—1968. *Economy and Society: An Outline of Interpretive Sociology*. New York: Bedminster.

Westermarck, Edward. 1968. *Ritual and Belief in Morocco*. New Hyde Park, NY: University Books.

8

Two Countries, Two Cultures

Clifford Geertz

Of all the dimensions of the uncertain revolution now underway in the new states of Asia and Africa, surely the most difficult to grasp is the religious. It is not measurable as, however inexactly, economic change is. It is not, for the most part, illuminated by the instructive explosions that mark political development: purges, assassinations, coups d'état, border wars, riots, and here and there an election. Such proven indices of mutation in the forms of social life as urbanization, the solidification of class loyalties, or the growth of a more complex occupational system are, if not wholly lacking, certainly rarer and a great deal more equivocal in the religious sphere, where old wine goes as easily into new bottles as old bottles contain new wine. It is not only very difficult to discover the ways in which the shapes of religious experience are changing, or if they are changing at all; it is not even clear what sorts of things one ought to look at in order to find out.

The comparative study of religion has always been plagued by this peculiar embarrassment: the elusiveness of its subject matter. The problem is not one of constructing definitions of religion. We have had quite enough of those; their very number is a symptom of our malaise. It is a matter of discovering just what sorts of beliefs and practices support what sorts of faith under what sorts of conditions. Our problem, and it grows worse by the day, is not to define religion but to find it.

This may seem an odd thing to say. What is in those thick volumes on totemic myths, initiation rites, witchcraft beliefs, shamanistic performances, and so on, which ethnographers have been compiling with such astonishing industry for over a century?

Or in the equally thick and not much more readable works by historians on the development of Judaic law, Confucian philosophy, or Christian theology? Or in the countless sociological studies of such institutions as Indian caste or Islamic sectarianism, Japanese emperor worship or African cattle sacrifice? Do they not contain our subject matter? The answer is, quite simply, no: they contain the record of our search for our subject matter. The search has not been without its successes, and our appointed task is to keep it going and enlarge its successes. But the aim of the systematic study of religion is, or anyway ought to be, not just to describe ideas, acts, and institutions, but to determine just how and in what way particular ideas, acts, and institutions sustain, fail to sustain, or even inhibit religious faith—that is to say, steadfast attachment to some transtemporal conception of reality.

There is nothing mysterious in this, nor anything doctrinal. It merely means that we must distinguish between a religious attitude toward experience and the sorts of social apparatus which have, over time and space, customarily been associated with supporting such an attitude. When this is done, the comparative study of religion shifts from a kind of advanced curio collecting to a kind of not very advanced science; from a discipline in which one merely records, classifies, and perhaps even generalizes about data deemed, plausibly enough in most cases, to have something to do with religion to one in which one asks close questions of such data, not the least important of which is just what does it have to do with religion. We can scarcely hope to get far with the analysis of religious change—that is to say, what happens to faith when its vehicles alter—if we are unclear as to what in any particular case its vehicles are and how (or even *if*) in fact they foster it.

Whatever the ultimate sources of the faith of a man or group of men may or may not be, it is indisputable that it is sustained in this world by symbolic forms and social arrangements. What a given religion is—its specific content—is embodied in the images and metaphors its adherents use to characterize reality; it makes, as Kenneth Burke once pointed out, a great deal of difference whether you call life a dream, a pilgrimage, a labyrinth, or a carnival. But such a religion's career—its historical course—rests in turn upon the institutions which render these images and metaphors available to those who thus employ them. It is really not much easier to conceive of Christianity without Gregory than without Jesus. Or if that remark seems tendentious (which it is not), then Islam without the *'ulama'* than without Muhammad; Hinduism without caste than without the Vedas; Confucianism without the mandarinate than without the Analects; Navaho religion without Beauty Way than without Spider Woman. Religion may be a stone thrown into the world; but it must be a palpable stone and someone must throw it.

If this is accepted (and if it is not accepted the result is to remove religion not merely from scholarly examination and rational discourse, but from life altogether), then even a cursory glance at the religious situation in the new states collectively or in any one of them separately will reveal the major direction of change: established connections between particular varieties of faith and the cluster of images and institutions which have classically nourished them are for certain people in certain circumstances coming unstuck. In the new states as in the old, the intriguing question for the anthropologist is, "How do men of religious sensibility react when the machinery of faith begins to wear out? What do they do when traditions falter?"

They do, of course, all sorts of things. They lose their sensibility. Or they channel it into ideological fervor. Or they adopt an imported creed. Or they turn worriedly in upon themselves. Or they cling even more intensely to the faltering traditions. Or they try to rework those traditions into more effective forms. Or they split themselves in half, living spiritually in the past and physically in the present. Or they try to express their religiousness in secular activities. And a few simply fail to notice their world is moving or, noticing, just collapse.

But such general answers are not really very enlightening, not only because they are general but because they glide past that which we most want to know: by what means, what social and cultural processes, are these movements toward skepticism, political enthusiasm, conversion, revivalism, subjectivism, secular piety, reformism, double-mindedness, or whatever, taking place? What new forms of architecture are housing these accumulating changes of heart?

In attempting to answer grand questions like these, the anthropologist is always inclined to turn toward the concrete, the particular, the microscopic. We are the miniaturists of the social sciences, painting on lilliputian canvases with what we take to be delicate strokes. We hope to find in the little what eludes us in the large, to stumble upon general truths while sorting through special cases. At least I hope to, and in that spirit I want to discuss religious change in the two countries in which I have worked at some length, Indonesia and Morocco. They make from some points of view an odd pair: a rarefied, somewhat overcivilized tropical Asian country speckled with Dutch culture, and a taut, arid, rather puritanical Mediterranean one varnished with French. But from some other points of view—including the fact that they are both in some enlarged sense of the word Islamic—they make an instructive comparison. At once very alike and very different, they form a kind of commentary on one another's character.

Their most obvious likeness is, as I say, their religious affiliation; but it is also, culturally speaking at least, their most obvious unlikeness. They stand at the eastern and western extremities of the narrow band of classical Islamic civilization which, rising in Arabia, reached out along the midline of the Old World to connect them, and, so located, they have participated in the history of that civilization in quite different ways, to quite different degrees, and with quite different results. They both incline toward Mecca, but, the antipodes of the Muslim world, they bow in opposite directions.

* * *

As a Muslim country, Morocco is of course the older. The first contact with Islam—a military one, as the Umayyads made their brief bid for sovereignty over Alexander's "all the inhabited world"—came in the seventh century, only fifty years after the death of Muhammad; and by the middle of the eighth century a solid, if not exactly indestructible, Muslim foothold had been established. Over the next three centuries it was rendered indestructible, and the great age of Berber Islam, the one which Ibn Khaldun looked back upon with such a modern blend of cultural admiration and sociological despair, began. One after the other, the famous reforming dynasties—Almoravids, Almohads, Merinids—swept out of what the French, with fine colonial candor, used to call *le Maroc inutile*, the forts and oases of the pre-Sahara, the walled-in rivers and pocket plateaus of the High Atlas, and the wastes of the Algerian steppe, into *le Maroc utile*, the mild and watered Cis-Atlas plains. Building and rebuilding the great cities of Morocco—Marrakech, Fez, Rabat, Sale, Tetuan—they penetrated Muslim Spain, absorbed its culture and, reworking it into their own more strenuous ethos, reproduced a simplified version of it on their side of Gibraltar. The formative period both of Morocco as a nation and of Islam as its creed (roughly 1050 to 1450) consisted of the peculiar process of tribal edges falling in upon an agricultural center and civilizing it. It was the periphery of the country, the harsh and sterile frontiers, that nourished and in fact created the advanced society which developed at its heart.

As time went on, the contrast between the artisans, notables, scholars, and shopkeepers assembled within the walls of the great cities and the farmers and pastoralists scattered thinly over the countryside around them naturally widened. The former developed a sedentary society centered on trade and craft, the latter a mobile one centered on herding and tillage. Yet the difference between the two was far from absolute; townsman and countryman did not live in different cultural worlds but, a few withdrawn highland groups perhaps aside, in the same one differently situated. Rural and urban society were variant states of a single system (and there were, in fact, a half-dozen versions of each). Far from unaffecting one another, their interaction, though often antagonistic, was continuous and intense and provided the central dynamic of historical change in Morocco from the founding of Fez at the beginning of the ninth century to its occupation by the French at the beginning of the twentieth.

There were several reasons for this. The first is that, as mentioned, the towns were at base tribal creations and, transient moments of introversion aside, largely remained so. Each major phase of civilization (and indeed most minor ones as well) began with a breaching of the gates by some ambitious local chieftain whose religious zeal was the source of both his ambition and his chieftainship.

Second, the combination of the intrusion into the western plains after the thirteenth century of marauding Bedouin Arabs, and the fact that Morocco is located not at the core of the grain-growing world but at its furthest frontiers, prevented the development of a mature peasant culture which would have buffered tribesmen from townsmen and allowed them, milking the peasantry of tribute or taxes, to go more independently along their separate ways. As it was, neither urban nor rural life was ever altogether viable. The cities, under the leadership of their viziers and sultans, tried always to reach out around them to control the tribes. But the latter remained footloose and refractory, as well as unrewarding. The uncertainty of both pastoralism and agriculture in this climatically irregular, physically ill-endowed, and somewhat despoiled environment impelled tribesmen sometimes into the cities, if not as conquerors then as refugees, sometimes out of their reach in mountain passes or desert wastes, and sometimes toward encircling them and, blocking the trade routes from which they lived, extorting from them. The political metabolism of traditional Morocco consisted of two but intermittently workable economies attempting, according to season and circumstance, to feed off one another.

And third, the cities were not crystal islands set in a shapeless sea. The fluidity of town life was hardly less than that of rural, just somewhat more confined, while the forms of tribal society were as clearly outlined as those of metropolitan. In fact, adjusted to different environments, they were the same forms, animated by the same ideals. What varied in traditional Morocco was less the kind of life different groups of people attempted to live than the ecological niches in which they attempted to live it.

Andalusian decorations, Berber folkways, and Arabian statecraft to the contrary notwithstanding, therefore, the basic style of life in, to use another term from the pointed rhetoric of the Protectorate, *le Maroc disparu*, was about everywhere the same: strenuous, fluid, violent, visionary, devout, and unsentimental, but above all, self-assertive. It was a society in which a very great deal turned on force of character and most of the rest on spiritual reputation. In town and out, its leitmotivs were strong-man politics and holy man piety, and its fulfillments, small and large, tribal and dynastic, occurred when, in the person of a particular individual, they momentarily fused. The axial figure, whether he was storming walls or building them, was the warrior saint.

This is particularly apparent at the great transitional points of Moroccan history, the recurring changes of political direction in which its social identity was forged. Idris II, the ninth-century builder of Fez and the country's first substantial king, was at once a descendant of the Prophet, a vigorous military leader, and a dedicated religious purifier and would not have amounted to much as any one of these had he not concurrently been the other two. Both the Almoravid and Almohad movements were founded—the first around the middle of the eleventh century, the second toward the middle of the twelfth—by visionary reformers returning from the Middle East determined not just to inveigh against error but to dismember its carriers. The exhaustion, in the fifteenth century, of the revolution they began, and the collapse of the political order that revolution had created, was followed in turn by what was probably the greatest spiritual dislocation the country has ever experienced: the so-called Maraboutic Crisis. Local holy men, or marabouts—descendants of the Prophet, leaders of Sufi brotherhoods, or simply vivid individuals who had contrived to make something uncanny happen—appeared all over the landscape to launch private bids for power. The period of theocratic anarchy and sectarian enthusiasm thus inaugurated arrested only two centuries later (and then only very partially) with the rise, under yet one more reform-bent descendant of Muhammad, of the still reigning Alawite dynasty. And finally, when after 1911 the French and Spanish moved in to take direct control of the country, it was a series of such martial marabouts, scattered along the edges of the crumbling kingdom, who rallied the population, or parts of it, for the last brave, desperate attempt to revive the old order, the Morocco that had, in the course of the previous half-century, begun slowly but inexorably to disappear.

In any case, the critical feature of that Morocco so far as we are concerned is that its cultural center of gravity lay not, paradoxical as this may seem, in the great cities, but in the mobile, aggressive, now federated, now fragmented tribes who not only harassed and exploited them but also shaped their growth. It is out of the tribes that the forming impulses of Islamic civilization in Morocco came, and the stamp of their mentality remained on it, whatever Arabo-Spanish sophistications urban religious scholars, locking themselves away from the local current, were able, in a few selected corners and for a few chromatic moments, to introduce. Islam in Barbary was—and to a fair extent still is—basically the Islam of saint worship and moral severity, magical power and aggressive piety, and this was for all practical purposes as true in the alleys of Fez and Marrakech as in the expanses of the Atlas or the Sahara.

* * *

Indonesia is, as I say, another matter altogether. Rather than tribal it is, and for the whole of the Christian era has been, basically a peasant society, particularly in its overpowering heartland, Java. Intensive, extremely productive wet rice cultivation has provided the main economic foundations of its culture for about as long as we have record, and rather than the restless, aggressive, extroverted sheikh husbanding his resources, cultivating his reputation, and awaiting his opportunity, the national archetype is the settled, industrious, rather inward plowman of twenty centuries, nursing his terrace, placating his neighbors, and feeding his superiors. In Morocco, civilization was built on nerve; in Indonesia, on diligence.

Further, not only was classical Indonesian civilization founded upon the rock of a spectacularly productive peasant economy, but it was not in the first instance Islamic at all, but Indic. Unlike the way it moved into Morocco, Islam—which arrived with genuine definitiveness only after the fourteenth century—did not, except for a few pockets in Sumatra, Borneo, and the Celebes, move into an essentially virgin area, so far as high culture was concerned, but into one of Asia's greatest political, aesthetic, religious, and social creations, the Hindu-Buddhist Javanese state, which though it had by then begun to weaken, had cast its roots so deeply into Indonesian society (especially on Java, but not only there) that its impress remained proof not just to Islamization, but to Dutch imperialism and, so far anyway, to modern nationalism as well. It is perhaps as true for civilizations as it is for men that, however much they may later change, the fundamental dimensions of their character, the structure of possibilities within which they will in some sense always move, are set in the plastic period when they first are forming. In Morocco, this period was the age of the Berber dynasties, which, whatever their local peculiarities, were at least generally driven by Islamic ideals and concepts. In Indonesia, it was the age (roughly contemporaneous, actually) of the great Indic states—Mataram, Singosari, Kediri, Madjapahit—which, though also importantly shaped by local traditions, were generally guided by Indic theories of cosmic truth and metaphysical virtue. In Indonesia Islam did not construct a civilization, it appropriated one.

These two facts, that the main impulse for the development of a more complex culture—true state organization, long-distance trade, sophisticated art, and universalistic religion—grew out of a centrally located peasant society upon which less developed outlying regions pivoted, rather than the other way around, and that Islam penetrated this axial culture well after it had been securely established, account for the overall cast Muhammadanism has taken in Indonesia. Compared to North Africa, the Middle East, and even to Muslim India, whose brand of faith it perhaps most closely resembles, Indonesian Islam has been, at least until recently, remarkably malleable, tentative, syncretistic, and, most significantly of all, multivoiced. What for so many parts of the world, and certainly for Morocco, has been a powerful, if not always triumphant, force for cultural homogenization and moral consensus, for the social standardization of fundamental beliefs and values, has been for Indonesia a no less powerful one for cultural diversification, for the crystalization of sharply variant, even incompatible, notions of what the world is really like and how one ought therefore to set about living in it. In Indonesia, Islam has taken many forms, not all of them Qur'anic, and whatever it brought to the sprawling archipelago, it was not uniformity.

Islam came, in any case, by sea and on the heels not of conquest but of trade. Its initial triumphs were consequently along the coastal areas rimming the tranquil Java Sea and its approaches the bustling ports, merchant princedoms actually, of northern Sumatra, southwest Malaya, south Borneo, south Celebes, and, most important of all, north Java. In the non-Javanese areas the new faith (new in form anyway; as it had come to the island not out of Arabia but India, it was not quite so new in substance) remained largely confined to the coastal areas, to the harbor towns and their immediate environs. But on Java, where the cultural center of gravity was inland in the great volcanic rise basins and where European presence along the coast soon became the commanding force, it had a rather different career. In the Outer Island enclaves it remained, or at least developed into, the sort of exclusivistic, undecorated, and emphatic creed we associate with the main line of Muslim tradition, though even there the entanglement with Indian pantheism, in both the archipelago and the subcontinent, gave it a perceptibly theosophical tinge. In Java, however—where, in the end, the overwhelming majority of Indonesian Muslims were to be found—the tinge became at once a great deal deeper and much less evenly suffused.

As the Dutch closed in upon Java from the seventeenth to the nineteenth centuries, a rather curious process of cultural and religious diversification took place under the general cover of overall Islamization. The indigenous trading classes, among whom Islam had taken its firmest hold, were driven away from international commerce toward domestic peddling, and thus away from the sea toward the interior; the highly Indicized native ruling classes were reduced to the status of civil servants, administering Dutch policies at the local level; the peasantry, drawn more and more into the orbit of a colonial export economy, folded back upon itself in a paroxysm of defensive solidarity. And each of these major groups absorbed the Islamic impulse in quite different ways.

The gentry, deprived of Indic ritualism but not of Indic pantheism, became increasingly subjectivist, cultivating an essentially illuminationist approach to the divine, a kind of Far Eastern gnosticism, complete with cabalistic speculations and metapsychic exercises. The peasantry absorbed Islamic concepts and practices, so far as it understood them, into the same general Southeast Asian folk religion into which it had previously absorbed Indian ones, locking ghosts, gods, *jinn*s, and prophets together into a strikingly contemplative, even philosophical, animism. And the trading classes, relying more and more heavily upon the Meccan pilgrimage as their lifeline to the wider Islamic world, developed a compromise between what flowed into them along this line (and from their plainer colleagues in the Outer Islands) and what they confronted in Java to produce a religious system not quite doctrinal enough to be Middle Eastern and not quite ethereal enough to be South Asian. The overall result is what can properly be called syncretism, but it was a syncretism the order of whose elements, the weight and meaning given to its various ingredients, differed markedly, and what is more important, increasingly, from one sector of the society to another.

* * *

In short, to say that Morocco and Indonesia are both Islamic societies, in the sense that most everyone in them (well over nine-tenths of the population in either case) professes to be a Muslim, is as much to point up their differences as it is to locate their similarities. Religious faith, even when it is fed from a common source, is as much a particularizing force as a generalizing one, and indeed whatever universality a given religious tradition manages to attain arises from its ability to engage a widening set of individual, even idiosyncratic, conceptions of life and yet somehow sustain and elaborate them all. When it succeeds in this, the result may indeed as often be the distortion of these personal visions as their enrichment, but in any case, whether deforming private faiths or perfecting them, the tradition usually prospers. When it fails, however, to come genuinely to grips with them at all, it either hardens into scholasticism, evaporates into idealism, or fades into eclecticism; that is to say, it ceases, except as a fossil, a shadow, or a shell, really to exist. The central paradox of religious development is that, because of the progressively wider range of spiritual experience with which it is forced to deal, the further it proceeds, the more precarious it gets. Its successes generate its frustrations.

Surely this has been the case for Islam in Morocco and Indonesia. And this is true whether one talks about that largely spontaneous, for the most part slower moving, spiritual evolution which took place from the implantation of the creed to somewhere around the beginning of this century or the end of the last, or about the painfully self-conscious questionings which, with accelerating speed and rising insistency, have been accumulating since that time. In both societies, despite the radical differences in the actual historical course and ultimate (that is, contemporary) outcome of their religious development, Islamization has been a two-sided process. On the one hand, it has consisted of an effort to adapt a universal, in theory standardized and essentially unchangeable, and unusually well-integrated system of ritual and belief to the realities of local, even individual, moral and metaphysical perception. On the other hand, it has consisted of a struggle to maintain, in the face of this adaptive flexibility, the identity of Islam not just as religion in general but as the particular directives communicated by God to mankind through the preemptory prophecies of Muhammad.

It is the tension between these two necessities, growing progressively greater as, first gradually and then explosively, the way men and groups of men saw life and assessed it became more and more various and incommensurable under the impress of dissimilar historical experiences, growing social complexity, and heightened self-awareness, that has been the dynamic behind the expansion of Islam in both countries. But it is this tension, too, that has brought Islam in both countries to what may, without any concession to the apocalyptic temper of our time, legitimately be called a crisis. In Indonesia as in Morocco, the collision between what the Qur'an reveals, or what Sunni (that is, orthodox) tradition has come to regard it as revealing, and what men who call themselves Muslims actually believe is becoming more and more inescapable. This is not so much because the gap between the two is greater. It has always been very great, and I should not like to have to argue that the Javanese peasant or Berber shepherd of 1700 was any closer to the Islam of al-Shafi'i or al-Ghazali than are the Westernized youth of today's Djakarta or Rabat. It is because, given the increasing diversification of individual experience, the dazzling multiformity which is the hallmark of modern consciousness, the task of Islam (and indeed of any religious tradition) to inform the faith of particular men and to be informed by it is becoming ever more difficult. A religion which would be catholic these days has an extraordinary variety of mentalities to be catholic about; and the question, can it do this and still remain a specific and persuasive force with a shape and identity of its own, has a steadily more problematical ring.

The overall strategies evolved in Morocco and in Indonesia during the pre-modern period for coping with this central dilemma—how to bring exotic minds into the Islamic community without betraying the vision that created it—were, as I have indicated, strikingly different, indeed almost diametrical opposites, with the result that the shapes of the religious crises which their populations now face are to a certain extent mirror images of one another.

In Morocco the approach developed was one of uncompromising rigorism. Aggressive fundamentalism, an active attempt to impress a seamless orthodoxy on the entire population, became, not without struggle, the central theme. This is not to say that the effort has been uniformly successful, or that the concept of orthodoxy that emerged was one that the rest of the Islamic world would necessarily recognize as such. But, distinctive and perhaps even errant as it was, Moroccan Islamism came over the centuries to embody a marked strain of religious and moral perfectionism, a persisting determination to establish a purified, canonical, and completely uniform creed in this, on the face of it, unpromising setting.

The Indonesian (and especially the Javanese) mode of attack was, as I say, quite the contrary: adaptive, absorbent, pragmatic, and gradualistic; a matter of partial compromises, half-way covenants, and outright evasions. The Islamism which resulted did not even pretend to purity, it pretended to comprehensiveness; not to an intensity but to a largeness of spirit. Here, too, one ought not to take the aim for the achievement, nor to deny the presence of unconformable cases. But that over its general course Islam in Indonesia has been as Fabian in spirit as in Morocco it has been Utopian is beyond much doubt. It is also beyond much doubt that, whatever they may originally have had to recommend them, neither of these strategies, the prudential or the headlong, is any longer working very well, and the Islamization of both countries is consequently in some danger not only of ceasing to advance but in fact of beginning to recede.

As far as religion is concerned, therefore, the tale of these two peoples is essentially the story of how they have arrived, or more accurately are in the process of arriving, at obverse forms of the same predicament. But, in some contrast to the way in which spiritual confusion is usually conceived in the West, this predicament is less a matter of what to believe as of how to believe it. Viewed as a social, cultural, and psychological (that is to say, a human) phenomenon, religiousness is not merely knowing the truth, or what is taken to be the truth, but embodying it, living it, giving oneself unconditionally to it.

In the course of their separate social histories, the Moroccans and the Indonesians created, partly out of Islamic traditions, partly out of others, images of ultimate reality in terms of which they both saw life and sought to live it. Like all religious conceptions, these images carried within them their own justification; the symbols (rites, legends, doctrines, objects, events) through which they were expressed were, for those responsive to them, intrinsically coercive, immediately persuasive—they glowed with their own authority. It is this quality that they seem gradually to be losing, at least for a small but growing minority. What is believed to be true has not changed for these people, or not changed very much. What has changed is the way in which it is believed. Where there once was faith, there now are reasons, and not very convincing ones; what once were deliverances are now hypotheses, and rather strained ones.

There is not much outright skepticism around, or even much conscious hypocrisy, but there is a good deal of solemn self-deception.

In Morocco this most frequently appears as a simple disjunction between the forms of religious life, particularly the more properly Islamic ones, and the substance of everyday life. Devoutness takes the form of an almost deliberate segregation of what one learns from experience and what one receives from tradition, so that perplexity is kept at bay and doctrine kept intact by not confronting the map with the landscape it is supposed to illuminate—Utopia is preserved by rendering it even more Utopian. In Indonesia it most frequently appears as a proliferation of abstractions so generalized, symbols so allusive, and doctrines so programmatic that they can be made to fit any form of experience at all. The eloquence of felt particulars is smothered in a blanket of vacant theories which, touching everything, grasp nothing—Fabianism ends in elevated vagueness. But, formalism or intellectualism, it really comes down to about the same thing: holding religious views rather than being held by them.

All this is, however, still but a crumbling at the edges; the cores of both populations still cling to the classical symbols and find them compelling. Or anyway largely so; the mere awareness on the part of those for whom the inherited machinery of faith still works passably well (which is probably the most it has ever done) that it does not work nearly so well for a growing number of others casts a certain shadow over the finality of their own perceptions. Even more important, those for whom the grasping power of the classical symbols has weakened have, with only scattered exceptions, not become impervious to that power altogether, so that rather than opting for an internal or an external approach to believing they fluctuate uncertainly and irregularly between them, seeing the symbols now as emanations of the sacred, now as representations of it. A few untroubled traditionalists at one pole and even fewer radical secularists at the other aside, most Moroccans and Indonesians alternate between religiousness and what we might call religious-mindedness with such a variety of speeds and in such a variety of ways that it is very difficult in any particular case to tell where the one leaves off and the other begins. In this, as in so many things, they are, like most of the peoples of the Third World, like indeed most of those of the First and Second, rather thoroughly mixed up. As time goes on, the number of people who desire to believe, or anyway feel they somehow ought to, decreases much less rapidly than the number who are, in a properly religious sense, able to. And in this rather demographic-looking fact lies the interest of religion for those of us who would like to uncover the dynamics and determine the directions of social change in the new states of Asia and Africa.

Alterations in the general complexion of spiritual life, in the character of religious sensibility, are more than just intellectual reorientations or shifts in emotional climate, bodiless changes of the mind. They are also, and more fundamentally, social processes, transformations in the quality of collective life. Neither thought nor feeling is, at least among humans, autonomous, a self-contained stream of subjectivity, but each is inescapably dependent upon the utilization by individuals of socially available "systems of significance," cultural constructs embodied in language, custom, art, and technology—that is to say, symbols. This is as true for religiousness as it is for any other human capacity. Without collectively evolved, socially transmitted, and culturally objectified patterns of meaning—myths, rites, doctrines, fetishes, or whatever—it would not exist. And when these patterns alter, as, given the impermanence of terrestrial things, they inevitably and indeed continuously do, it alters with them. As life moves, persuasion moves with it and indeed helps to move it. More bluntly, whatever God may or may not be—living, dead, or merely ailing—religion is a social institution, worship a social activity, and faith a social force. To trace the pattern of their changes is neither to collect relics of revelation nor to assemble a chronicle of error. It is to write a social history of the imagination.

* * *

It is this sort of history, condensed and generalized, that I am going to sketch for Morocco and Indonesia in the next two chapters and then use, in the final one, as the basis for some even less circumstantial comments on the role of religion in society generally.

In the next chapter, I will trace the development and characterize the nature of what we may call, to have a name for them, the classical religious styles in Morocco and Indonesia. As these styles were, like any styles, not born adult but evolved out of others, I shall not produce a timeless snapshot of something called "traditional religion" which, as the Moroccan idiom has it, "just came and was," but attempt to show how, gradually, variously, and with more than one detour and one delay, characteristic conceptions of the nature of the divine and the way in which men should approach it became reasonably well established in each of these countries.

To accomplish this it is necessary to do several things. First, the mere story of what came after what and when must be at least generally outlined; without sequence, descriptions of the past are catalogs or fairy tales. Second, the major conceptual themes which were in this way produced must be isolated and related to one another, and their symbolic embodiments, the cultural vehicles of their expression, must be described with some specificity, so that ideas are not left floating in some shadow world of Platonic objects but have a local habitation and a name. Finally, and perhaps most important of all, the sort of social order in which such ideas could and did seem to almost everybody to be not merely appropriate but inevitable, not commendable opinions about an unknown reality which it was comforting or prudential or honorable to hold, but authentic apprehensions of a known one which it was impossible to deny, must be depicted and analyzed. If Durkheim's famous statement that God is the symbol of society is incorrect, as I think it is, it remains true that particular kinds of faith (as well as particular kinds of doubt) flourish in particular kinds of societies, and the contribution of the comparative sociology of religion to the general understanding of the spiritual dimensions of human existence both begins and ends in an uncovering of the nature of these empirical, that is to say lawful, interconnections. The material reasons why Moroccan Islam became activist, rigorous, dogmatic and more than a little anthropolatrous and why Indonesian Islam became syncretistic, reflective, multifarious, and strikingly phenomenological lie, in part anyway, in the sort of collective life within which and along with which they evolved.

The fundamental alterations in this collective life over the past seventy-five or a hundred years, the movement toward what we vaguely and somewhat equivocally call modernism, in turn implied similar alterations in these classical religious styles, and it is to this—the interaction between religious and social change—that I will devote my third chapter.

The moving force of this still far from completed social and cultural metamorphosis is usually considered to be Western impact, the shaking of the foundations of traditional culture in Asia and Africa by the dynamism of industrial Europe. This is, of course, not wrong; but the energy of this external stimulus was converted, not just in Indonesia and Morocco but everywhere that it has been felt, into internal changes: changes in the forms of economic activity, in political organization, in the bases of social stratification, in moral values and ideologies, in family life and education, and, perhaps most critically, changes in the sense of life's possibilities, in notions of what one might hope for, work for, or even expect in the world. It is these internal changes, not, at least for the most part, European culture as such, to which religious change has been on the one hand a response and on the other an incitement. Only a tiny minority in either society has had any really intimate contact with European civilization, and most of that is either very distorted, very recent, or both. What most people have had contact with are the transformations that civilization's activities induced in their own. Whatever its outside provocations, and whatever foreign borrowing may be involved, modernity, like capital, is largely made at home.

The religious crisis in Morocco and Indonesia has been and is being generated in the internal confrontation of established forms of faith with altered conditions of life, and it is out of that confrontation that the resolution of that crisis, if there is to be a resolution, will have to come. If the term "modernization" is to be given any substantial meaning and its spiritual implications uncovered, the connections between changes in the classical religious styles and such developments as rationalized forms of economic organization, the growth of political parties, labor unions, youth groups, and other voluntary associations, revised relations between the sexes, the appearance of mass communications, the emergence of new classes, and a whole host of other social novelties must be discovered.

All this is, of course, generally known. What is not known, or anyway not very well known, are the particulars of the situation, and it is only through knowing the particulars that we can advance beyond the easy banalities of common sense. Blake's remark that there is no such thing as general knowledge, that all knowledge is knowledge of particulars, may be an exaggeration. But it is no exaggeration to say, at least so far as the sociology of religion is concerned, that there is no route to general knowledge save through a dense thicket of particulars. I shall try to keep the thicket as trimmed and well weeded as I can and to avoid telling you more about Indonesian shadow plays or Moroccan saint festivals than you care to know. Nor can I, in such a compass, discuss the nonreligious changes in any fine detail. But there is, in this area, no ascent to truth without descent to cases.

In the final chapter, at any rate, I will try to make something rather more broadly relevant out of all this closet-history and micro-sociology. Anthropology is, actually, a sly and deceptive science. At the moment when it seems most deliberately removed from our own lives, it is most immediate; when it seems most insistently to be talking about the distant, the strange, the long ago, or the idiosyncratic, it is in fact talking also about the close, the familiar, the contemporary, and the generic. From one point of view, the whole history of the comparative study of religion from the time Robertson-Smith undertook his investigations into the rites of the ancient Semites (and was dismissed from Oxford as a heretic for his pains) can be looked at as but a circuitous, even devious, approach to a rational analysis of our own situation, an evaluation of our own religious traditions while seeming to evaluate only those of exotic others.

The case is no different here. Moving from the special circumstances of Indonesia and Morocco to the new states in general, I hope to raise the suspicion that their predicament is also our own, that what they face we face, however differently we may formulate it or phrase our responses. I am not sure whether this will serve the Terry Foundation's stated purpose of "building the truths of science and philosophy into the structure of a broadened and purified religion," something I am not altogether certain is a good idea. But it ought at least to show those who would attempt such a valiant enterprise just what it is they are up against.

9

Islamic Movements: One or Many?

William R. Roff

Let me try to phrase the problem addressed in this essay as a series of linked questions. Does "Islam" constitute social relations in Muslim societies? If so, does it do so in ways that are common to all or most Muslim societies? If so, how can we best inquire into and understand the processes involved?

My own answer would be something like the following. All social action by Muslims, *acting as Muslims* (acceptors of the *shari'a*), is constrained by the objectively invariant prescriptions of "Islam," known to the believer first from the Qur'an and secondly (if more questionably invariant) the *sunna*. Though these prescriptions (and their elaboration by those learned in the *shari'a*) must be interpreted and applied by historically situated individuals (or collectivities), and hence do not exist outside of time or social context, it can be argued that they supply a major, sometimes determinative, part of the perceived objective conditions which direct or constrain action. Further, the common need to persuade, urge, teach, command, or reason with one's fellows in pursuit of proper Muslim action ensures the frequent iteration of prescription and its embodiment in argument and discourse. It is to this discourse, then, in all its complexity, and subject to its own rules, that we must turn in order to determine (if we care to) anything like common principles of Muslim social action. That all such discourse necessarily takes place in contingent and highly variable circumstances requires that the context and levels of the discourse, and *their* cultural and material constraints and determinants, be adequately discerned and understood. It is our apprehension of the simultaneous operation of the prescriptive and circumstantial conditions of action that may permit us to speak with some validity of a specifically Islamic constitution of social relations that can reasonably be held to apply to most if not all of "the Muslim world."

In a critical review not long ago of Ernest Gellner's *Muslim Society*, Jacques Berque wrote (1981, 1433) that "[the life of Muslim societies] is ordered—or disordered—in a perpetual debate between their principle and their reality, and any study of them which neglects one of these terms will lack either realism or intelligibility—by which I mean an intelligibility conceived in the same mode as the subject itself." It is this "intelligibility in the same mode as the subject itself" that must be our principal concern.

The answer to the question "Islamic movements, one or many?" plainly is (to my mind): both. That they are many is self-evident; that they should be perceived as one in any useful, interpretative sense, however, is much more problematic. It is easy to find unhelpful examples of what this perception can result in, whether it is constituted by orientalists about "the other"; stems from the ideologically formed views of political persuaders (be they Pan-Islam-fearful imperialists or wishful-thinking Khilifatists); or is the fruit of post-Marxist reflections on ideology and utopia (such as those of Russell [1920, 118–9] or Rodinson [1972, 154–6]). Though each of these positions, and their simulacra, would doubtless yield something to *verstehen* analysis, they are alike unhelpful in adopting or assuming a congealed and reified notion of "Islam" that takes little account either of real context or of the ways in which, starting from prescription, Muslims actually do construct, evoke, deploy, and accept the "Islam" from which they act, see themselves as acting, or argue that action should flow.

Historical or social enquiry based on examination of Muslim argument about these matters may well appear to reveal a plurality of Islams (see, for example, el-Zein 1977, 228, 242ff; Eickelman 1982, 1), but it seems clear that these Islams manifest in turn a shared repertory of principles of individual and collective action, of a kind that encourages us to explore not merely the intelligibility of Islamic imperatives for Muslims, but the comparability of the social dynamics that (notwithstanding the specificity of circumstance) result. Or to put the thing the other way round, though the real world (but note that just as there may be said to be many "Islams," there are many "real worlds" too) impinges on all human actors, not excepting Muslims— through social formations and relations of production that are at any particular moment given, through state systems and refractions of state power, and in other determinative (and over-determinative) forms—we may observe Muslims acting in ways for which they derive, and to which they give, force and meaning through a wide range of common, Islamically supplied (or enjoined) wellsprings of behavior and response.

One of the principal means of access we have to understanding of this response and its social dynamic is through the discourse of Muslims about (as Lenin put it from within another prescriptive tradition) "What is to be done?" It is therefore of primary importance to take seriously and in its own terms what Muslims, acting as Muslims, say, and not suppose that what they say "really" signifies something else.

Though doing this doubtless does not rule out Derridan or other semiotic approaches to "the text" of what is being transacted, I intend here simply the desideratum that, at the outset at least, what is said be taken at face value and in terms of its own intelligibility system, making the assumption that once familiar with much Muslim discourse, in many contexts, we can have fairly direct access to what and how it "means" for its utterers and auditors.

There is a tendency, not confined to studies of the Muslim world, to suppose that what the natives say is part of an innocent pathology, of an unknowing and essentially self-deceptive symptomology, to which only the trained observer-analyst can have the diagnostic key. This seems dubious, and indeed interpretatively unwise and impermissible if it involves disaggregation (rather than deconstruction) of the discourse, into parts or according to schema derived in extradiscourse terms. Lewis Hyde (1983; McGilchrist 1984, 77), in his recent book *The Gift*, contrasts the circulation of gifts among "primitive" peoples with the hoarding of those same gifts when they passed into the hands of the first anthropologists and were sent to the museums of the great universities. Much the same treatment has often been accorded to the conceptual currency of Muslims (and others), save that it has ended up on fixed deposit in the pages of anthropological (or, to be fair, Islamicist) monographs. If anyone should ask (as well they might, given the supposed nature of the category) why no "*abangan*" Muslims have been discovered in India (or, if it comes to that, in Malaysia or much of Indonesia), the simplest answer is surely that Clifford Geertz did his fieldwork in central Java. Not that that would end the matter.

Let me return, however, to the question of how we may usefully, at times, see the Muslim world whole, and find Islamic movements in some sense one. Or, to phrase the matter as I did at the outset, in what ways can it make sense to see "Islam" as constituting social relations in Muslim societies. If Muslim discourse, and the perceptions of constraint, moral imperative, and proper action that it embodies, is in fact central to any such enquiry, then one method of pursuing it might be to examine the discourse across a range of seemingly comparable, if in fact discretely various, historical circumstance. For instance, though there seems still to be a presumption among scholars that something called "Wahhabism" played a significant part in violent social upheavals occurring in many scattered regions of "the Muslim world" in the late eighteenth and early nineteenth centuries, it is actually not at all clear what, if anything, they truly had in common, in either impulse or content. What can one learn from looking at them in a comparative way, from the standpoint of the discourse among their Muslim protagonists—as well, obviously, as from whatever else we can know of the circumstances in which they occurred?

It is not hard to find idealist postulations of the wide significance of the movement described by its opponents as "Wahhabiya" and by its participants as *al-da'wa ila 'l-tawhid*; it is less easy to learn what precisely "Wahhabism" could have meant (and how) in local terms in places as diverse as the Nejd itself, West Sumatra, the Hausa states, and Bengal. To take only one recent if summary expression of the idealist view, Ali Merad (1977, 113), writing in a special issue of *Cultures* devoted to "Islam: The Perenniality of Values," and claiming that "the Wahhabis greatly contributed to restore the confidence of Muslim peoples and the dynamism they lacked," speaks of "the regenerating wind of Wahhabism...[sweeping] through the entire Muslim community," and sees "the Wahhabian impulse" as (quoting Iqbal) "the first pulsation of life in modern Islam." What can such an appeal to idea and sentiment possibly mean when examined in the immediate circumstances of peoples' lives across half the surface of the globe? Attempts to address this question have taken several forms, none of them (I think) wholly satisfactory.

On the assumption that it is the idea and its articulation that counts, but that (in good Islamic, not to say historiographical, fashion) the *isnad* (chain of authority) must be known, some effort has been made to reconstruct the intellectual milieu of late eighteenth- and early nineteenth-century Arabia (to which so many Muslims went to perform the *hajj* and to study), and to establish something substantial about the teachers and the taught and their links with a wider Muslim world. John Voll's essay on Muhammad Hayya al-Sindi and Muhammad ibn 'Abd al-Wahhab in eighteenth-century Madina is an important contribution in this respect, as is A. H. Johns' discussion of Ibrahim ibn al-Kurani (father of one of al-Sindi's principal teachers) and Ahmad al-Qashashi (Ibrahim al-Kurani's teacher), who through their student 'Abd al-Ra'uf al-Singkeli provide a connection with a somewhat earlier Sumatra (Voll 1975, 32–9; Johns 1978, 469–85). Both Voll and Johns help to provide a much clearer picture of the scholarly community of the late seventeenth- and early eighteenth-century Hijaz, drawn from many scattered parts of the world from the Maghreb to Persia, India, and Acheh, and linked by learning and *turuq* affiliation alike. Some of the ideational emphasis that emerge—among them a strong emphasis on *hadith* studies and on a purified Sufism associated perhaps mainly with the Naqshbandiya *tariqa*—certainly assist in establishing the lineaments of the dominant discourse that is being shaped.

The Nejd

But useful as this kind of study (and its necessary extension to more detailed examination of the writings and teachings of those involved) unquestionably is in elucidation of the intellectual matrices from which so much late eighteenth-century Muslim social thought seems to have sprung, it is a task that remains largely to be accomplished. For, as Voll notes (1975, 38–9), though many attempts have been made to portray the wider influence of "Wahhabi" ideology, "less has been done in analyzing the context out of which Wahhabism itself grew." Plainly, that context is not simply the cosmopolitan world of Mecca and Madina in the first half of the eighteenth century, but paramountly the more remote world of warring segmentary tribal lineages among the pastoral nomads of inner Arabia in the latter part of the century. For it was here, initially in the Nejd, that Muhammad ibn 'Abd al-Wahhab, gripped by his own sense of the gap between prescription and social reality in the lives of Bedu and townsmen alike, began to preach the kind of strict constructionism (an entirely appropriate term) to which in due course the eponym *Wahhabi* became attached, and found a patron and extender in Muhammad ibn Sa'ud, *amir* of the tribal group centered on the oasis settlement of Dir'iya.

The principal doctrinal elements of 'Abd al-Wahhab's teachings, and their expression in social and political institutions within the domains of the *muwahhidun* (unitarians), are tolerably well-known and understood, having been described (and to some extent set out) almost contemporaneously and often discussed since.[1] So also are the successful territorial campaigns of the Sa'uds, from the long struggle with Riyadh at the outset to the extension of Sa'udi influence over most of the peninsula up to Syria and the occupation of the Hijaz from 1803 to 1814. What we mainly lack, however, or so it seems to me, is any serious analysis of the dynamic of *muwahhidun* argument in the context of those social groups, institutions and processes that characterized eighteenth- and early nineteenth-century Arabia, from tribal organization, war and affiliation, to pastoral nomadism and settlement, trade and territory, and the politics of claimed Ottoman hegemony. The Wahhabi-Sa'udi conquest of Arabia was, of course, to a considerable degree a matter of warfare and submission, but it was warfare invested with moral argument, that made moral claims, and carried moral teaching. And it was teaching, one must assume, of a kind that carried meaning in terms of the time, place and context, timeless though its origins and *modus operandi* might claim to be, based on the seeking of God's will for man as set out in the revelation. *How* this teaching meant is likely to elude us unless we can apprehend both the circumstantial context in which it operated and the discourse that accompanied its contestation and acceptance.

These arguments are obvious enough, and offered not as in themselves any addition to interpretative understanding of "Wahhabism," but rather as an exemplification of the way in which interpretative understanding must proceed, and through which some comprehension of the social dynamic of Islamic argumentation may be obtained. When we move beyond Arabia, exactly the same considerations arise. But first let us look briefly at what is known about the substantive links between the Arabia of this time and the immediately relevant other parts of the Muslim world. Mervyn Hiskett (1962, 593) has said of the Fulani *jihad*ists, "it is impossible that they can have remained unaware of the 'innovations' in Arabia in their day," and we are quite familiar in a general way with the networks of communication which, through the *hajj*, peripatetic students and teachers, and affiliation with *turuq*, ensured a constantly renewed reportage of ideas and events from the Ivory Coast to Mindanao. More specifically, however, with respect to the "Wahhabi" movements we are considering here, the outbreak of the "Padri" revolt in Minangkabau has long been associated (with what validity may appear) with the "three *hajjis*" who returned there from Mecca in 1803, and the Fara'idi movement in East Bengal with the return of Hajji

Shariat Allah from twenty years in the Hijaz in 1818. And even in Hausaland (usually thought to be the most dubious of the cases) the return from his second *hajj* in 1786/87 of the Qadiriya Shaykh Jibril b. 'Umar, Usuman dan Fodio's most influential teacher, was followed by a marked intensification of dan Fodio's personal revelation and preachings, culminating in the *hijr* and *jihad* of 1804.

By themselves, however, such connections can be little more than inferential—in the real sense "accidental"—and indeed further enquiry readily shows that in all cases (especially perhaps those of Minangkabau and the Fulani) the apparent crucial moment turns out to be itself part of a somewhat longer local experience of social perturbation expressed in Islamic ways. Nor, from the standpoint of interpretative interest, is happenstance the point, any more than are calendrical occasion and the messianic expectations said to have been widely prevalent among Muslims at the turn of the *hijri* century in 1785 (as again in 1882, and some would say 1979). That there should be connections—between people and places, or times and events—is, of course, not without consequence, and their nature must where possible be accounted for and their ramifications explored. But the principal task remains that of trying to understand how, when invoked, Islamic imperatives come to have (or give) meaning for those involved.

The Padri Movement

The most careful and detailed examination that I know of the economic, social, and political context for a "Wahhabi" movement of the late eighteenth and nineteenth centuries is the study of the Padri movement recently published by Christine Dobbin, *Islamic Revivalism in a Changing Peasant Economy: Central Sumatra, 1784–1847.*[2] The part of central Sumatra known as Minangkabau consists of an extensive and well-populated highland massif, falling away abruptly to a narrow coastal strip on the west, and wandering off through swampy, riverine lowlands to the Malacca Strait in the east. Settled by agriculturalists cultivating wet and dry rice in the valleys and on the hill slopes of the massif, it had been connected to the outside world since at least the fifteenth century by a valuable trade in gold, mined in the highlands and taken out through west coast ports. Control of gold workings and trade routes (and from the sixteenth century, participation in the cultivation and marketing of export pepper) provided the basis for the Minangkabau state and underwrote one of the main forms of social differentiation. Another derived from the coexistence of two major principles of social organization, each with its own system of *adat* (Ar. *'ada*): that associated with the royal family, patrilineal in emphasis, and the "republicanism" of the majority of the population, expressed in non-territorial but land-owning matriclans. Minangkabau probably became Muslim in the course of the sixteenth century, initially through the west coast ports and those most involved in the commerce in gold (notably the royal family and traders), later among the generality of peasant agriculturalists through lineage Islamic functionaries and, at the village level, through the institution of the *surau* (young and unmarried men's houses), which increasingly became the focus of Sufi *turuq* and schools.

The decline of the gold workings in the latter half of the eighteenth century, accompanied by a collapse of the pepper market, placed great strains on Minangkabau economy and society, loosening political ties, aggravating regional imbalances, and assisting the penetration of society by forces associated with the rapid growth of a new export crop, *Arabica* coffee (itself perhaps introduced, coincidentally, by returned Mecca pilgrims). Coffee did best on marginal land, on hill slopes above the previously more prosperous lineage-controlled *sawah* (wet rice) lands. Its cultivation brought into being new wealth, creating tensions between *sawah* lineages and land-short coffee growers, as well as between villages competing for boundary land. It fostered the entry into commercial activity of new groups of intermediate traders and carriers, distinguished from the old gold route trading elite and their royal family patrons. Market centers established in the highlands became the locus not simply of new wealth but of forms of economic and social behavior not previously manifested or sanctioned, from a cruder individualism to banditry, rampant gambling, and associated evils. In these circumstances, Dobbin (1983, 126) argues, it was the *surau* that emerged as an alternative to lineage institutions for regulating society's affairs, especially with respect to dispute settlement and with an altogether new emphasis on the *shari'a* rather than *adat* as the supplier of codes of conduct.

The first Islamic "renewal" in Minangkabau dates from about 1784, when the Shattariya *surau* of Tuanku Nan Tua, in the Agam district, began to function as a major source for the teaching of a revived Islamic jurisprudence in the practical context of conflict over trading and land matters among neighboring villages, to the extent that by the 1790s Nan Tua had become known as "the patron of the traders" (Dobbin 1983, 127). Similar developments are documented for elsewhere in the region, as is a marked increase in the pilgrimage to Mecca by those benefiting from the new wealth. One of the famous "three *hajjis*" who returned in 1803, Haji Miskin, had been involved in Tuanku Nan Tua's renewal movement before his departure, and now proceeded to teach what Dobbin terms "Wahhabi" doctrines in one of the newly prosperous coffee-producing villages, urging adherence in all respects to a *shari'a* derived solely from the Qur'an, requiring the substitution of plain white clothing (and the veiling of women) for native dress, strict performance of the *salat* and other *'ibadat*, and the prohibition of cock-fighting, tobacco and opium smoking, and *tuak* (rice wine) drinking. Subsequently, under the patronage of another major Shattariya teacher, Tuanku Nan Rinceh, the local struggle was extended in a more general "*jihad*," accompanied by much violence, to spread these teachings, and the adoption of the *shari'a*, administered by specially appointed *qadis*, to regulate all matters of property and commerce. The civil strife that resulted in Agam persisted for six years, and was later replicated in other major areas of Minangkabau, until involvement by the Dutch in the 1820s altered the whole character of the affair.

One might, perhaps, do more than Dobbin has chosen to do to disinter the detail of the discourse among Muslims that accompanied the Padri movement. Though the materials are limited, it is clear that there was much debate, much appeal to authority of varying sorts within the Islamic tradition itself, much discussion of proper *modus operandi*, and the argument might with advantage be treated somewhat more coherently in its own terms, and less derivatively. But her account comes a great deal nearer than most (whether of this movement or others) to situating the discourse in a closely examined context of socio-economic change, and to taking seriously the dialectic that results. While it may not be necessary (and at times perhaps not even helpful) to see the movement as "Wahhabi," there can be little doubt that despite the great contextual differences it was remarkably similar to that of the *muwahhidun* in its impulses and argument, in its capacity to create and convey meaning for its followers through Islamic imperatives, and can best be understood, in a comparative way, in such terms.

The Fara'idi Movement

Can one say the same of Hajji Shariat Allah's Fara'idi movement in East Bengal, launched in 1821? It may be worth noting at the outset—for again the contexts are very different—that where Tuanku Nan Tua became known to his supporters as "the patron of the traders," Hajji Shariat Allah was derided by his opponents as "the *pir* of the *julahas*" (spiritual mentor of the [poor] weavers) (Ahmad Khan 1965, 86). The establishment of East India Company control over Bengal in the 1770s, and the introduction of a British-devised system of administration in place of the supplanted Mughal one, had profound effects especially on land tenure and revenue collection, transforming the basis of the state from what may be termed a tributary mode of production to a rentier capitalist one. In brief, the Mughal *zamindars* (ideally, the revenue-collecting agents of the state, though with certain accrued hereditary rights over land as well) became, through the "permanent settlement" of 1793, proprietors of the land, liable only for regular and fixed payments to the state. Furthermore, in the space of a few decades only, with the Mughal upper class (for the most part non-Bengali in origin, and Persian and Urdu-speaking, but Muslim) pushed aside and much of their lands resumed, the *zamindars* were drawn increasingly from among Calcutta-based, Hindu merchant collaborators with the Company, set thereby over a largely Muslim peasantry reduced to the status of tenants-at-will. Two further economic changes greatly affected the condition of the predominantly Muslim poorer classes of the delta, peasant and artisan. The loss of Britain's colonies in the Americas led at the turn of the century to the emergence of East Bengal as a major center for the cultivation of indigo by British plantation interests, with oppressive effects on land use and tenant conditions; and metropolitan policies concerning the manufacture, import and export of cloth goods led to the rapid decline and eventual extinction of the Bengal cotton- and silk-weaving craft industry. The net effect of half a century of Company rule was the impoverishment of the poorer classes of Muslims, especially in the delta areas of East Bengal, and the erosion of social ties between the peasantry and the erstwhile (now much reduced) Muslim official and landowning classes.[3]

Shariat Allah had been born into a *taluqdar* (petty landowning) family in the delta district of Faridpur in 1781. In 1799, at the age of eighteen, he went to Mecca with his Calcutta teacher of Persian and Arabic, Mawlana Basharat 'Ali, who, it is said, had become "disgusted with the British regime and decided to emigrate to the holy city" (Ahmad Khan 1965, 3). He remained in the Hijaz for nineteen years (save for two years at al-Azhar), became a student in most of the Islamic sciences of Shaykh Tahir al-Sunbal al-Makki (of whom little is known), and was initiated by him into the Qadiriya *tariqa*. He returned briefly to Bengal in 1818, and then in 1821 for good. Appalled at the state of Muslim belief and practice in his native land, with its emphasis on shrine worship and *pir* veneration and its adulteration by Hindu and other custom and ritual, he began to preach a renewed Islam purified of *bida'* and insistent upon proper performance of the fundamental duties of the faith (*fara'id*, hence the name by which the movement became known). His following is said contemporaneously to have grown rapidly, embracing by the 1830s about one-sixth of the rural population (Taylor 1840, cited in Ahmad Khan 1965, 12). At the same time, it brought him into conflict with the Hindu *zamindar*s, over non-payment of "idolatrous" taxes, and with more traditional Muslim leaders on a variety of issues, not least his proscription of *pir* veneration (he claimed for himself only the title *ustaz*, teacher) which undercut the basis of much rural spiritual authority. Where specifically state power was concerned, Shariat Allah's requirement of his followers that Friday congregational (*juma'*, *jam'*) and *'Id* (festival) prayers not be held in villages and towns in a Bengal effectively stripped under Company rule of its legitimating Islamic authority (*amir* and *qadi*) can be seen as having political implications, though there is some difference of opinion over whether it was directed more against the British or against a local Muslim leadership perceived as errant or absent.

The transformation of the Fara'idis from communities of personally purified Muslims based on repentance (*tawba*), observance of the *fara'id*, and strict avoidance of *shirk* (polytheism), into a more direct and militant expression of economic and social discontent of a kind quickly characterized as "Wahhabi" was largely the work of his son, Muhammad Muhsin al-Din Muhammad (better known as Dudhu Miyan), who returned from some five years in Mecca in 1836 (four years before his father's death), and proceeded to supply the movement with organization and structure which transcended its original impulse. Building on the first, local level *panchayats* (village councils) set up by his father as teaching centers, and on the idea of a solidarity community of believers, he established an elaborate network of authority, with himself as *ustaz* (after 1840) and a hierarchy of advisory *khalifa*s (deputies) at the center, superintendent *khalifa*s at district level, and unit *khalifa*s in village and town ward. Authority was expressed through both *siyasa* and *dini* structures, the former to recruit fighting groups through which to assert directly the rights of cultivators and artisans against *zamindar*s and forced-contract indigo planters; the latter to govern *fara'idi* communities, with unit *khalifa*s acting as *imam*s and *qadi*s, overseeing *zakat* and *'ushr* collection, and responsible for the provision of community *astanas*, used among other things for visiting teachers and for the regular performance of Qadiriya *dhikr*. In the course of the twenty years from Dudhu Miyan's return to Bengal and the outbreak of the "Indian Mutiny," the Fara'idis grew considerably in numbers, and were increasingly involved in organizing and channeling agrarian protest throughout East Bengal, continually coming before the British on charges of public violence and luddism, and perceived as having established among themselves to a threatening degree an *imperium in imperio*.

Any brief summary of the kind given above must do violence to the complexity of social reality. The Fara'idis were by no means the only Muslim renewal movement to become resoundingly active (and to be labeled Wahhabi) in early nineteenth-century Bengal, and the later set debates (*bahas*) between these several tendencies, together with the *puthi* literature that reflects them (perceptively discussed by Rafiuddin Ahmed (1981) for the second half of the century), was plainly an important part of a larger "Islamization" process that was under way. Similarly, the Hindu context of social action was altogether more subtle than this summary can convey, and the sharpening of boundaries between Hindus and *sabiqi* Muslims (traditionalists, "syncretists"— read "*abangan*"?) is obviously more than a matter of emerging conflict between the poorer (not solely Muslim) classes and the *zamindar*s (not all of whom were Hindu). Much remains to be known, too, in a sociological way, about the Fara'idi leadership, as well as that of similar movements.

My present concern, however, is simply to raise the question, not to my mind yet answered by the literature, of how, for the Fara'idis, leaders and followers, fara'idi prescription operated within the given socio-economic and cultural circumstances, and, from the outset of Shariat Allah's mission, to enjoin and to give meaning to personal and social action in such a way as to render comprehensible in its own terms the social dynamic that resulted. This question certainly cannot be answered by application of the term "Wahhabi," but it is not very satisfactorily addressed either by predominantly materialist or instrumental interpretations of the movement, persuasive as these may be as glosses after the fact, pointing to the attraction of a textually validated Islamic equalitarianism for caste-like (and out of work) weavers; to the appeal of the Qur'anic *ayat*, "Whatever is in the heavens and in the earth belongs to Allah" (Qur'an 2:129 and 4:131; cf. Ahmad Khan 1965, 114), as a charter for oppressed peasants; or to the interests served by social mobilization for ousted elites suffering from relative deprivation.[4] What one needs, it may rather be maintained, is to know more of the discourse that accompanied, and formed the burden of, fara'idi prescription. In fact, this may not be very easily supplied. The most detailed and carefully argued discussion of the Fara'idis, that by Muin-ud-Din Ahmad Khan, is able to reproduce very little of it, especially from the early period, having to rely largely on later emanations from the movement (in the form of *fatawa*, *puthi* literature, hagiographies and the like), together with some contemporary report ánd the counterblasts of such prominent opponents as Mawlana Karamat 'Ali. But the question is worth addressing, and could with profit be pursued.

The Fulani *jihad*

Turning, briefly, to the last of my examples, what is perhaps most striking about the Fulani *jihad*, in contrast to the Padri and Fara'idi movements (or that of the Nejdi *muwahhidun*) is the abundance of contemporary documentation produced by its protagonists. One of the consequences of this is that it has been possible for students of the movement to produce descriptive and interpretative accounts which draw heavily, indeed rely considerably, on the writings of those who took part. Not surprisingly, such accounts tend to see and explain the *jihad* in substantially local, though not thereby wholly *sui generis*, terms. One might be inclined to think that, had this been possible for the Padri and Fara'idi movements, they would less often be labeled "Wahhabi" and more readily discussed in terms of their explicit impetuses. No doubt overmuch should not be made of this, for the *jihad*ists too had significant links with the Sufi and Hijazi intellectual circles of the time (and they too were aware of the turn of the Islamic calendar), but it comes as a useful corrective.

The Fulbe (Hausa: Fulani) of the central Sudan in the eighteenth century were a mainly transhumant pastoralist, clan-organized people, speaking the Fulfulde language, who, tracing their origins to the western reaches of the medieval Saharan kingdom of Mali (where they claimed a measure of Berber descent), had migrated from the fifteenth century on into the Hausa-speaking country east of the middle Niger. Here on the scrubby savannah lands of the Sahel, they grazed their cattle and moved among the settled agriculturalist population, owning at least nominal allegiance to the Hausa chiefs of more than a dozen principalities, half of which were in some sense Muslim and half not. The Islamic religion, and with it a substantial measure of Arab culture (not least the Arabic language among the learned), seems to have been strongly present in the central Sudan from about the early sixteenth century, associated especially with traders seeking gold and slaves and (in due course) with literati seeking patronage at Hausa courts. Nuclei of Islamic communities existed in the walled towns of the region, from which some influence extended to the surrounding "mixed" communities, and there was in addition a constant traffic through the region of Muslim scholars, students and teachers, seeking each other, going on and returning from the *hajj*, engaged to some degree in trans-Saharan trade, affiliated from the eighteenth century with one or another Sufi *tariqa*, and teaching wherever they could. The Islamic presence, like the population generally, may thus be said to have had its settled and its peripatetic components.

Among the Fulani, many but not all of whom were Muslim, was one clan or sub-clan that had a particular association with and commitment to Islamic learning. These were the *Torodo* (pl. *Torodbe*), originally from Futa Toro in western Senegambia, where their kinsmen had been involved in earlier West African *jihad*s against non-Muslim hosts or neighbors, establishing state-like Imamates in Futa Toro, Bondo and Futa Jalon in the early and late eighteenth centuries. The Torodo Fulani, who had migrated a thousand miles to the east in the fifteenth century, centering themselves on the northern Hausa kingdom of Gobir, lived both settled and peripatetic lives, as scribes, counselors, and teachers at the court and in the towns, and as itinerant scholars (*mallams*) living from time to time in smaller settlements and villages but constantly on the move. Though their primary constituency, outside the towns, was among the Muslim cattle-Fulani nomads, they had some following also among those of the Hausa peasantry who had become in a measure Muslim, and in often (though not always) close association with the nomadic Tuareg of the northern marchlands, especially the latter's *Ineslemen* (*mallam*) lineages.

There are some indications that in the late eighteenth century endemic, incipient, or potential systemic stresses between the several groups comprising the Gobir (and other Hausa) polities were in the process of exacerbation. Fulani nomadic pastoralists, despite a tendency to concentrate in the outer reaches of the Hausa kingdoms, were always liable to conflict with the settled Hausa peasantry over access to grazing land and water supplies. Subjected to state cattle taxes seen as burdensome (and to the *mallam* Islamically improper), their problems in this respect were certainly less than those of the Hausa cultivators, the objects of frequently discriminatory and oppressive taxes on land and produce by their rulers. Fulani and Hausa alike were prey to slave raiding, an immemorial problem given fresh edge in the late eighteenth century by the acquisition of firearms by the court-sanctioned raiders. Tuareg nomadic herdsmen, growing in number, felt increasingly impelled to move from the northern Sahel to better southern pastures. As one historian (Waldman 1965, 344) has said, "At the end of the eighteenth century, Hausaland was filled with people dissatisfied with the Hausa order" and ready to join movements of protest. In this context, it was the Fulani, and especially the Torodo Fulani *mallam*s, who were best able to find both ideology and structure for such protest: ideology through an Islamically argued need for change, structure through their own and associated clan solidarities and their network of long-distance teaching and exchange.

The course of the movement brought into being by Usuman dan Fodio ('Uthman b. Muhammad Fudi), and his brother Abdullahi and son Muhammad Bello, has been frequently and well described,[5] and will not be set out at any length here. Usuman, son of a learned (Ful., *fudiye*) Torodo *mallam*, was born in a village in northern Gobir in 1754. Educated into the tradition by his father and uncles, he later (1779) became the student of the militantly rigorist Tuareg Shaykh Jibril b. 'Umar al-Aqdasi, not long returned from Mecca and Cairo, who initiated him into probably three Sufi *turuq*, notably the Khalwatiya and Qadiriya, both then part of the purified Sufi response to *muwahhidun* strictures on excesses (and the latter the *tariqa* of the *fara'idi* Shariat Allah).[6] Among other teachers of consequence were his cousin (or maternal uncle)

Muhammad al-Raj, who taught him al-Bukhari, having studied *hadith* in Madina with Abu'l Hasan al-Sindi, a pupil of the Muhammad Hayya al-Sindi who had taught 'Abd al-Wahhab ('Abdullah ibn Muhammad Fodio 1963, 95). In 1774, aged twenty, Usuman dan Fodio began his own peripatetic teaching, first in Gobir and then in neighboring states, both among the Muslim Fulani and among those, Hausa as well as Fulani, who had not yet "smelt the scent of Islam." Encouraged by wide success as a teacher, and an extirpator of laxity among the "mixers," he sought out the nominally Muslim ruler of Gobir, "to [explain] to him the true Islam and [order] him (to observe it) and to establish justice in his lands" ('Abdullah ibn Muhammad Fodio 1963, 86). Some years later (in 1787 or 1788) he and numerous other *mallam*s confronted the ruler at the *'Id al-Adha* festival, and obtained from him a list of promised concessions to Muslim subjects of the state. He continued to teach, to travel, and to win a following. From 1789 onwards, Usuman was vouchsafed a succession of personal visions, in which first the Prophet Muhammad appeared before him, and then, in 1794, 'Abd al-Qadir al-Jilani, founder of the Qadiriya order, who gave him a green robe embroidered with the *shahada* and a "sword of truth" to unsheath against the enemies of Allah.[7] Relations between a new and less secure Gobir ruler (acceded 1796) and the Muslims deteriorated until, in 1804, modeling himself on the Prophetic tradition, Usuman dan Fodio declared a *hijr* to the borders of the kingdom, from whence was launched the *jihad*, led in the field by his brother Abdullahi and son Muhammad Bello, that several years later resulted in the establishment of what became known as the Sokoto caliphate or empire. Though the kernel of the *jihad* forces were drawn from the *mallam*s, the rank and file support, as it accumulated, was extremely heterogeneous, from Fulani (and Hausa) Muslims to previously non-Muslim groups which for many and diverse reasons became caught up in the struggle.

Usuman dan Fodio throughout much of his life from the early 1790s (he died in 1817) committed a great deal of his teaching and argument to writing, a corpus of materials added to by Abdullahi dan Fodio, Muhammad Bello and others of his Companions (as well as by those court-appointed *mallam*s with whom he debated), so that we have an extraordinary quantity of Muslim discourse on which to base understanding of the imperatives claimed by the movement, and how they spoke to those who became its adherents.[8] Though most of Usuman's writings were in Arabic, he wrote also (especially in verse) in Fulfulde and possibly also in Hausa, presumably to reach a wider audience. The works ranged from emotional Sufi poems and simply expressed teachings of the *'aqa'id* to carefully argued expositions of his theological beliefs and political views. They extend in time from his *Ihya al-sunna wa ikhmad al-bid'a* (Revivification of the sunna and extinction of innovation), which in a largely non-polemical way set out in 1792 to correct the practice of Muslims in his own place and time, through the *Masa'il muhimma* (Important matters) of 1803, which presaged the need for *hijr* and *jihad*, to the 1806/7 *Bayan wujub al-hijra 'ala 'l-'ibad* (Explanation of the obligation of *hijr* for the worshipers) and *Kitab al-farq bayna wilayat ahl al-Islam wa bayna wilayat ahl al-kufr* (Book of the difference between the government of the people of Islam and the government of the unbelievers) in the post-*jihad* period, together with discussions in poems and elsewhere (notably in the 1811/12 *Siraj al-ikhwan* [Lamp of the brethren]) of himself not as *Mahdi* but as the calendrical *Mujaddid* (Renewer), and of the crucial distinction (in the context of any argument for *jihad*) between sinners and apostates or unbelievers.[9]

The Dialectic

Faced with this mass of detailed, socially embedded Muslim discourse—to which must be added the biographical accounts and didactic writings of Abdullahi and others, and the contemporary histories—simplistic evocations of "Wahhabism" necessarily dissolve. But as they dissolve, and with them the implied claims they make to a special sort of *a priori* inherent universalism, they draw fresh attention, in virtue of the very specificity of the discourse and its circumstance, to the *modus operandi* by which particular Muslims, utterers and auditors, find meaning in or create meaning from a commonly shared, Islamically derived repertoire of imperatives to personal and social action. It is in the intricate analysis of the dialectic between any given, historically evolved set of structural relations—be they those of the Nejdi *muwahhidun*, Padris, Fara'idis, or Fulani—and the transcendental prescriptions as understood by those involved (a dialectic accessible through, and only through, what the natives say) that the oneness of Islamic movements may at times be usefully discerned. It is a oneness residing not in any supposed essential features of "Islam" (for in this sense it has none, and must be construed) but in the logic of relations between the meanings given to prescription and those given to circumstance; between, for Muslims, as Berque suggested, their principle and their reality.

I have tried in this paper to address these questions by looking at some of the roughly contemporaneous movements often described as "Wahhabi." One might equally well, I suppose, have taken the "Salafiya" movements of a century later, or, if it comes to that, something nearer our own day. My argument, if it has any validity at all, is not dependent upon cases. The "Muslim world" today is at least as various as it was at the end of the eighteenth century (and is, of course, not only, or always, the Muslim world, but part of the "capitalist periphery," of the "Third World," of "post-colonial state systems," and much else, depending on the lens one chooses). It is quite as interconnected as it was then, and presumably much more so. The *hajj*, Sufi *turuq*, learning in Mecca and Madina and at al-Azhar, have not been supplanted, but they have had added unto them, magnified by the explosion of communications to which we have all been subjected, International Islamic Universities in at least three other countries, international *da'wa* organizations, the Organization of the Islamic Conference, the Islamic Development Bank, Qaddafi's secret legions, and a lot more. The context of Muslim discourse (in the sense in which I have been speaking of it) and its external constraints have as a result become infinitely more complex. But the task and the challenge of understanding and interpreting that discourse remain, it seems to me, much the same, as do the means of undertaking the task.

I shall end with a reflection that may or may not be pertinent, and is commonplace enough in its way. Not long ago I found myself sitting one Friday at midday in the garden outside the Badshahi Mosque in Lahore, waiting for a friend. Because he was late, I was able to sit there throughout the *juma'* prayer, and in due course to listen to the *khutba*. My knowledge of Urdu is negligible, but I found it was not hard to follow, in general terms, what the *khatib* was saying, and how he was saying it, in an address concerned largely with the Soviet occupation of Afghanistan, and with what must, by Muslims, be done. I could follow what he was saying for several reasons. First of all, because the shape of the *khutba* and its rhetorical style were familiar; secondly, because as in all such addresses the speaker illustrated his argument by frequent quotation from the Qur'an, given in Arabic and then translated into the vernacular; and thirdly, because, though I was outside the mosque and could see nothing of what was going on, I was acutely aware that I was present at a performance in which the speaker, and an audience vocal in response, were together engaged in an exercise the general drift of which did not elude me. Obviously, had I understood Urdu, or indeed had better Arabic, had I been present in the mosque and been able to observe, and had I known something about the *khatib*, his own background, his relation to his parishioners and to the state (and all the other things that Patrick Gaffney is looking at so carefully in his essay), I should have been rather better able to "analyze the discourse." My capacity to analyze it at all, however, is not the point, but rather the certain fact that it might equally well have been taking place (on whatever subject, or indeed on Afghanistan) in Jakarta, Kuala Lumpur, Dacca, Delhi, Qum, Cairo, or Kano, and that Muslims from any or all of these places would have grasped its import much more readily than I. If there is not an "Islamic world," perhaps at times not even a "Muslim world," there is an evident world of Muslims, to whom Muslim discourse speaks.

Notes

1. See, especially, O'Kinealy 1874, 66–82; Burckhardt 1831, 96–357 (esp. 131–62 on government, administration of justice, and revenue collection); Brydges 1834, II, 7–164ff. (esp. 115–27 on administration of justice); Raymond 1925; Niebuhr 1792, II, 130–36. The principal secondary account is presumably Rentz 1948; but cf. also Rentz 1972, 54–56. Materials in Arabic unavailable to me include 'Abd al-Wahhab, n.d. (cited in Al-Yassini 1982, 83); 'Abd al-Wahhab 1955 (cited in Zaharuddin 1979, 156); al-'Uthaymayn, n.d.; and *Majmu'ah al-rasa'il* 1928–31 (the last two cited in Voll 1982, 361).

2. Dobbin 1983. See also Hollander 1857, vol. V (being an account in Malay by a participant, with Dutch translation); de Stuers 1849–50, 2 vols.; and Stein Parve 1855, 245–78. Cf. also Cuisinier 1959, 70–88; and Abdullah 1966, 1–24.

3. For an account of this process, see Mallick 1961 (esp. chap. II); and cf. also Kaviraj 1982 (esp. chap. I).

4. For an interpretation of this kind see, e.g., W.C. Smith 1963, 178; and the recent study by Samad 1983.

5. The principal accounts are Last 1967, Part I, 1–62; Hiskett 1973; Martin 1967, 13–35. Cf. also Waldman 1965, 333–55; M.G. Smith 1966, 408–20; and the useful short account in Hiskett 1976, 131–51.

6. Martin 1967 provides the best discussion of the Sufi background; and cf. also Martin 1972, 300–5.

7. Hiskett 1973, 66, quoting Usuman's late-written Wird; and cf. also the earlier Fulfulde verse, translated into Arabic by 'Abdullah ibn Muhammad Fodio 1963, 105–7.

8. For lists, finding aids, and descriptive accounts of this literature, a large part of which exists only in manuscript, see Last 1967, xxv–lvii, 236–54; Balogun 1975, 177–83; Tapiero 1963, 49–88. The general bibliographies in Last 1967 and Hiskett 1973 contain details of most of the material that has been published or translated. Cf. also Hiskett 1975; and Bivar and Hiskett 1962, 104–48.

9. Usuman's *Ihya' al-sunna*, published in Cairo in 1962, is summarized and in part translated in Balogun 1975, 49–81; his *Kitab al-farq* is published in translation, with parallel text, in Hiskett 1960, 558–79. Hiskett 1973 contains numerous and extended passages of translation from Usuman's writings; cf. also 'Abdullah ibn Muhammad Fodio 1963. Usuman's own account of his life, written originally in Fulfulde, is published in translation, with a photocopy of the text and a transliteration, in al-Masri, Adeleye, and Hunwick 1966, 1–36. Cf. also Arnett 1922, which contains a paraphrase and in parts a translation of the *Infaku 'l-Maisuri* of Sultan Muhammad Bello. On the specific question of the argument for *jihad*, see Martin 1967, 50–97; and cf. Willis 1967, 395–415.

References

'Abd al-Wahhab, Muhammad Ibn. 1955. *Kitab al-tawhid*. Cairo.

—n.d. *Mu'allafat al-shaykh al-imam Muhammad ibn 'Abd al-Wahhab*. 12 vols. Riyadh: Islamic University of Imam Muhammad Ibn Sa'ud.

'Abdullah ibn Muhammad Fodio. 1963. *Tazyin ak-waraqat*. Ed. and trans. M. Hiskett, with parallel Arabic text. Ibadan: Ibadan University Press.

Abdullah, Taufik. 1966. "Adat and Islam: An Examination of Conflict in Minangkabau." *Indonesia* 2: 1–24.

Ahmad Khan, Muin-ud-Din. 1965. *History of the Fara'idi Movement in Bengal (1818–1906)*. Karachi: Pakistan Historical Society.

Ahmed, Raffiuddin. 1981. *The Bengal Muslims, 1871–1906: A Quest for Identity*. Delhi: Oxford University Press.

Arnett, A. J. 1922. *The Rise of the Sokoto Fulani, being a paraphrase and in some parts a translation of the Infaku'l Maisuri of Sultan Muhammad Bello*. Kano.

Balogun, Ismail A.B. 1975. *The Life and Works of 'Uthman dan Fodio*. Lagos: Islamic Publications Bureau.

Berque, Jacques. 1981. "The Popular and the Purified." *Times Literary Supplement*, December 11: 1433.

Bivar, A. D. H., and M. Hiskett. 1962. "The Arabic Literature of Nigeria to 1804: A Provisional Account." *Bulletin of the School of Oriental and African Studies* 25: 104–48.

Brydges, H. J. 1834. "A Brief History of the Wahauby." In his *Account of His Majesty's Mission to Persia in the Years 1807–11*, vol. II, 7–164ff. London: James Hohn.

Burckhardt, J. H. 1831. *Notes on the Bedouins and Wahabys*. London: H. Colburn and R. Bentley.

Cuisinier, Jeanne. 1959. "La guerre des Padris (1803–1838–1845)." *Archives de Sociologie des Religions* 7: 70–88.

Dobbin, Christine. 1983. *Islamic Revivalism in a Changing Peasant Economy: Central Sumatra, 1784–1847*. London: Curzon Press.

Eickelman, Dale F. 1982. "The Study of Islam in Local Contexts." *Contributions to Asian Studies* 17: 1–16.

Hiskett, Mervyn. 1960. "Kitab al-farq: A Work on the Habe Kingdoms Attributed to 'Uthman dan Fodio." *Bulletin of the School of Oriental and African Studies* 23: 558–79.

—1962. "An Islamic Tradition of Reform in the Western Sudan from the Sixteenth to the Eighteenth Century." *Bulletin of the School of Oriental & African Studies* 25: 577–96.

—1973. *The Sword of Truth: The Life and Times of Shehu Usuman dan Fodio*. New York: Oxford University Press.

—1975. *A History of Hausa Islamic Verse*. London: School of Oriental and African Studies.

—1976. "The Nineteenth Century Jihads in West Africa." In *The Cambridge History of Africa*, vol. V, 131–51. Cambridge: Cambridge University Press.

Hollander, J. J. 1857. "Hikajat Sjech Djilal Eddin Tuanku Samiang; verhaal van den aanvang der Padri-onlusten op Sumatra." In idem, ed., *Maleisch Leesboek voor Eerstbeginnenden en Meergevorderen*, vol. V. Leiden: Brill.

Hyde, Lewis. 1983. *The Gift: Imagination and the Erotic life of Property*. New York: Random House.

Johns, A. H. 1978. "Friends in Grace: Ibrahim al-KuranI and 'Abd al-Ra'uf al-Singkeli." In *Spectrum: Essays Presented to Sutan Takdir Alisjahbana on his Seventieth Birthday*, ed. S. Udin, 469–85. Jakarta: Dian Rakyat.

Kaviraj, Narahari. 1982. *Wahabi and Farazi Rebels of Bengal*. Delhi: Peoples' Publishing House.

Last, Murray. 1967. *The Sokoto Caliphate*. London: Longman.

McGilchrist, L. A. 1984. Review of Lewis Hyde, *The Gift: Imagination and the Erotic Life of Property*. In *Times Literary Supplement*, January 27: 77.

Majmu'ah al-rasa'il. 1928–31. *Majmu'ah al-rasa'il wa masa'il al-Najdiyyah*. 4 vols. Cairo: Matba'ah al-Manar.

Mallick, Azizur Rahman. 1961. *British Policy and the Muslims in Bengal, 1757–1856*. Dacca: Asiatic Society of Pakistan.

Martin, B. G. 1967. "Unbelief in the Western Sudan: Uthman dan Fodio's Ta'lim al-ikhwan." *Middle Eastern Studies* 4: 50–97.

—1972. "A Short History of the Khalwati Order of Dervishes." In *Scholars, Saints, and Sufis,* ed. N. Keddie, 275–305. Berkeley, CA: University of California Press.

al-Masri, F. H., R. A. Adeleye, and J. O. Hunwick. 1966. "Sifofin Shehu: An Autobiography and Character Study of 'Uthman b. Fadl in Verse." *Research Bulletin, Centre of Arabic Documentation (Ibadan)* 2: 1–36.

Merad, Ali. 1977. "Reformism in Modern Islam." *Cultures* 4: 108–27.

Niebuhr, M. 1792. "Of the New Religion of a Part of Nedsjed." In his *Travels through Arabia*, II, 130–6. Edinburgh: R. Morison & Son.

O'Kinealy, J. 1874. "Translation of an Arabic Pamphlet on the History and Doctrines of the Wahhabis, written by 'Abdullah, grandson of 'Abdul Wahhab, the founder of Wahhabism." *Journal of the Asiatic Society of Bengal* 1: 66–82.

Raymond, Jean. 1925. *Mémoire sur l'origine des Wahabys, sur la naissance de leur puissance et sur l'influence dont ils jouissent comme nation. Rapport de Jean Raymond date de 1806* ... Cairo: Societé Royale de Géographie d'Egypte.

Rentz, George S. 1948. "Muhammad ibn 'Abd al-Wahhab (1703/04–1792) and the Beginnings of Unitarian Empire in Arabia." Unpubl. Ph.D. dissertation. Berkeley, CA: University of California.

—1972. "Wahhabism and Saudi Arabia." In *The Arabian Peninsula: Society and Politics*, ed. D. Hopwood, 54–66. London: Allen & Unwin.

Rodinson, Maxime. 1972. *Marxisme et Monde Musulman*. Paris: Ed. du Seuil.

Russell, Bertrand. 1920. *Bolshevism: Practice and Theory*. New York: Harcourt, Brace & Rowe.

Samad, Abdus. 1983. "Dynamic of Ascriptive Politics: A Study of Muslim Politicization in East Bengal." Unpubl. Ph.D. dissertation. New York: Columbia University.

Smith, M.G. 1966. "The jihad of Shehu dan Fodio: Some Problems." In *Islam in Tropical Africa*, ed. I. M. Lewis, 408–20. London: Oxford University Press.

Smith, W. C. 1963. *Modem Islam in India: A Social Analysis*. Repr. Lahore: Ashraf. London: rev. ed. 1946.

Stein Parve, H. A. 1855. "De secte der Padaries (Padries) in de bovenlanden van Sumatra." *Tijdschrift voor Indische Taal-, Land- en Volkenkunde* 3: 245–78.

de Stuers, H. J. J. L. Ridder. 1849–50. *De Vestiging en Uitbreiding van de Nederlanders ter Westkust van Sumatra*. 2 vols. Amsterdam: Van Kampen.

Tapiero, N. 1963. "Le grand shaykh Peul 'Uthman ibn Fudi (Othman dan Fodio)...et certaines sources de son Islam doctrinal." *Revue des Etudes Islamiques* 21: 49–88.

Taylor, James. 1840. *A Sketch of the Topography and Statistics of Dacca*. Calcutta: G. H. Huttmann, Military Orphan Press.

al-'Uthaymayn, 'Abdallah al-Salih. n.d. *Al-shaykh Muhammad ibn 'Abd al-Wahhab, hayyatuhu wa fikruhu*. Riyadh: Dar al-'Ulum.

Voll, John. 1975. "Muhammad Hayya al-Sindi and Muhammad ibn 'Abd al-Wahhab: An Analysis of an Intellectual Group in Eighteenth Century Madina." *Bulletin of the School of Oriental and African Studies* 38: 32–9.

—1982. *Islam: Continuity and Change in the Modem World*. Boulder, CO: Westview Press.

Waldman, Marilyn. 1965. "The Fulani jihad: A Reassessment." *Journal of African History* 6: 333–55.

Willis, John R. 1967. "Jihad fi sabil Allah: Its Doctrinal Basis in Islam and Some Aspects of its Evolution in Nineteenth Century West Africa." *Journal of African History* 8: 395–415.

al-Yassini, Ayman S. 1982. "Saudi Arabia: The Kingdom of Islam." In *Religion and Societies: Asia and the Middle East*, ed. C. Caldarola, 61–84. Berlin: Mouton.

Zaharuddin, M. Z. 1979. "Wahhabism and its Influence Outside Arabia." *Islamic Quarterly* 23: 146–57.

el-Zein, Abdul Hamid. 1977. "Beyond Ideology and Theology: The Search for an Anthropology of Islam." *Annual Review of Anthropology* 6: 227–54.

10

Islam in Contemporary Southeast Asia: History, Community, Morality

Barbara D. Metcalf

The broad themes that resonate throughout this collection are ones shared by many societies in recent times. They reflect the extent to which religious symbols and issues have come to the fore in public life and provide a language for issues of citizenship, ethnicity, shared histories, and morality. Thus, even what might be thought to be intimate issues of family ceremony or dress may now be linked to corporate issues of community and political orientation. If we look for "Islam" in the late twentieth century, one arena of central importance turns out to be the institutions of the nation-state. The meaning of being "Muslim" in that sense, as the marker of a citizen or of a politicized ethnic group, is profoundly new. And just as many of the specifics of the debates described in this volume (Hefner and Horvatich 1997) are much the same as those conducted by Muslims elsewhere, the kinds of issues engaged in these debates are ones shared by modern societies everywhere.

This argument stands in marked contrast to what is perhaps the characteristic Western interpretation of Islam in public life. That interpretation insists above all on quintessential difference and continuity, failing to recognize what is new in the meaning and deployment of Islamic symbols and failing to recognize what is shared. In that regard, Dale Eickelman's (1992) argument recognizing the modernity of the very concept of "the Islamic state" is particularly important. Europeans and Americans on the whole have a blind spot in relation to Islam and tend to posit it as a retrograde, oppressive, and anarchic threat. The essays in this volume belie that interpretation and, far from suggesting that Southeast Asia is unique ("not really Muslim"), should encourage us to rethink our approach to Islamic societies overall.

In the American case, a distorted view of Islam continues to be a serious handicap to a rational Middle Eastern policy. Nor is this interpretation only Western: there are Indians who justify the virulent anti-Muslim behavior in their country in terms of the great danger of worldwide Islamic "fundamentalism" from Israel to India itself. The essays in this volume provide lines of analysis that challenge the interpretation of a frightening, monolithic Islam, ones that are relevant to Muslim societies generally, not only to Southeast Asia. They encourage us to ask two sets of questions: How and in what settings is an Islamic language deployed? And is "Islam" in fact different from other historic religious traditions?

At first blush, the chapters seem to fit into the narrative of Islamic power and difference, many structured around themes of Islamic "resurgence," "reactualization," "renewal," and so forth. In each of the countries studied, the Philippines, Malaysia, and Indonesia—whether the Muslim population is 5 percent, 52 percent, or 90 percent of the whole—the story in the last two decades seems broadly the same. In each case, states or provinces have increasingly supported Islamic programs in such arenas as law and economics; individuals increasingly demonstrate public behavior marked as Islamic in behavior and dress; and Islamic organizations directed to politics, social welfare, and preaching seem to proliferate. One might well conclude that these changes demonstrate an Islamic identity and power long waiting to emerge. But by examining these changes in detail we learn, on the one hand, of the historical shallowness of politicized Islamic communities and, on the other, of the complexity and, indeed, often the familiarity of the social and ideological projects—not reducible to state terrorism or "*jihad*"—in which Islamic symbols find expression.

Narrating Histories

Nothing makes clearer the power of the historical myths that shape political loyalties than the fact that they are taken as natural and prima facie factual. Histories are at the core of nation-state identities and form a major strand in constructing, sustaining, and contesting those identities. Benedict Anderson has pointed to the essential irony in these stories: they are new in modern times but they must be told as if they were very old (Anderson 1983). In these stories a religion may even be equated with citizenship itself.

To cite a comparative case, India is particularly striking in the extent to which a historical myth, its fundamental lines evolved during the colonial period, has come to the fore in public life. In that story, part of virtually everyone's "common sense," "Muslims" and "Hindus" are taken as the significant markers of identity throughout the long period of the past thousand or so years. "Muslims" are "foreigners," who "penetrate" and "invade," and their monuments are deemed an extrusion symbolizing the shame of invasion. Forgotten are the pluralism and fuzziness of earlier societies, the shifting boundaries of cultural regions that render problematic notions like "foreign," the presence of Muslims in the subcontinent from roughly the same period as other migrants/invaders from what is now outside India, the shifting alliances defined not by religion but by interest, and the intermarriage and conversion that make it impossible to equate genes and culture. The British first told the story of two communities and foreign invasion as they constructed a history of "India" and justified their place in it; nationalists in turn utilized the story to explain cultural decline and to claim nationhood (Irschick 1994).

History has since become a basis for political argumentation on moral grounds by making "original" occupation (already problematic, as noted above) a justification for entitlements and rights. Against this basis, other arguments that ignore this "history"— current legal claims, the social good, justice, archeological conservation—have little play. The story ceased to be abstract on December 6, 1992, when Hindu nationalists destroyed the sixteenth-century mosque at Ayodhya and justified their action, and even the anti-Muslim violence that followed, as necessary to restore the pristine cultural shape of the nation as a whole (Gopal 1991; van der Veer 1994).

In Southeast Asia, particularly in Malaya and the Philippines, colonizers and colonized have told similar stories in which "Muslims" as a historically continuous community have played a part. The chapters on the Philippines richly illustrate the modernity, "inventedness," and utility to ethnic and national projects of this kind of linear narrative. Thomas McKenna (1997) convincingly argues that the notion of a coherent Muslim identity, forged in religious wars with Spain, contravenes substantial evidence of long periods of peace, of the lack of an *'ulama'* class ranged against the Spanish, and of intersultanate rivalry that meant frequent alliances on the part of the sultanates with Spain. Instead, the colonial power, in this case the United States, saw a coherent "Moro" identity—assumed on Orientalist grounds to be of necessity embryonic and only needing encouragement—as a fundamental fact of Filipino history and sought to use it as the foundation for democratic participation.

It is modern education and the opportunities of modern politics, not atavistic religious antagonism, that forge a Muslim identity, at least among certain elites, in the colonial and postcolonial state. Despite an officially secular school policy, we hear of Carpenter (governor of Mindanao/Sulu, 1914–1920) wanting to educate Muslims "in the positive aspects" of their religion and Kuder (a superintendent of schools, 1924–1941) again pushing education and links to cultural artifacts like the *Arabian Nights* so that students in colleges come to see themselves as "Mohammedan Filipinos." Boundaries are drawn to create an area with "Moro" courts and a Moro municipality. With independence, Muslim leaders focus on "rationalized emblems of a single Muslim ethnic identity," as McKenna puts it, as a way to project Muslim power; and, whether as politicians or as rebels, they deploy the heretofore pejorative Spanish label "Moro," a label Patricia Horvatich (2002) shows to be largely irrelevant to ordinary Muslims in everyday life.

Thus Muslim politicians and civil servants and, after 1972, rival elites give legitimacy to their claims for political clout or autonomy by reading back into history a solidarity only now, haltingly, having any meaning at all. Even today, according to Horvatich (2002), a Maranao, a fellow Muslim Filipino, is as foreign and frightening to a Sama as is a Christian Filipino. Sama depend on the Filipino state to protect their interests against the long-dominant Muslim Tausug. Yet Muslim politicians claim a primordial, essential Muslim nation, even as they contend with the claims of Filipino nationalists who counter with an equally primordial, pre-Christian and pre-Muslim, identity that they call on "backward" Muslims to embrace.

Although only alluded to in the essays in this volume, Malay history bears much the same burden of reified communities and the moral claims of presumed prior residence of Malays, in contrast to putative immigrants, who bear the further taint of colonial association. "Malays" are homogenized and elevated to privilege by their status as "sons of the soil." A Sumatran who arrived yesterday achieves that distinction. A Chinese whose ancestors came five hundred years back is a mere migrant.

These narratives set the framework for defining the nations in which Islamic symbols, institutions, and communities have become so significant. Even in Indonesia, whose national myths typically allowed for more pluralism, an Islamic discourse and Islamic programs have in the past two decades increasingly come to the fore.

National Politics

In each of these settings, underpinned to varying degrees by historical stories of primordial community, there has been a move from "vertical" identifications as subjects of patrons and notables to "horizontal" ethno-religious community (cf. Anderson 1983). Roy Ellen, speaking of Malaya, called precolonial Islam an "idiomatic convenience" deployed, for example, in festivals used to reaffirm loyalty to chiefs (Ellen 1983, 74). In the Indian case, the Mughal Empire, far from being an "Islamic state," operated like other early modern polities on the fundamentally secular basis of loyalty. Only if a non-Muslim went into opposition would he be signaled as a *kafir*; and Muslim as well as non-Muslim opponents in warfare would be subject to *jihad* (Eaton 1994).

The settings conducive to moving from this kind of sociopolitical organization to a pattern of religiously defined community identity are those of modernity: the colonial state, the nationalist movements, the ethnic competition characteristic of interest competition in nation-states with limited resources, and the cultural bonds forged in transnational flows of education, travel, personnel, and resources. Although some chapters in this volume treat the deeply important colonial context as laying the foundation for the new religious communities, most focus on the frameworks offered by the contemporary states that provide a context and even support for the new ethnicities.

That these Islamic movements and identities flourish in modern social contexts is suggested by the importance of educational centers, including international centers, for fostering a self-conscious Islamic religious style (Eickelman 1993). It is in colleges in the Philippines that young men come to think of themselves as Muslim Filipinos. Nur Misuari got his start through a university scholarship, and the public school supervisor, Haji Hussein, spread the teaching of the Ahmadiyya movement to receptive teachers in Tawi-Tawi. It is at al-Azhar, in the 1960s and after, that a new Filipino clerical class is forged with a vision of Islamic reform. In Malaysia, higher education not only provides the context in which modern Muslim identity is forged, but, as Shamsul A.B. (1997) shows, the academic discipline pursued actually influences individuals' response (moderate or radical) to the *dakwah* movement. The dominant figures in Islamic intellectual circles in Indonesia all seem to have U.S. advanced degrees. Beyond travel for education, we hear of travel for work to Sabah and the Middle East, and travel for pilgrimage and business. While the setting for Islamic reform and ethnicization is the nation-state, what happens in the nation-state is profoundly influenced by what happens outside its borders.

As significant as the newness of these communities is the fact that the bonds may be as much ethnic as Islamic. Here too the Philippines serves as a useful example, since the "Moro" rebellion was initially driven by a nationalist/regional program, not an Islamic program, at the elite level and by bonds of kin and community at an individual level. Outsiders may often impute a religious program—the genesis of Pakistan is a good example when in fact goals are primarily the political interests of those who happen to be Muslim.

All three states, Malaysia, the Philippines, and Indonesia, have seen their interests bound up in patronizing and controlling expressions of Islam. Malaysia, as Clive Kessler has argued (1993), may be "secular" at the federal level, but it contains a system where provinces may well be engaged in religious activities, and, at the central level as well, there have been recent initiatives in support of an Islamic university, Islamic economics, Islamic courts, and a civil law that "implicates" *shari'a* at the expense of a shared "life world" for all Malaysians. In the Philippines a 1976 settlement brought federal support for Muslim personal law, Islamic banking, and even a mosque built by patronage from Marcos himself. In Indonesia, after what appeared to be suppression of Islamic symbols in the first decade of the New Order, there have now been a range of initiatives supporting Islamic practices, restricting Christian missionaries, building mosques and *madrasa*s, and identifying state officials with voluntary Islamic organizations.

There has been in each state a kind of homogenizing of what is defined as Islamic, rather like what Romila Thapar has spoken of as "syndicated Hinduism" in the Indian case (Thapar 1985). In both cases, the "flattening" of local and sectarian differences is intimately linked to the project of forging a national culture. In this respect, the quotation from Wilkinson (1906) that Michael Peletz (1997) cites—"The native...is becoming less of a Malay and more of a Mussulman...his racial laws are being set aside.... His allegiance is being gradually transferred from national to Pan-Islamic ideals"—is, in fact, quite wrong, for the process has turned out to be the invention of the Malay "Mussulman" race as metonym precisely for the nation.

An Islamic discourse has come to dominate public space so that resistance, as Peletz (1997) argues for Malaysia, becomes the morally ambiguous resistance to Islam itself. In this Malaysia would appear to resemble Pakistan in the period inaugurated by Zia ul Haq in 1977, when all participants in public life had to embrace an Islamic vocabulary lest they be charged with opposing Islam (Metcalf 1987). In the cases described by Peletz, it would appear that people come to associate Islam with state control, tainted by U.S. government support, intruding into intimate dimensions of individual lives, including family law, surveys of economic transactions, limits on women's dress, imposition of corporal punishment, and restrictions on local customs. Martin Rössler's village-level study in Indonesia (1997) seems much the same: villagers empty the mosque when an official enjoins Ramadan attendance, and everyone resists turning over the *'id al-fitr* offerings to officials. Islamic movements, like Nahdlatul Ulama in Indonesia, that disassociate themselves from formal participation in government thus remove themselves from association with distasteful state control.

A corollary to state use and "syndication" of Islam would appear to be the traditionalizing and encapsulating of local cultural forms. *Wayang* produced in hotels and theaters, described as the embodiment of "tradition," or, in Whalley's example (1993), Minang clothes regarded as "ethnic dress" worn on special occasions, are no longer culturally central except as a necessary foil to "modernity," here in the form of "Islamic modernity."

In the case of Indonesia, it would appear that the withdrawal of organizations from active politics or the creation of new organizations with "constructive" rather than political programs has made it possible for Islamic activities and ideologies to flourish without the taint—though the tension is always there—of undue association with the state, its at least potential oppression, and its apparently inevitable corruption. Andree Feillard (1997) argues that by this disassociation with politics since 1984, Nahdlatul Ulama has gained considerable legitimacy, proliferating organizations for women and youth, serving as a moral force to shape government policy, and stimulating Islamic change at the local level ("more mosques, fewer dogs"). Robert Hefner (1997) similarly charts the influence of ICMI, the new Association of Indonesian Muslim Intellectuals (1990), which declares itself apart from politics even while involving government figures in the quest to capture the moral imagination of the urban middle class living in a context of rapid economic change and polarization and the spread of consumer culture. It is in the context of this activity that the Indonesian state, what-ever its Pancasila rhetoric, has successfully identified itself with a range of Islamic symbols and institutions.

If these Muslim communities are new, so too are the other identities, national and local, with which they interact. Patricia Horvatich (1997) has underlined how being

Sama must not be understood to be the old, primal identity but is itself the result of active fostering—drawing boundaries, writing books, staging performance, creating university study programs—in the context of economic and political rivalries within the nation-state. The contested statement "I was a Malay before I was a Muslim," described by Kessler (1993), recalls another widely quoted statement by a Pakistani politician, "I am a six thousand years old Pushtoon—a thousand year old Musalman, and a twenty-seven year old Pakistani."[1] The truth is that, as markers of politicized communities, all these terms are equally new.

Moral Communities

Both the activist movements and the nation-states they operate in are engaged in defining the principles of behavior, law, and morality that guide everyday life. Overall there has been an increasing utilization of Islamic idioms within the institutional structure of the nation-states coupled with a transition within the society to more self-conscious scrutiny of what are taken to be normative Islamic practices.

In part this transition is linked to greater mobility and sociopolitical integration within a society as a whole. Put simply, there are a range of practices engaged in uncritically that serve to structure rural society: patterns of feasting and reciprocity that define social relations among the living and the dead. These practices are "Muslim" in that Muslims engage in them and may, in an unsystematic, even unself-conscious way, see them as conducive to sustaining the moral community. In contrast are a range of practices that are anything but unself-conscious: they are measured against rationalized principles of what is taken to be "Islam" properly understood. Those who identify with these "reformist" principles may often be people engaged in larger social arenas. In John Bowen's Gayo setting (1997), those who espoused these principles as early as the 1930s typically were engaged in commerce, lived in multiethnic settings, and were fluent in the language that was coming to be called "Indonesian." Both systems can be seen as underpinned by values, even Muslim values. Both offer status and prestige in one setting but not the other.

The new values were defended, in a characteristically Islamic style but not by a defense of "Islam" as such—that comes later. Rather, arguments were conducted at a more fine-grained level. Thus, to take John Bowen's issue (1997) of *ushalli*, the objection might be that "it is against the *shari'ah* to make requisite that which is optional." The objection to feasting or *wayang* might be "it is against the *shari'ah* to waste money," "to go into debt unnecessarily," "to create a venue where men and women mix inappropriately," "to absorb people in activities that distract them from required worship," and so forth. This goal of such critical weighing, in which the issue of acting always out of good intent (*ikhlas*) and obedience, and not out of self-interest in any sense, including the pursuit of a good reputation based on following old customs, is to foster a religion of individual responsibility and "portability" delinked from local bonds of time, place, and ritual specialists. This process and the modes of argumentation are ones that cut across Muslim societies.

Muslim religious styles may seem to vary infinitely, but there are shared languages, institutions, and approaches that some members of societies may share across wide geographical boundaries at any given time. This style of *shari'a*-based reasoning is certainly one, and may not be as specific to Gayo, for example, as it seems. Thus, the *Fatiha* for the dead, with accompanying food, in the Indic context is subject to much the range of interpretation as death ceremonies in Gayo. Critics will insist that it is an attempt to reach the dead, to bring them their favorite foods, or, in the case of powerful figures, an effort to win their goodwill and intervention in worldly needs, all this in ways that risk the worship owed to God alone. Those committed to the practice might insist on normatively acceptable arguments: that the *Fatiha* merely seeks intercession with God who is alone powerful or that it is the recitation of sacred texts whose merit accrues only to the reciter, and so forth. In the course of contention, the meaning and moral underpinnings of customary practices also change (Metcalf 1990).

The issue of the salience of social context for different religious values is nicely illustrated in Martin Rossler's vignette of the funeral of the sister of Banci, the former traditional priest who by 1991 had become involved in the "new Islam," which the local imam insisted was inappropriate in the village and belonged in the towns. Banci, it turned out, had been influenced by his own town-based brother, and, while he managed to conduct the funeral as he wished, other relatives, for whom such behavior threatened their values and networks, performed the traditional rituals secretly. Adherence to normative practices can also be a route to social mobility when those practices are associated with the pious and the well-born. Correct practice distinguishes one from peasants. We may well use Bowen's Weberian language of "elective affinity" of certain social realities for certain religious styles.

"Reformist modernism," again to use Bowen's term, may also distinguish one from the cosmopolitan, or secular, or Westernized elites, a fault line illustrated in Whalley's discussion of Minangkabau (1993). In Indonesia, as described by Hefner, a goal of the Islamically oriented has been to "convert" the secular Javanese elites. Educated professional women can distinguish themselves from such suspect values in part by their dress. This has also been true in Pakistan, where a particular target of the Islamists has been the Westernized women who are seen as a threat to all society (Metcalf 1987).

The focus of much moral argument, in both Southeast Asia and the Subcontinent, has, in fact, been issues of gender. Control of women's behavior and restrictions on women's dress have become centrally important public symbols of an Islamic society. Whalley has described the choices of dress styles available to urban, educated women, especially unmarried women, as they seek to manage a public image of themselves as both modern and moral (1993). On the whole deeply concerned with sustaining the status of their natal lineage, they now do so not in the old way of marrying appropriately, but in a new way by behaving and dressing in a morally acceptable style while earning an independent livelihood. Whalley, citing Errington, underlines that elaboration of female difference through dress is a recent development in Southeast Asia in contrast to an emphasis on distinction by class.

Bowen's study of reform in Gayo, like my own of Deoband in India, finds—surprisingly, given our stereotypes about Islam and women—that women and men are conceptualized as essentially identical, open to the same kind of teaching, responsible for the same kind of behavior. The elaboration of female difference, both bodily (undergirded with Western pseudoscience on subjects like menstruation) and moral, attributing to women the heretofore unknown quality of innate spirituality, comes with the more political movements of the twentieth century, like that in the Subcontinent led by Mawdudi. In Gayo, women were apparently not only invited to participate in the reformist religious style, but were themselves among the poets who spread the teachings. In Minangkabau, as early as the 1920s women were being trained to be good Muslims and civil servants and professionals: it is the Indonesian state that now wants to narrow the scope of women's activities primarily to the home. Even so, in Indonesia today women are active and well known among public preachers and preach not only to other women but to mixed audiences. The contemporary attention to distinctive women's roles is not "traditional" but embedded in the construction of national states.

What is the Nature of Islamic Difference?

This brief review of some of the themes in this wide-ranging collection of essays may suggest some points to counter the kinds of assumptions that are so widespread in our society. First, the fact of "horizontal" Muslim solidarities, of "ethnic" or "nationalist" Islam, is as modern as the nation-states in which Muslims are embedded. Muslim communities, above all communities motivated by ideological programs, are not age-old. If many Muslims today talk of the distinctiveness of Islam as a "complete way of life," we must recognize that as one contemporary trope and then take account of the multiplicity of Islamic positions that range from those who envisage utopian communities to those who insist that to sacralize the state is *shirk*. Christianity is no more uniformly committed to a separation of religion and politics than Islam is to a single religious order. What is more totalistic than the Puritan fathers, the Spanish inquisition, or the pre-Emancipation British exclusions?

Second, the public use of Islamic symbols and the forging of Islamic solidarities are often part of profoundly modern projects shared across nations. We have seen in the Philippine case the extent to which Muslim solidarities are used as a basis for participation in the modern state, much as other ethnic solidarities are elsewhere. The Moro Islamic Liberation Front uses the language of democratic egalitarianism in opposing the *datus*: "good people with good minds have had little chance for success"—this resonates more with America as a land of opportunity than with the Qur'an. The *datu* answer similarly reflects a liberal democratic view, in this case directed to the separation of religion and politics: "if the *ulama* form the political leadership, there will be no one to preach.... We do not want to create ayatollahs." Islam provides a language for political participation and competition.

It also provides a language for debating values in public life and for defining the respective authority of individuals, civil society, and the state. Even without invoking Harvey Cox, the ICMI vision of individual personal ethical cultivation and the espousal of issues like "human rights" bespeak cosmopolitan moral values and would be at home with other movements challenging states and societies dominated by corruption and consumerism everywhere. An ICMI leader like Nurcholish Madjid is part of a transnational conversation, engaged in, in the United States, by intellectuals like Robert Bellah, who seek to foster the institutions of civil society as the locus of transcendent values and commitments that in turn influence the state. Robert Hefner suggests that Indonesia provides "an alternative ideology of what the nation should become" for those who expect secularism inevitably to triumph. But Islamic movements like this one in Indonesia are also an "alternative" to those who identify Muslim movements only with reaction and terror.

It matters that these societies are Muslim above all because of the awareness and links they have with each other. But it is, in the end, the participation in patterns common with other cultural, religious, and nationalist groups, not their specificity, that comes out most clearly in this collection. Bowen, with his interest in whether there are universal forms of the modern person; Hefner, exploring the nature of Indonesian civil society; and the authors of all these essays invite us to make the kinds of investigations of contemporary Islamic movements and styles that can profitably be compared with other, non-Muslim societies. The very process of doing that, in contrast to the stereotyping and demonizing of Islam that is so widespread, will illuminate our study of Southeast Asian societies as well as of other societies, including our own, engaged with common problems of social change and pluralism.

Note

1. The quotation is from Wali Khan in his affidavit to the supreme court in 1975, cited in Mortimer 1982, 216.

References

Anderson, Benedict. 1983. *Imagined Communities: Reflections on the Origin and Spread of Nationalism.* Rev. ed., 1990. London: Verso.

Bowen, John R. 1997. "Modern Intentions: Reshaping Subjectivities in an Indonesian Muslim Society." In *Islam in an Era of Nation-States: Politics and Religious Renewal in Muslim*

Southeast Asia, ed. Robert W. Hefner and Patricia Horvatich, 157–82. Honolulu: University of Hawai'i Press.

Eaton, Richard M. 1994. *The Rise of Islam and the Bengal Frontier, 1204–1760*. Berkeley and Los Angeles, CA: University of California Press.

Eickelman, Dale F. 1992. "Mass Higher Education and the Religious Imagination in Contemporary Arab Societies." *American Ethnologist* 19/4: 643–55.

___ 1993. "Southeast Asian Muslims from a Middle Eastern Perspective." Paper presented at conference on "Islam and the Social Construction of Identities: Comparative Perspectives on Southeast Asian Muslims." School of Hawaiian, Asian and Pacific Studies, University of Hawai'i at Manoa, August 4–6.

Ellen, Roy F. 1983. "Social Theory, Ethnography and the Understanding of Practical Islam in South-East Asia." In *Islam in South-East Asia*, ed. M. B. Hooker, 50–91. Leiden: Brill.

Feillard, Andrée. 1997. "Traditionalist Islam and the State in Indonesia: The Road to Legitimacy and Renewal." In *Islam in an Era of Nation-States: Politics and Religious Renewal in Muslim Southeast Asia*, ed. Robert W. Hefner and Patricia Horvatich, 129–56. Honolulu: University of Hawai'i Press.

Gopal, Sarvepalli, ed. 1991. *Anatomy of a Confrontation: The Babri Masjid-Ramjanmabhumi Issue*. New Delhi: Penguin Books India.

Hefner, Robert W. 1997. "Islamization and Democratization in Indonesia." In *Islam in an Era of Nation-States. Politics and Religious Renewal in Muslim Southeast Asia*, ed. Robert W. Hefner, Patricia Horvatich, 75–128. Honolulu: University of Hawai'i Press.

Hefner, Robert W., and Patricia Horvatich, eds. 1997. *Islam in an Era of Nation-States: Politics and Religious Renewal in Muslim Southeast Asia*. Honolulu: University of Hawai'i Press.

Horvatich, Patricia. 1997. "The Ahmadiyya Movement in Simunul: Islamic Reform in one Remote and Unlikely Place." In *Islam in an Era of Nation-States: Politics and Religious Renewal in Muslim Southeast Asia*, ed. Robert W. Hefner and Patricia Horvatich, 183–206. Honolulu: University of Hawai'i Press.

—2002. "The Martyr and the Mayor: On the Politics of Identity in the Southern Philippines." In *Cultural Citizenship in Island Southeast Asia*, ed. Renato Rosaldo, 16–43. Berkeley: University of California Press, 2002.

Irschick, Eugene F. 1994. *Dialogue and History: Constructing South India, 1795–1895*. Berkeley and Los Angeles: University of California Press.

Kessler, Clive S. 1993. "Reactualizing Islam in Our Times: Faith, Law, and the State in Malaysia." Paper presented at conference on "Islam and the Social Construction of Identities: Comparative Perspectives on Southeast Asian Muslims." School of Hawaiian, Asian and Pacific Studies, University of Hawai'i at Manoa, August 4–6.

McKenna, Thomas M. 1997. "Appreciating Islam in the Muslim Philippines: Authority, Experience, and Identity in Cotabato." In *Islam in an Era of Nation-States: Politics and Religious Renewal in Muslim Southeast Asia*, ed. Robert W. Hefner and Patricia Horvatich, 43–74. Honolulu: University of Hawai'i Press.

Metcalf, Barbara D. 1982. *Islamic Revival in British India: Deoband, 1860–1900*. Princeton, NJ: Princeton University Press.

—1987. "Islamic Arguments in Contemporary Pakistan." In *Islam and the Political Economy of Meaning: Comparative Studies of Muslim Discourse*, ed. William R. Roff and Dale F. Eickelman, 132–59. London and Sydney: Croom Helm.

Metcalf, Barbara D., ed. and trans. 1990. *Perfecting Women: Maulana Ashraf 'Ali Thanawi's Bihishti Zewar*. Berkeley and Los Angeles: University of California Press.

Mortimer, Edward. 1982. *Faith and Power: The Politics of Islam*. New York: Vintage Books.

Peletz, Michael G. 1997. "'Ordinary Muslims' and Muslim Resurgents in Contemporary Malaysia: Notes on an Ambiguous Relationship." In *Islam in an Era of Nation-States: Politics and Religious Renewal in Muslim Southeast Asia*, ed. Robert W. Hefner and Patricia Horvatich, 231–74. Honolulu: University of Hawai'i Press.

Rössler, Martin. 1997. "Islamization and the Reshaping of Identities in Rural South Sulawesi." In *Islam in an Era of Nation-States: Politics and Religious Renewal in Muslim Southeast Asia*, ed. Robert W. Hefner and Patricia Horvatich, 275–306. Honolulu: University of Hawai'i Press.

Shamsul A. B. 1997. "Identity Construction, Nation Formation, and Islamic Revivalism in Malaysia." In *Islam in an Era of Nation-States: Politics and Religious Renewal in Muslim Southeast Asia*, ed. Robert W. Hefner and Patricia Horvatich, 207–30. Honolulu: University of Hawai'i Press.

Thapar, Romila. 1985. "Syndicated Mokhsha." *Seminar* (New Delhi): 14–22.

Van der Veer, Peter. 1994. *Religious Nationalism: Hindus and Muslims in India*. Berkeley and Los Angeles: University of California Press.

Whalley, Lucy. 1993. "The Politics of Minangkabau Women's Dress." Paper presented at conference on "Islam and the Social Construction of Identities: Comparative Perspectives on Southeast Asian Muslims." School of Hawaiian, Asian and Pacific Studies, University of Hawai'i at Manoa, August 4–6.

Wilkinson, Richard J. 1906. *Malay Beliefs*. London: Luzac.

11

Beyond Orientalism?
Max Weber and the Displacements of "Essentialism"
in the Study of Islam

Armando Salvatore

The Orientalist Heritage and Weber's Essentialization of Islam

It is our claim that Western patterns of cognitive domestication of the Islamic Orient are worth being analyzed through the major historical displacements of models of essentialization. This analysis can help relativize, and historically situate, the contention made by the critique of Orientalism about Orientalism's inherent "essentialism," and finally show that essentialism is a fundamental constraint of cross-cultural cognizance. The following reconstruction of the trajectory of essentialism will be centered on Max Weber's treatment of Islam within his comparative sociology of religion, as well as on the resulting emergence of "Weberism"[1] as the pivotal conditioning force, until the late sixties at least, and not only in the West, behind each effort to make sense of "modern Islam" and its alleged "failure." The essay will culminate in the examination of the final crisis of the Weberist equilibrium in the hermeneutics of Islam. This crisis has legitimated new ways of "thinking" or "rethinking" Islam, although no new equilibrium, or paradigm, in the hermeneutics of Islam has been established until now.

The genesis and the evolution of the space of interaction between the "West" and "Islam," and how it acquired "transcultural"[2] properties, is crucial for understanding what kind of influence it had on the shaping of an Arab-Islamic collective identity taking the form of a "framework of universal reference." The emergence of a framework of reference which entails a universal character is a major medium of what we call political-intellectual modernity, in the sense that it reflects a "consensus of communication" (Bourricaud 1987, 19–20) built on the will of rejecting unconditioned loyalty to established hierarchies and establishing new, "public," communication patterns which refer to a wider, "willed" community, a "society" or "nation," and aim to shape and transform it. On the other hand, the intellectual distinction always needs an external Other in order to construct a framework of universal reference. In the Western case, the view of the Islamic Orient, its "orientalization," was crucial for defining the Western path of modernity (Salvatore 1995).

It is not by chance, remembering Montesquieu, that the question "How can one be a Persian?," reflecting a sense of amazement towards the inexplicable otherness of non-Westerners, was first posed in the context of the Enlightenment (see Bourricaud 1987, 14–15). This is the crucial point where we can see how what is called essentialism is indispensable to the making of a modern distinction, where the distinction cannot exhaust itself in its reference to an *ancien régime* or to a backward culture or class, but requires a game of exclusion in universal terms, of confrontation with an ultimate type of otherness. The making of one's own universal reference has to be made through a negative reference to *another* universe. The transcultural dimension has its roots in this paradox of two opposing "universes."[3]

At the origin of the game of opposing essentializing attitudes between the "West" and "Islam" there is an obvious phenomenon: the preliminary construction of a Self–Other polarity in medieval Christian Europe, due to the experience of a menacing, neighboring "world of Islam." A similar, specular construction also characterized the opposite side, reinforced, since the era of the Crusades, by signs of a possible reverse in the power relationship between the two worlds, which was, up to that moment, favorable to Islam. We can admit that in this pre-modern stage Other-constructions are still defensive, not broadly instrumentalized and still tightly dependent on the protection of a Self defined by the past. But the dichotomization of the broader universe of experience, which led Christian Europe to conceive Islam as an anti-Christian apostasy (see Daniel 1966), was about to acquire a new meaning as Europe began to perceive itself as bound to a fate of progress, evidenced by its growing power in controlling nature, territories and, eventually, enemies. This is to say that the rather obvious ethnocentrism which animates different cultural groups or worlds throughout their history, as a consequence of the need to build and reproduce their collective identities, is not identical throughout its different phases.

The term essentialism as applied to cross-cultural knowledge normally stresses the (over)-simplifying aspect of the cognitive process of constructing a Self–Other polarity. We would like, however, to focus on the opposite dimension of it, on its relationship to "complexity," as complementary to simplification. If we consider that the modern intellectual attitude reflects on alleged social complexity, which has to be accounted for and appropriated by way of knowledge, the role played by an "essence" is that of delimiting the field and the scope of the domestication of the Other. This enterprise entails selecting and collecting proof, in the form of "sources" which, being disparate, have to be reduced to a common denominator. "Defensive" ethnocentrism does not depend on these constraints; it does not need to play with essences, since the substance of the problem of defining an identity is virtually given along lines dictated by the "inside–outside" polarization, and does not tend to change very quickly, thereby generating hermeneutic dispersion. Of course, the game of essentializing Islam was already flourishing in late medieval Europe, to the extent the creation of a European self-understanding was already in motion. But as long as communication across the two religious–cultural universes was sporadic, the task of defining the Other was almost automatically given by the "primordial" impulse of drawing boundaries, and did not need to engage in any essentializing game.

If an ethnocentric view is quite common, as part of the game of stabilizing identities, the intellectual practice of "essentializing" should be assessed as typical of a modern self-understanding and self-confidence. The absence of an "Occidentalist" equivalent of Western academic Orientalism is no proof against the existence of more or less standardized essentializing intellectual practices on the Islamic side,[4] obviously taking no neatly specular attitude to the "West," due to the power asymmetry between both sides, where power has to be seen primarily in the selection and control of sources, as well as in appropriate techniques for their scrutiny.

The trajectory of German Orientalism during the last century (the most important national branch, from the point of view of the influence on Weber) demonstrates (Stauth 1987) that however empathic and sympathetic the single scholar may have been toward Islam,[5] academic Orientalism was to fulfill a specific function within a sort of division of labor with other branches of study. Among these, sociology was gradually gaining ground over historiography, by putting new questions of method to the former, as how to make the Self–Other polarity scientifically intelligible. While sociology was engaged in explaining why the West ("we") had grown modern and rational, Orientalism had to account for why the Islamic Orient, in spite of its bright past civilization, had become at some point in history tendentially static and incapable of moving ahead.

The real basis of the academic division of labor was not between units of analysis considered at the same point in time and then made comparable, but between modern history on the one hand, and ancient texts, on the other. At the level of method, the contrast was between an expanding range of socio-historical tools suitable to account for such a "complex" historical phase, on the one hand, and a basically philological method borrowed from the study of antiquity, on the other. In other words: precise limits were set at the level of method to the factor of empathy, and its accompanying ambiguities.[6]

As clear, in their identifying power as Self-definitions and Other-definitions, the labels "Islam" and "West" operate today and fulfill the role of discursive constraints, so little effort has been made in elucidating the salient passages in their parallel making. This is all the more surprising since these categories are indispensable to the Western discourse of modernity. Our hypothesis is that formative needs of the discourse of modernity were met by the division of labor between mainstream sociology and Orientalism, with the work of Max Weber intervening, at a crucial stage, in systematizing the link. Thus, in order to understand our heritage of the Western process of knowing-essentializing Islam, it is crucial to reassess Weber's handling of Islam within the framework of his unique contribution. This is of foremost importance for its impact not only on the social sciences (where in fact the influence of the two other "founding fathers" of sociology, Marx and Durkheim, may have been greater), but also on the basic self-understanding of the "West" as such.

For this purpose, a quick look at the genesis and evolution of academic Orientalism in nineteenth-century Germany is more than useful, since German Orientalism was to exert an influence on Weber, a fact which is easily understood, since Weber's achievements at large are to be read in the context of specifically German conditions of production of academic knowledge and engagement in politics. What, however, makes this reconstruction of the crucial passages in the academic division of labor in Germany relevant for the fate of Western knowledge and the Western attitude towards the Islamic Other in general, is the fact that the subsequent making of "Weberism" is in no way an exclusively German phenomenon.[7]

The German Orientalism which forms the background of Weber's study of Islam was well-rooted in an academic and cultural environment epistemologically dominated by positivism (Stauth 1987, 9). It was already a kind of "sociologized" Orientalism, in that it employed a "systematized apparatus of social categorization" (Abaza and Stauth 1990 [1988], 210). Weber's dependence on German Orientalism was also due to the fact that he used—for understandable reasons, because of the wide scope of his work—almost exclusively secondary sources. In fact he was very modest about the scientific status of his comparative studies, which he assessed as problematizing investigations (Schluchter 1987, 106; see also below).

Islam was included in both main projects that the leading German sociologist conducted in parallel (drawing on the same sources) between 1911 and the beginning of World War I; the first (*Die Wirtschaftsethik der Weltreligionen*, included in the first volume of the *Gesammelte Aufsätze zur Religionssoziologie*, hereafter RS) devoted to the inner motivations, the second (*Die Wirtschaft und die gesellschaftlichen Ordnungen der Mächte*, which was posthumously included in the second part of *Wirtschaft und Gesellschaft*, hereafter WuG) to the external conditions of the evolution of *Kulturreligionen*. It is interesting to note that in the first work Islam is absent, along with Christianity, from the published version. From Weber we know directly that the essay should have culminated with the cultural-religious units that he considered as the closest to modern Western Christianity, i.e., in the order: ancient Christianity, talmudic Hebraism, Islam and Oriental Christianity (Schluchter 1987, 20–22). It seems that among all non-Christian units Islam was taken as the one of most immediate importance, probably even more than Hebraism, if the order of the units in the statement cited is not casual.[8] Weber deemed Islam as relevant for the central concern of his work (the reconstruction of the reasons of the uniqueness of Western development) both at the level of historical "preconditions" for the Western path and of contrastive specificity to it (Schluchter 1987, 21).

It is a bit of a mystery why, despite Weber's allusion to this project, no manuscript explicitly dedicated to Islam was found in his *Nachlass*. Whatever the solution to this enigma,[9] it is certain that aside from some short, but very significant, hints regarding Islam in the later version of the RS, the bulk of Weber's treatment of Islam is found in the corpus of texts devoted to external conditions rather than in those relating to internal motivations.[10] Furthermore, the position of Islam in comparative perspective is not, in the available texts of WuG, of the kind suggested by Weber's statement. On the other hand, the fact that Weber still considered Islam crucial to his comparative project well after he ceased to study it around 1914 (Schluchter 1987, 23–24) is proved by clear allusions in the Foreword to the RS, written after the end of the [First] World War.

We only know that it was Weber's intention to inscribe his study of Islam in an explicitly comparative framework focused on the development of models of rationality, and that the paradox of this largely innovative purpose was that Weber's undertaking was dependent on Orientalist frameworks of categorization.[11] This dependence is evident in the fact that at the time he decided to expand his sociological study of religion[12] toward the "Orient," Weber adopted "world religions" as units of analysis, and even exceeded the Orientalist tendency to overaggregate religious-cultural units.

It is the special typological interest in the seeming similarity between Islam and Calvinism that (in the opinion of Schluchter) was as interesting for Weber as it only concerned some aspects of "surface" concerning both units (Schluchter 1987, 24). That is to say, Weber was interested in showing, by way of a contrastive comparison,[13] how some distinctive features that at first sight were common to Islam and Calvinism, could not be considered responsible for the particular performance of Calvinism in terms of rational *Lebensführung* ("life conduct"), and especially from the point of view of the *Wirtschaftsethik* ("economic ethic"). This operation was grounded on the presumed evidence (which was not further questioned) that *Islam has not gone that way*. We can say that the extent to which Weber's handling of Islam was predetermined by his own concern for reconstructing the reasons for Western uniqueness (Turner 1991 [1983], 43) was well beyond the Eurocentric constraints already embedded in the Orientalist paradigm, as shown by the lack of isomorphism between the two units of comparison. In spite of the clearly unhistorical character of this peculiar comparison, the resulting view of Islam will have an enduring impact on the Western observer, as we will see, since it will entitle him at the outset, on the basis of the claim of uniqueness, to observe, know and define Islam.

According to Weber, what Calvinism and Islam seem to have in common is the absolute character of the faith in God's transcendence (Schluchter 1987, 36).[14] This distinctive element (which is common to old Hebraism as well) results in the absence of a solution to the question of theodicy, the problem of the justification of God especially with regard to the existence of evil in this world. Under the heading *Das Problem der Theodizee*, Weber first provides a general definition of each ethical prophecy as a step toward the rationalization of the idea of God; but he then stresses the tension between the path toward ever more stringent forms of transcendent monotheism and the reality of the world's imperfection.[15] The tension reflected by such a religious rationalization carried to the extreme limits of monotheistic assertion (something in which Islam is probably unequalled, thereby surpassing Calvinism itself) is finally assessed as the crucial living feature of such "advanced" religions.[16]

Essentialism at Work: The Joint Making of the "West" and "Islam"

In the most accurate work produced until now on Weber's view of Islam, Wolfgang Schluchter reaffirms the basic coherence of this view, looking at it from within the logic of argumentation. Our interest here is to reassess it from a more external perspective, one concerned with checking how the motivational and epistemological perspective of the Western student of Islam influences the final hermeneutic product, thereby giving the transcultural space the particular imprint it bears today. It seems that Weber constructed the difference between Islam and Calvinism, beyond the surface of their similarities, by attributing to the former, as a solution to the aforementioned problem, a plain predeterminism endowed with a generic cosmological dimension devoid of any forceful stress on salvation, whereas the specificity of the latter was seen in its production of a coherent doctrine of predestination (Schluchter 1987, 39).

Overt directness in the definition of the God–man relationship, instead of subjective labor, is the key peculiarity of Islam as reflected by Weber's contention that the concept of salvation in its ethical dimension is alien to this religion (WuG, 375).[17] Islam's alleged imperviousness to the notion of salvation is highlighted in strict relation to the postulation of the inherent political character of Islam. But this deficit, coherently with the nature of the essay where this judgment is included,[18] is again to be explained by the overly "material" character of Islam as "standisch orientierte Krieger-religion" and "Herrenreligion" (WuG, 375). Here, as elsewhere, the consideration of the *Geist* component (as opposed to *Form*) of Islam, or the central Weberian question of the axis of the relationship between religious ethic and *Lebensführung*, remains largely unproblematized. The problem is that Weber considered the "Meccan component" in the making of Islam as merely a provisional, volatile "phase," thereby disregarding its enduring impact on the Islamic symbolic-communicative system. That the outcome of Weber's search for the "true" origin of Islam is the definition of the "essentially political character" of Islam's regulations for this world's life (WuG, 375) is not surprising.

The particular reason for Weber's selective characterization of Islam is probably due to his concern for explaining the undeniable "success" of early Islam coupled with Islam's alleged historical failure to develop rational capitalism.[19] This explanation was a sociological reformulation of the traditional Orientalist scheme of success-and-failure as rise-and-fall, in "civilizational" terms. A crucial medium of explanation was the stress on the centrality of *jihad*[20] in the possibility of existence of that "belated" religion and revelation ("Spätling des vorderasiatischen Monotheismus": WuG, 375). While on the one hand Weber's view of Islam's trajectory was dependent on the assumption of the enduring primacy, in Islam, of the shift from the eschatological Meccan period to the political Medinan phase,[21] on the other it referred to an undoubtedly crucial aspect of early "Islamic" history—territorial conquest and the distribution of the resulting benefits—that is devoid, nonetheless, of any solid direct reference to the Qur'an and its *din*.[22] Weber was willing to draw the generalizing conclusion that the motivational strength of Islamic doctrine is only found in extraordinary situations, typically in wars (by virtue of the incentive of achieving either booty or "a sensual soldiers' paradise": WuG, 376).[23]

Weber intends to show that the "innerwordly asceticism" of Islam radically diverges from that of Calvinism,[24] which has produced the rational work ascetics that is Weber's central concern. In this sense, his position poses no immediate prejudice against an assessment of "intellectual modernity" in the Islamic case. In fact the very attitude to cyclical reform in Islamic history, that Weber is very close to admit, has been precisely the basis of one famous claim that Islam has a particular predisposition to modernity (Gellner 1981), according to a "minimalist" concept of this, which avoids approaching the question of "structural" modernity in "strong"— either Marxian or Weberian—terms. Ernest Gellner maintains that the cyclical movement of reform and renewal in Islam, a phenomenon indispensable for its very reproduction, became at a certain moment in history capable of culminating in a more encompassing and enduring Reform (or era of Reform), imbued with a spirit of universal reference in modern terms.[25] What is interesting to note is that this stress on Islam's capability of cyclical reform is already present in Weber, but formulated in purely negative terms, in relation to its alleged deleterious influence on "rational" daily *Lebensführung*, which is the crucial medium between religious ethic and the model of *Wirtschaften*.[26]

The analysis of "life conduct" is, instead, virtually absent from Weber's treatment of Islam. In Weber, as well as in Weber's specialized interpreters (and even stronger in "Weberism"), Islam's cyclical motion is assessed as the negation of the systematic and rational shaping of life conduct, which is the epitome of Western modernity brought about by Protestant asceticism (RS I, 125). Weber maintains that even when this rational element is at least partially present in Islamic history, it immediately turns the ethos of the *Lebensführung* into political action (Schluchter 1987, 44). Through this interpretation the syndromatically political character of Islam was firmly established, with enduring consequences, as we shall try to show, on the reshaping of the transcultural space for the rest of our century (Salvatore 1995).

We should not forget, however, that Weber clearly aspired to go beyond the explanation of the genesis of rational capitalism, in order to account for the whole of the uniqueness of Western culture, including Western science (in the largest sense of the word, but as rooted in academic institutions). This is shown by the statement: "only in the West there is 'science' in the developmental stage, to which we nowadays attribute 'validity'" (RS I, 1), placed at the very beginning of the RS (thereby reflecting the position of the last Weber.)[27] The problem is that Weber did not deal with this last topic extensively. This incongruence has probably had crucial consequences, since the general impression of comprehensiveness of Western uniqueness in Weber has helped shape the aspect of Weberism that claims the Western exclusiveness of rational science and the Enlightenment and equates this with intellectual modernity at large.[28] Weber did not succeed in incorporating an adequate treatment of knowledge in his general comparative approach, and in the particular case of Islam a specific thematization of knowledge and science is totally absent. This double deficit is precisely what would make Weber's heritage, intended as a concrete corpus of studies, unsuitable for assessing Islam's capacity to generate intellectual modernity.[29]

In synthesis, there seems to be an increasing tendency in Weber, through the years of his comparative work, to attempt to fit Islam into a contrastive role with Calvinism as the quintessence of Western *Geist* and achievement, even more so since Islam *seemed* to be grounded on very similar doctrinal settings. It is probably of great significance that this tendency reaches its apex in Weber's additional statements concerning Islam in the revised edition of the *Protestantische Ethik* (hereafter, PE) (Schluchter 1987, 111, n. 84).[30] These passages, due to the centrality of the PE in the Weberian heritage (independently of the fact whether this is justified or not in the light of a more careful consideration of the whole of Weber's work), have probably been determinant in forging Weberism. In attempting to demonstrate, in the case of Calvinism, how far predestination, through the doctrine of *Doppeldekret* and the *Bewährungsglaube*, was from producing fatalism, Weber needed to refer to a cultural-religious "type" with concrete historical rooting that could be considered liable to fatalism in "routine" times, due to a kind of alleged pseudo-predestination doctrine that was simply a form of predeterminism devoid of any substantial anchoring in a subjective strive for salvation.[31] This is not to say that in Weber the treatment of Islam is purely instrumental as in the case of Weberism, but, rather, strongly "oriented." This "orientation" appears more cogent in Weber than in nineteenth-century Orientalism by virtue of the combination, in the former, of the sociological explicitation of a "global" approach in a comparative perspective with the "parochial" concern for Western (or even German) developmental paths (see Turner 1990, 353). The methodological dimension of this kind of sociologization of "the question of Islam" is made explicit by Weber himself, where he admits, in the opening sentence of the introduction to the RS,[32] the heuristic Eurocentrism underlying his comparative undertaking.[33]

The essentialism of classic Orientalism was still operating within a rather personalized attitude toward the establishment of a distinction toward the Islamic Orient. In an older, but still most valuable, academic study on Orientalism (Waardenburg 1963) that considers five leading Orientalist scholars,[34] the function of the search for an essence is highlighted by focusing on the psychological mechanisms of approaching a religion other than one's own in terms of "understanding." According to this reconstruction, it appears clearly how at the source of essentializing procedures there are the individual concerns of the researcher, and how their outcome is almost regularly the definition of a very static essence (Waardenburg 1963, 325–28). This provides a valuable insight into the living *methodos* (hence not merely method in a technical, or in this case philological, sense) of classic Orientalism.[35] In the case of Weber, and taking into account his public engagement in German national politics of his time, the original concern was much more consciously formulated in terms of a Western, or more specifically German national, concern, and the outcome was a dynamic essentialism, combining understanding and explanation, internal (subjective) and external (objective) variables, *Geist* and *Form*, with an undeniable primacy of the first component: a method suitable to the study of how discontinuities can arise from continuities, and that in so doing reflected the crux of social sciences at large, their combination of compelling essentialism and analytic vocation.

We have seen, however, in the case of Islam, how the dynamic property of Weber's refined essentialism aborted to a large extent. But even more important is that Weber's "upgrading" of such an essentialist method was paralleled, in studying Islam, by a loss of analytic depth in defining the tensions inherent in the unfolding of an Arab-Islamic subjectivity.[36] It is symptomatic that Weber felt obliged to pay homage to the older division of labor with Orientalism that he seemed to violate.[37] His tribute to the competence of the specialist cannot be regarded as a mere lip-service. Weber felt the obligation to openly justify this dependence on Orientalism, since ethnography could have constituted an alternative reference for him.[38] But Orientalist philology and historiography was precisely what he needed, since his focus was on the life conduct of cultural elites.[39]

By this inevitable focus on the *Kulturträger* we see how Weber's combination of approach and *Fragestellung* provided a powerful key to identify patterns of intellectual modernity in extra-European cultural units, including Islam. He certainly lacked, however, the appropriate sources and focus, as he did not concentrate on those phenomena in the eighteenth and nineteenth centuries which have now become a privileged object of attention by some "revisionist" historians (see Gran 1979, Peters 1980 and Schulze 1990). This is in fact a category of phenomena which nineteenth and turn-of-the-century Orientalism was only marginally able or willing to approach.[40] If Weber's claim of the Western monopoly of science[41] can be accepted with some restrictions, it is simply mistaken that the press as a social phenomenon is an exclusively

Western endowment (RS I, 3), and we know the importance of the role of the press in creating a public arena of competition and allowing the formation of a "consensus of communication" grounded on a framework of universal reference. In summary, Weber inherited from nineteenth-century Orientalism a selective historical focus, along with a predetermination of cultural units in religious terms that in the case of the Oriental units, and in particular of Islam, was too strictly dependent on the Western historical point of observation.

The essentialism resulting from the combination of the focus on "civilizations" and *related*, functional selection of textual sources was "upgraded" by Weber to a study of the development of forms of subjectivities and, within them, of rationalities. But the hard nutshell of essentialism was not eliminated, could not be eliminated, if we assess the previously mentioned introductory paragraph of Weber's *Vorbemerkung* as setting the stage for comparative cultural studies guided by culturally specific concerns. Essentialism is, in fact, an inescapable feature of modern intellectual constructions, even an *a priori* of modern cognizance, at whatever level of analysis and abstraction it locates itself. In historical perspective, the extent to which Weber makes explicit and requalifies essentialism can be considered as marking the threshold to the opening of a genuine transcultural space between the "West" and "Islam," where the intellectual concern for the Other is openly assessed as crucial for understanding and defining the Self. As we will see, the making of Weberism will impoverish the qualitative elaboration of this concern, but will not change its nature.

The Formation and Success of "Weberism"

Although Schluchter has claimed that Weber's analysis of Islam has not produced any major impact on both the Orientalist and sociological study of Islam (Schluchter 1987, 84), this is true only within certain limits, in the sense that for decades hardly any student of the Islamic Middle East accurately elaborated Weber's fragmentary— but indeed coherent and compulsive—references to Islam, even less so in the context of Weber's more general *Fragestellung*. For precisely this reason Weber's influence on Islamic studies has taken the form of "Weberism," which is a phenomenon of broader cultural range.[42] It consists in a trivialized version of the Weberian heritage that is often, but mostly anonymously, opposed to Marxism, and that operates through the authoritative "cover" provided by Weber's work on every Western—not only academic—cognitive undertaking which is engaged in defining patterns of distinction toward the Other, non-Western world, and first of all toward the part of it that is most relevant for the shaping of the Western self-image, the Islamic Orient.

It is no mere speculation that different schools tried to "use" Weber, without really grasping the original features of his approach. Most prominent in the making of Weberism is the Parsonian reading of Weber, which, as revealed by distortions and even omissions in his own English translation (Gordon 1987, 313), made an adaptative misuse of Weber, moved by the urge of securing a rash and stable consolidation of a sociological theory in post-World War II America. From the point of view of the study of Islam, Weberism helped reshape the Orientalist tradition in conformity with the American hegemonic position and the new character of hegemony exercised (Salvatore 1991, 37–53). This process led to the establishment of "Middle East Studies" as the most prominent branch among "Area Studies" (Binder 1976), at least from the viewpoint of the urgencies of foreign policy.

This division of the social sciences in a mainstream branch studying differentiation and "complexity" in modern society and an "Area Studies" branch devoted to the study of would-be societies still largely in a phase of undifferentiated traditionalism (as well as to the task of providing the theoretical tools to help them in modernizing), reflects Weberism as operating in Parsons, and cannot be explained solely through his adoption of a Durkheimian perspective.[43] It is worth remembering, in this context, how within the academic setting in the social sciences in post-World War II America, a new division of labor was achieved that overcame the previously mentioned chronological incongruence of object (as well as of the method applied) entailed by the older division of labor. The disciplinary field of the scientific representation of Self and Other was unified.

The immediate reason for this achievement can be found in the strong American perception, after the war, of "one world," with America at its center. But at the very source of such active universalism there was, paradoxically, the "American exceptionalism" (Hartz 1955) which allowed the view that change is not only possible, but easy to carry out everywhere (Packenham 1976 [1973], 18–20), so that if "our world" imposes itself as the prototype of modernity, the Other has to modernize, *is to be modernized* (cf. Lerner 1964 [1958]). Very roughly, but without distorting the self-understanding of the division of labor, we can say that the reflection on the Western "prototype" provided a theory of "structural" modernization and of "political development," whereas the reflection on the Other was finalized to define the field of tension between traditional cultures and strivings for modernization, as well as to suggest strategies of application of modernization theory in concrete cases.

If we remember Weber's already quoted introductory sentence in the RS (and Schluchter's interpretation of it), the unavoidable character of "heuristic Eurocentrism" emphasized by Weber is associated with the awareness of the danger to shift from this toward a "normative Eurocentrism."[44] The occultation of heuristic Eurocentrism behind the screen of objectivist social sciences in the case of post-war American neo-Orientalism results in a swift conversion to a normative Eurocentrism. Weber's sentence can be seen as foreshadowing the subsequent success of Weberism and its influence: this is in fact characterized by not making explicit the epistemological constraint visibly highlighted by Weber.[45] But Weberism was also made possible by virtue of disregarding other clear and insistent warnings in Weber's *Vorbemerkung* to the RS, concerning the status of his own comparative studies. Besides being inescapably constrained on a heuristic level (with the already mentioned consequence that his handling of Islam was more than "oriented": RS, 13), Weber stresses, towards the end of his life, that his comparative research has a markedly pioneeristic character[46] and should be assessed as such. It almost seems that Weber, conscious of the representative strength, for Western concerns, of his remarkably innovative approach, appeals to future social scientists for working out creatively its heritage, and against stiffening it in a doctrine. He seems to warn against Weberism.

We cannot, however, ascribe to Weberism alone the responsibility for a "maximalist" conception of modernity, the view of this as an integrated package. While on the one hand Western uniqueness does not necessarily imply, for Weber, that the way to rational capitalism cannot be found under different conditions and stages in other cultures, he tends, nonetheless, to see this uniqueness in the shaping of an anthropological type that cumulates paths of rationalization along lines that cannot be reduced to simple "structural" modernity. In this sense he reshapes the moral claim to distinction inherited from the Enlightenment according to criteria which are compatible with—although not reducible to—the positivistic method of inquiry (see Hennis 1987 and Gordon 1987, 295). This is probably the reason why Weber failed to make clear that rationalist disenchantment (as identified with structural modernity, i.e. the modernity of capitalism and bureaucracies) was possible to endure, in the long run, only through an intellectual game of rationalist *reenchantment* consisting in intellectual modernity and the ensuing construction of frameworks of universal reference. The prime interest here is not represented by the points addressed by later critiques of Weber (see below) on whether and for what reasons Islam is unlikely to produce structural modernity,[47] as embodied in the model of "*Wirtschriften* rationality" necessary for capitalism. What mostly matters is the fact that the Enlightenment as the epitome of the "intellectual turn" corresponded to the presumption of asserting Reason in the realm of politics, where Reason is nothing but an "ideological" transfiguration of the rationality of *Wirtschriften*. One could even say that, in this game, the stress laid on Western structural modernity and disenchantment is only a card played to assert the greatly enchanted vision of Western uniqueness.[48]

The making of Weberism out of Weber's variegated corpus of investigations does not seem to have been analysed as a distinct phenomenon. Specialists of Weber are keen on reconstructing the correct interpretation of his work, so that Weberism is only touched upon in its negative side, as a mistaken interpretation, or oversimplification of Weber's *Fragestellung*. The position taken in the present study is that the reasons for Weberism matter in themselves, and we believe that these reasons can be only grasped within the context of the development of Orientalism, through its different phases, during the last two centuries. A suggestion of something very close to, but not identical with, what we call Weberism is given us by Colin Gordon when he affirms that "Weber is...innocent...of the so-called Weberianism that adopts a uniform, monolithic conception of historical phenomena of rationalization" (Gordon 1987, 294). He inscribes this claim in the broader discussion, initiated by Wilhelm Hennis, of how Weber's "true" *Fragestellung* would be *Lebensführung* (intended also, or mainly, in an ethical sense), and not *Entzauberung*, as reflected in Weberism,[49] so that the "maximalist" separation between a traditional and a modern universe of meaning would *not* be part of the proper Weberian heritage (312). We basically agree with this claim, but not without the important limitation that, given Weber's treatment of Islam, a maximalist view of modernity is, paradoxically, what Weber cannot avoid producing when adopting the kind of "oriented" perspective that characterizes his own comparative work. We would revise Gordon's position by saying that Weberism arises out of *the extent* to which Weber *failed* to fulfill his project of a "comparativist approach to different rationalization phenomena" (294) which aimed at finding out "that different societies arrive at [the] threshold [of modernity]...endowed with variable levels of capability for negotiating it successfully" (312–13).

The Crisis of Weberism and the Limits of Anti-essentialist Critique

Once the links of continuity and discontinuity between Orientalism, Weber and Weberism have been sketched, the examination of the first attempts to "critically" analyze Weber's view of Islam can be useful for elucidating when, how, and in which cultural climate the Weberist equilibrium in the transcultural space began to be shaken.[50] Maxime Rodinson's *Islam et capitalisme* (Rodinson 1966) attacked Weber's view of Islam as an ideological construction functional to establishing the superiority of Western rationality and, in the final analysis, the Western monopoly upon modernity. This attack is in itself a crucially important sign of the incipient crisis of Weberism as well as of the corresponding transcultural equilibrium. Rodinson's essay in fact touches on the most delicate point of Western essentialism, much more than any "direct" critique of Orientalism was able to do, such as an earlier essay by Anouar Abdel-Malek. This had the merit of producing an already lucid diagnosis of the problem of essentialism, as well as of the related focus on units (language, religion) detached from any solid reference to a broader societal evolution (Abdel-Malek 1963, 113–4).[51] This diagnosis provided the basis for the much later Saidian initiative, but failed to tackle the actual core of the problem, as represented by Weber's mediation.[52]

It is true that Rodinson's essay showed a tendency to oversimplify Weber's arguments, and not to contextualize Weber's view of Islam within the rationale of his work.[53] All these flaws notwithstanding, or even by virtue of them, the work of the French Orientalist signals the emergence of all urgent will to liberate Orientalism from the suffocating embrace of Weberism. If leveled not against Weber, but against Weberism, most of Rodinson's claims are justifiable. It is interesting that Schluchter, commenting on Rodinson's central argument that stressed the bent for rationality embedded in the Qur'an, discovers that the conclusions attained by the French scholar do in fact conform to Weber's own emphasis on the rationalizing potential of Islam

(Schluchter 1987, 88). The grip of Weberism on Orientalist science was probably so tight that it constituted a hindrance to reading Weber by paying enough attention to those interpretative elements where his hermeneutic Eurocentrism was potentially no prejudice against a fair assessment of Islam.[54]

The next major critique to Weber's study of Islam appeared some years later. The change in motivation and perspective in Bryan Turner's *Weber and Islam* (Turner 1974) shows that at that time Weberism began to be recognized as such (although it was not given such a name). Turner's original intention was "to write a very general work on Islam which could be directed at undergraduate sociology students" (Turner 1974, 1). So he came to the idea of "using" Weber, but he had to recognize that it was not possible to do this without oversimplifying Weber's sociology, thereby falling, as we could say, in Weberism. The task required, on the contrary, a reinterpretation of Weber and of his view of Islam, an operation that was almost automatically a challenge to Weberism, a phenomenon which post-Weberian sociology of religion had contributed to legitimize, to the extent it never approached Islam directly. The crucial difference to Rodinson's undertaking is that, while the French scholar defied Weberism directly, whilst presuming to criticize Weber, in Turner's case the lower urgence—since he was no Orientalist—to free the study of Islam from the grip of Weberism turned out to be (through the uneasiness at the keeping silence of sociology of religion on Islam) a stimulus for providing an attempt to restore the "true" Weber, beside Weberism.

Turner's book complemented the mounting criticism towards the self-understanding of the Western path of development (a phenomenon which passed a critical threshold by the early seventies) with an indictment of the crucial component of the entire transcultural equilibrium, in the form of Weberism.[55] This is well reflected in Turner's discovery of the vice of origin of Weberism that was present in Weber himself: that in the case of the study of Islam the German sociologist "inconsistently applied in practice those methodological and philosophical principles which he declared were crucial to an adequate sociological approach" (Turner 1974, 3). It is significant that Turner's conclusion combines an innovative strength in transcending Weberism and a keeping subordination to the neo-Orientalist consensus that dominated the study of Islam during the sixties, as postulating the potentially universal character of modernity, due to the Western irradiation of modernizing impulses. This combination is summarized in Turner's statement that "Islamic reformers in the modern world have adhered to a strikingly Weberian view of social development. This results from the fact that many of the intellectual elite of reformist Islam received their training in Europe or accepted a European view of world development... Weber's view of motivation came to fit the Islamic case as the result of cultural diffusion" (175).

By the mid-seventies the critical position was able to establish itself as an official reality in the academic landscape of Middle East Studies, and triumphantly announced the end of Orientalism and the rise of "political economy" (Owen 1975, 109). This result was achieved through the initiative of a group of scholars which had become "increasingly dissatisfied with the state" of Middle East Studies, and whose aim was "to encourage the production of theoretically relevant work informed by a critical appreciation of the Middle East and its history" (Asad and Owen 1975). The instrument of this enterprise was a new journal called *Review of Middle East Studies* (RMES), which was published twice during 1975, following a seminar held at Hull University in September 1974.

The leaders of the initiative did not conceal their ambition to conceive the undertaking as a "series of critiques which...will eventually include most of the important and influential works within modern Middle East Studies." In fact the two issues published in 1975 already tackled (obviously in a "critical" vein, as witnessed by the titles of most contributions) such representative authors belonging to the broader Orientalist tradition as Kedourie, von Grunebaum, Gibb, Cohen, Hodgson, Vatikiotis, Binder, Lewis, and Rodinson himself, accused by Roger Owen, the leader of the RMES group, of having been caught by the same essentialist logic present in Weber (Owen 1976). The interest in this critique is that it addressed the unit of analysis, or rather the principle itself of isolating units presumed to incarnate cultural subjectivities. Rodinson himself is stigmatized as Weberian.[56]

Many contributions in the RMES issues reflect the illusion that a "de-orientalization" of Middle East Studies could be carried out through sweeping away the essentialism connaturated in Orientalism and replacing it with allegedly objective methods of investigation based on the "political economy" paradigm.[57] Although not trivially Marxist, the scholarly campaign staged under the leadership of Roger Owen failed to stress what Marxism has in common with Weberism in its effort to explain the absence of capitalism in Islamic societies: both conceptualize Islam as a series of gaps (Turner 1978), thereby complementing the Orientalist stress on Islam's insufficiencies in religious eschatological terms.

The convergence between Marxism and Weberism[58] lies in their pointing to a sort of "institutional deficit," where the absence of a bourgeois culture is explained through the absence of autonomous cities, of a bourgeois class, of a rational bureaucracy and so on. Or, more vividly: the absence of "civil society," which has been a key-concept in modern intellectual distinctions since the Enlightenment, compatible with both a Marxist and a Weberist perspective. This concept acquires sharp contours only by virtue of a comparison with its antithesis, the realm of Oriental despotism or Oriental patrimonialism, where a true social differentiation and intellectual distinction is deemed impossible. In so far as "civil" refers to the painful making of subjectivity, in the sense appropriated by Norbert Elias when speaking of "civilization process" (Elias 1976 [1939]), "Oriental" becomes the negation of "civil," where the non-isomorphic character of the opposition of predicates does not diminish, but enhances the depth of the polarity.

What was missing both in Owen and in Turner was a problematization of the limits of being anti-essentialist. And this has proven to be the most enduring flaw of every kind of Orientalism critique. A more recent case is worth being analyzed in order to show how such a limit is actually reached. Commenting rather incidentally on Weber's *Vorbemerkung* to the RS, Sami Zubaida maintains the possibility of a non-essentialist path of historical analysis, however likely it may be to slip into essentialist procedures, a case that he sees epitomized precisely in the famous introductory essay written by the German sociologist (Zubaida 1989, 129–30). By so doing, Zubaida neither falls into a wholesale simplification of Weber's approach, as did Rodinson, nor forces the interpretation of Weber's method toward the establishment of the primacy of structural-institutional factors, as in the case of Turner, but tries to maintain a truly Weberian equilibrium.

Although very conscious of the potential value of the Weberian heritage in its particular emphasis on questions of *Lebensführung*, Zubaida still seems much more preoccupied with Weberist degenerations. The consequence is that he neglects Weber's quasi self-denunciation of essentialism at the beginning of the *Vorbemerkung* of the RS, and indulges in sketching, in rather obscure terms, what a non-essentialist method should look like,[59] thereby reproposing the fragile "alternative" advanced in the mid-seventies by the RMES group and elegantly avoided by Said. Zubaida's perspective, and in fact the whole discussion conducted by many scholars on essentialism, suffers from a mono-dimensional concept of this cognitive phenomenon: it looks for this in its apparent unfolding, but not in the historically cultural-specific genesis of the method of knowledge applied by students of Islam or the Middle East.

Essentialism is not limited to the cases where the essence is externalized, but is also at work when the search for an essence is kept internal to the implicit claim for the universal validity of the method chosen, as in approaches influenced by the "political economy" paradigm. In other words: an approach in terms of "understanding," like the classic Orientalist one, places the essence ("Islam" as the antithesis of the "West") very visibly in the middle of the argumentation, while patterns of explanation focusing on "structural" factors conceal the essence in the definition of variables, and particularly of the independent ones, which are an emanation of Western self-understanding through the medium of historically successful conceptualizing patterns. In both cases, the essence is constituted by how the Self (the "West") is constructed. The indictment of the first, "classic" case of interpretative essentialism on the ground that it explicitly revolves around the essence of "Islam" obscures the extent to which "Islam" merely derives from the construction of the "West," a construction which is also determinant in the second, "sociological" model of essentialism.

The circular motion of the Orientalism debate is probably due to the tendential equation between Orientalism and essentialism, as well as to the desperate effort to go beyond Orientalism by suppressing essentialism. But all we can do is to be transparent about where our essentialism is located and how it unfolds, and how the logic of "making a difference" is constructed, with its self-sustaining emphasis on itself as "method" that grounds the "object" of the research. This process does not follow the strict "necessities" of explanation, but depends on the hermeneutic logic of an understanding that is always primarily Self-understanding.

One can of course object, without necessarily sticking to universalist positions, that this second kind of essentialism ("explanatory" essentialism) is in fact no real essentialism, but only a perspective influenced by a good deal of ethnocentrism. It is true that our definition of essentialism certainly depends on conceiving the "essence" not necessarily as an entity with a given name, but as the product of a cognitive mechanism of "reductive" constitution of the object of a "discipline" on the basis of subjective concerns. Thus our definition of essentialism is a "maximalist" one, which has the curious property of filling our minimalist definition of intellectual modernity as inscribed in the construction of collective identities. Modernity as the "fact," essentialism as its cognitive "tool." This extremely schematic statement can acquire some plausibility if we circumscribe it to the process of reciprocal knowledge, definition and cognitive domestication which takes place between cultural "universes" which are capable to produce, at some time in history, by virtue of inner impulses or external stimulation (or a combination of both), frameworks of universal references. This is the game of opposing essentialisms which has constituted such entities like the "West" and "Islam."

This perspective can be more easily accepted if we focus on Weber, as a leading thinker in Western ethical anthropology whose entire work was sustained by a particularly intense elaboration on the category of "our concern." He epitomizes the centrality of Western essentialism in the intellectual construction of the modern world, as well as the long-term vulnerability of this centrality to the tensions produced within the transcultural space between the "West" and "Islam."[60]

Notes

1. This is the phenomenon of the acceptance of trivialized versions of Weber's typological classification for setting modern Western society apart from all that is "traditional," in the Western past but especially in the contemporary non-Western world.
2. This term refers to a dimension of communication across cultures, hence "crosscultural," where it is not merely "exchange" of meaning to link both sides of a space of interaction, but their tendentially reciprocal concern for the Other as an instrument for defining the Self. In a more mature stage of the evolution of a transcultural space, whose probably unique example is the transcultural space between the "West" and "Islam," there can also be phenomena of merging of meaning through both sides of the space, up to the point when the location of the original source of a certain meaning is either no longer possible, or has become irrelevant. We consider the emergence of the "transcultural" properties of the space between the "West" and "Islam" as the consequence of a long process that reached its crucial phase after the zenith of classic European Orientalism, from Weber's study of Islam in the framework of his comparative sociology up to the crisis of the resulting "Weberism."
3. The focus on this game of opposing essentialisms as one of "uniqueness"—making risks obscuring the "sub-universal" variety and mobility of identity references. But the relevance

of the corresponding frameworks is of a markedly formal nature, claiming validity through their game of reciprocal reference by virtue of distinction.

4. A direct consideration of these practices cannot be part of the present work. It is clear, nonetheless, that after the eighteenth-to-nineteenth-century turn in the power balance, the modalities of relational essentialism were destined to deeply differ in rationale and format among the two "universes." Only studies on the working of these modalities during the formative period preceding the turn (seventeenth and eighteenth centuries) could prove the existence of rather "inherent" differences.

5. The empathy factor should be considered an almost technical variable intervening in essentializing procedures, and is hence not only not incompatible with, but even functional to Orientalism (Waardenburg 1963).

6. That such a division of labor was still existing at the time of Weber is clearly reflected in the Foreword to Weber's studies in the sociology of religion, the *Gesammelte Aufsätze zur Religionssoziologie* (hereafter RS: see below for a further discussion of this point). Of course this schematization of the division of labor does not do justice to the process of cross-fertilization between the two branches which began before Weber's intervention (see Stauth 1987, 13).

7. One of the well-known reasons for the transformation of German problematics into broader Western concerns was the wave of emigration of German-speaking scholars to the USA in the thirties. This was also the trajectory of the Orientalist Gustave von Grunebaum, who best incorporates the passage from classic European Orientalism to American post-war Middle East Studies.

8. Schluchter evidently does not intend to go so far in asserting the privileged place of Islam in Weber's comparative vision, as he writes that "[die] Rekonstruktion [der okzidentalen Entwicklung] legt sowohl aus genetischen wie aus typologischen Gründen den Ausgriff auf Judentum und Islam nahe" (Schluchter 1987, 14), thereby equating the importance of Islam and Hebraism.

9. Did he allude to it "programmatically"? Was this manuscript nothing but the pages devoted to Islam present in WuG?

10. Of course the partition is in no way rigid, due to the interplay of both sets of factors according to Weber's own original theoretical stance, an interplay reflected not only in the *Wirtschaftsethik*, but also in the revised version of the *Protestantische Ethik*, hereafter PE.

11. He knew some Hebrew, but no Arabic.

12. As we know from Marianne Weber: "Als er dann (etwa um 1911) die religionssoziologischen Studien wieder aufnimmt, zieht es ihn in den Orient" (quoted in Schluchter 1987, 18).

13. This becomes particularly stringent in some points of the revised edition of the PE.

14. "Eine solche Gotteskonzeption beschneidet die Heilsbedeutung aller Vermittler, seien sie personaler oder institutioneller Natur" (WuG, 346).

15. "Je mehr [die Prophetie] aber in der Richtung der Konzeption eines universellen überweltlichen Einheitsgottes verläuft, desto mehr entsteht das Problem: wie die unge-heure Machtsteigerung eines solchen Gottes mit der Tatsache Unvollkommenheit der Welt vereinbart werden könne, die er geschaffen hat und regiert" (WuG, 315).

16. "Gerade weil dieser Glaube *keine* rationale Lösung des praktischen Theodizeeproblems enthält, birgt er die grössten Spannungen zwischen Welt und Gott, Sollen und Sein" (WuG, 317; this passage is also quoted in Schluchter 1987, 37).

17. This is a key statement of those pages of WuG, included in the section entitled "Die Kulturreligionen und die Welt", where Weber tackles Islam most extensively.

18. This essay is more inclined to stress "external" variables.

19. This is a claim that in no way has the status of an ascertained fact. For the first major challenge to it in historiographic terms see Gran 1979.

20. "Der islamische Glaubenskrieg noch mehr, weil noch ausdrücklicher, als derjenige der Kreuzritter...war eine wesentlich an feudalen Renteinteressen orientierte Unternhemung zur grundherrlichen Landnahme" (WuG, 289).

21. The distinction was already well consolidated in the works of Goldziher and Wellhausen, from which Weber probably drew (Schluchter 1987, 51).

22. As Schulze has ironically observed (Schulze 1992, 106), the "text" that legitimated and recorded the very concrete goal of Islamic conquest was not the Qur'an, but the *diwan* (register of rendits). Weber's incongruous shift in attributing the "search for rendits" to Islam is recognized by Schluchter (Schluchter 1987, 64).

23. "Daher entfaltete die Pradestination im Islam ihre Macht zwar stets erneut in den Glaubenskämpfen, wie noch in denen des Mahdl, büsste sie dagegen mit jeder 'Verbürgerlichung' des Islam ein, weil sie keine inneralltägliche Lebensmethodik stiftete wie im Puritanismus" (WuG, 347).

24. "Aber [Islams Askese] ist eben Askese des Kriegslagers oder eines kriegerischen Ritterordens, nicht mönchische und erst recht nicht bürgerliche asketische Systematik der Lebensführung—immer nur periodisch wirklich herrschend und stets zum Umschlagen in Fatalismus disponiert" (WuG, 376).

25. On this point see also the even more stringent reformulation in Gellner 1992.

26. This medium has been recognized as Weber's central *Fragestellung*: see Hennis 1987, 12. On this point Schluchter seems to agree with Hennis, their reciprocal polemic attitude notwithstanding.

27. The *Vorbemerkung* to the RS is in fact among the last textual traces left by Weber.

28. Gellner has recently tried to show (Gellner 1992) how it is possible to conceive of Western science as unique (something relativists are not convinced of) without at the same time denying Islam the ability to produce a modern framework for universal reference.

29. This evaluation does not preclude the possibility of seeking inspiration in Weber's method for a study of historical sociology on the genesis of Islam's own "intellectual turn."

30. See in particular the following statement: "Im *Islam* sind...fatalistische Konsequenzen angetreten. Aber weshalb? Weil die islamische Vorherbestimmung *prädeterministisch*, nicht prädestinatianisch, auf die Schicksale im *Diesseits*, nicht auf das *jenseitige* Heil bezogen war" (RS I, 102, n. 2). For supporting this judgement Weber referred to an unpublished dissertation thesis of 1912 which dealt with the predestination doctrine in Islam and Christianity.

31. See also WuG, 346–47, where the argumentation on the status of Calvinism's predestination also shifts almost automatically to an explicit reference to Islam.

32. "Universalgeschichtliche Probleme wird der Sohn der modernen europäischen Kulturwelt unvermeidlicher—und berechtigterweise unter der Fragestellung behandeln: welche Verkettung von Umständen hat dazu geführt, dass gerade auf dem Boden des Okzidents, und nur hier, Kulturerscheinigungen auftraten, welche doch—wie wenigstens wir uns gerne vorstellen—in einer Entwicklungsrichtung von *unwerseller* Bedeutung und Gültigkeit lagen?" (RS, 1; see Schluchter 1987, 96 and 121 for the interpretation of this statement).

33. Instead of insisting, as Said and Saidists have done (see various essays in Hussein et al. 1984), on the continuity of Orientalist essentialism through different stages, we wish to

stress the discontinuities recognizable within the "iron cage" of modern essentialism. Crucial to the understanding of the Weberian turn is the highlighting of the shift of essentialist method it represented, and the further shifts it foreshadowed, firstly through the creation of Weberism, and ultimately through its crisis.

34. Among whom three who had a major impact on Weber: Christian Snouck Hurgronje, Ignaz Goldziher and Carl Heinrich Becker.

35. In fact Waardenburg is quite sympathetic to this tendentially empathic strategy, and he only suggests that the researcher should try to keep "open" the essence "discovered": "L'essence d'une religion doit rester une question ouverte" (Waardenburg 1963, 327).

36. This is best shown by returning to Ignaz Goldziher, whose thematization of the relation between *muruwa* (the Bedouin virtue of valor and honor) and *din* (Stauth 1987, 12–13) produced insights into the relations between pre-Islamic Arab customs, the ethical character of Muhammad's prophecy and the "resulting" dimension of Islam's warriors' ethos along lines of explanation whose analytic value is certainly higher than in Weber's study of Islam, even from a perspective of "historical socio-anthropology."

37. "Nur den Fachmännern steht ein endgiiltiges Urteil zu. Und nur weil, begreiflich erweise, fachmännische Darstellungen mit diesem besonderen Ziel und unter diesen besonderen Gesichtspunkten bisher nicht vorlagen, sind sie überhaupt geschrieben worden" (RS I, 13).

38. In fact he envisaged a more systematic re-elaboration of his entire work in the sociology of religion, supposedly to attempt to make up for the incompleteness of the study of Islam, to be carried out also by resorting to ethnographic sources (RS I, 15).

39. "Weil es hier gerade auf die Zusammenhänge der religiös bestimmten Ethik jener Schichten ankommen musste, welche 'Kulturträger' des betreffenden Gebiets waren. Um die Einflüsse, welche *deren* Lebensführung geübt hat, handelt es sich ja" (RS I, 15).

40. The "dialogue" that few Orientalists of that time initiated with contemporary Islamic reformers lacked the necessary focus on the social conditions of intellectual thought. John Lewis Burckhardt (1784–1817), who lived in the Middle East at the beginning of last century, at the same time Orientalism began to take a solid institutional form in the European academic landscape, represents the probably most prominent exception to the Orientalists' lack of insight into contemporary politics in the region. And it is certainly symptomatic that he studied in particular, through "field work" (by not being an Orientalist in the conventional sense), the *Wahhabi* movement, that can be considered the proto-modern movement in the making of an Arab-Islamic framework of universal reference. A later "proto-ethnographer," William Robertson Smith (1848–1894), further enhanced the scholarly, systematic profile of his field work, although he kept a more solid rooting within the Orientalist establishment (Eickelman 1981, 31–35).

41. "Nur im Okzident gibt est '*Wissenschtaft*' in dem Entwicklungsstadium, welches wir heute als 'gültig' anerkennen" (RS I, 1): the location of this sentence at the beginning of the *Vorbemerkung* reveals the importance for Weber of this aspect of modernity which he partially neglected.

42. It is worth remembering that Said himself, at the same time that he renounced focusing analytically on the issue (however formulated) of Weber and Weberism with regard to Islam (probably because he was not primarily interested in studying discontinuities), explicitly recognized, although very briefly, its importance: "Although he never thoroughly studied Islam, Weber nevertheless influenced the field considerably" (Said 1978, 259). A leading historian of the Middle East has been even more outspoken: "Until the last few decades, the great majority of studies of social movements in Islamic societies tended

(either implicitly or explicitly) to be situated within the Weberian tradition, though often without much methodological self-awareness" (Burke 1988, 20).

43. On the genesis and evolution of Middle East Studies in the central socio-politological field see Binder 1976.

44. As expressed by the clause "wie wenigstens wir uns gerne vorstellen": see note 32.

45. This occurs in the probably most visible place in his entire work, since those who want to read the famous PE, first read the introduction to the RS, whose opening sentence tackles the question of Eurocentrism.

46. "Bescheiden," "provisorisch," and "dazu bestimmt, bald 'überholt' zu werden" (RS, 13–14).

47. This is a problem not directly tackled by Ernest Gellner in his essays on Islam that are connected with the Weberian problematic. He seems in fact to take for granted that there was no inherent obstacle in Islam and its *Wirtschriftsethik* against rational capitalism. Gellner's thesis is that upon a more attentive, less pre-oriented look into the historical unfolding of Islam's ideology Weber should have seen in it—all obvious differences notwithstanding—substantial (and not just merely exterior) affinities with Calvinism as to the presence of rationalizing impulses (Gellner 1981). More recently Gellner has stated that "Weberian sociology leads us to expect a certain congruence between a modern economy and its associated beliefs and culture. The modern mode of production is claimed, above all, to be 'rational'... If this is indeed what a modern economy demands, and, above all, if this is what is required by the process of construction of a modern economy (and perhaps also of a modern polity), then reformist Islam would seem custom-made for the needs of the hour. In fact, given the congruence between what Weberian sociology would lead one to expect, and what is offered by High and Reformist Islam, there is a bit of a puzzle concerning why Muslim economic performance is not rather more distinguished than it actually is... But whatever the state of the economy, there cannot be much doubt about the present situation in the ideological sphere" (Gellner 1992, 21). This argumentation should be interpreted in the following way: that the Weberian method of analysing conditions of modernity is substantially fine, that Weber's own application to Islam was basically wrong, but that one still feels uneasy with this "non-integrated" modernity of Islam, although it is preferable not to invoke the nineteenth-century colonial impact of Europe to explain either the partial structural modernization of Islamic countries, or, inversely, their aborted autonomous path of economic modernization (as is usual in comparing the different fate of Egypt and Japan in the first half of the nineteenth century). Gellner's socio-anthropological models concerning Islam are valuable attempts to be Weberian by carefully avoiding Weberism.

48. One of the leading figures of the first generation within the establishment of American "Middle East Studies" provides a sort of self-diagnosis of Weberism at work in the hermeneutics of Islam: "the criticisms [of Islam] were not based on any scientific findings regarding the prerequisites of development. They rather reflected the self-image of Western society and those values to which the dominant classes were inclined to attribute the success of the systems they dominated" (Binder 1988, 210).

49. Weberism can be considered responsible for the "semantic banalization" of the concept of *Lebensführung*, transformed into the label "way of life" (see Gordon 1987, 313).

50. It is not our goal, therefore, to establish the extent to which these attempts were vitiated by insufficient knowledge of Weber's work, as Schluchter has done with unrivaled ability in the essay here frequently quoted (Schluchter 1987). The problem is that Schluchter, after stressing both the importance of Islam for Weber and its quantitatively disappointing treatment in the whole of his work, does not deliver any substantial answer to this apparent

contradiction. Schluchter seems rather preoccupied with showing how, aside from some understandable mistakes, Weber's view of Islam was basically correct because it was substantially coherent with his own method, and did not contradict basic Orientalist knowledge. We have observed that in trying to interpret and, to some extent, expand Weber's interpretation of Islam (especially in its characterization as *Kriegerreligion*), Schluchter often quotes contemporary works written by authors who are among those most exposed to "indictments" of Orientalism, in the Saidian sense (these are Patricia Crone and Daniel Pipes: see Said 1986 and Sadowski 1993). Without intending to comment on the substantial terms of the polemic on Orientalism, we can take this clue as supporting the claim of the influence of Weberism on neo-Orientalist science, and also of how the critique of Orientalism should be read in the context of the more encompassing crisis of Weberism.

51. Another well-known attempt to criticize Orientalism by a Muslim scholar located in the West (Tibawi 1964) is less relevant for us, because to a large extent it is still inscribed within a "traditional" Muslim apologetic perspective.

52. The first public sign of malaise within the transcultural equilibrium was given by the *Colloque sur la Sociologie Musulmane* held in Brussels in 1961 (also mentioned in Abdel-Malek 1963). Abdel-Malek had the merit of making clear with argumentative strength, two years later, that the question transcended the level of academy, and that there was a crucial link between the crisis of Orientalism and the collapse of the colonial system: "la crise frappe au coeur de l'orientalisme: depuis 1945, ce n'est pas seulement le 'terrain' qui lui échappe, mais aussi les 'hommes,' hier encore 'objet' d'étude, et, désormais, 'sujets' souverains" (1963, 109). Apart from the content of this claim, which Abdel-Malek tries to support by an analytic reference to the development of Orientalism and its shift into neo-Orientalism, it is relevant to note that as an Arab intellectual he consciously attempts to upset the status quo in the transcultural space, so paving the way for the later Saidian enterprise. The superficially optimistic character of the critique lies, in contrast to what Said will do, in challenging the ethnocentrism of Western universalism by maintaining a thoroughly universalistic approach through reference to a generic "Marxism" as an instrument against the dominant Weberism.

53. According to Schluchter, the essay even contained outright mistakes and showed a basic ignorance of Weber's work (Schluchter 1987, 86–88).

54. Writing at about the same time as Rodinson, Albert Hourani was much more fair towards Weber, stating that the fact "that Islam is seen as virtually a pure type of warrior-religion runs counter not only to what is now known and thought about it, but also to Weber's own sense of the complexity of the particular existent being... [in fact] his typology was never modified to take account of the specific features of Islam" (Hourani 1980 [1967], 71). Aside from pointing out the instrumental use of Islam, Hourani recognizes that the study of Islam in Weber was intrinsically not suitable for enriching his comparative sociology, according to its rationale of discovering "types" of man. Compared to Rodinson's intervention, these remarks are far less relevant to the evolution of the transcultural space, since they are quantitatively limited and indeed do not grow out of an immediate concern with Weberism. They nevertheless reflect a lucid view of Weber's "position" in the history of Western thought, and consistently suggest the origin of the incongruence in Weber's handling of Islam that was to encourage the rise of Weberism.

55. That this was Turner's conscious intention is revealed by the subtitle of the book, *A Critical Study*.

56. "Once again something called 'Islamic civilization' or the 'Muslim world' is compared to something called Europe or the Christian world" (Owen 1976, 93).

57. After a good start the initiative slowed down. A second volume published in 1976 was followed by silence in 1977. An additional issue published in 1978 in a more modest vein signaled that beyond its original, pretentious claims of overcoming essentialism, the initiative had already fulfilled its function of clearly and publicly formulating the rupture of the Weberist equilibrium in the transcultural space. But the most spectacular sign of the rupture, in its manifold directions of influence, was represented by Said's *Orientalism*, published in the same year. This book, however, did not thematize Weberism in any remarkable form.

58. This convergence has been recently given an additional emphasis by Bryan Turner (Turner 1990, 353) after he had firstly tried (Turner 1974) to read Weber in quasi-Marxian terms, and later attempted to perform an anti-Orientalist task through rescuing and developing, in an Althusserian mood, the supposedly non-Orientalist core of the Marxist system (Turner 1978).

59. Zubaida's alleged anti-essentialist recipe consists in the effort "to show how, for any given social formation, a series of historical conjunctures, each with its own patterns of socio-political processes, have led to a distinctive configuration" (1989, 129–30).

60. It has been claimed that Weber believed that "what distinguishes modern man from all others...is his 'essentialistic' attitude towards all prevalent spheres and territories of social action," and that Weber himself "was not just reconstructing the relationship between Christianity and modernity," but in fact incarnated the culmination of "a transposition of Christianity into modernity" (Abaza and Stauth 1990 [1988], 217).

References

Abaza, Mona, and Georg Stauth. 1990 [1988]. "Occidental Reason, Orientalism, Islamic Fundamentalism: A Critique." In *Globalization, Knowledge and Society*, ed. Martin Albrow and Elizabeth King. London: Sage.

Abdel-Malek, Anouar. 1963. "L'Orientalisme en crise." *Diogène* (October): 109–42.

Asad, Talal, and Roger Owen. 1975. "Introduction." *Review of Middle East Studies* 1.

Binder, Leonard. 1976. "Area Studies: A Critical Reassessment." In *The Study of the Middle East: Research and Scholarship in the Humanities and the Social Sciences*, ed. Leonard Binder, 1–28. New York: John Wiley and Sons.

—1988. *Islamic Liberalism: A Critique of Development Ideologies*. Chicago and London: University of Chicago Press.

Bourricaud, Francois. 1987. "Modernity, 'Universal Reference' and the Process of Modernization." In *Patterns of Modernity*, ed. Samuel Noah Eisenstadt, 12–21. London: Pinter.

Burke, Edmund III. 1988. "Islam and Social Movements: Methodological Reflections." In *Islam, Politics and Social Movements*, ed. Edmund Burke III and Ira M. Lapidus, 17–35. Berkeley, CA: University of California Press.

Daniel, Norman. 1966. *Islam and the West: The Making of an Image*. Edinburgh: Edinburgh University Press.

Eickelman, Dale F. 1981. *The Middle East: An Anthropological Approach*. Englewood Cliffs, NJ: Prentice-Hall.

Elias, Norbert. 1976 [1939]. *Über den Prozess der Zivilisation: soziogenetische und psychogenetische Untersuchungen*. Frankfurt: Suhrkamp.

Gellner, Ernest. 1981. "Flux and Reflux in the Faith of Man." In E. Gellner, *Muslim Society*, ch. 1. Cambridge: Cambridge University Press.

—1992. *Postmodernism, Reason and Religion*. London: Routledge.

Gordon, Colin. 1987. "The Soul of the Citizen: Max Weber and Michel Foucault on Rationality and Government." In *Max Weber, Rationality and Modernity*, ed. Scott Lash and Sam Whimster, 293–316. London: Allen and Unwin.

Gran, Peter. 1979. *Islamic Roots of Capitalism: Egypt, 1760–1840*. Austin and London: University of Texas Press.

Hartz, Louis. 1955. *The Liberal Tradition in America: An Interpretation of American Political Thought since the Revolution*. New York: Harcourt, Brace, and World.

Hennis, Wilhelm. 1987. *Max Webers Fragestellung: Studien zur Biographie des Werks*. Tubingen: Hans Mohr.

Hourani, Albert. 1980 [1967]. "Islam and the Philosophers of History." In A. Hourani, *Europe and the Middle East*, 19–73. London: St. Anthony's.

Hussein, Asaf, et al. 1984. *Orientalism, Islam and Islamists*. Brattleboro, VT: Amana Books.

Lerner, Daniel. 1964 [1958]. *The Passing of Traditional Society: Modernizing the Middle East*. Glencoe: Collier-Macmillan.

Owen, Roger. 1975. "The Middle East in the Eighteenth Century—an 'Islamic' Society in Decline?: A Critique of Gibb and Bowen's 'Islamic Society and the West.'" *Review of Middle East Studies* 1: 101–12.

—1976. "Islam and Capitalism: A Critique of Rodinson." *Review of Middle East Studies* 2: 85–94.

Packenham, Robert A. 1976 [1973]. *Liberal America and the Third World: Political Development Ideas in Foreign Aid and Social Science*. Princeton, NJ: Princeton University Press.

Peters, Rudolph. 1980. "*Igtihad* and *taqlid* in 18th and 19th Century Islam." *Die Welt des Islams* 20: 132–45.

Rodinson, Maxime. 1966. *Islam et capitalisme*. Paris: Seuil.

Sadowski, Yahya. 1993. "The New Orientalism and the Democracy Debate." *Middle East Report* July: 14–21.

Said, Edward W. 1978. *Orientalism*. London: Routledge and Kegan Paul.

—1986. "Orientalism Reconsidered." In *Literature, Politics and Theory*. Papers from the Essex Conference 1976–1984, ed. Francis Barker et al., 210–29. London and New York: Methuen.

Salvatore, Armando. 1991. *Ruolo egemonico e modernizzazione in "Medio Oriente." II dilemma degli aiuti economici americani in Egitto*. Napoli: Ferraro.

—1995. *Islam and the Political Discourse of Modernity*. Reading: Ithaca Press.

Schluchter, Wolfgang. 1987. "Einleitung. Zwischen Welterberung und Weltanpassung. Überlegungen zu Max Webers Sicht des frühen Islams." In *Max Webers Sicht des Islams*, ed. Wolfgang Schluchter. Frankfurt: Suhrkarnp.

Schulze, Reinhard. 1990. *Islamischer Internationalismus im 20. Jahrhundert: Untersuchungen zur Geschichte der Islamischen Weltliga*. Leiden: Brill.

—1992. "Islam und Herrschaft. Zur politischen Instrumentalisierung einer Religion." In *Der Islam im Aufbruch? Perspektiven der arabischen Welt*, ed. Michael Luders. Munich: Piper.

Stauth, Georg. 1987. *Civilizing the Soul: German Orientalists*. Germany: University of Bielefeld, Working paper.

Tibawi, A. L. 1964. *English-speaking Orientalists: A Critique of their Approach to Islam and the Arabs*. London: Islamic Cultural Centre.

Turner, Bryan S. 1974. *Weber and Islam: A Critical Study*. London and Boston: Routledge and Kegan Paul.

—1978. *Marx and the End of Orientalism*. London: Allen and Unwin.

—1990. "The Two Faces of Sociology: Global or National?" *Theory, Culture and Society* 7: 343–58.

—1991 [1983]. *Religion and Social Theory*. London: Sage.

Waardenburg, Jean Jacques. 1963. *L'Islam dans le miroir de l'Occident*. Paris and The Hague: Mouton.

Weber, Max. 1922. *Gesammelte Aufsätze zur Religionssoziologie*, I. Tübingen: Hans Mohr.

—1976. *Wirtschaft und Gesellschaft, Grundriss der verstehenden Soziologie*. 5th ed. Ed. Johannes Winckelmann. Tübingen: Hans Mohr.

Zubaida, Sami. 1989. *Islam, the People and the State: Essay on Political Ideas and Movements in the Middle East*. New York and London: Routledge.

PART III

RELIGION

12

THE MUSLIM EAST AS IT PRESENTS ITSELF

Duncan Black Macdonald

What I desire to put before you now is Islam as it will always present itself. As it has always presented itself, perhaps I should say; I know nothing about the future. But, at any rate, it will portray Islam in its broad outline; as you may see it in any Muslim land; in its spirit and not in its details. In a word, I would display and turn before you, if I may so put it, the many colored globe of Muslim life and thought— for remember that there is life and there is thought there too—and show to you Islam in certain of its permanent and outstanding phases and aspects.

But when I say Islam, what does that mean? I can best bring its meaning home by saying that Islam for the Muslim means formally and historically the same thing that the word Christendom does for us. It is the broadest of all expressions for them; just as Christendom covers all our thought, all our life, all our history. It is a unity to them, a unity more absolute than the term Christendom covers for us; but it is a unity of the same nature; and only as you look at it in that way—as a unity and not as a multitude of details—can you possibly get any idea of its real, essential character.

What, then, I am now going to put before you is simply this Islam, and I desire to show you some of its phases and aspects, such as may be suggestive of the whole, such as may open up, and that especially for the missionary, what lies under that term Islam. It will, then, be for you who may be interested in the Muslim world and may be looking toward a missionary career to follow this up. I suggest to you a beginning and a search, and I put before you some examples.

But, again, in these examples I fear that I must be personal in tone. What I have to say to you is not drawn only from what I have read; it is drawn also from what I have seen; from the contact which I have had with Muslims. It would have been impossible for me, I am free to admit, to deliver this course of lectures in their present form a year ago; and it was only by the permission and help of the Seminary, which enabled me to pass a year in Muslim lands, that the way was opened and that much of such insight as I have gained was made a possibility. I shall, therefore, have to draw very largely in the future upon my own personal experiences. I shall need to ask your indulgence for much introduction of myself in describing the people I have met and the things I have seen. And, with that, I must also beg of you to believe that when I put before you any anecdote, it is absolutely the fact as it came to me; that in no way, in no degree, have I touched up my experiences in order to make them more telling.

But above all, I would hear and throughout suggest and entreat sympathy. I would lay emphasis on the great facts of religious unity between us and the Muslim world, and not upon the points of controversy that may arise. It is my endeavor and desire, as you will see, to say here what may help the missionary to understand Islam, rather than what may be of direct advantage to him in order to convert Islam. After he understands, he may know how to deal with the problem; but my first purpose is to help him—so far as is in my power—to understand; and an understanding can be reached only by thorough, entire sympathy, by sinking the points of difference and holding the points of unity.

For example, several times in my wanderings I was brought into contact—religious contact—with darwishes. Among them I met with as true hospitality, as fervent religious feeling as I have anywhere experienced. Their method of life and their ideas I will take up hereafter in detail. At this point, I would allude only to the sympathy and openness with which they spoke with me upon religious things—the broad religion of the spirit, be it always understood. I will admit that I was exceedingly careful not to speak of Muhammad as "The False Prophet"—as I have heard too many do—and when they spoke of my Father in Heaven as *Rabbuna*, "Our Lord," I took their words according to the meaning, and together we were able to speak of Our Lord, meaning God Most High, and thus meet upon a common plane.

Further, it is certainly true that many things in the world of Islam were a great deal more open to me, that much more was shown to me and said to me, coming as I did as a wandering scholar amongst them, a student of Arabic and of their religion, than if I had been recognized by them as a missionary. But, at the same time, I am persuaded that these things could be more open, more accessible to a great many missionaries than they are. It all lies in the attitude.

Let me now take up some examples of such contact, such reaching and touching the Muslim world in what I would call a sympathetic way. For many people sympathy means weakness. I confess to having a weakness for saints. They make the romance of the religious life, and their biographies—try, for example, *The Golden Legend*—move in an air as remote from our treadmill existence as *The Arabian Nights*, and yet are instinct with spiritual realities and vitalizing energies. For them the ancient world is ever fresh and young, and the Spirit of God still broods visibly over it. The milk of Paradise is on their lips and they hear the footsteps of the Almighty. There is nothing too wonderful to happen to them, and through everything that happens they look straight back to God. But of such absolute saints we, in these western lands and in our harder age, can know alive but few, and I, for my part, have had to fall back upon dead saints, and of these Islam has furnished me with an abundance.

Before I went to the East at all, I had come to know a good deal about some of the more important saints of Islam; I had read their books, had studied their lives and ideas and had come to respect and esteem a great many of them, in a very high degree. When I, then, found myself on Muslim soil, the possibility was opened to me of visiting the tombs of those saints whom I thus knew through books and whom I respected and reverenced. What was I to do? The course that I followed, a course which I believe was perfectly right under such circumstances, was to visit them frankly in reverence, and I found that the fact that I did so—that I behaved, as my Eastern friends would say, like a religious-minded man and a gentleman—helped me indefinitely in my intercourse with Muslims.

There is one usage, for example, that is of rule when visiting the tombs of Muslim saints. You advance to the railing that surrounds the tomb, you hold it in your right hand—in the East you do everything public with the right hand—and you recite the *Fatiha*, the first chapter of the Qur'an, which holds pretty much the place with the Muslim that the Lord's Prayer does with us. Now let me recite to you a translation of the *Fatiha*. It runs thus:—*In the name of Allah, the merciful Compassionator! Praise belongeth unto Allah, the Lord of the Worlds, the King of the Day of Doom. Thee do we serve and of Thee do we ask aid. Guide us in the straight path, the path of those to whom Thou hast been gracious, not of those with whom Thou art angered or of those who stray. Amen.*

I do not know how strict theologians would regard my action; but I confess I found no difficulty at all when I had come to the tombs of these saints, in reciting the above prayer according to usage. Very frequently there would be an inscription on the door of the tomb asking, "O thou visitor to my tomb, forget me not with a pious petition, but lift up thy hands unto the Lord and recite the *Fatiha* for me." I do not know whether the saints in question were much benefited by this. I do not know whether any one of those standing by were especially spiritually benefited by it. I do know, however, that I was benefited by feeling the nearness of the spiritual kindred of all that call upon the Lord, and I know, too, that those Muslims who saw me do this or who knew that I did it, felt that here was a spiritual unity, that this man, Christian though he might be, reverenced their saint and knew what it meant to recognize holiness and the life hid in God.

For example, in the neighborhood of Jerusalem, on the Mount of Olives, there is what is called the Mosque of the Ascension. It is a very curiously sacred place, because it is holy ground for both Muslims and Christians. Islam does not accept the crucifixion; it, therefore, does not accept the resurrection, but it does accept the ascension. It holds that Christ ascended into one of the heavens, which one is a matter of dispute, and is there even now, although it will not put it in the form that He sat down at the right hand of God the Father Almighty. Along the walls of the mosque there are altars for each one of the Christian sects, and upon Ascension Day their priests are admitted to the mosque and it is free to them to celebrate upon their own altars. When I went to that mosque and visited it as one of our sacred spots, I found that there was near it a darwish monastery—I have learned since that in former times it was an Augustinian Abbey—and, as I did almost always on such occasions, I visited the monastery also. I was received there in the most friendly manner. There was a young man sitting at the door of the monastery repeating or reciting the Qur'an, with the book spread open upon his knee, but reciting it, as they commonly do, from memory, and when I came to stand before him, with lifted hand I repeated the common prayer that would bring us both together.

Again, on another occasion in the neighborhood of Cairo, at the tomb of the great mystical poet, 'Umar ibn al-Farid, I found the same observance of the greatest possible value. I remember when I advanced in the fitting manner towards the grated window which looks in on the tomb of the saint, hearing whispers from the Muslim guardians of the tomb, "He knows what is the right thing to do. He has a sense of reverence." The same thing happened when I visited, in Cairo, the tomb-mosque of the great mystical saint, al-Sha'rani; I did it with as great reverence for the man, for his work and personality, as I have ever felt at any tomb to which my steps have been led. Of course, I might say that I was careful in all this to pick my saints. There are many saints in the Muslim calendar, as in that of Christendom, that I could not visit with any reverence at all. They may have had their redeeming qualities; but these did not appeal to me. But there are many saints—and this is my point—with regard to whom I felt and feel that there is a perfect possibility for the most absolute Christian to visit their tombs and to feel that he is visiting the tombs of good men, and I am persuaded that my being able to do so suggested nothing to the Muslims that were with me, but simple unity and charity. It is perfectly true that occasionally some may have thought that I was personally inclined towards Islam. If they did, I could not help it. But here is a curious illustration which shows how such a thing could arise only in the case of the ignorant.

I came to a saint's tomb at Tiberias. The tomb itself was nothing more than a rubbish heap, as the tombs, even of the saints, tend to become in the East; in fact I came upon it unawares. I had no knowledge that there was any saint's tomb there, until I heard my guide being abused by some one for permitting me to enter the sacred precincts. What did my guide say? Well, very nearly in part, the words of the elders about the centurion. "He loveth our people, and the Lord may open his heart to Islam." Such cases were rare; but the cases of mutual understanding on the basis of differing faith were not rare.

I am perfectly conscious, of course, that a missionary might hesitate to follow such a method as this in the country of his labors; but I can imagine also that a man of strong personality, and sympathetic genius, one of the giants of the mission field of whom we have known many, such a man might do it and still remain a missionary and all the better a missionary for it. He would not fear all the time lest he should be misunderstood. The people around him would know well what kind of a man he was and why he did this thing.

But now I must turn from these preliminaries. I have been endeavoring in them to give some clue as to the way in which I approach my subject. It is the sincere way of sympathy; the broad way of unity; the honest way of endeavoring to understand from within.

What is the first thing—the first thing outstanding and to be reckoned with—that meets any one who studies Islam on the spot, whether he be a student or a missionary or simply a traveler? I think that it is what can only be described, most unhappily but truly, as a conspiracy of misinformation. All seem to be leagued together to this end, to tell you the thing that is not. And this conspiracy of misinformation is so fundamental, is so subtle, goes through so many phases of life, is so constant, that the student or the missionary will have to deal with it throughout his entire residence in the East. It is not a thing that you meet on the threshold and then pass beyond. It must always be reckoned with.

Now, because it is so fundamental and constant, I must spend a little time over it. This is not a case, understand, of paying too much attention to the statements of the common dragoman; even the rawest Cook's tourist, whom the native calls a "Cookee," has learned to distrust him; nor is it the case of the mercenary hanger-on upon missions, and so far as my experience goes I do not think there are so many of these as is commonly supposed; nor is it even in general a case of the Oriental desire to please. It goes a great deal farther and a great deal deeper. Even Europeans who have been long in the East are themselves dragged into it and come to be inconceivably reckless in their statements. Here is an example.

In all the Muslim countries or towns that have been taken by force of arms from unbelievers it is a custom that the *khatib*, the preacher who delivers the Friday prayer-sermon, should carry in his hand a sword and should lean upon it in preaching as though it were a staff. That holds true only in such towns as have been taken by force of arms. When, then, I began to try to get some first-hand information about this, I immediately met with the most extraordinary nest of fabrications. One man, a man of high position in Cairo, a European who had spent there the greater part of his life, who had been in intimate contact with Muslims precisely on that side of things—mosques and religious observances—and who, you would have imagined, should have known about this if any one did, this man assured me gravely that it was a Muslim custom to shake this sword to the four winds of heaven as a sign that Islam must conquer all the world. Now, there is absolutely not a word of truth in that. The sword is used as a staff and as a staff only. Of course, it is also a symbol of the historic conquest of that place where it is used.

Another bit of curious misinformation that I gathered with regard to this same thing was that the Muslims did not like Christians to see this sword. I was induced, for a time, rather to believe that there must be something in this second point because, when being shown different mosques and enquiring as to this thing and that, I experienced difficulty in obtaining a sight of the sword used by the *khatib*. And when the guardian of a mosque did finally show it to me—there it was of painted wood only—I thought I saw a somewhat suspicious smile upon his face. But that idea, again, I discovered in time was absolutely false. There is no such feeling regarding the *khatib*'s sword. Let me illustrate to show how false it was.

In the course of my wanderings, I came to Nablus, the ancient Shechem, and there I had peculiar opportunities of access to the mosques. Now Nablus has the reputation of being a very fanatical town, a town where Christians are in danger of being ill-used and will certainly not be received in a friendly fashion. I myself had no experience of the kind. For example, in the great mosque, when I began to speak—of course in Arabic—with the men whom I met there about the different parts of the building and their use, they showed me the sword—in this case a real sword—and made me tell them what the usage regarding it was, where it was used and where not. It was for them, evidently, a kind of examination in Muslim science, and when I had passed, they at once received me with open arms. I was an obvious *kafir* in an egregious sun-helmet and with a Baedeker in my pocket, but I was not entirely uneducated. A teacher in the College or *madrasa* connected with the mosque led me into his private room and we had some interesting talk on theology and metaphysics; but as to the sword, there was not a trace of evidence that there was any secrecy about it.

Again, when the caravan of pilgrims for Mecca sets out from Cairo, there accompanies it what is called the *mahmal*. It is a small, square palanquin, mounted on the back of a camel; a kind of a camel-carriage in a very conventionalized form in which a woman might possibly travel. Few foreigners in Cairo seem to know what is its purpose or meaning. I was told that in this palanquin, a thing of limited size and carried on the back of this one camel, there was packed the covering called the *kiswa*, or robe, which is spread over the Ka'ba at Mecca and which is renewed every year—a most obvious absurdity. One lady even assured me, and this is an illustration of how careful you must be in accepting information from what seems a certain source, that she knew that such must be the use of it because she had been told so by the French tutor of one of the sons of the Khedive. She may have misunderstood him; but if he did tell her that, then he was very ignorant or else he was lying. The fact about this palanquin is that it is simply a symbol of sovereignty. Historically it is a conventionalized reproduction of the palanquin in which the Mamluk queen Shajarat al-Durr—the same who held St. Louis to ransom—made the pilgrimage to Mecca. It now takes the place of the Khedive himself going on pilgrimage to Mecca, and it is very much the same thing, one might say, as when in old-fashioned England a man who could not go to a funeral sent his carriage by way of showing respect. When the *hajj* caravan sets out from the great square under the citadel at Cairo, the Khedive solemnly gives over the halter of this camel into the hand of the Amir al-Hajj, the leader of the pilgrimage, and thus constitutes him his representative on the journey. Similarly, he receives back the halter when the *hajj* returns.

These are cases due to foreign ignorance; but even the native scholar may supply misinformation. It may be unintentionally. With one of my Cairo friends, a graduate of Azhar University, I had a great deal of trouble once in getting at a certain doctrine. He could not remember the point I was trying to develop or any passage bearing upon it. He had never seen it in any theological book. But that was only a curious example of what you might call the Oriental possibility of passing things over. I had, eventually, to show him the doctrine in the *Ihya'* of al-Ghazali, a regular authority at the Azhar. Again, another case, and this time intentional. When I was reading with a distinguished scholar a commentary upon the Qur'an, we came to the passage which I have already translated to you as "The Lord of the Worlds." Now, the universally accepted interpretation of that phrase—accepted by all Islam—is that "the worlds" are the three classes of intelligent beings, mankind, the angels and the jinn, the genies of our old *Arabian Nights*. But my guide had no intention of saying anything in my presence that would expose to the ridicule of an unbeliever the superstitions and weaknesses of the Muslims. I could get nothing more from him in interpretation of these words than that they meant "everything." *Kull shay'* he said again and again, and further than that he would not.

This misinformation is so thorough, goes so deep, is given to you with such an air of certainty, that I must confess that, though I had been reading Arabic and Muslim theology for some twenty-five years, I was staggered at several points before I discovered what were the possibilities in the case, and was for some weeks in doubt as to whether my Arabic authorities might not have misled me. But when it came to getting information upon questions of fact—not of theology or anything of that kind but of historical events in the past and situations and attitudes in the present—I was driven, at last, to absolute agnosticism. How did the different officials stand with Lord Cromer? What of the Khedive's matrimonial experiments? I was told so many opposing things and that so dogmatically, that I had to give up trying to reach anything upon which I could depend as to such points.

The thing is not simply untruthfulness, it is a strange carelessness as to fact. On one side, the Oriental and the Orientalized European has a feeling of, as you might say, "What does it matter anyway?" It is the slackness of one for whom this world is only the fleeting show of a phantasmagoria. And he recognizes it himself. The phrase by which the Cairene is known and by which also he himself marks his typical representative like the Spanish, "*Quien sabe?*" is *Ma'alesh*, "It doesn't matter." "What indeed." It is as though he asked, "does really matter in this world?" And, on another side, he has the creative imagination of a child. If the Oriental does not know what you ask him, he will create something for you, and he is so well pleased with his creation that it becomes solid and real in his eyes. This he does, apparently, with a good conscience because it fills a vacuum of knowledge, a thing which he, like nature, abhors. So far as I can remember, I met only one man who was prepared to say, "I do not know," and, most astounding of all, that was a donkey-boy. When questioned as to the names of mosques or tombs, he would pause and think, and at last, if need were, come to the point of admitted ignorance. But the dragoman, be it noted, always knows.

Now, there follows this; and it is the moral. There is danger for the missionary of believing too much, and there is perhaps greater danger of his becoming cynical and believing nothing at all.

The practical consequence is that the man who is prepared to believe anything on less than the word of a dozen witnesses should never go to the East. Nor should the man go who is inclined to hold that all men are liars, and to become soured in consequence. You have got to take things as you find them and keep an open mind. And let me add to this a still more practical suggestion. It is eminently desirable that missionaries, before they reach the East and are plunged into its chaos of misinformation, should have learned at least enough of Islam to maintain a cautious attitude. I have known cases where such errors, remaining inveterate, have biased better knowledge for years. This, then, is one outstanding aspect of the East, and, I think, the first that will meet any one who begins to look at all into the subject.

Another is the Oriental's assured feeling of religious superiority. It is a somewhat galling thing to us of the West to meet people who dare, calmly, unquestioningly, without imagining that there can be a shadow of doubt, to look down upon us and to say, "But you cannot know this; we know, we understand." Their certitude is as absolute as that of Browning's *Abt Vogler*, "'Tis we musicians know." But such is, undoubtedly, the fundamental attitude of the Muslim East towards Western religious life.

Here are two illustrations. At the Congress of Orientalists held at Algiers in April, 1905, Prof. Karl Vollers read a paper on the origin of the Qur'an. His thesis was that the Qur'an, as we have it at present, in its precise wording and grammatical form, did not proceed from Muhammad; that the language which Muhammad used had been of a colloquial type; and that it was later, at the hands of editors, that the Qur'an had been put into the careful grammatical form which it at present has. This thesis was, certainly, new and strange, and European scholars are not yet, by any means, ready to accept it. But how was it received by Muslim scholars? For the first time, at Algiers, a large number of these were present at the Congress of Orientalists. Professor Voller's paper raised with them tremendous opposition. One thing was clear: the world of scholars in Islam had not yet reached the point of objectively discussing anything looking towards religion, so that the remotest approach to a Congress of Religions would be utterly impossible if Muslims were to form part of it. One Muslim, whom I afterwards met in Egypt, delivered a long and personal address against Professor Vollers, and finished with this, "In the matter of the Qur'an we will take nothing from a stranger." He was prepared—they are all prepared—to learn from Europe and America anything dealing with the material side of life. Such things of the world do not really matter, of course; but when it comes to religion, when it comes to the world of religious thought, there the Muslim must stand alone. He is superior to all Christians; knows it; feels it. No Christian can really feel the things of God as he does.

Again, another example of the same. One of my Muslim friends, with whom I came to be on a very pleasant personal footing, was in conversation with me in his house, and the talk drifted towards philosophy. He asked me, "What is the present tendency of philosophy in Europe?" That was rather a large question, especially as I had to answer it in Arabic, and I was afraid that I might use terms which would mislead him. I ventured, however, to tell him that I thought that the tendency in Europe was distinctly towards an idealistic position. But how was I to express "idealistic position"? I used the term Sufism, but went on to guard myself by explaining that I did not use it in the Muslim sense but in the sense in which it might have been employed by Plato. He nodded his head very approvingly, and said that he had no idea there was so much right philosophical feeling left in Europe. Evidently what I had said took more or less of a load from his mind. These people, he thought, are not so much left to themselves after all. So, at every turn, if you get into any real contact with the religious minded Muslim, you will meet with the feeling that religion is of Islam and not of the outside world.

Let me take one other aspect of Islam. For it I ask you to go with me to Cairo, to the windswept, bird-haunted mosque of Ibn Tulun. That mosque, as it stands at present, is probably the oldest left in Egypt, and one of the oldest in the Muslim world. It is a great square courtyard surrounded by deep colonnades and has not, for many generations, been used for worship. Now, when you enter it, all that you find of signs of life are the footprints of birds marked in the soft, fine sand that covers all the courtyard and their cries as they hover and dart overhead. The roar of the city without dies away; within is silence. There it lies in the midst of Cairo, abandoned, full of crumbling memories, a monument of the past to the grandeur of those who built it. In its prayer-niche, towards which during centuries millions of the faithful must have bowed in the worship of Allah, I found some Arabic verses which had been written in pencil in 1877, by a certain Darwish Mustafa. They are deeply significant for the attitude of Islam to the world and to Allah. They run as follows:

Where are the kings and those who peopled the earth?

They have left what they built in it and what they
peopled.

And have become a pledge of the grave for that which
they wrought.

They have turned to decayed bones in it, after they
had been forgotten.

Where are their armies which repelled not and availed
not?

And where is that which they gathered in the earth
and that which they treasured?

There came to them the command of the Lord of the
Throne in haste,

And there availed them from it neither wealth nor
fortress.[1]

Such is the burden of all Muslim thought. One generation cometh and another goeth; but Allah abideth for ever. Nothing else is sure; nothing else permanent. "Oh, where are kings and empires now?" is ever recurring on Muslim lips; but those other lines which mean so much to Christendom, "But, Lord, thy Church is praying yet, To endless years the same," could be repeated by Muslims, if at all, only with grave differences of meaning. The conception of the Church Militant, a Church in travail, laboring, striving for an unaccomplished ideal, is foreign to all Islam. The Muslim world is the Muslim Church, not any encircling mass to be leavened and conquered by that Church, then to abide as a Church Triumphant. That world and Church, rather, are fleeting, evanescent, a mere shadow-show cast upon the screen of existence, while Allah is the only reality. God has not tabernacled in human flesh for Muslims, nor does He as the Holy Ghost still dwell in men and thus make them partakers of the divine nature. They remain His creatures always, of a dependent existence, to be swept, in the end, from the board of life. It came easily, therefore, to some Muslim sects to teach that at the last heaven and hell with their dwellers would be destroyed and Allah would remain enthroned alone, even as He had been in the beginning.

Here, perhaps, we find the absolute, the essential difference between Islam and Christianity.

Note

1. I do not know who was the author of these lines. They are quoted also in *The Arabian Nights*, Bulaq edition, II, 45; see, too, Lane's *Arabian Nights*, III, 127.

13

THE SPECIAL CASE OF ISLAM

Wilfred Cantwell Smith

So far we have not dealt with the Islamic situation. This particular case has been reserved for separate treatment because it is both unusual and intricate. It is in some ways different from the others, and in some ways similar. On both scores it is illuminating.

We may take the differences first, since they lie closer to the surface. The first observation is that of all the world's religious traditions the Islamic would seem to be the one with a built-in name. The word "Islam" occurs in the Qur'an itself, and Muslims are insistent on using this term to designate the system of their faith. In contrast to what has happened with other religious communities, as we have partly seen, this is not a name devised by outsiders, those inside resisting or ignoring or finally accepting. On the contrary, it is they who proclaim it, and teach it to others. Indeed, Muslims are zealous in their campaign to persuade the rest of the world to abandon other spontaneous names for their "religion" (such as "Muhammadanism") in favour of this proper one, which they proudly bear.

This name for their religious system, moreover, has the sanction not only of the Muslims and their tradition but, they aver, of God Himself. God is presented as announcing: "This day I have perfected your religion for you, and completed My favour unto you; and have chosen for you as a religion *Islam*" (Qur'an 5/3). Again, it is written: "Verily, *the* Religion in the eyes of God is Islam" (Qur'an 3/19). Such verses, which we will later carefully reconsider, are basic for many a Muslim. The assurance of divine approval could hardly be more squarely based, more explicit.

Secondly, we may note a further point, which the Qur'an verses just cited also illustrate. This is that the Arabic language has, and has had since the appearance of Islam and indeed from shortly before, a term and concept that seem to be quite closely equivalent to the Western "religion." Indeed this word—namely, *din*—is used in all the various senses of its Western counterpart. It carries the sense of personal religion: the classical dictionaries give *wara'*, "piety" as an equivalent, a word that never has a systematic or a community meaning and that cannot have a plural. It carries also, however, the sense of a particular religious system, one "religion" as distinct from another. In this sense it has a plural (*adyan*). This plural is not in the Qur'an, but is traditional. Furthermore, the word in its systematic sense can be used both ideally and objectively, of one's own religion and of other people's, the true religion and false ones.

In fact, it may be used of these both at once. Muslims quote classical verses from the earliest period that affirm that "the religion of Muhammad [is] the best of the religions of mankind." I have previously suggested that such a conception is remarkable, especially for an early period. In Latin, as we have observed, a plural *religiones* was common, but it referred to rites and observances, and the plural was regularly used with one specific God. The Christian Latin writers used the plural to refer to what might today be called in the singular the pagan religion (or, cults) of the Greco-Roman world; they also use the singular, and sometimes the plural, for their own Christian rites or worship. I have not, however, come across any instance where a Christian writer of that period uses a plural to designate his own and the outsiders' religious systems collectively and simultaneously. That "Christianity is one of the religions of the world" is a concept that, as we shall see in our next chapter, is still resisted. No early Church Father, so far as I have discovered, can conceptualize his situation in this way. To do so involves a notion that there exists a series of phenomena of essentially the same kind. Of them one may be affirmed to be the best, as in the Arabic verse just cited; but it is the best of its kind, not something *sui generis*.

To return to the Arab singular, *din*. We may note that this is used, finally, of religion as a generic universal, in both senses: as generalizing personal religiousness or human piety at large, and as generalizing the various systematic religions as ideological or sociological structures.

The Muslim world, then, is definitely and explicitly conscious of something that it calls, and is persuaded that it ought to call, a religion, as one among others but in its own case one given as such by God. Further, it is emphatic in naming that religion "Islam," holding that God Himself has so named it.

Lest there be any doubt that it is systematic religion that is so named, we may note the practice of Muslim use of the word *nizam*, "system," in connection with "Islam." This is conspicuously prevalent in Urdu but is affirmed also by religious leaders in the Arab world.

The West's adoption of the term "Islam" to name the religion of the Muslims is a process still going on. It began only recently. For, on more careful examination, it turns out that in this case also outsiders did invent a name for the system and applied it; those within did resist. The difference is that their resistance is now proving successful. The West became aware of the religious communities of India and China and their traditions only in relatively modern times, through Western exploring: whereas with the Islamic it came into immediate contact, and conflict, from the beginning. Europe has throughout been aware of what it now calls Islam. For long, however, it was not aware of and certainly did not use this name. And to be quite accurate, since conceptions are relevant to perceptions, one should say rather that Europe was aware of the Muslim community. To a very limited degree and rather hazily, distortedly, it was aware also of some of its ways and notions.

In the Middle Ages, the common European practice was to refer to the sect or heresy of the Saracens. After the Renascence and Reformation, when the term *religio* was coming into currency for these purposes, one finds the phrase "the religion of the Saracens" and by now, also, "... of the Tartars and Turks." More impersonally, substituting an adjective for a noun that names the people, one gets "Mohammedan religion" and the like in the Enlightenment. As we noted earlier, the systematic term "Mohametanism" is found in English in 1612, "Muhammedrie" in 1613; two centuries earlier than comparable names for any other Eastern system. "Islam" is first used in English, curiously, for "Muslim": "the Islams, that is, Catholike or right-believing Musulmans" (1613); this persisted into the nineteenth century: "Thou art . . . an Islam in thy creed" (1814).

Various other names for the adherents of this community, chiefly varieties of either "Muhammadan," the Western term, or "Muslim," the internal one, appear fairly early in the modern period.

In the eighteenth century, a term "Islamism" was introduced, and is still used in modern French. We shall later recognize by inference that there is some validity in this, even though it seems awkward to us now.

In the nineteenth century and into the twentieth, the chief term in English was "Muhammadanism" (in a cheerful variety of spellings), as the established subject entry for library catalogs, encyclopedia articles, book-titles, and the like. At the present time, chiefly since World War II, this is giving way in Europe and America to "Islam." The transition is being pushed partly by Muslims themselves, partly by Westerners who have lived among them, and not least by orientalists. The argument for it turns basically and simply on the point that this is the proper name used by the Muslims themselves. Its use by outsiders, therefore, is urged as both more courteous and more correct.

The Islamic tradition, then, we would suggest, seems to be unique in this matter of having its own name. If our whole argument has any validity, one must suppose that this may not be insignificant. We may well then ask the question, *Why*? Wherefore is it an exception to the general rule? What is involved in the fact that this particular religious community differs from all the others on this point?

The matter, I believe, is indeed significant. I suggest that there are two fundamental considerations to be brought to bear on it.

The primary observation is perhaps a retort: Why not? In the comparative study of mankind's religious history, certainly one of the first considerations must be to recognize and to take seriously the fact that the various religious traditions are different. They are different not only in detail but in basic orientation. Each is unique. Each is an exception on some quite fundamental matters to any generalizations that one might make about the others. Christians at times have devoted a good deal of vigor to insisting that, or to asking whether, Christianity is unique. Of course it is unique; every religious tradition is unique. Each is unique in some quite special way. One of the first illusions that must be dropped in such comparative study is that of imagining that all the traditions are of a given form, are varieties on a single theme. One must come to recognize—and it is not always easy—that not merely do they propound differing answers but rather that often they are asking different questions.

Islam, it could be argued, may well in fact be characterized by a rather unique insistence upon itself as a coherent and closed system, a sociologically and legally and even politically organized entity in the mundane world and an ideologically organized entity as an ideal. This could be seen as true in ways deeper and more patterned than pertain to the self-consciousness of any other religious group—true particularly of standard orthoprax Islam, with its dominating concept of law (*shari'a*). If so, it would be one of the matters to which the Sufi mystics' emphasis through the centuries could be seen as an alternative or supplement—if not in protest against it, at least as an attesting to a less impersonalist, less formal concept of Islam.

This much, at least, is clear, or can be fairly readily shown: that the various religious traditions of the world do in fact differ among themselves in the degree to which each presents itself as an organized and systematized entity. If this be so, then one of them may well be, must be, the most entity-like. One could suggest that Islam, it so happens, is that one.

To anyone who knows India it is evident that both Christian and Islamic ideals are much more coherent and consolidated matters than the religious orientation of Hindu India can readily appreciate. Again, the "three religions" of China are, as we have noted, less distinct, less mutually exclusive, are more amorphous, than Muslims or the West can usually appreciate. One may suggest that the Islamic tradition is even more "morphous", if one might use such a term, than is the Christian. If it be true that the forms of the religious life of the world differ, it may be taken as simply a datum of observation that Islam is more reified than any other of the world's great living faiths.

Our second consideration is of another order. It is historical. If the Islamic tradition appears both to its adherents and to some outsiders to be more reified than others, one may ask how this has come about. On inquiry, it turns out that, like everything else on earth, there is an historical process by which this situation came to be what it is.

Actually, I discern three historical processes. The Islamic world over the centuries proves to have been subject to the pressures of three processes of reification.

An examination of these not only helps to explain and clarify the peculiarity that we have noted, but also reveals that this is not nearly so deep-rooted nor so essential as at first might appear. Historically, it turns out that the Muslims are different from the rest of us not enigmatically, but have been involved rather, though as is to be expected in their own particular way, in the same kinds of development as has mankind at large. Indeed it turns out that the particularities of their rather special reificationist trends are related to the particularities of their specific involvement in the totality of world history. What makes the Muslims specifically different from other groups is the very fact that makes them generically the same as other groups; namely, that they are persons living *sub specie aeternitatis* in concrete and particular historical situations.

The first process of reification that has impinged on Islamic development is a very long-range one. To apprehend it one must go far back in Middle Eastern history, and bring to awareness trends that are less generally known than their major consequences warrant. Our exploration of these will prove rewarding for the light that they throw not only on the Islamic tradition, elucidating the context in which this arose, but also on the world religious situation. For as we shall see, pre-Islamic developments in the Middle East set a context for the religious history of much of the world. They elucidate in part the emergence of a differentiation of man's major religious traditions. A recognition of this would seem, indeed, to make incipiently possible a unified view of man's religious history on a world scale.

The Islamic is historically the youngest of the world's major religious traditions. It was proclaimed by Muhammad and accepted by its early adherents in a world in which religious communities in our systematic sense, organized as independent entities, were already in evidence. Jewish and Christian self-consciousness had become accepted facts, and the existence of their groups had become part of the accepted outlook of the area. Formal conceptualization among these groups, we have seen, was not yet as much developed as it was later to become. Yet the innovation was well established of a demarcated religious grouping, separating off those of a common religious loyalty from others among whom they lived. We saw that when it was launched in the Mediterranean world the Church was a novel kind of religious form. Its missionary zeal, its openness to individuals from all varieties of traditional background and from all places, on the one hand, and its sharp metaphysical rejection, on the other hand, of those who did not join, instituted a new phenomenon in society. At about the same time, the Roman Empire forcibly ejected the Jews from their homeland yet they continued to subsist as a widely scattered yet religiously integrated community bound only by the system of their faith. This too was a novel phenomenon. The independent religious community had been born.

And it had been noted.

By Muhammad's time not only had these developments begun to impinge a little on Arabia, fairly significantly on its more alert and sensitive minds; also, they had sunk deeply in the mentality of those more urban areas such as in Egypt and Syria where the formative centuries of the new Muslim community's history were to be centered. In addition, there had been further and more elaborate evolution in this realm both of life and of thought, further east. Not only Judaeo-Christian developments but those of other traditions, other communities as well were important in the areas into which the Muslims from Arabia carried their new message and in which they constructed its early elaborations. Indeed, in some eddies of these new eastern developments a few levels even of Arabian life can be seen to have become involved, already in Muhammad's day.

To inquire into this whole development takes us into a cultural tradition, centered chiefly in Iran and the Tigris-Euphrates valley, that for many centuries had been religiously and intellectually effervescent. Its role in the general stream of man's religious history is greatly more formative than has usually been recognized, far outside its own borders.

* * *

With this awareness, then, of historical and linguistic context, we are ready at long last to return to the question of the rise of Islam, and to our question of how to understand its apparent divergence in form from man's other major religious traditions. Do the reificationist trends of the Middle East that we have discerned help to clarify this?

For the Muslim, the argument becomes delicate here, since the issue raises questions of the relation between revelation and history—between the timeless truth that God discloses and the concrete, limited situation at a particular time and place in which the revelation takes place. This is in a sense one aspect of the issue of our entire study. The delicacy at this particular point for Muslims lies specifically in the fact that, since we are discussing the history of ideas and the terms used to express them, we touch upon the relation between religious truth and religious language. This involves a characteristic and profound article of faith with Muslims.

The seriousness of this matter is evinced in the traditional Islamic refusal that the Qur'an be translated. This is reasonable in so far as words that God has chosen are not to be thought interchangeable with those that are human constructs. We have been assuming throughout our study that words used in particular historical situations may be treated as expressive of ideas in men's minds, and that these ideas may not be final characterizations of the universe in which we live. Phrased theologically, we take seriously the possibility that the terms that men use may not necessarily formulate concepts in the mind of God. A plea for a critical reappraisal of concepts presupposes that we may be the victims, and may become the masters, of human ratiocination.

The Muslim, of course, is as ready as is anyone to admit that human conceptions may fall short of perfection, and even of adequacy. But the *terms* in which he conceptualizes the world are given to him in the Qur'an.

For him these terms do stand for concepts in the mind of God. They are ultimately valid and permanent. It would be intolerably arrogant for him to think of criticizing or improving upon them, and fatuous for him to think of rejecting this gift.

He does, however, have an acknowledged problem in ascertaining, so far as he is able, what these terms may mean. The Muslim and the rest of us, therefore, join company again at this point, especially in so far as one may give one's attention to the problem of what meaning the words of the Arabic language had for the Arabs of the time and place in which the Qur'an is presented as having been revealed. The need to ascertain this has been a standing demand of Muslims themselves, as requisite for Qur'an understanding. To it, modern students add the historical question of how these words came to have those meanings.

For the meanings of words, like everything else in the life of the pre-Islamic Arabs, were of course the product of an historical evolution up to that time. And they were the result of various influences, including some from outside their traditional environment. Men's concepts change, and these men's were changing, partly under the impact of new ideas, partly under the impact of new experiences, new things that they saw.

Furthermore, the convinced Muslim and the outside observer may join forces also in endeavoring to ascertain what, whether rightly or wrongly, particular persons at particular times have in fact understood given words to mean. Apart from the question as to what a term or text properly and truly signifies, what it ought to mean, there is the mundane question of what it actually has meant in the minds of actual men. This, both he and the historian may agree, has varied. It is also empirically ascertainable. The true meaning of a given passage may be transcendentally given, but the actual meaning to particular persons has been historically conditioned, and may be historically elucidated. The historian may help the theologian, perhaps, if the latter would like to put it thus, to understand why men have misunderstood.

One need not assert, therefore, what a Muslim would inevitably and vigorously reject, that the text of the Qur'an was influenced by Manichee ideas or that the essential form of Islam is to be understood in terms of Persian concepts of religion. Yet one may proffer the suggestion that some Middle Easterners in the early days of the Muslim community, when they heard the Qur'an or thought about Islam, were influenced in their understanding of the one or conception of the other by such pre-Islamic pressures.

This much, at least, would seem clear: that a few sophisticates and cosmopolitans among the Hijazi Arabs who first heard a new faith being preached by Muhammad and first saw the movement that gathered round him and his message, and many among the subsequently Arabic-speaking groups in the cities of Syria and especially

Iraq and Iran who received the new teachings into their society or their hearts, were presumably mentally somewhat prepared to perceive as such a new religious system.

In this light, the significance is more apparent of the fact that we earlier stressed: that by the seventh century AD the Christian and the Jewish religious traditions were not only facts but had become defined and self-conscious communities and to a significant degree were also explicit, systematic ideas. This was true in general, and was beginning to be true also in Arabia. That is, they were facts and ideas in the light of which the Islamic message was preached and was received. Further, in the wider Middle East in which that message was presently elaborated, there were still other religious traditions known and communities organized, and ideas of them were still more systematic.

A Muslim might phrase this differently; by saying, for instance, that this was the particular time and place that God chose for His final proclamation to mankind. In the Arabic environment in which the Prophet delivered his message, two organized religious communities of the new type were already conspicuous, the Christian and the Jewish; and the new community and its faith, while actually different in form and in substance, yet patently appeared a member of the same general species. Again a Muslim might formulate the proposition in different words, but the facts are not in dispute: it is sound Islamic doctrine that the Jewish, Christian, and Islamic as historical systems are variations on a single theme.

With this historical overview, also, one may perhaps understand that, in a way that is not true of any other great religious leader of the world except Mani, Muhammad to some seems self-consciously and deliberately to have set about establishing a religious system. He might be said to have believed himself called upon by God to do just that. In a sense one could characterize him as, after Mani, the only "founder of a religion" who knew what he was doing. Muslims themselves regard God as the founder of their religion in its ideal sense, but Muhammad (under God's guidance) as manifestly the founder of it as a sociological system and historical phenomenon, and withal as executing that assignment in a very clearheaded and careful way.

We have already observed that it is hazy thinking to speak of Guru Nanak as "the founder of Sikhism," or Lao Tse and Chuang Tse of a Taoist religion; the same applies in some degree to K'ung, to Gautama the Buddha, to Moses, and to Jesus. It is both theoretically and historically of moment that these men were concerned with communities; yet they did not preach abstract or consolidated systems. One cannot imagine Plato talking of "Platonism"—he was talking about the universe. Jesus was not interested in Christianity, but in God and man. He could not have conceptualized "Christianity." Muhammad, on the other hand, seems to some observers and to some Muslims to have known what he was about when he talked of Islam.

One finds him taking steps, at first incidentally rather like other religious leaders, but later in a careful and calculated way, to organize a community socially, legally, and politically, as the expression of a religious idea. This has had, we believe, large consequences. The *Sangha* is important to Buddhists, certainly; and the Church to

Christians—important religiously. Moreover, men like Durkheim have drawn attention vividly to the intimate tie between the religious and the sociological universally. Nevertheless the role of the *umma*, the Islamic community, in Muslim life is distinctive and crucial. And I have argued elsewhere that Muslims find more religious significance in their community's history than is true of any other religious group. It would appear that here is something fundamental to the uniqueness of the Islamic among the religious orientations of the world. It would appear also that this may be related to the uniquely deliberate implementation of a sociological-system concept of religion by the Prophet.

Germane to all this is a further point on which we have had occasion to touch more than once: that a religious system appears as a system, an intelligible entity susceptible of objective conceptualization, primarily to someone on the outside. In the light of this, an historian may find it illuminating to observe that the Islamic seems to be the only religious movement in the world that arose historically not primarily out of a reform of the indigenous religious tradition of the people to whom it was presented. It arose, rather, among, and was preached to (a Muslim might say, God revealed it among) a people for whom it was the reform of outsiders' religious traditions.

What non-Muslims call the Jewish-Christian impact on Islam, but what to those within is postulated rather as a transcendent connection, has often been studied. We may quote some words of a scholar very decidedly a non-Muslim, but among nonbelievers one of the most careful students of the externals of the Qur'an:

> From the fact that Muhammad was an Arab, brought up in the midst of Arabian paganism and practising its rites himself until well on into manhood, one would naturally have expected to find that Islam had its roots deep down in this old Arabian paganism. It comes, therefore, as no little surprise, to find how little of the religious life of this Arabian paganism is reflected in the pages of the Qur'an .... Even a cursory reading of the book makes it plain that Muhammad drew his inspiration not from the religious life and experiences of his own land and his own people, but from the great monotheistic religions which were pressing down into Arabia in his day. (Jeffery 1938, 1)

The phrasing here is very much that of an outsider; the passage will be offensive to Muslims. Yet it expresses how an outside historian views something that to them is in fact obvious anyway, namely that the Prophet's message was delivered to the Arabs as a reformulation not primarily of their own, idolatrous, religious tradition but of the tradition of Christians and Jews, which in Muslim eyes needed reforming. In an historian's eyes it is the adaptation to its people of a reform of outsiders' traditions.

The gulf that separates how the same facts appear to a Muslim and to an outside observer, to those who are and to those who are not *engagés* in a tradition, is itself of major significance, and is relevant to the course of our whole argument. The concept of a religious system is inherently different for those who stand outside.

For our immediate purposes, this point is relevant for what the word *din* might mean to those Arabs who were not Christians and Jews. Here would seem a second factor in the potentially reificationist conceptualizing of Islam by those among whom its message was proclaimed. First, as we have seen, of all the major religious communities of the world today the Islamic is the only one that has come into historical existence this side chronologically of that period in human history when schematized religious systems had evolved, and in that part of the world where the process of systematizing them was developing. Secondly, we have seen that the practice of naming a religion and conceptualizing it systematically is appropriate primarily for outsiders, for those for whom it is not a medium of faith; and the Islamic is the only religious movement in the world that was launched by a reformer and accepted by a people standing outside the tradition (in this case the two traditions) being reformed.

Reference

Jeffery, A. 1938. *The Foreign Vocabulary of the Quran.* Baroda, India: Oriental Institute.

14

Religion is a Different Matter

Charles Le Gai Eaton

Other subjects may lend themselves, in varying degree, to objective study, and in some cases personal commitment serves only to distort what should be a clear and balanced picture. Religion is a different matter because here objectivity only skims the surface, missing the essential. The keys to understanding lie within the observer's own being and experience, and without these keys no door will open. This is particularly true of Islam, a religion which treats the distinction between belief and unbelief as the most fundamental of all possible distinctions, comparable on the physical level to that between the sighted and the blind. Believing and understanding complement and support one another. We do not seek for an adequate description of a landscape from a blind man, even if he has made a scientific study of its topography and has analyzed the nature of its rocks and vegetation. In Islam every aspect of human life, every thought and every action, is shaped and evaluated in the light of the basic article of faith. Remove this linchpin and the whole structure falls apart.

For the unbeliever this article of faith is meaningless and, in consequence, nothing else in the life of the Muslim makes sense. Even for the faithful Christian the "sublime" and the "mundane" relate to different dimensions, and he is disturbed by any confusion between the two. Islam does not recognize this division. For the Muslim, his worship and his manner of dealing with his bodily functions, his search for holiness and his bartering in the market, his work and his play are elements in an indivisible whole which, like creation itself, admits of no fissures. A single key unlocks the single door opening on to the integrated and tight-knit world of the Muslim.

That key is the affirmation of the divine Unity, and of all that follows from this affirmation, down to its most remote echoes on the very periphery of existence, where existence touches on nothingness. Islam is the religion of all or nothing, faith in a Reality which allows nothing to have independent reality outside its orbit; for if there were such a thing, however distant, however hidden, it would impugn the perfection and the totality of that which alone is.

It follows that one cannot speak of Islam without adopting a specific point of view and making that point of view quite explicit. This book is written by a European who became Muslim many years ago, through intellectual conviction and within the framework of a belief in the transcendent unity of all the revealed religions. The word "convert" implies the rejection of one religion in favour of another, but mine was an act of acceptance which carried with it no corresponding act of rejection other than the rejection of the secular, agnostic world of thought in its entirety.

One who enters the community of Islam by choice rather than by birth sinks roots into the ground of the religion, the Qur'an and the traditions of the Prophet; but the habits and customs of the Muslim peoples are not his. He lacks their strengths and is immune from their weaknesses; immune, above all, from the psychological "complexes" which are the result of their recent history. He does not become a mimic Arab, since he knows that Islam, as a world religion, owes both its endurance and its rich fabric to the entry, century after century, of outlanders: Persians, Berbers, Mongols, Turks, Indians, Malays, Africans. These outlanders often broke the mold cherished by the Arabs, but they vivified the religion, and with it the culture and society that are stamped with its mark. Islam has created an immediately recognizable design for human living, but the way in which this design has been filled out and colored has differed widely from one region of the *dar al-Islam* (the "House of Islam") to another; the peacock's tail has been spread over the world.

The European or American who has come to Islam in this way stands astride the oldest frontier in the world, the frontier that has separated Islamic civilization, first from Christendom and later from the post-Christian world, for some thirteen centuries. This is in many ways a strange position to occupy because the frontier runs between two areas of reciprocal incomprehension, and to be at home in both is, in a sense, to commute between different planetary systems. The Westerner's inability to understand the Muslim is matched by the Muslim's incapacity to understand the Westerner. Those who stand astride the frontier find themselves obliged to act as interpreters between two different languages and must themselves speak both with adequate fluency.

The Western Muslim does not change his identity, though he changes his direction. He is dyed with the colour characteristic of the culture into which he was born and which formed him; he asks the questions which this culture asks; he retains a sense of tragedy and of the world's ambiguity, with which the European tradition is imbued but which is strange to the traditional Muslim, and he is still haunted by the ghosts of

Europe's past. Ancestral voices familiar to his kind are not silenced, but he has distanced himself from them.

The Semitic mind and temperament are legalistic by nature and a certain literal-mindedness is characteristic of the Muslim. The European, on the other hand, is more concerned with the spirit than with the letter of the law, and he inevitably brings something of this bias with him into Islam. This may even be the most useful contribution he can make to his adopted faith in an age of change and fluidity, in which the outworks of religion are eroded by the times so that it is necessary, as never before, to establish what are the essentials of the Faith and to hold fast to them. To say this is not to suggest that any part of the total structure is unimportant, but only to emphasize that when a castle is under siege, and alien forces have scaled the outer battlements, one must be ready to man the inner defences.

This book is written for those whose minds have been shaped by Western culture. Given that the contemporary world, as it now exists almost universally, is entirely a product of that culture, I write as much for those of my co-religionists who have received a "modern" education as I do for non-Muslims. Among the former there are already quite a number who have rediscovered the religion into which they were born as a result of seeing it through foreign eyes; no longer convinced by the traditional arguments of their Faith, which sufficed while Islam was a closed system, they have had to dive deep and travel far in order to return to their origin. They will assess this book in the light of their knowledge of the religion. But the non-Muslim who has an interest in understanding Islam, but who lacks the time and the inclination to read and compare a number of books, has every right to ask whether what he is told is authentic and, in a general sense, "orthodox."

No simple answer can be given to this question. It is difficult to provide a universally acceptable definition of Muslim "orthodoxy," a term for which there is no precise equivalent in the Arabic language. There is no ecclesiastical hierarchy in Islam (whatever may be the appearances in Shi'a Islam as we find it in Iran), no ultimate doctrinal authority other than that of the Book itself, the Qur'an. What I believe or what the next man believes, provided we stay within the framework of the religious Law, is largely a matter of personal insight, so long as we do not depart too far from the consensus of the community (assuming that such a consensus exists, and this is an open question today).

If, however, we borrow what is essentially a Christian term, it can be said that Sunni orthodoxy emerged in the tenth century AD, taking shape over the next two hundred years; and that it emerged as a consensus following a middle way between conflicting points of view, which threatened to tear the community apart. Leaving room for wide variations of opinion, it was achieved in reaction against narrow and exclusive views of what constituted orthodoxy and of what entitled a man or woman to belong to the *umma*, the sacred community of Islam. A Muslim, by this definition, is anyone who is able to make the confession of faith in sincerity; to say seven words, and to mean them. *La ilaha ila Allah; Muhammadun rasul Allah*: "There is no divinity but (or 'if not') Allah: Muhammad is the messenger of Allah." And since human beings cannot read the secrets of hearts, the judgement as to sincerity rests only with Allah.

In practice few would accept that this suffices, unless it is taken to include all the consequences which flow from the simple affirmation of faith. The Muslim believes in One God, who is all-powerful and has no partner; believes in His messengers, sent to mankind for their guidance from the beginning of time; believes that Muhammad closed the cycle of messengers and that there can be no further revelation of the divine Law after him; believes that the Qur'an is the Word of God, unaltered and unalterable, and believes in the obligation to conform to the "Five Pillars," which are the confession of faith, the five daily prayers, payment of the poor-due, the fast of Ramadan, and performance of the Pilgrimage to Mecca by those physically and financially able to undertake it. A Muslim may neglect one or more of the pillars (except the first) and still be counted as a believer, but if he denies their necessity he has placed himself outside the community.

The Qur'an itself offers a broad definition: "The messenger believes in that which has been revealed to him from his Lord, as do the believers. Each believes in Allah and His angels and His scriptures and His messengers—We make no distinction between any of His messengers—and they say 'We hear and we obey.' Forgive us, 0 Lord. Unto Thee is the journeying." A further condition, however, follows from this. If membership of the community of believers requires acceptance of the Qur'an as the revealed Word of God, then denial of any part of the Qur'an or of any statement made in the Book may be assumed to call belief into doubt. This is so, and yet we have here an area of ambiguity. Certain verses, particularly those relating to matters of law, are plain enough, but there are many parts of the Qur'an which lend themselves to a variety of interpretations; and indeed it is said that, in principle, every single verse contains layer upon layer of meaning. It is natural that there should have been wide variations in interpretation, variations which have, on the whole, been accepted, provided they did not contradict the literal meaning.

This is why the common sense which has constantly re-asserted itself against the passions and follies of fanaticism throughout the history of Islam inclines towards the broad definition of "orthodoxy," leaving the final word with the consensus of the community. But the battle for tolerance and the broad definition has never been finally won, and this is particularly clear at the present time when for various reasons, including what may be called an "identity crisis," many Muslims have taken refuge in narrowness and literalism. Since each particular group holds to its own narrow corridor, the *umma* as a whole is troubled by bitter and unnecessary conflicts of opinion. The Muslim who writes or speaks about Islam today may expect to be accused of *kufr* (unbelief) or *bid'a* (innovation) by one group or another, not unlike the Christian who, in former times (when religion was still a matter of life or death, salvation or damnation), walked a tightrope over the abyss of "heresy." He accepts these accusations with as good a grace as he can muster, detecting in them symptoms of weakness rather than strength.

So far as "innovation" is concerned, it would in fact be very difficult to introduce any new element into Muslim thought—even supposing that one wished to do so—but it is easy to re-introduce much that has been forgotten or overlooked in the course of time. It happens often enough that, flushed with what we take for some new insight into the religion, we find that this very idea was put forward by such-and-such a Muslim thinker a thousand years ago; and this is as it should be.

While on the one hand the Western Muslim's "orthodoxy" may be questioned by the more hidebound among his co-religionists, he is likely, on the other, to be accused by non-Muslims who have had some contact with the Islamic world of "idealizing" Islam and presenting a view of the Faith which is contradicted by the perceived facts. These facts, however, relate to practice not to principles, and he is under no obligation to defend or to attempt to justify the manner in which the religion is practiced in a particular period of history by those of its adherents who catch the light and attract attention. Where human beings are concerned, good men and good women are by no means thick on the ground, but vice always pays its tribute to virtue by masquerading behind the mask of religion or—more recently—of some political ideology, and both wickedness and stupidity walk the streets more confidently when decently clothed.

It would be foolish and, to say the least, counter-productive to seek arguments to excuse divisions within the *umma*, wars between Muslim states, the brutality and hypocrisy of certain national leaders, the corrupt practices of the rich or the hysteria of zealots who have forgotten the fundamental law of Mercy and the binding obligation to make use of the gift of Intelligence. We live in an age of *fitna*. This term is usually translated as "civil commotion." An alternative translation might be "fermentation," and it is a characteristic of the process of fermentation that the scum rises to the surface.

At the same time it must be borne in mind that, despite the fairly recent division of the *umma* of Islam into nation states, Muslims still tend to identify a man in terms of the religion into which he was born rather than in terms of his nationality or racial origin. Since they find it difficult to grasp the fact that there are people in this world who do not even profess to believe in God—any God—they habitually refer to all Europeans and Americans as "Christians" (it is quite common to hear the late Adolf Hitler cited as an example of how wickedly Christians can behave). By the same token, everyone who happens to have been born into the Islamic world calls himself a "Muslim." Westerners take this designation at its face value, and shabby little tyrants who are as distant from Islam as was Hitler from Christianity are seen as "Muslims"; the religion as such is judged—or misjudged—in terms of their behavior.

Beneath the surface, however, and invisible to the casual observer, there exist a vast number of simple men and women who remain exemplary Muslims and who redeem Islam today as they did in the past, as do the mystics, whose selfless thirst for God reduces the sins of the mighty to little more than a rude irrelevance. Islam is not always discoverable in the hands or the hearts of its leaders or of its official spokesmen, but those who seek it will find it.

They will find it expressed in many different forms. The central theme of any serious study of Islam must be unity in diversity. Muhammad was an Arab and the Qur'an is quintessentially an Arabic scripture, expressed in a language which contains within its own structure an implicit view of reality. From this point of view every Muslim is in a certain sense "Arabized," but although this has created a recognizable pattern in the various textures of Islamic civilization, it has not extinguished a rich cultural diversity shaped by racial and historical differences. The principles of the religion and of the law derived from it are simple, but no limit can be set to the variety of their applications.

In what follows I hope, God willing, to show what it means to be a Muslim, and to consider doctrine, history and social life in the light of the Revelation which is the source of the Faith, as it is of the civilization and culture constructed by human beings, good and bad, wise and foolish, out of the materials crystallized from that source. But the whole, which reflects the divine Plenitude, cannot be caught in any net of words. To every statement I would gladly add a formula of great significance in the Islamic context, a formula which means that God knows best, that He alone knows, and that those who speak or write must always keep in mind their relative ignorance and the limitations of their perspective, just as the living must always keep death in mind. *Wa Allahu a'lam.*

15

Official, Popular, and Normative Religion in Islam*

Jacques Waardenburg

1. A Medieval Muslim View

In his *Kitab iqtida' al-sirat al-mustaqim mukhalafat ashab al-jahim* (Book of the Necessity of the Straight Path Against the People of Hell) (Memon 1976), Ibn Taymiyya (1263–1328 CE) combats what may be called "popular religion" among Muslims in his time. He treats such popular religion as a kind of *'id* (festival) in the widest sense of the word, at a time, in a place or with a ritual that cannot be considered lawful according to the *shari'a* (religious law). These religious celebrations consequently have no divine sanction and in his view ought to be forbidden and suppressed. Ibn Taymiyya is thinking here of *mawlid al-nabi* (the birthday of Muhammad, a feast unknown in early Islam) and of the participation by Muslims in certain parts of Christian festivities or in festivals celebrating the forces of nature (for instance in springtime with symbols of creativity, rebirth, and new life) as they exist in countries south and east of the Mediterranean. But he is also thinking of saint veneration and the veneration of the dead, where human beings take another human being as a possible intercessor with God and even as a potential granter of wishes. All these forms of popular religion are *bid'a* (innovation) introduced outside and beyond what true Islam prescribes and allows.

Ibn Taymiyya was not the first jurist-theologian who objected to popular religion in Islam, but he was one of the first who wanted to prove methodically that such forms of popular religion are incompatible with the Qur'an and the *Sunna* (religious tradition of early Islam based on the words and deeds of the Prophet) and contrary to the explicit formulations of the *shari'a* and of *kalam* (theological thinking). The jurists before him and the state authorities had never given official recognition to such manifestations of popular religion, but they had been quite lenient in practice and had looked upon their occurrence with indulgence. However, a puritanical mind like Ibn Taymiyya's, with a deep belief in Islam as the religion of *tawhid* (testifying to the perfect Unity of God), had the ability to draw out the implications of this with the utmost clarity. He judged definitively that such popular religious practices promote idolatry, that they are conducive to *shirk* (associationism, or polytheism in the widest sense of the word), and that they are thus by their very nature antithetical to religious truth as proclaimed in Islam. Popular religion should be suppressed by the state authorities, and Ibn Taymiyya demanded that they do so.[1]

Like others before him, Ibn Taymiyya explains the occurrence of such popular religion as borrowings from other religions, in particular from paganism as it existed before Islam in Arabia and elsewhere, and from Eastern Christianity with its rituals, feasts, and veneration of saints. He does not deny the existence of the forces that are venerated or feared but he defends the supreme reality of God's might and power which alone deserves to be venerated and served. He is particularly vehement in his attacks on ideas and practices that had developed in Islam in connection with the belief in the intercession of one human being for another. Such a belief shifts a person's faith from the Creator to a creature and tends to do away with the essential disparity between the Creator and the creature. In the first case, it leads generally to *shirk* and in Sufi mysticism to the doctrine of *walaya* (sainthood, saintship), and in the second case to the Sufi doctrine of *ittihad* (mystical union of humans with God).[2]

It is important to note that the jurist-theologian Ibn Taymiyya thought what he was doing in defending true Islam against human accretions was *mutatis mutandis* the same as what Muhammad had done in defending true *tawhid* against human distortions and deformations. Just as Ibn Taymiyya saw practices of religious festivals and intercession in popular religion as deformations of true *tawhid*, Muhammad had seen a number of beliefs and practices of Judaism and Christianity as deformations of true *tawhid*. From a Muslim point of view, Judaism and Christianity, like most religions other than Islam, can be considered "popular" deformations of the one true religion. There is something sacred about the unity and uniqueness of God that should be defended against such human deformations, which in their essence go back to *shirk* and *ittihad*. The problem of normative and popular religion has been formulated in the Muslim community in its own terms as a fundamental one, of a juridical and theological nature. The normative and official religion is that of true *tawhid*, and although Islam has no "official" organization of its own, throughout Islamic history this *tawhid* has been upheld by Muslim religious scholars in opposition to the popular religion with forms of *shirk*. However, what can be said about popular religion in Islam from a scholarly point of view is another question.

2. Popular Religion in Islam

2.1. Popular Forms

When Europeans visited Muslim countries up to the early twentieth century and in some cases up to World War Two, they often reported about Islam and described it as a number of customs and practices, beliefs and loyalties that would now be called "popular Islam." A basic human interest in what is visibly different from one's own society and in the exotic generally, as well as other interests, may have drawn the attention of the visitors especially toward popular forms of Islam,[3] but it is fair to say that the latter must have been much more abundant at that time than today. One may speak on the whole of a certain decline of popular Islam since the modernization of Muslim countries started, with more schooling and greater literacy, with a more rationalized way of life, and with the penetration of Western ideas. The political independence of these countries has led to a massive impact of state-supported ideologies, which are by their nature inimical to popular religion and tend to play it down as "folklore." One may think also of new waves of purification of Islam, like the earlier one of Ibn Taymiyya, which have arisen through the reformers since the end of the nineteenth century or through more fundamentalistic ideologies that are text-oriented and call for a return to the true Islam of the Qur'an and *sunna*.

We can classify the most striking forms of popular Islam in the following way:

1. celebrations of *rites de passage*;
2. celebrations of the sequence of the seasons of nature and of the weeks, months, and years;
3. communal celebrations outside the seasons that secure the coherence of the group, such as pilgrimages, tribal elections or celebrations of particular families or classes within the tribe;
4. ways in which a particular religious significance has been bestowed on individuals (Sufi *shaykh*s, *ashraf* [descendants of Muhammad], *mujtahids* [innovating scholars], and other prominent religious leaders) either during their lifetime or after their death, leading then also to saint veneration and the veneration of the dead;
5. forms of religious behavior that arise in response to unforeseen events and crises, such as natural disasters and catastrophes in the social order or in individual life;
6. specific and not officially recognized religious forms that may occur among Muslim women, in Muslim festivals (musical performances, forms of *dhikr* or "mentioning the name of God," cults with emotional religious expressions), in the institution of new Muslim feasts (like that of *mawlid al-nabi*), in certain Muslim ways of life (circumcision, the use of protective objects as amulets, forms of "magical" action);

7. ways of life and ideas in explicitly religious groups (*turuq* or mystical brotherhoods, Muslim "brotherhoods" and "societies");
8. religious customs confined to specific Muslim communities, for instance various "sects" (Kharijis and groups of Shi'is), or to Muslim communities in specific regions, especially outside the heartlands of Islam.

Although such forms of popular Islam may sometimes constitute a sort of alternative religion, in nearly all cases they have an important cultural and social structural function within the total life pattern of the societies concerned. They frequently provide a sacral structure for communal life, aid in the face of the practical problems of individual and social life, and offer possibilities for more religious natures to express and realize themselves. They are part and parcel of traditional Muslim societies.

2.2. Popular Movements

Things take on a slightly different aspect if one considers popular movements instead of forms. Throughout Islamic history, a number of movements of clearly Islamic inspiration have arisen but have had little to do with the recognized Islamic religious leadership. Although they are only remotely related to the forms of popular Islam just mentioned, they should be taken into consideration as well in any discussion of what is to be understood by popular religion in Islam. Indeed, as Dr. Kenneth Brown suggested in a letter to me, Islam itself can be called a "popular" movement at its inception.

1) First, one thinks of the various more or less popular movements that opposed the Umayyad dynasty (661–750 CE) and its governance, inasmuch as these movements were religiously motivated and touched larger sections of the Muslim population. One may think of the participants in the "great *fitna*" (discord) with Mecca as its center against Damascus (681–92 CE), the *mawali* (newly converted Muslims admitted as client members to Arab tribes) claiming equal rights with the older Arab-born Muslims, and other religious opposition groups, partly sectarian, asking for a greater stress on the role of Islam in state affairs than the Umayyads (with the exception of 'Umar II, 717–20 CE) were willing to concede. Such movements finally contributed to the downfall of the Umayyad dynasty in the 'Abbasid revolution.

2) One can think of other religiously motivated groups in the first centuries of Islam that were able to mobilize significant segments of the population for their religio-political protests and ideals: Kharijis, Shi'is of various persuasion with their popular uprisings in Baghdad, Sunni groups that could be mobilized by their leaders to oppose the Shi'is, and other dissidents in the streets. Best known among them is the Hanbali mob, which did not hesitate to march through the streets of the capital to ask for the liberation of Ahmad ibn Hanbal, who was imprisoned in the 840s because he held to his belief in the uncreated nature of the Qur'an against the official stand of

the Caliph, who propounded the createdness of the Qur'an. In such popular movements, the influence of the ordinary Qur'an reciters is noticeable, and in later eighth to tenth-century Baghdad, religious issues were very much the concern of the people and may have constituted the core of popular Muslim movements. In this context, one must also mention religious-social protest movements against 'Abbasid governance, like those of the Zanj (ninth century CE), African slaves in southern Mesopotamia who had become Muslims, of the Mazdakites (eighth century CE), and other opposition movements (like the Khurranites) in Iran, of the Qarmatians (tenth century CE) in Northeast Arabia, and others whom, although defending or appealing to Muslim ideas and practices, the ruling dynasty could consider as being close to religious nihilists.

3) One cannot help but think of the Sufis and the Sufi brotherhoods (*turuq*) that absorbed great numbers of people and instructed them religiously. In contrast to the official, normative Islam of the *'ulama'* (religious scholars, jurist-theologians), the Islam of the mystics can rightly be held to have been a lived, popular, and even "alternative" Islam.[4]

4) There were religiously motivated, more or less violent popular movements of various kinds: (a) militant religious movements proclaiming *jihad*, sometimes with Mahdist claims, for instance the eleventh-century Almohads in Morocco and later in Spain, the activities of the Shehu Usuman Dan Fodio in West Africa at the beginning of the nineteenth century, and the Mahdist movement in the Sudan at the end of that century; (b) movements of resistance, at least in the beginning stages, against Western ideological intrusion and political interference in the nineteenth and the beginning of the twentieth century; (c) Muslim brotherhoods active in a number of countries after World War Two and opposing too secular a conduct of affairs of state, especially after the achievement of independence.

5) Twentieth-century political movements like that of Pan-Islamism, the Caliphate Movement in India in the twenties, various independence movements and broader movements against the West or states like Israel or India. They refer to Islamic ideals and values, are often of a militant character, make a broad appeal to the Muslim masses, and have as such a "popular" character.

6) The peaceful expansion of Islam in South and Southeast Asia, in Africa South of the Sahara, and in East Africa, mainly through trade and Sufi preaching, had an essentially popular character and, certainly in the beginning, had little connections with the "official" circles of the leading *'ulama'*.

7) The banner of Islam could always serve as a popular symbol against adherents of other religions, in situations of tension and conflict both within and outside of Muslim territory.

A number of these popular movements were quite powerful and brought about political changes. They lacked the static character of the popular forms of Islam described in the previous section. In its movements, popular Islam has always been exceedingly dynamic, exerting a strong emotional appeal liable to bring about changes and to adapt itself to new circumstances. It has promoted the expansion of Islam and its defense against potential enemies.

2.3. Some Characteristics of Popular Islam

Both the forms and the movements just described have appealed to something in the people, which has shown itself to be deeply sensitive and very much alive. They appealed to a whole set of emotions, values, and ideals that may have remained under the surface in everyday life but that could manifest themselves in situations of stress and need, in festive celebrations, in fundamental religious rituals, and in metaphysical orientations. Such values and ideals are transmitted in the ordinary situations of life and constitute a kind of "invisible religion" of a communal nature, which is difficult for the outside observer to grasp but which can always be invoked in connection with actions and solidarities deemed to be properly "Islamic."

This popular kind of Islam may be far both from the religious Muslim scholars (*'ulama'*), and the cultural elite in general, and also from the political, especially the central state authorities. Among the people the feeling often prevails that there is too much injustice in society and state and that a properly Islamic order and way of life are lacking because of negligence on the part of the authorities. The local horizon and the disproportion between Islamic ideals and actual political and social realities may account for a certain aloofness of popular Islam from state affairs, but also for the occasional outburst of religiously motivated movements in times of crisis. This is all intimately connected with the economic situation of the groups concerned; socio-economic and human sufferings determine to a large extent what kinds of protest actions can occur, mostly with an appeal to Islamic religion or an Islamic ideology. In the former colonies, for instance, a Muslim population often tended to gather against the Western administration under the banner of Islam. This is as much a part of popular Islam as is the folklore that strikes the visitor's eye.

Popular Islam seen in this way is less static than it seems at first sight. It is responsive in various ways, mostly difficult to perceive, to external events and changes that occur in society. It contributes to shaping communal moral consciousness among the people with a constant reference to Islam and its religious and moral values. In its political manifestations, it may take violent forms at times and then be suppressed by the authorities. In its daily occurrence, however, it tends to be looked down upon by the more enlightened Muslims, modernists, religious scholars or otherwise, who see it as a kind of folk religion or as evidence of primitiveness. Popular Islam changes considerably with the growing literacy of the population and many aspects of it seem to disappear; in fact it has been most important in preliterate, traditional Muslim societies. As an expression of a communal and sometimes even collective Islamic consciousness and solidarity, however, it continues to exist in all Muslim communities.

2.4. Popular Islam within the Framework of Practiced Islam

What has been said earlier about popular Islam can be expanded now within a larger framework. First, until the moment when it is reduced to the level of folklore, popular Islam appears to be an essential part of Muslim societies and can perform various functions in social and individual life. Second, much of what is called "popular" Islam is in fact a concrete (medical, political, social, and so on) use of particular elements of the many symbols and symbolic actions that Muslims of various orientations consider as belonging to Islam. Popular Islam then comes down to a particular kind of "practiced" Islam. Interactions between official and popular Islam can be largely understood as an interaction between the more theoretical considerations of the religious scholars and the more ritual and practical activities in Muslim societies, both justifying themselves by means of Islamic religion. Third, specific psychological motivations, forms, and movements of popular Islam vary widely according to their social function and practical effects among men and women, Bedouin, peasants and townfolk, different classes, and particularly different regions with varying cultural traditions. In many cases, a functional symbiosis can be recognized between a particular kind of practice of popular Islam and the way in which official Islam is represented in a given society.

I shall now give three examples of forms of Islam that are part and parcel of practiced Islam but that cannot be called "popular" Islam as described above.

1) The development of mysticism and the place of Sufi piety in Islam place the problem of popular Islam in a wider framework. The origin of Sufism was quite "orthodox"; it started as the consistent application of religious norms contained in the Qur'an and the early *Sunna*. As it developed, it took its own course, assimilating influences from outside, and even came close to becoming a kind of "alternative" Islam alongside the normative Islam as defined by the scholars. By the end of the twelfth century CE, however, through the influence of al-Ghazali (1058–1111 CE), except for extreme mystical positions that explicitly contradicted official doctrine, it was incorporated within the mainstream of Islam, which had to be expanded accordingly. The Sufis considered themselves to represent a profounder Islam than the *'ulama'*, because they paid attention to its inner aspects, spirituality, and religious experience. In practice, Sufism gave rise to a kind of popular Islam that stresses miracles and the veneration of saints. Parallel to particular groups' acceptance of individual Sufis and their doctrines, in the social realm the religious brotherhoods or Sufi orders (*turuq*) were admitted into the mainstream of Islam and Muslim societies. These brotherhoods became intimately connected with certain geographical areas (including quarters of towns), professions, and social classes, and at certain times and places some of them had so much influence that they could almost be considered part of official Islam.

The existence of Sufism in Islamic history is also important from another point of view. Sufi writings and the history of the different *turuq* are the principal sources for our knowledge of personal religious life and experience in Islam. Indeed, Islam, as it was actually lived in the past, is difficult to discover. Most texts deal with the norms that should be adhered to and followed; the evidence about what people really believed and did is dispersed through historical, literary, and religious writings. Even if theologians like Ibn Taymiyya criticized certain abuses in their time, the precise extent to which such customs were actually practiced cannot be gauged. The influence of Sufism on everyday religious life in most places seems to have diminished significantly since the nineteenth century, whether because of the movements of return to a pure or purified Islam, the "scriptural" movement of the reformers who restored the authority of Qur'an and *Sunna* against that of the Sufi *shaykh* or the traditional *'alim*, the political use of Islam as an ideology, or the development of modernization through rationalization with its critical tendencies with regard to religion.

2) Just as Sufism is more than popular Islam, so the Shi'a cannot be simply reduced to a kind of popular Islam. In fact, the Shi'is explicitly claim to represent true Islam and deny that the Sunnis do so. From the Shi'i point of view, represented by nearly ten percent of Muslims, it is the Sunnis who represent a kind of "popular" Islam in the sense that they do not recognize the proper authorities (*Imams*) and that they lack deeper knowledge and insight. The Sufis have also leveled this last reproach against Sunni Islam, that is, that it has reduced religion to outward forms and legal distinctions, to the detriment of spirituality.

3) Another element that came to Islam after its early beginnings, but that cannot simply be regarded as popular religion although it bears traces of it, is the customary law (*'ada*) prevailing in particular in areas islamicized later. Elements of Byzantine law that prevailed in the Near East before the Arab conquest found their way into Islamic customary law. In areas that are more on the periphery, like India, Indonesia, and Africa south of the Sahara, great parts of locally valid customary law have been retained and function in a way that is complementary to the *shari'a*. In a strict sense, this could be called "popular" religious law, but since it was recognized by the local Muslim judiciary, it became "official" in the same way as parts of Sufism became "official" when they were recognized as a valid complement to the legal and doctrinal injunctions of Islam.

The acceptance of ancient Arab customs in official Islam presents a special case. On the one hand, the notion of a charismatic leader, as seems to have been alive in South Arabia, has been applied by the Shi'is to Muhammad, his son-in-law 'Ali, and the latter's descendants. The popular custom of looking at the leader in this way became an essential element of Shi'a Islam. On the other hand, one may think of the way in which Muhammad himself promoted the ancient popular Arabian ritual of the *hajj* to a prescribed ritual duty of Islam.

We can go even further. From the point of view of the history of religions, it can be argued that historical practiced Islam is largely an Arab variant of more general religious notions and practices that were current in the Near East in the sixth and seventh centuries CE, if not earlier. One can think of the idea that prophethood is needed for law-giving and founding or "restoring" a religion, or that the authority of a scripture rests on revelation. Even the concept of a universal religion and what it meant for the community of its adherents had been in the air centuries before Muhammad started his preaching.

It may be concluded that the typically "popular" forms and movements in Islam can be put within the wider framework of practiced Islam. Moreover, this practiced Islam should be seen in the wider context of practiced religion at given times and places.

3. Official Religion and its Representatives in Islam

Since there is no worldwide organized religious institution in Islam that can establish what is to be considered "official" Islam, the question arises whether we can speak here of official religion at all and, if so, what may be the criteria of calling something "official Islam" with a recognized leadership.

In medieval Islamic thought, the term "official" Islam is applied to what is religiously lawful and what, consequently, enjoys divine sanction. Its contents are held to go back to the Qur'anic text considered "revelation" and ancient *Sunna*. Phrased differently, all that goes back to something that is religiously authoritative like a revelation whose faithful transmission is authoritatively guaranteed, and that is expressed in an authoritative way, enjoys religious authority and can be called official and normative Islam. In Muslim terms, revelation is the true official and normative religion. Whenever a community fails to transmit and apply this revelation faithfully in its social and individual life, ignorance and error prevail.

Juridically speaking, official religion implies that qualified people in certain offices can perform specific activities that are religiously binding and juridically valid. For example, the *'ulama'* establish the conditions for a *jihad* and the caliph carries it out, the *mufti* gives responses (*fatwas*) to legal questions and the *qadi* administers justice. In other words, to carry out certain activities with a religious bearing, a certain office or status is required and it is through religious law that one can know what "official" status is needed in these cases and which prescriptions apply.

Theologically speaking, opinions on religious subjects, too, are officially valid only under certain conditions. Such opinions need to go back to the Qur'anic text and ancient *Sunna*, thus being connected with revelation, and be supported by the *ijma'* (consensus) of the faithful or at least of the qualified specialists. The religious opinion of a single individual can only obtain an official, that is, recognized and authoritative character if it is based on data contained within the revelation. If, however, such a person has immediate access to revelation, like a prophet, or is recognized by *ijma'* as a *muhyi al-din* (literally a "reviver of religion") or as a *mujtahid* (independent scholar) in Shi'i Islam, he is not obliged to prove this separately for each of his opinions although he can be asked to do so.

From this point of view, acts and opinions become official only under specific conditions established by religious law. The early Fatimid rulers in Tunisia in the first half of the tenth century could be seen as adhering to a "popular" Shi'i religion until the moment that the ruler was proclaimed the only legal caliph. At that moment he took on an official capacity. The Umayyad ruler in Spain obtained this capacity when he proclaimed himself "orthodox" (Sunni) caliph not long afterwards. In a similar way, customs and opinions became valid, authoritative, and "official" in the sense that they should be adopted within the Muslim community as soon as qualified *'ulama'* considered them to be "Islamic." The process of assimilating data from outside the community and giving them an Islamic label, first in the form of a *hadith* and later by a *fatwa*, is in the first place a legal validation, so that Muslims can practice them. In this way they are "officialized."

In social practice, however, there was another criterion for "official" Islam besides the theological and juridical considerations just mentioned. In fact, official Islam has been held to be that kind of Islam whose representative leaders stood close to the state authorities and supported them with a religious legitimation. This state of affairs has to do with the fact that at least Sunni Islam does not know a separate "official" spiritual institution. The caliph, for instance, was not a spiritual head of the community; he was only held to create the external conditions under which the *shari'a* could be applied. The *'ulama'* could only formulate the content of the *shari'a*, and not impose it. It was left to the believers individually—as well as to the Muslim community as a whole—to follow its injunctions. Only the Shi'is expected their *Imam*—the technical term for caliph also among Sunnis—to be the spiritual as well as political leader of the community.

The relationships between the jurist-theologians and the political state authorities and their division of tasks have been shaped through history. It was only for a few decades that the caliph, as the political head of the community, also took responsibility for the content of law and religious doctrine. This happened when al-Ma'mun (813–33), together with Mu'tazilite theologians, proclaimed the doctrine of the createdness of the Qur'an as "official" and when he instituted a *mihna* (inquisition) against this doctrine's opponents. A few decades later, the caliph al-Mutawakkil (847–61) and more traditionalist theologians revoked this doctrinal position. Subsequently, the state authority kept aloof from problems of the content of law and religious doctrine, at least in Sunni Islam. For political reasons, the sultan, on behalf of the caliph, reinforced the Sunni institutions in the second half of the eleventh century, and, in practice, brought them under state control in those areas where the caliph still ruled.

A century later, in 1171, Salah al-Din (Saladin) imposed Sunni Islam instead of the Shi'a in Egypt and Greater Syria. At that time, the educational program of the *'ulama'* in the *madrasas* had become largely standardized by "official" teaching of religious law and doctrine, and those who had finished their religious studies could be assumed to become loyal servants of the caliph or other head of state. Later, in the Ottoman Empire, the relationships between the jurist-theologians and the government officials would be carefully institutionalized and a certain equilibrium established between the sultan and the *shaykh al-islam*. The state itself was then ruled largely by non-religious *qanun* legislation promulgated by the sultan alongside the *shari'a* as the official religious law. As a religion, Islam remained more or less helpless against the interest of the state. This has increased with the creation of national states in the twentieth century.

Since the twelfth century, the predominance of Sunni Islam has been assured in Muslim states. Exceptions were Iran where Twelver Shi'i Islam has dominated since the sixteenth century, Yemen that had other kinds of Shi'i Islam, and Oman with its important Ibadi community. The Sunni *'ulama'* had to accept their dependence on the state while being aware that this situation left much to be desired for a complete implementation of the *shari'a*. The Shi'is, in general, have been more demanding toward the state authority than the Sunnis.

In conclusion, "official" Islam has become ever more conditioned by state interests. It would be unjust to say that in Sunni Islam the opinions of the leading *'ulama'* were official merely because they were close to the state authorities. The principal reason why their opinion had an "official" character in the Muslim community was their own religious learning, their upholding of the *shari'a* as an absolute norm, and the very fact that their opinions were accepted by *ijma'*. That they also had a number of interests in common with the state authorities reinforced, however, their official status and contributed to the recognition of their views and opinions as "official" Islam. The links between the jurist-theologians and the state have been severed to some extent with the rise, especially in the twentieth century, of "Muslim" states that are no longer based exclusively on *shari'a* principles and that have their own power structures. Still, a basic loyalty of the *'ulama'* to the state remains. In the "Islamic" states, which apply *shari'a* prescriptions beyond family law, the weight of the *'ulama'* is of course greater in state affairs.

We have already mentioned that individuals can be recognized as having a personal religious authority. For scholars, this is true if the *ijma'* of the community of scholars explicitly or implicitly recognizes them as such because of their learning in religious matters. It was assumed that each century had its *muhyi al-din* whose authority must be recognized. This happened, for example, to al-Ghazali. For mystics, on a spiritual level, the procedure was in a way easier. The recognition of a spiritual authority by a great number of followers, in fact the members of his Sufi *tariqa*, was sufficient to give his words and deeds an "official" authority within the *tariqa*. Saintly figures were also recognized by Muslims outside a particular *tariqa*.

To sum up, religious leaders in Islam derive their authority in religious matters not from a religious organization or an established institution, but from the knowledge they have of the data of revelation, that is to say from their religious learning, or from spiritual insight. The knowledge *'ilm* pertains to Qur'an and *Sunna*, *fiqh* and *kalam*. The spiritual insight (*ma'rifa*) pertains to one's own experience, especially in Sufi traditions. Such insight (*ma'rifa*) differs from knowledge (*'ilm*). The Shi'a recognizes moreover the spiritual authority of the descendants of the prophet (as *Imams*) and of certain recognized independent religious scholars (*mujtahids*).

4. The Concept of Normative Islam

After having discussed what is to be considered "official" religion in Islam, I would like to suggest the use of a concept that is more suitable and more applicable to the study of Islam as a religion. Since one of its characteristics is the constant search for clear norms for human life, it is often better to speak of "normative" than of "official" Islam linked to state interests. "Normative Islam" is that form of Islam through which Muslims have access to the ultimate norms that are valid for life, action, and thought. At once the polarity becomes evident between this normative Islam and the Islam that is in fact practiced.

The formal basis of normative Islam for all Muslims is what Muhammad as a prophet and leader of the community is held to have instituted as Islamic religion, especially through the revelation he brought (the Qur'an) and the example he gave in words and deeds (the ancient *Sunna*). After his death, it was only the religious scholars, and specifically the jurist-theologians, who could establish, mainly on the basis of Qur'an and *Sunna*, what duties were incumbent on Muslims. In this way, a tradition of normative Islam crystallized in the first centuries. One of the ensuing problems of later times has been to decide how rules that once were formulated as part of this normative Islam can be reinterpreted, changed, or even abrogated in accordance with the particular needs and problems of later times. In classical Muslim terms, normative Islam is the *shari'a*.

Since there is no organizational institution, normative Islam, once formulated, can be enforced only indirectly. We have seen the duties of the *'ulama'* and of the caliph in this respect. In general, the pressure of ordinary people faithful keeping to tradition, the *ahl al-sunna wa'l-jama'a*, has been instrumental in the upholding of normative Islam. Periodically, however, movements have arisen throughout the history of Islam that call for purification and reform, for going back to Qur'an and *sunna*. These movements impose strict standards of conduct as well as the elimination of new and "foreign" elements that have insinuated themselves into "original" Islam and corrupted it. Through an appeal to revealed Scripture and tradition, the whole community is then morally and socially placed under the rules of strict normative Islam. No Muslim, however, can be forced to follow the *shari'a* completely, although certain religious duties ought to be performed by everyone.

Certain factors work or have worked in favor of an implementation of this normative Islam. One of them was the Islamization of the Middle East at an early date and in an intense form; the further a region is from the heartlands of Islam, the more local customs may survive.

Another factor is the degree to which this normative Islam has been rationalized by the religious scholars and is presented and accepted as a coherent system. A particular kind of rationalization takes place today in the development of new Islamic ideologies and their presentation of Islam as a single coherent view of life and world. Rationalization is typical of Islam as a scriptural religion that lays a heavy accent on knowledge and reason. But the development of a scholastic rational system may also have indirectly favored, as a reaction, the occurrence of a less rationally-aligned, more "spiritual" or more "popular" Islam that better satisfies nonrational human needs.

A third factor promoting the influence of normative Islam is popular literacy. Throughout Islamic history and certainly in all reform movements, learning to read and write Arabic as the language of the Qur'an has been stressed and a religious school system teaching Islam has functioned from the very beginning. The importance of education in Islam is again closely connected with its having a scripture containing the basic norms that the faithful should know.

A fourth important factor is political unity. Different ethnic communities and other socio-cultural groups tend to develop their own diverging cultures that also have their own religious forms. Since unity of religion is an important factor in political stability, governments of larger Muslim countries have tried to promote in various ways a certain unity and uniformity of Islam within their countries. As a consequence, the normative Islam advanced by the religious scholars has often received support from the state authorities and became "official." In fact, different kinds of Islam are often connected with different political structures, with their own social, economic, ethnic, geographical, and historical backgrounds. A good example is the enforcement of Twelver Shi'i Islam by the Safavid dynasty in sixteenth-century Persia, as opposed to the official position of Sunni Islam in the Ottoman empire, Persia's natural enemy.

A fifth factor is geographical location. In certain cases, isolated areas such as desert regions have favored an implementation of normative Islam, not only in hope of restoring Islam as it was in Arabia at the time of the prophet and the first caliphs, but also because in such regions there were hardly any influences from outside until the mid-twentieth century. Whether the Bedouin individually have always been an example of a *shari'a*-oriented life to their fellow-Muslims is another question.

Generally speaking, in order to establish itself, normative Islam needs specific institutions like mosques, religious schools, jurisdiction with Islamic personal law, provisions to keep the ritual laws regarding food, rules of worship and fasting, and so on.

In my view, the concept of "normative" Islam is scholarly better suited to the data and structures of this religion than the concept of "official" Islam that is linked to state recognition. It can be used without prejudice for all Muslim groups that appeal to Islam as their norm for individual and social life. The concept is a formal one, and consequently can be applied to the different kinds of Sunni and Shi'a Islam as well as to Khariji, 'Alawi, and Ahmadi Islam, all searching to implement "Islam." Furthermore, all that has been said earlier about the relationship and interaction between popular and official Islam holds even more true for that between practiced and normative Islam. The search for the ultimate norms of normative Islam is incumbent not only on the religious leadership but on Muslims generally including intellectuals. Elements from outside or new elements can become part of normative Islam, but they may pass first through life practice. In Muslim societies, normative and popular practiced Islam appear to fulfill complementary functions, so that they should not be seen as completely separated from each other.

5. Conclusion

Seen in retrospect, Islam has shown a tendency, especially in its first centuries, to increase the volume of what is religiously authoritative. The same holds true for those regions in which Islamization has taken place and when; the weight of authoritative Islamic religious tradition has become ever heavier. After the first centuries of Islam, we also find a stabilization of the status and role of the religious scholars.

Not only practiced Islam but also normative Islam as it is perceived by people—what Islam is held to prescribe—is subject to changes. They may arise out of purifications in connection with a return to Qur'an and *Sunna* or to pure *tawhid*. They may also arise out of adaptations to new situations, for instance as a consequence of modernization processes that lead to new interpretations of the cultural and religious heritage. Changes in normative Islam could be due to rational thought but they have seldom come about through the direct influence of other religions. Such changes were due only to a limited extent to the influence of popular Islam, since this tended to lead a life apart from the centers of religious learning and from modern society. The increasing modernization of society, however, has influenced both practiced and normative Islam. On issues like personal status (marriage, repudiation, inheritance, and so on), however, a confrontation of "modernity" with normative Islam could well occur.

It will have become clear that, in the absence of an "official" institutional organization in Islam, the relationships between official and popular, and between practiced and normative religion become more subtle. They are closely related with the political relationships, in particular those between state and society, in each country. In the absence of an organized religious authority, in present-day states different kinds of official as well as popular Islam can be established or grow and different views can be held about what normative Islam prescribes as an absolute norm. This demands a relative tolerance that was not displayed by some Hanbali reformers like Ibn Taymiyya. It also demands a certain understanding that popular Islam must keep within its own sphere of life and not compete with official Islam as far as the general issues of the Muslim community are concerned. On the whole, modern states have increased their social and political control over expressions of popular Islam and have suppressed its extreme forms. In the event of unrest and disorder, the state authorities can intervene.

A further consequence of the fact that Islam has no institutional religious organization is that it has a somewhat amorphous character in its relations with the "outside" world, including religions that happen to have such an organization. Representatives of the latter tend to look to the guardians of official Islam, that is to say the *'ulama'*, as representative Muslims. Beyond these circles of specialists, however, the contacts between adherents of Islam and other religions actually have taken place much more in the sphere of social and cultural life and of practiced, even popular Islam.

Our main conclusion is that, until recently and still today in certain regions, Islam has been an agglomeration of very different kinds and sorts of religion. A certain unification, but also a new differentiation of them, is taking place now, due among other things to the media and means of communication and especially to present-day social movements and political developments in Muslim countries. As a result of important changes in these countries, Islam can now function in new ways not always easy for Islamicists or political scientists to understand. There is reason to assume that a century ago, official Sunni Islam was much less known and spread in Muslim societies than today. It was in fact restricted to a limited number of communities; especially outside the towns and the heartlands, many Muslim communities had in practice a kind of popular religion with only a veneer of official Islam. This situation may have been still more prevalent in former centuries. It indirectly suggests the limits of the influence of the religious scholars within the world of Islam, even if they succeeded in having normative Islam accepted as an absolute norm in all Muslim societies.

It was apparently the "fundamentalist" Hanbali reforms and the reform movements of the nineteenth and twentieth centuries that intensified and rationalized the permanent tension between normative and practiced Islam. They also rationalized the tension between the existing official, state-linked Islam and their own proposals for a reformed Islam, denying some or all of the claims of this official Islam.

Such tensions are inherent to Islam even if we concede that each expression of normative Islam is in fact a particular interpretation and application of Islam as an absolute norm. Whenever the people felt that a Muslim society was moving too far from normative Islam, a reform movement could start that claimed to be going back to the Qur'an and *sunna* and to be restoring the true original Islam, possibly with the help of arms. It would seem that the interplay between the more or less "fundamentalist" reform movements with their call "back to true Islam!," often supported by some *'ulama'*, on the one hand, and popular religion's recapturing of its lost terrain in due time with its appeal to satisfy specific religious needs, on the other hand, is one of the fundamental structures of this religion. The tension between "modernizing" initiatives adapting religious prescriptions to the demands of the time and traditional structures from the past is typical of modern times.

The tension between the absolute norms of "normative" Islam (however considered) and empirical reality appears to be a third basic structure. Against any given socio-political reality, recourse is always possible to absolute norms—such as justice—for human life and society. Seen in this light, normative Islam will endure, even if only a few Muslims actually would live up to it, because it can always be recognized as an absolute norm that puts reality under judgment.

Throughout its history, Islamic religion has shown great leniency toward the weakness of human beings in the face of both the harshness of reality and the high demands of religion. Perhaps Muslims did not experience the tension between normative and practiced Islam as a failure of their religion or a proof of human sin, but rather as an indication of human weakness. But this tension and the ensuing problems are precisely what will interest an Islamicist concerned with "official" and "popular," "practiced" and "normative" religion in Islam.

6. Appendix: A Note on the Contexts of Earlier Research on Official and Popular Islam

The distinction made in Islamic studies between official and popular Islam can be traced back in European scholarship to at least the middle of the nineteenth century. I think of Edward William Lane's account of the "popular" manners and customs of the "modern Egyptians" (1836). The interest in Islam as a religion expanded then in various ways and its scholarly study increased in scope and improved in quality through more methodical and disciplined approaches. An important factor contributing to this development of Islamic studies was that scholars had gained access to new sources, through the discovery and edition of little-known manuscripts and through more direct contacts with lived, practiced Islam. The question is whether there were reasons, apart from the nature of the available sources, why the distinction between an official and a popular Islam has been stressed so much.

6.1. Most important perhaps was the *situation of scholarly research* at the time. The study of Islam took place in various disciplines. There was the quickly developing textual research opening up an enormous literature, religious and otherwise, written by Muslims over a period of some thirteen centuries. This textual research presupposes a sound knowledge of the major languages of Islam, in the first place Arabic, to which Persian and Turkish and much later Urdu were added. Attention was of course first directed toward those texts considered to be authoritative religious documents from the first centuries of Islam, starting with the Qur'an. These texts continued to be authoritative during the whole history of Islam, and it could easily be assumed that they represented a kind of official Islam in written form, providing the norms and truths according to which the faithful should live.

Historical research was to correct this impression by showing for instance that doctrines had varied according to schools, times, and places and that not all texts were of the same importance. It was clear that the history of Islam as a religion was much more than just the history of its religious literature. Historical research on Islam is concerned with historical realities and events, including the historical and social setting of the texts, the schools that acknowledged or rejected their authority, the debates on issues held to be relevant, and the different ways in which these texts were used. Historical studies show that different groups in Islamic history had defined "official Islam" in different ways and that it was not foreseeable at the outset what would later come to be "orthodox" and what would be considered sects. Such studies could also investigate the historical developments that caused particular opinions and doctrines to be "officially" recognized as well as the contrast between official Islam as expressed in the religious texts and historical reality.

Another correction to a too literary conception of "official Islam" was made by anthropological and sociological fieldwork in given Muslim communities. Here much stress was placed on the religion as it was actually found and observed, on the norms and ideals that existed and were in fact valid among the people, and on the connections between this lived religion and the societies the people belonged to. Here another unilateral view arose, since social scientists rarely knew the authoritative texts of Islam and the historical development of its law and doctrine. They tended to stress popular Islam as they found it with all its "primitive" elements, at least as they appeared to the eyes of a Western observer, often to the exclusion of the doctrines of the official Islam which clearly were not applied as they ought to be. For anthropologists, popular Islam was then the real Islam of the people, and official Islam was considered to be the religious norms and ideals of some remote theologians and jurists.

There were other reasons, too, that could easily prejudice the proper scholarly study of Islam, including the relationship between official and popular Islam. These reasons have to do with the particular situation in which the observers and scholars stood and that led to certain tendencies of research of which the observers themselves may have been aware only on certain occasions.

6.2. The *political situation* in which scholars had to work at the time implied a strong separation of "theory" (scholarship) from "practice" (application). Scholars in the universities concentrated in their study of Islam mainly on textual and historical research; they rarely went to Muslim countries and then largely to consult manuscripts. On the other hand, scholars working on contemporary Islam and who did research in the field were mostly in direct or indirect government service; they often worked in close contact with the Western colonial administrators on site.

The study of the "practice" of Islam was not a matter of complete indifference to the Western colonizing states. In fact, such studies provided a considerable amount of factual information about the Muslim inhabitants, which could be very useful for the administration concerned, whether in Morocco, Libya, India, or Java. In much of this research there was an implicit assumption that the links between the particular Muslim country and the mother country in Europe should be continued as they existed.

Moreover, those developments in the Muslim country should be supported that were profitable or at least not harmful to the interests of the mother country. Consequently, not only the colonial administration but also the scholars connected with it mostly had a negative view of any Muslim movement that opposed the Western mother country, and indeed of all forms of Islam that implied a threat to the colonial power's rule.

So there was a definite interest in establishing an opposition between "medieval" Islam and modern civilization, in accentuating the "primitive" and "exotic" sides of Islam, and in showing the discrepancy between this "real," lived Islam and the "official," normative Islam of the books. Muslim rebellions or the Pan-Islamic movement could create nervousness among administrators and field Islamicists alike, and even Islamic self-confidence could irritate the Westerner. In quite a few descriptions, support was given to the simple people's folk religion as a factor of stability and to mystical Islam as an otherworldly and finally harmless outlook on life and reality; the more challenging demands of official Islam were then considered inapplicable norms stemming from a medieval tradition.

It was true, of course, that only a small part of the *shari'a* was applied and that the lived religion differed greatly from what the norms prescribed. Western scholars were rightly struck by these facts. Their mistake, however, was that they nearly always took the given facts and the *status quo* as the point of departure for their interpretations. They did not inquire about the deeper reasons for apparent discrepancies or about whether there were not more complex relationships between official and popular Islam than could be seen on the surface. They did not see Muslims as actors in their own right.

In fact, before World War One, it seems to have been almost impossible to imagine that there might be a living official Islam with its own dynamic and inspiration, that there might be an interaction between this normative Islam and popular, practiced Islam, and that a network of structural relationships might come about between different forms of Islam and deeper social and political aspirations that were alive in Muslim societies. Did scholars at the time not realize that it was to some extent the colonial or half-colonial situation itself that drove Islam into becoming largely an "underground" religion and that Islam's vitality was to a large extent paralyzed by this situation as well as by the rapid secular modernization process? A certain number of Islamicists specialized in Islamic and *'ada* law, which were of immediate interest for the judiciary; it has been correctly observed that there were more jurists than anthropologists studying living Islam at the time.

Only now, at a relative distance, can we see the ways in which the colonial situation and the interests of colonial administrations conditioned scholarly investigations at the time. The nearly absolute opposition found between the "theory and practice" of Islam, between normative and popular Islam, seems a case in point. Western students of Islam—to the degree that they are not politically involved in other ways—are able to view contemporary developments of Muslim societies more impartially when their governments are less immediately involved in the internal affairs of Muslim countries.

6.3. We must also take into account the religious situation in which scholars interested in Islam as a religion had to work up to the mid-twentieth century. This situation was marked by the expansion of Western Christianity through missionary efforts. People connected with the missions tended to separate Islam as a religion and faith from its social reality; otherwise a religious change or conversion from Islam to Christianity could scarcely be envisaged. The fact that in the West religion was often considered a system of norms, ideals, and spirituality existing, so to say, in itself may have contributed to regarding Islam in the same light.

Parallel to the colonial bias, there was thus a certain religious bias in the study of Islam. Moreover, Islam as a religion had a largely negative connotation in Europe at the time. In the study of Islam as a religion there was frequently an implicit rule that those aspects that looked positive from a Christian point of view should be studied attentively; the aspects that looked negative could be used as an argument against Islam and for Christianity. When possible, those religious developments were to be supported that favored missionary work or that at least would not harm Christianity. There could not but be an instinctive antipathy among Christians toward any kind of Islam that openly opposed Christianity and a kind of implicit hatred could arise against violence in the name of Islam and those forms of Islam that threatened the expansion of Christianity. In a number of cases, this meant a certain deprecation of normative Islam, whose norms were shown either of low standard or not to be applied in practice. The miseries of the people were often attributed to Islam and the "primitive" aspects of popular Islam were stressed.

Whereas the colonial situation stressed the contrast between Western culture—in this case the mother country—and Islam, the missionary situation stressed the contrast between Christianity and Islam. Both schemes implied that Islam was in a crisis, lifeless, or even at its end. The "practice" of Islam was shown not to correspond with what the "theory" or doctrine prescribed and this practice was a sad spectacle.

In a way, the failures of scholars interested in Islam as a religion were more tragic than the failures of scholars involved in their own government's interests. The latter could hardly arrive at true knowledge, because of external, mainly political, conditions, whereas the former could hardly perceive correctly what religious Muslims would be willing to tell them about their religion and faith, because of their commitment to their own religion's missionary work. In neither case could justice be done to Islam as a lived religion, and so the problem of official and popular Islam—and of what was really going on in the Muslim communities—could not be handled properly. In various ways, the political and religious situation at the time before independence made disinterested scholarly research of Muslim communities extremely difficult.

6.4. The handicaps scholarly research suffered from because of the existing political and religious situation were all the greater since no correction could be made by scholars who were Muslims themselves. There were at the time very few Muslims in a position to know the approaches of Western scholarship, to discuss and possibly contradict Western interpretations of Islam, and to be taken seriously on this score by Western scholars.

Muslim scholars of Islam were working at the time within the normative system of Islam itself. Their protests against Western interpretations were expressed in terms of another discourse than that of Western scholarship and could easily be treated by the latter as Islamic apologetics. Those Muslim scholars of Islam who had been trained in Western scholarship nearly always studied Islamic texts and history. They were hardly interested in popular, more or less "primitive" forms of Islam that were alien to the modern world and from which they probably wanted to keep aloof both as Muslims and as educated scholars.

In the situation of the time, with Western attacks on Islam, Muslim scholars could not but have a tendency to defend Islam as a norm and as an ideal, which they themselves had a vital interest in separating from practiced Islam. Because of their "defensive" situation, it was practically impossible for them to do justice to the problem of the relationship between official and popular Islam.

These and other factors may explain to some extent why previous studies, especially before World War Two, bringing together so much factual information about Islam, could make only a modest contribution to the understanding of official and popular, practical and normative Islam and their complex mutual relationships.

Notes

* This contribution is a revised version of a paper "Official and Popular Religion as a Problem in Islamic Studies," Waardenburg 1979: 340–86. Islam as a religion is here taken in the broadest sense as the religion of people who define themselves as Muslims.

1. This in fact was done by the Wahhabis, who adhered like Ibn Taymiyya to the strict Hanbali *madhhab* (juridical school). In a way, they applied a certain number of Ibn Taymiya's ideas. See chapter entitled "The Wahhabis in Eighteenth and Nineteenth Century Arabia" in Waardenburg 2002.

2. On Ibn Taymiyya's attitude to speculative and more popular Sufism, see Memon 1976: 26–46 and 46–85 respectively.

3. For the attitude of Western scholars to the opposition between official and popular Islam, and some reasons for it, see the Appendix, "A Note on the Contexts of Earlier Research on Official and Popular Islam," at the end of this article.

4. So for instance Gibb 1975: chapter on "Sufism," 86–99.

References

Gibb, Hamilton Alexander Rosskeen. 1975. *Islam: A Historical Survey*. 2nd ed. (1st ed. titled: *Mohammedanism*). London, Oxford and New York: Oxford University Press.

Lane, Edward William. 1836. *An Account of the Manners and Customs of the Modern Egyptians*. London: Charles Knight & Co.

Memon, Muhammad Umar. 1976. *Ibn Taimiya's Struggle against Popular Religion: With an Annotated Translation of his* Kitab iqtida' as-sirat al-mustaqim mukhalafat ashab al-jahim. Religion and Society 1. The Hague and Paris: Mouton.

Waardenburg, Jacques D. J. 1979. "Official and Popular Religion as a Problem in Islamic Studies." In *Official and Popular Religion: Analysis of a Theme for Religious Studies*. Religion and Society 19. Ed. Pieter Hendrik Vrijhof and Jacques D. J. Waardenburg. The Hague: Mouton.

—2002. *Islam: Historical, Social and Political Perspectives*. Berlin and New York: Walter de Gruyter.

16

The Limits of Islamic Orthodoxy

Norman Calder

I will begin by setting out what it is that I am not going to discuss in this essay.[1] The word "orthodoxy" means "right teaching"; but observing Islam, I am not in a position to judge between Sunnism and Shiʿism, to say whether one of them is orthodox and the other the non-orthodox tradition. What I think will be the case is that within the Sunni tradition, or within the Shiʿi tradition, there might be some sense in which that tradition defines for itself a set of right beliefs and does not go very far beyond them. The question I want to ask here is: what are the outside limits of "right belief" for the Sunnis?

F.M. Denny, in his *An Introduction to Islam* [New York: Macmillan, 1985], claims that "orthodoxy" is not the best term to use when characterizing Islam; it is better to use the term "orthopraxy" meaning right practice. I do not think that this is true. From the point of view of a sociologist, it may well be true that in a given Muslim society there are practices which are rejected by that society. But I do not think that the practices of any particular Muslim society will represent orthopraxy, the focus of what it is to be a Muslim. In fact, theologically, it is clear that the Sunni tradition does not allow practice, works, to be taken into consideration in the definition of a Muslim. In order to achieve salvation as a Muslim, one has to have right belief in some sense or another. If one has right belief, wrong actions are not a barrier to achieving salvation. One may go to hell for a short time, but all times are short by contrast with eternity, and all Muslims, or all Sunni Muslims, who have faith—I am not quite sure where the limits lie here—are guaranteed eventual arrival in Paradise, perhaps after a period in Hell suffering the consequences of their bad deeds. But their bad actions do not stop them from being Muslims. The Muslim jurists are careful to distinguish between those who fail, let us say, to pray five times a day—they do not cease to be Muslim—and those who deny the incumbency to pray five times a day who might be apostates. So I do not think that Islam, either in its social practice, or in its theological and intellectual traditions, is a religion of orthopraxy; it is a religion of orthodoxy. There is a right teaching somewhere which we might find inside Sunni Islam defined in a particular way, and inside Shi'i Islam defined in a different way.

One of the places we might look to discover the right teaching of Islam is to those books which are called *'aqida* or *'aqa'id* in Arabic. The word means "creed" and the books (often booklets or pamphlets or even sections within larger books of a different genre) set out the agenda of beliefs that represent being a Muslim. There is a genre of such works which have been produced by both the Sunni and the Shi'i tradition. To move away from Islam for a moment to the Roman Catholic tradition. The Roman Catholic Church has a creed, a set of beliefs, "I believe in one God, the Father," and so on, which is recited every day at the Mass. It derives from a number of Councils which were held in the fourth and fifth centuries. In the first five centuries of Christianity, there was debate about what it was you had to believe to be a Christian, and finally at, say, the Council of Chalcedon, a form of the creed was agreed on, under the authority of that Council and the Pope who convened it. Since then it has stayed exactly the same. For the last 1500 years, the same creed has been recited in the Mass day after day, week after week, century after century. The Catholics achieved that kind of focus and continuity because they have a formal hierarchy consisting of the pope, cardinals, archbishops, bishops and priests, who can be summoned together in order to make final and binding decisions about the articles of faith and the mode of their expression.

Islam, by contrast, does not have such a system of authority.

There has never been a council in Islam and there are no clearly articulated hierarchies. In fact, we cannot find a single Muslim (or Sunni) creed which is believed in by all Muslims. There are probably hundreds of Muslim creeds; certainly dozens can be found in, for example, the university library at Manchester. Each of these creeds is written by a particular jurist; so we can find the creed of al-Tahawi, the creed of Ibn Taymiyya, the creed of al-Ash'ari, and the creed of Abu Hanifa. We can look at them and ask: where is the right belief of Muslims? The answer, however, would seem to be that there is not one. There is al-Ash'ari's view about right belief, al-Tahawi's view, Ibn Taymiyya's view, and so on. Throughout Islamic history there are different creeds written out by different scholars. The significant creeds are those that emerge within a discursive tradition, through an informal, consensual acknowledgement of value that is quite different from the formal procedures of the Roman Catholic hierarchy.

The creeds that were thus produced in Islam had, of course, much in common, not least the components of the *shahada*, the belief that God is one and Muhammad is the messenger of God. But there were also more recondite beliefs—for the Sunnis, for example, that God has real attributes and the Qur'an is the uncreated word of God. These are central focuses of the creed; but how that creed is expressed varies from person to person. How high up on the agenda of faith a particular item is brought changes from time to time. Sometimes it may seem that an issue thought to be primary in one century is gradually displaced, moves towards the bottom of the list, and may fall off the list altogether. For example, the earliest Muslim creeds have a great deal to say about faith and works, whether works count towards faith. The issue was contentious, but in the end an established pattern of variation emerged. There seemed to be agreement that works count towards getting quickly to heaven (though God's mercy and the Prophet's intercession were also important), but they do not count decisively in the question of whether one can achieve salvation. For the Sunni tradition, faith alone guarantees salvation, and the limit of faith is *shirk* or polytheism. Those who avoid *shirk* will go to heaven eventually.

There remained significant and articulated differences about the definition of faith and its consequences, even within the Sunni tradition. The question, however, became unimportant and did not have to be expressed in every creed; it certainly was not expressed at all in some later creeds. But since the creeds form a tradition of literature, a continuous and authoritative tradition, the issue could always be revived, and be invested with a new significance. This is one of the patterns of flexibility that lies in the Muslim tradition; certain items on the agenda of faith move up and down the scale of importance, perhaps lose their significance, but may later recover and require re-expression, and must then be re-expressed in a manner that is not inconsistent with the decisive presence of a literary tradition.

Every Muslim agrees that God is one, but how does one express this? Ibn Sina or Avicenna, as he came to be known in medieval Europe, produced a philosophical definition of God as the necessary existent (*wajib al-wujud*), a phrase which did not immediately find acceptance in Sunni theological circles. However, through the influence of those scholars who admired the philosophers, and especially through the influence of Fakhr al-Din al-Razi (d. 1209) who was clearly fascinated by Avicenna's writing in spite of its dubious status as an articulation of right belief, the notion of God as the necessary existent became acceptable to Sunni Islam. In later creeds, even of the Sunni tradition, God is not only one but also the necessary existent.

Thus, there are patterns of development in the articulation of right belief, and there are acknowledged areas of dispute internal to the community. Both the agenda of relevant items and the way of expressing individual items may change with the passage of time. Where then precisely is orthodoxy? Does it lie in this or in that articulation of the creed, in this or in that century, in this or in that terminology?

Just to simplify things for the moment, let us say that it lies inside the discursive tradition of jurists who write creeds. As you see, I come back here to a set of ideas that I have already introduced in contrasting Islam with Roman Catholicism, that Muslims are caught up in a discursive process, an ongoing process of interpreting their own past. They seem not to—and this may be a great advantage—come down to established formulae that are going to last for 1500 years, but to provisional assessments. No matter how vehement, forceful, elegant or sophisticated the articulation of this or that scholar, no matter even how influential, it is not a final articulation. The scholars of the community, in consultation with one another and listening to one another, gradually develop, change and move—though, perhaps, not too far. There is always a core of belief which is there: the belief that God is one, Muhammad is the messenger of God, and that God, in some more or less mysterious sense, has attributes which can be named and numbered.

The question of what Muslims meant by God's attributes was always a difficult one, but it is not possible here to illustrate how the scholars expressed their understanding of this belief. Possibly even more difficult was the question of the Qur'an and its status as, in some sense, the uncreated word of God. There is some evidence that, since the late nineteenth century, the question of whether the Qur'an is the uncreated word of God has moved down the agenda, perhaps indeed dropped off it. Many Sunni Muslims today do not even know that this was an important item of their credal system. Indeed, some major writers have suggested that it is not only unimportant but quite unnecessary to claim, in any sense, that the Qur'an is the "uncreated" word of God. And yet that was one of the most important and top-ranking elements of the creed at various times in the past.

We come back then to the general point that the creed is a set of beliefs, elaborated in a discursive tradition by scholars, who are committed to and engaged with the tradition as the core of orthodoxy. But what are the limits, the outside limits, of this orthodoxy? When does one drop off the edge, as it were, and stop being a Sunni Muslim? At this point, let me relinquish the question and try a different approach. For even if we concede that the literary tradition of creeds represents the core of orthodoxy, there is something unsatisfactory about the concession. Something seems to have been left out: I mean the law. Islam, it seems obvious, is a religion of which the central theological feature is the law, and yet the creeds scarcely mention the law. It is a striking fact that many law books (both *furu'* and *usul*) contain expressions of creed, but the creeds do not contain expressions of law. There is perhaps a significant symbolism in that fact, in the context of our question about the outer limits of orthodoxy. Books of law contain expressions of the creed, but not vice versa (unless of course some formulation of the injunction to obey God and his prophets be seen as just this).

If we are looking for a definition of orthodoxy, we ought to look for one which includes at least some reference to the law. So here I will draw a line under everything I have said so far, and start again from a different angle. From a purely abstract point of view, we might be able to categorize religious belief amongst all peoples at all times in terms of a limited number of typological headings. Let me make an effort in that direction. I shall even claim, for the limited purposes of this paper, that all possible forms of religious belief can be caught under the following five headings: scripture, community, gnosis, reason, charisma.

Some people claim that the way towards knowledge of God is through scripture, that God has revealed His own being through a set of written texts which we can call scripture or "revelation." Others claim that God's self-revelation to man is not through scripture, or not primarily through scripture, but through the community, that one particular community has been chosen by God and within that community correct belief will be articulated and preserved, because that community is guarded by God and preserved from error. A third group claim that the way towards knowledge of God is through "gnosis"—I am using that word here to stand for mystic knowledge, as when a particular person, a holy man, claims that he can, through prayer, ascetic exercises or whatever, achieve direct communication with God. A fourth group claim that the way towards understanding God is by using reason, and that human reason is an adequate way to gain a complete knowledge of God. Perhaps the Islamic philosophers are an example of this point of view. Finally, there are communities which state that God has appointed, throughout the generations, one particular person to express and guard His message, claiming perhaps that this person has special charisma and knowledge of God, and that he is, in some sense, protected by God and given right belief.

Now, what I have done is set out five categories which, at least in theory, we can look upon as pure categories. Theoretically, there might be a religion which says that the only way God reveals Himself to man is, let us say, through charisma, that is, through the choice of a particular man who is the leader of the community and who will tell the community about God and their duties towards Him. But in practice, most religions are mixtures of the five categories. Religions will both have a scripture which is God's revelation and, perhaps, a theory that inside the community there will always be right belief and, perhaps combined with that, a suggestion that there will be some people in the community with direct contact with God, mystically. All the great religious traditions of the world, like Hinduism, Islam and Christianity, in fact, have all five elements in various mixtures. And the same is likely to be true, within Islam, in relation to the two great orthodox traditions of Sunnism and Shi'ism. We can, further, usually pinpoint within a large religious tradition certain movements that correspond to particular items in that five-part epistemology that I have just presented. If we ask ourselves how we have knowledge of God, the question leads, I think, to this kind of epistemological typology, and I suspect that every religion could be analysed in terms of these five epistemological categories.

Within Islam, the Twelver Shi'a and the Isma'ili Shi'a in their various forms are communities which lay stress on charisma as being, in various degrees, the highest and most important form of our achieving knowledge of God. Within Islam, there are two communities again, two sets of people, who lay great stress on reason as the means for our achieving knowledge of God. One is represented by the philosophers like al-Farabi and Avicenna. The other significant group is the Mu'tazila, a historical group who flourished in the ninth and tenth centuries, and for some centuries thereafter. They are rejected by the Sunnis because, in their view, the Mu'tazila overstress the role of reason. In an Islamic context, the term gnosis refers, of course, mainly to the Sufis.

Where do the Sunnis lie in this epistemological spectrum? The reader will perhaps already sense the direction of my argument. I wish to claim that the Sunnis lie somewhere between scripture and community, or rather that they encompass both categories. By so doing, I go slightly against the way some Western scholars present Sunni Islam. In general, they seem to present Sunni Islam as a community which relies on scripture. But I think they have not taken enough note of what actually happens when Muslims are engaged in thinking about, expressing and developing their religion, and that we have here a religion whose major understanding of God is expressed through acknowledgement of what happens inside the community, the ongoing community. In fact, I wish to claim of Sunni Islam that it is more a religion of community than of scripture.

What are the major components of Sunni Islam? This religion states that at a certain point in history, God sent a prophet called Muhammad. He was not the first prophet; there were many prophets before him: Adam, Noah, Abraham, Moses, Jesus. In fact, there were many besides that familiar list, for it is said that there were 124,000 prophets altogether. Of these, some 300 (Ibn Qutayba says 315 in his *Kitab al-ma'arif*) brought a scripture of some kind. As a result of these prophets, and in particular the Prophet Muhammad, we have scripture or revelation. Divine intervention in history, manifested in God sending prophets to diverse human communities through the ages, culminated, and in some sense ceased, with the mission of the Prophet Muhammad. As a result of his mission, the whole of humanity—for his summoning the whole of humanity was one of the distinctive qualities of Muhammad's mission—was left with two bodies of texts, the Qur'an and the *hadith*. These are, for Sunni Muslims, the content, the manifestation, of revelation. These are the texts to which Muslims appeal when they are expressing and interpreting their faith.

These texts are the residue of salvation history. I use the term "salvation history" here to indicate that part of history which is brought forward by a religious tradition as being somehow part of the definition of that religion. When young Muslims are brought up, they may be taught their local or national history at school, but as Muslims they are also taught about Adam, Noah, Abraham and all the prophets, as well as the life of Muhammad, at an appropriate level for youngsters. There are stories of the prophets for children and there are stories of the prophets for adults. These stories are the central components of salvation history for Muslims. As a result of salvation history (a history which has now come to an end because Muhammad was the last, the seal, of the prophets) we have revelation, scripture. The precise term is not important here. The reference is to a bundle of texts which constitute authority. Out of these, at least in theory, the Muslim community derives a theology and a system of law, both explained and justified by reference to the Qur'an and the *hadith*, through engagement in the exegetical process.

Some Muslims would say, with justification, that what they derive from scripture and revelation is, in fact, a way of life. And this is true in so far as the interpretation of scripture and revelation leads to the whole practical and historical experience of the Muslim community. But I want to focus here on the intellectual experience of the Muslim community and on that aspect of their faith which claims that out of revelation, that is, the Qur'an and the *hadith*, come the intellectual traditions of theology, law and exegesis. It is, in fact, possible to propose that the whole intellectual tradition of Sunni Islam can be encapsulated in a list of literary genres, these being the genres, the traditions of writing, through which the Sunni community has given expression to its understanding of its relationship to God and His Prophet. Rather schematically presented, the complete list (and I emphasize that I am referring here specifically to the Sunni community) is as follows: *qisas al-anbiya*; *sirat al-nabi*; Qur'an; *hadith*; *fiqh*; *kalam*; *tafsir* and *sharh al-hadith*.

The *qisas al-anbiya* (literally, "tales of the prophets") refers to a literary genre which offers a retelling of salvation history for Muslims. A continuation of this aim, but a different genre (different that is by the nomenclature of the literary tradition itself), is discovered in the *sirat al-nabi* literature. This offers a biography of the Prophet Muhammad. There are, of course, many different realizations of the tales of the prophets, as there are many realizations of the biography of Muhammad. Each generation rewrites these materials differently. Later generations draw upon and comment on the works of earlier generations. Each generation deals differently with the fact that some are intellectuals and some are five-year-olds. For a five-year-old, you tell the stories of the prophets and the biography of the Prophet Muhammad in a very different way from when you are dealing with people older, more educated or more intellectual.

The body of revelation in Islam is represented by the Qur'an and the *hadith*. Beyond these, and in some way exegetically linked to them, there are the great intellectual genres of *kalam* which is Islamic theology, *fiqh* which is Islamic law, *tafsir* which denotes commentaries on the Qur'an, and *sharh al-hadith* which denotes commentaries on *hadith* literature. The fact that the Muslim community produced commentaries not only on the Qur'an but also on the *hadith* is a reminder that both these sources have the status of revelation, both requiring to be interpreted in search of meaning and significance.

Now, if you go to any traditional Muslim library, and in particular to a Sunni Muslim library, I think you will find that a majority of the books in such a library, in so far as they relate directly to religion, can be accommodated under these broad generic headings. In order to make that claim absolutely certain, I would have to add a commentary on my own categories. For example, one of the problems facing the Muslim community was that of setting the limits on acceptable *hadith*. There are a great many collections of *hadith*, some of which are central and universally accepted, while others are recognized as of immense and undisputed importance, and there are still others which have a marginal status and are a focus of discussion. So, one feature of Muslim tradition is that it acknowledges an indeterminately large body of *hadith* literature. Associated with this body of literature is a method of critical assessment which, in turn, is embodied in literature. There is a range of books and types of book which offer views on how to pass judgments on *hadith*. The most important of these books are perhaps those known generically as books of *jarh wa ta'dil*, books that offer a methodology for categorizing the transmitters of *hadith*, and so permitting an assessment of the *hadiths* themselves. For the purposes of this paper, I want to bundle all the books of this type under the general heading of *sharh al-hadith*, just as I want to classify here the many different types of books that deal with the Qur'an, including specialist studies of its vocabulary, literary style, the incidence in it of abrogation, or such large studies as al-Suyuti's overview of the Qur'anic sciences (*al-Itqan fi 'ulum al-Qur'an*), as all part of *tafsir*. This is not a resource of despair—for the genres of Islamic religious literature could be more discriminately analysed and categorized—but a matter of practical convenience.

My aim in delineating these genres, and in proposing that they form the bulk of the contents of a traditional library, is to suggest that the limits of Islamic orthodoxy are expressed in this list. This is what Islam, or specifically Sunni Islam, in its broadest sense, is about. It is about everything contained in the *qisas al-anbiya*, *sirat al-nabi*, the Qur'an, *hadith*, *kalam*, *fiqh*, *tafsir* and *sharh*. Anything that is brought in under these headings and held inside the discursive tradition of Muslim literary experience belongs within the limits of Islamic orthodoxy. And these are discursive limits, for the question of what can be held inside these works is not fixed by reference to one work, or the works of one century, one school or one geographical region. The canon of literature which expresses the orthodox tradition of Sunni Islam is fairly clear in its central components—and even there such controversial and apparently irreconcilable figures as Ibn Taymiyya and Fakhr al-Din al-Razi must be held inside the tradition—but it offers almost limitless extension in the direction of minor and contested figures, who might always be drawn nearer or further from the center as time and scholarship move.

In such a large tradition, where the center is in debate and the boundaries are contested, is anything, one may wonder, excluded? Can this exploration of the limits of orthodoxy demonstrate that some particular belief or set of beliefs falls outside of those limits? Let us consider, for a while, *tafsir*. *Tafsir* is a term that designates, in one range of use, commentaries on the Qur'an. A work of *tafsir* will contain the whole text of the Qur'an, divided up into segments; the commentator will present a segment and then he will tell you what the segment means—except that he will not tell you what the segment means; he will tell you what the people before him said the segment meant. Works of *tafsir* characteristically consist of reports intimating that so and so said that this part of the Qur'an means such and such. One finds a very similar phenomenon, a similarly literary format, in works of *fiqh*. The single text is broken up by the operation on it of time and scholarship. The possibility of a single meaning is lost, the message is rendered into fragments, and all the fragments are brought into the present, because we find that a single verse of the Qur'an may have ten different scholars commenting on it with ten different views as to what it means. There will be limits, but there is a tendency, as time passes, for the meanings of the Qur'an to grow bigger. And there is also a tendency for Muslims not to comment directly. When a scholar writes a large *tafsir*, he explores the views of earlier authorities, including of course the views of the Prophet himself, the views of his Companions, the views of the next generations, until at the end, he might say "And my view is ..." or "My preferred view is ..." thus expressing preferences within the tradition rather than pinning down the meaning of the Qur'an. It almost never happens—in fact, I would go so far as to say that prior to the nineteenth century it does not happen—that a Muslim scholar sits down with the Qur'an and, using his own intellect, literary skills and imagination says "I think it means X." When such a thing did happen, the scholar in question usually became open to accusations of heresy.

One man who did this is, perhaps, the Bab, I mean Sayyid 'Ali Muhammad Shirazi (d. 1850), the founder of the Babi movement, and indirectly, of the Baha'i faith. The Bab wrote a *tafsir* of the *Surat Yusuf* (Sura 12) of the Qur'an. What he seems to have done is to express his opinion, at least in the end. There are, in his work, some vestiges of what might be called the orthodox technique, but in the end he simply used the Qur'an as a prompt to express his own religious experience. In the course of his lifetime, he was both perceived to be, and in the end claimed to be, the founder of a new religion. It was a deviation from orthodoxy, an abandonment of tradition, which is symbolized in his failure to acknowledge in his *tafsir* the experience of the community—I mean here the intellectual experience represented in generations of exegetical activity. It is perhaps odd, and it does not sound like the religion we so often hear about, and yet it is insistently the case: the intellectual tradition of Islam is one which makes it a requirement that each succeeding generation look at and take into consideration the work of the preceding generations. It is not a religion which, from generation to generation, goes back to the original words of scripture and revelation. When a scholar makes this attempt to go back to the original sources and to look at them with an unprejudiced eye (if there is such a thing), people are not sure about this and, as in the case of the Bab, he is liable to rejection.

Even when people are less radical than the Bab, they still get pushed aside. Consider the fate, for example, of those movements within Islam called the Zahiri and the Salafi. The terms can be translated, respectively, as Literalist (implying a return to the literal meanings of the revealed texts) and Primitivist (a return to the values of the early community). The terminology records the perception of the mainstream tradition in respect of these minor traditions. They were perceived to have a backward orientation, an orientation towards the verbatim words of scripture or the primitive community. The main tradition was represented by the great schools of law (Hanafi, Maliki, Shafi'i and Hanbali) and by the main theological traditions (Ash'ari and Maturidi). The Salafi thinker, Ibn Taymiyya, who lived in the thirteenth and fourteenth centuries, has had a tremendous influence on twentieth-century Islam; but he had very little influence in the centuries after his death. In the nineteenth century his thinking was revived and discovered to be a good thing, although earlier he was not regarded as a good thing.

Let me return to my assessment of the contents of a traditional Muslim library. Those who are familiar with such a library may have noticed that there is one major literary genre, one that has a significant presence in a Muslim library, that is missing. It is the genre of *tabaqat* ("generations"), biographical works, and I missed it out deliberately because, in recalling it now, it helps to make my point. One of the most productive literary genres in Islam, the *tabaqat* literature, though it has many specialist divisions, conforms basically to a single format: it chronicles the transmission of knowledge through the generations. Whether dealing with jurists, exegetes, experts in *hadith* or with all types of scholar, such works offer a diachronic realization of Islam; an assertion that the essential message is preserved, not solely within the revealed texts, but in the teaching about these texts that is transmitted from generation to generation through the ages. The genre of *tabaqat* is an essential part of the religious self-expression of Muslims, and as such it tends to confirm what I have been suggesting, that Sunni Islam is a religion in which although everything in one sense is taken back to scripture, in another sense it is ongoing. It is a religion which seems to demand of its participants that appropriate acknowledgement be granted to the community as it develops through time (and as it is represented by scholars). Every later participation in the forms of literature—and it is through established literary forms and genres that thought takes place—every later statement of faith or assessment of meaning in the Qur'an, takes into account the earlier statements worked out by the community. The epistemological categories of scripture/revelation and community are always balanced inside Sunni Islam, and always balanced, I would say, in favor of community, not scripture.

This does not quite end the problem. I have not yet, as it were, reached the limits of orthodoxy. My first step is to suggest that the limits of orthodoxy are represented by what is, or what can be contained within, the broad literary tradition that I have identified in the preceding paragraphs. But this literary tradition contains references to other literary traditions. For example, it contains references to the writings of the Mu'tazila, to the philosophers, to the Sufis, and sometimes to the Twelver and Isma'ili Shi'is. And it seems to me that we might attempt to define the limits of orthodoxy not only by saying that it is here, inside the literary tradition of the Sunni community, but also that it is there, in those aspects of the other traditions which seem to be necessary for the Sunnis to define their own position. There is a sense in which the preservation and recall of the Mu'tazili position on God's attributes constitutes the necessary ground of the Sunni position. Certainly, there are very few attempts to state the Sunni position on the divine attributes which do not explicitly recall the Mu'tazili position, making it the focus of fine distinctions which distinguish and clarify the Sunni position. The explicit acknowledgement of parallel and erroneous traditions is a part of the orthodox tradition. And the articulation of orthodoxy could not be achieved without a discursive exploration of the boundaries that separate the orthodox tradition from those traditions that are acknowledged to deviate from it.

What is at issue can be caught in the notion of "intertextuality," a term that denotes the way that texts refer to other texts. The reference to other texts can be implicit—in the sense that a novel implies the existence of a whole genre of such things—or it can be explicit. The implicit references are more interesting but also difficult to assess. What is clear and immediately useful for our present investigation is the fact that inside this body of literature, that which constitutes Sunni orthodoxy, are numerous explicit references to that other body of literature, the works of the Mu'tazila, the philosophers, the Shi'is and the Sufis. In so far as such explicit references are helpful and accommodating, then these alternative traditions are being given a place in orthodox Islam, in this context Sunni Islam. In so far as they are explicitly rejected, we are approaching a definition of the boundaries of orthodox Islam.

Now, as far as I have ever been able to ascertain, in so far as the Sunni tradition mentions anything about the Isma'ilis, it is with clear and explicit rejection. One of the clearest boundaries of Sunni Islam is that which separates it from the Isma'ili faith. It is just possible that, in the eleventh century, when al-Ghazali attacked the Ta'limiyya, as he called the Isma'ilis of his day, he was moved by his sense of the strengths of their philosophy to build up parallel strengths in his depiction of Sunnism, but there has been very little subsequent acknowledgement of the Isma'ilis. Unlike, say, the philosophers, Isma'ili writers do not become a significant part of the discursive move towards self-definition by later Sunni thinkers. It is also true that the Twelver Shi'is are not particularly referred to, and not particularly liked in general, within that body of literature. From a Sunni point of view, the basic Shi'i error, their refusal to acknowledge the historical succession to the Prophet Muhammad, is frequently acknowledged, and this is, of course, a fundamental part of the depiction of Sunni tradition. But the great tradition of Shi'i writers, whether on law, theology or philosophy, remains almost unacknowledged within the Sunni tradition. In fact, I would be tempted to say that the epistemological category of charisma, as I have defined it above, is very clearly outside the boundaries of Sunni Islam, except possibly at a popular level where it has tried to accommodate certain beliefs about the exceptional status of 'Ali b. Abi Talib, though these are in a Sunni context often assimilated to Sufism rather than Shi'ism.

The Sunni tradition of *kalam* refers to the Mu'tazila frequently and tries to derive a kind of shifting position in which certain of the views expressed by the Mu'tazila are more or less acceptable to Sunni Islam. Some scholars such as Ibn Taymiyya were extremely negative about the Mu'tazila; on the other hand, another Sunni theologian, Fakhr al-Din al-Razi, was much more accommodating. He found it necessary to cite, explain and clarify a great deal of the Mu'tazili tradition in order to assess its compatibility with the Sunni tradition. Unlike Ibn Taymiyya, he is not vehemently negative about this alternative tradition, but rather holds on to it, makes it a means whereby to discover and express the possibilities of Sunni Islam. In one other way the Mu'tazili tradition produced books that were accommodated inside Sunni Islam. A famous example is the Mu'tazili exegete, al-Zamakhshari (d. 1144). Although his *tafsir* contained Mu'tazili ideas, it contained also so much that was good, so much that was interesting to the Sunnis, that they began writing commentaries on al-Zamakhshari's work in which they took seriously what he had to say. Here then, at the boundary between Sunnism and the Mu'tazila, the line is not so clear. There is a sense in which the boundary is discursive, such that certain patterns of advance and retreat can be noted and mapped. The Mu'tazili tradition, in some way, is a part of the history of Sunnism and a permanent element in Sunni self-definition.

How about the philosophers? Al-Ghazali, famously, set out reasons why the philosophers were unacceptable to him, but in so doing established for them an important place on the defining fringes of orthodoxy. And not everyone agreed with all of al-Ghazali's strictures. Again, Fakhr al-Din al-Razi is an important figure here. Fascinated by the work and the arguments of Avicenna, he wrote a summary of the *Tanbihat wa'l-isharat*, Avicenna's last and possibly his most brilliant literary achievement. By that very fact of writing a summary, Fakhr al-Din indicated that he, a Sunni theologian, was taking on board at least some of what Avicenna had to say, and, indeed, many of the ideas and much of the terminology of Avicenna appear in Fakhr al-Din's *tafsir*. Thus, a great deal of philosophical terminology and thought crept into the Sunni tradition and became internal to that tradition. Of course, it was not absolutely internal, because other Sunni writers disliked the philosophers intensely, notably Ibn Taymiyya. So inside Sunnism we have a kind of "yes" and "no" with regard to both the philosophers and the Mu'tazila; and in that sense reason as an epistemological category has a significant place, albeit a highly qualified place, within Sunni Islam.

What about gnosis? Here, let me just say that, as far as I can see, from the twelfth century onwards, slowly but insistently, there emerges an increasing quantity of favorable reference inside that body of Sunni literature to the literature representing Sufism. Again, it is Ibn Taymiyya who represents the opposition movement. He clearly felt strongly that the Sufis, in some respects, were a danger to Sunni Islam. But that negative evaluation was matched by more positive evaluations elsewhere, above all perhaps by a general tendency in the major juristic schools to acquiesce in the religious aspirations of the Sufi tradition. By the nineteenth century, there had emerged a long tradition of references and statements which indicate that Sunni Islam, as represented by that body of literature defined above, is at ease with gnostic literature, as represented by a long, continuous tradition of specialist works, beginning with figures like Abu 'Abd Allah al-Muhasibi, Abu Nu'aym al-Isfahani, Abu Talib al-Makki, al-Qushayri and others, and finally embracing Ibn al-'Arabi, who as *al-shaykh al-akbar*, "the greatest shaykh," becomes a symbol of Sufi literature in its most sophisticated and, perhaps, its most dangerous form. In spite of this, he is, on the whole, approved of.

That last point may be illustrated very briefly by reference to a Hanafi juristic work of the nineteenth century: the *Hashiyat radd al-muhtar* of Ibn 'Abidin (d.

1842), which is a commentary on a commentary on an epitome of the law—the layered glosses of the work incidentally neatly illustrate the stress on continuity, on preserving the tradition, on acknowledging diachronic continuity, which I have already identified as an essential part of the Sunni religious experience. But here I want to note more specifically a couple of contexts in which Ibn 'Abidin makes explicit intertextual reference to works of the Sufi tradition. In a brief biographical reference to Abu Hanifa, founder of the Hanafi school of law, Ibn 'Abidin recalls the information, well-established by his time, that amongst those who followed the great *imam* in his juristic methodology were many of "the noble friends of God," including Ibrahim b. Adham, Ma'ruf al-Karkhi, Abu Yazid al-Bistami and other famous Sufis. In proceeding to make some remarks on these figures, Ibn 'Abidin mentions the works of Abu Nu'aym al-Isfahani and al-Qushayri. By citing these works, he establishes that they too belong to the constellation of authoritative sources that validly tell us about the experience of the (Sunni) Muslim community. He is telling his readers not only that some of the most important early mystics who were contemporary with Abu Hanifa learnt their law from him, but that the literature through which the Sufi tradition gives expression to its identity is acceptable to that tradition within and through which Ibn 'Abidin gives expression to his identity. Both the story (history) and the intertextual reference signal an alliance between the juristic school of Abu Hanifa and the mystic tradition as represented by even al-Bistami, who was often looked upon with suspicion because he held rather extreme mystic views. The story of Abu Hanifa's relationship with mystics was developed still further, with special reference to al-Shadhili, eponym of one of the most powerful mystic orders of the nineteenth century. And so we see that there developed a kind of narrative tradition, a set of stories, which signal the relationship between Sufism and Sunni Islam. In a different context, Ibn 'Abidin takes up the question of the acceptability of the teachings of Ibn al-'Arabi. It cannot be said that he offers an easy acquiescence in the problematic philosophy of the great mystic, but he does offer a kind of acquiescence, a modulated recognition that there is nothing essentially alien to Sunni Islam in the ideas of Ibn al-'Arabi, if correctly understood.

In conclusion, let me offer a final statement about the limits of orthodoxy in Sunni Islam. At an intellectual level, the limits of orthodoxy are represented by the contents of that set of books defined above as constitutive of a traditional Sunni library, together with such aspects of the alternative traditions (Shi'is, Mu'tazila, philosophers, Sufis, etc.) as are acknowledged in the primary set. My own, in this context necessarily broad, analysis of these books permits a kind of conclusion, namely that Sunni Islam is primarily a religion of community, scripture and gnosis, marginally of reason, and hardly at all of charisma. The primary elements are community and scripture (in that order I am sure), because they are the fundamental epistemological categories of Sunni literature. Gnosis has to be added and brought up to a primary position because, on balance, the body of Sunni literature acknowledges the religious validity of the Sufi experience, though its expression depends on a different set of literary texts. The totality of the experience available to a Sunni Muslim includes both the scholastic tradition or, if you like, the exegetical tradition represented in the former body of literature, and the mystic tradition represented in the tradition of Sufi literature.

In coming to these conclusions, I am conscious of a difficulty, namely that the situation I have described is not demonstrably true of the twentieth century. As a university teacher, teaching "religion" within a secular educational system, I am concerned not with the discovery or the evaluation of religious truth, but rather with the analysis of texts. In an academic context, it seems to me, I can say nothing about the existence or the nature of God, or the possibility of salvation. About the nature of texts and the arguments, about the beliefs and opinions that mold them, I can say at least a little. It is even possible, in this context, to formulate questions about religious experience which permit of answers that are within the sphere of academic analysis, answers that might be demonstrably true or false, or at least, more or less adequate to the situation analyzed. In this context, students come from all over the world, including all parts of the Islamic world, to participate in this exercise of academic analysis. In proposing, year on year, to read with my students either this book or that, I can choose, without difficulty, texts which are a great pleasure for me to read and a great pleasure for them to read. They are the texts which constitute the intellectual heritage of Muslims throughout the world, and for non-Muslims too they are a part of the human heritage, a part which we too can share and enjoy, even if we do not have faith. Whether Muslim students come from Saudi Arabia, Malaysia or Africa, or even Iran with its predominantly Shi'i tradition, they are happy to read any work, from any of the literary genres that constitute Sunni Islam. But should I propose to read Ibn al-'Arabi, I would certainly meet with some resistance, with some intimation that this is not central to, or even perhaps is not, a part of the Islamic tradition. That is, there is a tendency for some contemporary Muslims to reject one major part of the historical experience of their community. This—and here I take off my academic hat and, with due apology, put on a judgmental one—seems to me on the whole not a very healthy tendency. I am inclined to think that if you have a rich, complex and varied tradition, the needs of the twentieth century hardly indicate that it should be restricted; rather, that it should be accepted in all its richness. Contemporary Muslims are, as it were, offered by their tradition a massive, complex, sophisticated heritage, a generous profusion of modes of religious fulfillment, and any step towards making that heritage smaller must be a bad thing.

If we ask why there is a tendency for at least some modern Muslims to make their heritage smaller, we will I think find that it goes back to a very great man and a very important thinker, Muhammad 'Abduh (1849–1905). He wanted to reform Islam and make it relevant to the modern world, and the method he chose was a method of rejection. It had some very positive results, but one of the things he rejected was the whole mystic tradition. He claimed that much mystic lore was nonsense, *khurafat*; he called upon his followers not to listen to mystics and to get rid of them. One can perhaps understand what he meant in terms of what mystic traditions were like, or how they appeared, in the late nineteenth century, but nonetheless it is not a particularly good point of departure for Muslims today trying to find their way forward as Muslims. Muhammad 'Abduh also, in fact, initiated a novel stress in the area of scripture versus community. I am inclined to say that the reality of the Islamic (Sunni) tradition is that they combine the epistemological characteristics of scripture and community, while laying greater stress on community. Muhammad 'Abduh implied that Muslims, in order to accommodate themselves to the nineteenth and twentieth centuries, should go back to the beginning. The products of the great intellectual tradition were not to his mind so very wonderful; for him, much of what these jurists and theologians had produced was of little value; they could be safely and wisely discarded. The community should go back and start all over again with the Qur'an. The relevant juristic hero for Muhammad 'Abduh was not Abu Hanifa, Malik, Shafi'i or even Ibn Hanbal, great figures though they all were; it was Ibn Taymiyya. And his usefulness was that he offered a scourge for the intellectual tradition and a banner for revivalism; he represented, par excellence, the Salafi (Primitivist) tendency in Islam.

Now, perhaps Muhammad 'Abduh was right; perhaps this was a necessary way forward, a retreat the better to advance. But on the whole, I would be inclined to say that, at that point of transition, Islam started to become a smaller tradition; and that, in some respects, sadly, Muhammad 'Abduh is the cause of a smaller, more limited Islam than that which was on offer before, and which remains on offer inside not simply the Sunni scholastic (exegetical) tradition, but also inside those other traditions which the Sunni tradition hauls in its wake—the precious baggage, the inescapable burden, of experience.

Note

1. Some of the ideas discussed in this paper have been more formally developed in Calder 1997.

Reference

Calder, Norman. 1997. "History and Nostalgia: Reflections on John Wansbrough's *The Sectarian Milieu." Method and Theory in the Study of Religion* 9: 47–73.

17

Defining Islam in the Throes of Modernity

Abdulkader I. Tayob

The twentieth century has witnessed tremendous change in how religious traditions like Islam cohere. The issue has been important for those who wish to define and understand Muslims, and also for Muslims themselves, who wish to live by the teachings of their religion in a modern world. For the former, the challenge lies in presenting a precise and succinct picture of a complex human phenomenon; sometimes, they may even dare to predict future trends. For insiders, the major transformation of the twentieth century demands a reorientation and rejuvenation of ideals and principles. This essay argues that, in spite of postmodern criticism, the search for a key Islamic category continues unabated. With all its imperfections, Islam affords both observers and insiders an opportunity to search for a core interpretative category or truth. Islam remains a coherent social category insofar as it represents a search for meaning and value in a changing world.

Is the Category of Islam Coherent?

Many objections have been raised against the glib and disingenuous use of Islam as a generalized category. Some suggest that one cannot even speak of historical entities that are wholly or predominantly determined by Islam. Islamic leaders, communities, cities, and symbols are merely conceptual categories that unduly privilege the cultural and religious over the social and political. As concepts, they reside properly in the minds of their producers but obscure the nature of historical and social realities. Since the notion of the Islamic city has received considerable attention from Weberian scholars, it provides a useful illustration of this level of criticism. Weberian scholars have tried to form an understanding of the Islamic city in comparison with and as distinct from the European city. As the social foundation of capitalism, industrialization, and modernity, the city has become a compelling category in understanding social formation and development. The judgment, generally, has been that, compared with the European city, the Middle Eastern entity may not be called a city. Bryan Turner, the Weberian interpreter of Islam par excellence, characterized the Islamic city as "aggregates of sub-communities rather than socially unified communities" (Turner 1974, 99). Aside from the negative view evidenced in this statement, the debate about the Islamic city has also produced some interesting ways of understanding the unique "social aggregates" in Islamic civilization. Noticing the non-European character of Cairo, Baghdad, and Damascus, scholars of Islam have talked about the unique nature of Islamic cities. Ira M. Lapidus, for example, has produced extensive surveys of the great metropoles of the Islamic Near East, and has shown how the *'ulama'* prevented them from disintegrating. The cohesiveness of the Islamic city was not dependent on institutions but on "patterns of social activity and organization which served to create a more broadly based community, and this community was built around the religious elites" (Lapidus 1967, 107). Concurring with this view, Muddathir Abdel-Rahim, from among Muslim scholars, has suggested that the *shari'a*, the most prominent activity engaged in by the scholars, acted as a determining social institution for the form of the city (Abdel-Rahim 1980).

More recently, postmodernists have challenged the fundamental assumptions of the search for the elusive Islamic city. In general, they regard with suspicion and skepticism attempts to define a social aggregate by its cultural and religious identity. Islam, in their view, was not a "monolithic force" that shaped manners and customs, much less the nature of a complex city (van Leeuwen 1995, 154–5). Rejecting the perceptive observations of Lapidus, van Leeuwen regards any city to be consisting of "the various statuses of space, the regimentation of space within urban environments, the influence of social relations on spatial organisation, the role of spatial structures in the exertion of power, or the focuses of intertwining networks in spatial organisation." The special case of cities occupied by Muslim peoples are but a measure of the "integration of several urban centres within one system which determines their type, and in this process cultural factors are only one of many causes," with the possibility of "differences and divergent developments" (van Leeuwen 1995, 158). Clearly, from this perspective, it makes no sense to speak of an Islamic city with religion as its most distinctive feature. The religiocultural aspect of social forms is only one of several features, and cannot be used as a point of identification. Calling something an Islamic city, Islamic bank, or Islamic science implies that Islam is its major determining factor. In reality, according to the postmodern critique, such naming only hides and obscures other characteristics like ethnicity, ideology, and historical circumstances that equally determine social formation.

In my view, such a critical deconstructivist approach to social forms is extremely one-sided. While it clearly shows how social scientists and historians impose categories on the subject matter at hand, it fails to consider how the actors themselves work with such symbols. In some postmodernist discourse, therefore, the Islamicity of social forms and actors is completely erased. While the modernist formulation, in its search for a unique European city, presents Islam as the extreme other, postmodernist discourse fails to acknowledge the way in which indigenous actors create and contribute to the symbolic formation of society. No matter how elusive its character, the Islamic city—much like the Islamic leader, ritual, or court—is one of those compelling symbolic categories by which Muslims create history. The task of the social scientist is to locate these symbols in their broader social context, not to dissolve them, for this would be tantamount to denying social agency. The frustration of Weberian expectations leads to the dissolution of all social agency, and to the resultant neglect of how indigenous actors contribute, positively or negatively, to the creation of social entities. When we consider the example of the Islamic city, for example, we note how Muslim jurists, in their attempt to define Friday worship, debated the meaning of social units. Friday worship was only required when a sufficiently large community was settled in a particular area. This is not to say that power relations between religious and political leaders had no impact on their jurisprudence. Postmodernist discourse would, however, deny the reality of powerful cultural and—in this case, religious—influences.

A second criticism of the generalization and undue universalization of the category of Islam comes from those who would rather speak of *islam*s rather than *Islam*. In their view, the normative definition of Islam within social formations should be the responsibility of theologians, who set the limits of orthodoxy and orthopraxy. Historians and social theorists have no business to determine what individual or group is pure, syncretistic, hybrid, or sectarian. The social scientist that recognizes and acknowledges a true and pure center in comparison with an impure periphery denies the plurality of meanings. When he or she privileges the central and original as orthodox and the peripheral and subsequent as heterodox, he or she takes a role no different from the theologian's. The social scientist must give up this bias toward orthodoxy and reveal the subject as one of many possibilities. "There are as many *Islams* as there are situations that sustain it," declares Aziz al-Azmeh in an apt formulation of this position (1993, 1). At one level, this criticism of Islamic determinism is not too different from the postmodernist critique of Van der Leeuwen. In his book, *Islams and Modernities*, al-Azmeh argues that Islamic cultures must be deconstructed, that critical reflection must "contextualize [them] into the flow of historical and social forces, and thus deculturalize and demystify them." And yet al-Azmeh speaks of *islam* as the identity of a particular type of law, for example. While criticizing the tendency in Western media and academia to portray Islam as a monolithic phenomenon, he does not completely debunk the notion of unique Islamic realities: "Muslim reality in Britain is, rather, composed of many realities, some structural, some organisational and institutional, but which are overall highly fragmentary" (al-Azmeh 1993, 4). In spite of his deconstructivist approach, al-Azmeh can still discern social formations that can be called *islamic*. He does not question the continued use and meaning of *islam*, even in the plural, and fails to spell out clearly what justifies his use of *islam* as such. While he talks of the unacceptability of the use of *Islam*, he does not convincingly provide a justification for the use of *islam(s)*.

If the *Islamicity* of social forms remains imprisoned in the mirror of Western categories, it would be better to drop it altogether. Such "imprisonment" is characteristic of some of the Western approaches to Islam, which, one might add, have gained popularity among Muslims as well. The scramble for Islamic science, social sciences, and banks is partly due to the inherently reactionary nature of such Muslim approaches. On the other hand, the term *Islamicity* itself cannot be so easily discarded, as is assumed in some radical postmodernist discourse. In the rest of the paper, I would argue that the use of the term Islam(ic) is helpful in understanding certain societies and their institutions, and, more important, in understanding the redefinition of a religion by its followers in a changing world. Attempting to understand societies and their institutions is bit hazardous since social scientists run the risk of subsuming a social reality to its cultural or religious root. This subsumption, however, is unavoidable if one is trying to understand a society, community, or group in its cultural or religious dimension. But in trying to understand a group's redefinition of its religion, there is no alternative to the use of the category of *Islam* by Muslims. Combining these two senses of *Islam*, I will try to show the validity of the search for meaning by Muslims and social scientists.

In Search of Modern Islam

As one surveys the discourse on Islam in the second half of the twentieth century, the presence of the terms *Islam* and *islam(s)* in it cannot be overlooked. Cultural categories and symbols are deeply ingrained in both society and academia. Islamic symbols have refused to disappear from Muslim homes, places of worship, and personal lives in the age of modernity or postmodernity. Muslim intellectuals like Fazlur Rahman, Isma'il R. al Faruqi and Seyyed Hossein Nasr have tried to make sense of the social and philosophical challenges of modernity. On the other hand, social scientists and historians such as Clifford Geertz, Dale E. Eickelman, and Muhammad Asad have suggested critical indices for understanding the meaning of modern Islam. Both the insiders and the outsiders grapple with the same phenomenon—the presence of religious symbols in a multitude of social contexts of the modern world. This essay examines well-known definitions of Islam in the context of social change. Rahman, al Faruqi, Nasr, and Mohammed Arkoun are prominent Muslim intellectuals who have given expression to their understanding of Islam during the second half of the twentieth century. This essay situates their attempts in light of Ernest Gellner's and Armando Salvatore's analyses of the meaning of Islam in the modern world.

In the 1960s and 1970s, most scholars thought that the end of religion in general and Islam in particular was inevitable. Under the advance of science and secularization, it was thought that religious traditions like Islam were bound to become either personal-faith orientations or totally irrelevant. But Gellner's close analysis of Muslim social organization and his perception of diversity within Islam led him to a different conclusion. In his collection of essays, *Muslim Society*, he went so far as to say that Islam "alone may maintain its pre-industrial faith in the modern world" (Gellner 1981, 4). He suggested that precisely because of modernity and secularization, the Islam of the literate and urban classes would prosper against the decline of the Islam dominated by holy lineage and its privileges. The hierarchical organization of society based on nearness to the Prophet and saints was unable to resist the egalitarian force of urban Islam. According to Gellner, the Islam of the urban and literate classes, after having remained for centuries at the mercy of autocratic rulers and puritanical Bedouins, would finally triumph.

Taking into consideration the social organization of cities and tribes, and the forms of Islamic life, Gellner proposed a model to explain how "ecology, social organization, and ideology interlock in one highly distinctive civilization." The model "explains *how* their distinctive fusion produced its stabilities and tensions, and continues to influence the various paths along which it is finally entering the modern world" (Gellner 1981, 85; author's emphasis). Gellner's thesis was built on the work of Ibn Khaldun as well as modern sociologists like Max Weber and Talcott Parsons. He drew a sharp distinction between Islam in urban centers and Islam in rural areas. The Islam of the city is literate, trade-dependent, egalitarian, and sober; tribal Islam is based on widespread illiteracy and has a pastoralist lifestyle and a hierarchical understanding of reality (Gellner 1981, 99–100). In Ibn Khaldun's understanding of social organization, the vigor and puritanism of the peripheral rural Islam forces itself onto towns and cities, which are suffering from degeneration in the forms of political weakness and moral decay. The purity of tribal organization, as also the cohesion and moral rectitude of that organization, invigorates urban life. For Gellner, the advent of modernity ushered in a "continuation and completion of an old dialogue between orthodox center and deviant error, of the old struggle between knowledge and ignorance, political order and anarchy" (Gellner 1981, 4). Now, however, the towns were able to centralize more efficiently, and were thus able to stem the tide against tribal Islam and prevent its periodic domination. Furthermore, the legal, rational Islam of urban societies was compatible with modernity and modernization, as contrasted with the mystical and superstitious character and hierarchical organization of rural Islam. According to Gellner, Ibn Khaldun's cyclical view of Islamic history was arrested by modernity. With the rise of literacy, scientific endeavor, and effective transportation, modernization favored urban Islam, giving it a sense of supremacy and moral privilege it had never enjoyed before.

Taking into consideration the complexity of Sufi organizations, *'ulama'* guilds, and political authorities, Gellner showed how Islam and its various interpretations played a vital role in maintaining the social equilibrium. Gellner has been criticized for emphasizing the difference and separation between the urban and the rural (Cornell 1998). As Vincent J. Cornell points out, the forms of Islam in town and rural contexts were more interdependent than Gellner seems to suggest. This means that the debate within Islam will not simply be a battle between town and country, and that knowledge of the social location of Islam is not sufficient for purposes of understanding contemporary change. Conspicuously missing in Gellner's interpretation was the manner in which Muslims were responding to the new political realities of the modern state and to postcolonialism. Gellner was right about the resilience of the Islamic symbols, but mistaken with regard to the triumph of a reformed urban Islam that was compatible with modernity. While urban Muslims have, by and large, adapted to modern life, some of them have become extremely sectarian in their approach. The latter have not emerged from the rural areas, as happened previously, but from the urban centers characterized by widespread unemployment, overcrowded slumps, and a disaffected middle class. The political contest in postcolonial Islam, therefore, is not between a mystical, illiterate, and rural *islam* and an urban *islam* with opposite characteristics, but between competing interpretations of urban *islam*. The insightful comments of Gellner call for another look at the specific details, and particularly at what the religious symbols signify in contemporary Muslim society.

A more recent attempt to understand Islam in the modern political process has been undertaken by Armando Salvatore in his search for modernization in a multicultural world. Even though both Gellner and Salvatore recognize the resilience of Islam in the modern world, Salvatore's conclusions are completely different from those of Gellner. In *Islam and the Political Discourse of Modernity*, Salvatore analyzes the meaning of Islam in the public and political discourse of Arab societies. He traces the development of this Arab discourse to the nineteenth century, when scholars first came into direct contact with Europe and began to address the question of the meaning of Islam. He follows this trajectory to the end of the twentieth century, viewing it as a series of hermeneutic circles of public discourse that problematized the meaning of Islam. The circles include nineteenth-century reformists and twentieth-century Islamists (like Yusuf Qaradawi), and also take into account contemporary debates about the relevance of the Islamic heritage for Arab public life. In discussing each of these circles, Salvatore reveals how, at the level of public discourse, scholars were grappling with issues of social and political concerns using the language of religion. Running concurrently with these circles of Arab discourse were, according to Salvatore, Western circles of discourse which tried to make sense of the Arab world. The primary focus of Salvatore's work does not lie in the detailed, substantive arguments for the viability of Islam in the political process. Amidst this welter of debate, he discovers the formulation of a modern political subjectivity:

It is my claim, however, that the measure of the political, and its consecration as an autonomous hermeneutic factor within the interpretive field of political Islam, is not primarily established by an objective assessment of which political acts are performed in the name of Islam in Muslim societies, but by the way it provides a contrastive image for a redefinition of Western political subjectivity in times of crisis. (Salvatore 1997, 143)

Without going into finer details of modern Islam, Salvatore identifies a level of subjectivity in the discourse that, he says, affords a critical insight into the role of Islam in public life. He believes that such a level of subjectivity implies the presence of an alternative trajectory of modernization to that of the West. His analysis focuses on the emergence of the subjective self that Charles Taylor, among others, identifies as the principal distinction of European modernization (Taylor 1989). Using such a category, Salvatore's analysis breaks through the sensationalized media accounts of medieval barbarism and tradition usually associated with Islam, evaluating the discourse of Arab Islam as public discourse. Unlike Gellner, moreover, he provides a deeper sense of how modern Muslims are making sense of their history. Salvatore's analysis of Islam in public life clearly recognizes the potential of religious discourse in producing modernization. A comparison may be ventured. Gellner discussed the trajectory of modern Islamic developments from the perspective of secularization theory, which regards modernization as a systematic process of disenchantment. Thus, according to Gellner, the urban institutions of Islam seemed most compatible with modernity. Salvatore, on the other hand, regards the distinctive trait of modernization to be the emergence of subjectivity. In his approach, therefore, the discourse of Islamization was the product of a shared hermeneutic space and manifested a unique subjectivity in modern Islam.

It seems to me that there are two major criticisms that can be made of Salvatore's analysis. First, the absence of popular Islamic discourse in his analysis leaves us with a partial view of the meaning of Islam among the highly literate, elite section of Arab society. The works of Arkoun, Abu Zayd, Hasan Hanafi and Jabiri treated by Salvatore are of great signification in public discourse. The substantive arguments of Islam in historical, literary, and hermeneutic perspectives may reveal the level of subjectivity in the debate. Modern Islamic public discourse, however, goes beyond the subjectivity displayed by these hermeneutic circles. The shift from public discourse to the religiopolitical discourse of apostasy—a shift that took place in the case of Abu Zayd, for example—seems to remain unaccounted for in Salvatore's analysis. The public discourse of Islam and the Islamic heritage could easily degenerate into a politicization and abuse of religion. And the meaning of Islam in public life is to be found equally in the political hermeneutic of Islam, as well as in the slogans of street politics.

The second criticism against Salvatore's approach concerns the pitfalls he wants to avoid: the details of modern Islam, which is so often caricatured in popular conceptions of Islam. Gellner's analysis provides a social theory for the dominance of urban

Islam, while Salvatore's study puts the focus on the emergence of a political process within urban Islam. Salvatore clearly identifies the content of what Gellner expected of urban Islam. What is not so clear, however, is whether such an interpretation of Islam would be compatible with modern, global expectations. In particular, would it be acceptable in a global, pluralist world if Muslims, or any other religious or cultural group, decided that it has a unique understanding of human rights, ecological management, and the like? It seems that such specific details cannot be left out in the attempt to understand Islam in the modern world. In order to answer such questions, we need to go one step further and look at the specific meaning of Islam espoused by Muslims. This examination will complement the analysis of Gellner and Salvatore, who seem to focus, respectively, on the broad social parameters of modern Islam and on modern Islamic discourse. I would like to focus, in light of the social parameters outlined by Gellner and Salvatore, on the modernized discourse of Muslim intellectuals.

Modern Islam

Intense debate and dissension characterize modern Islamic writings. Muslims agree on certain fundamental beliefs, but disagree on the forms of worship, the ways of understanding the Qur'an, and the paths to religious and social reconstruction. Theoretically, a comparison could begin anywhere—with the Islamic approaches to gender, political liberalism, socialism, or civil liberties. Such comparisons have been made with varying degrees of success. I would suggest, however, that we ought to begin by asking how Muslims themselves understand Islam. In addition to Salvatore, Wilfrid Cantwell Smith and Dale Eickelman and James Piscatori have pointed out reification of Islam as a substantive category in Muslim discourse (Eickelman and Piscatori 1996; Smith 1978). It would be a useful exercise to conduct a survey of how key Muslim intellectuals have defined Islam in recent years. Such a survey is likely to confirm the general conclusions of Gellner and Salvatore in unexpected ways, and also point to ways in which we can continue the debate on the nature of modern Islam.

The books and articles of Fazlur Rahman do not deal with the question of Islam as a descriptive or interpretive category. However, it is clear from his writings, one of which is a book entitled *Islam*, that he sees no problem with the hermeneutic complexities of defining Islam. In his *Islam and Modernity*, Rahman tackles the issue of the hermeneutic of reading by briefly considering the views of the German philosopher Gadamer. Gadamer's approach to reading, history, and literature is marked by the importance he assigns to the role of the reader and her context, and may be regarded as the forerunner of the deconstructivist and postmodern approaches to philosophy and religion. Rahman rejects Gadamer as hopelessly subjective, and opts for the possibility of reconstructing the past on the basis of the mind's ability to apprehend reality, including the present and the past (Rahman 1982, 8–9). Rahman seems to have been guided by his study of Islamic philosophy, wherein he investigated the meaning of the intellect and its relation to prophecy (Rahman 1958). Since the intellect was believed to be engaged with abstract entities, which included perceptions both of the past and of the present, the identity of the past and the present was readily assumed. Rahman's idealist position offers him a justification for assuming a fundamental essence of Islam, traced from the beginning to the present.

But Rahman is clearly not interested in history for itself. His hermeneutic is "concerned with an understanding of [Islam's] message that will enable those who have faith in it and want to live by its guidance—in both their individual and collective lives—to do so coherently and meaningfully" (Rahman 1982, 4). Rahman is acutely aware of historical change, and rejects the wholesale duplication of early Islamic social forms in the modern worlds. Thus, as early as 1965, he argued in *Islamic Methodology in History* that the social forms of early Islam were "absolutely irrepeatable" since the earliest Muslims also approached the Qur'an and the *sunna* in a creative manner:

> if we are able to live as progressive Muslims at all, viz., just as those generations met their own situation adequately by freely interpreting the Qur'an and Sunnah of the Prophet—by emphasizing the ideal and the principles and re-embodying them in a fresh texture of their own contemporary history—we must perform the same feat ourselves, with our own effort, for our own contemporary history. (Rahman 1965, 178)

Rahman was careful to exclude religious obligations, but believed quite passionately that it was the responsibility of Muslim scholars to search for the principles and values that lay at the heart of Islamic teachings. For Rahman, the key elements of the "original experience of Muhammad" were the absolute belief in one God and the Last Day, and the implementation of socioeconomic justice. These basic elements led to moral action in the world (Rahman 1982, 13–14). The "properly moral" was the fundamental basis of Islam—it was that special quality that corresponded to faith in an extrahistorical and transcendental being (Rahman 1982, 5). It is not surprising, therefore, that Rahman identified the root problem of modernity to be its secularism, which "destroyed the sanctity and universality [transcendence] of all moral values" (Rahman 1982, 15). Moral action, as opposed to secularism, enabled Muslims to transform the world and human society to reflect the values of justice and equity. Rahman rejected the notion that Islam was a remnant of the past. The principles and values of Islam offered hope for modern life.

We now turn to an activist scholar who sought to present Islam as a viable civilizational foundation for Muslims in the modern world. Isma'il Raji al Faruqi seemed at times to reject, but at times to endorse, the modernity of the West. His work on Islam includes an essay on Islam (1974) as a contribution to a volume on world religions, an introduction to *Islam* (1979), and a comprehensive work entitled *The Cultural Atlas of Islam* (1986); the last-mentioned book was coauthored with his wife shortly before their brutal, untimely death. In some respects, al Faruqi came close to endorsing the results of Rahman. Speaking of Islamic law, he said:

> The revelation acknowledged, further, that the law is susceptible to change in time and place, conditioned as it must be by the status quo of the addressees. The needs of various societies must determine the nature of the laws they may be expected to observe. The principles of the law and its ends, on the other hand, stand above change and must remain the same throughout creation, since they represent the ultimate purposes of the Creator. (Al Faruqi and al Faruqi 1986, 108)

Like Rahman, al Faruqi stressed the underlying principles of Islam. But while Rahman focused on the combination of religious and socio-political principles of revelation, al Faruqi's principles were more theological and philosophical. Al Faruqi was certainly not opposed to social justice, but social justice did not take center stage in his thought. The essence of Islam, according to al Faruqi, is *tawhid*, affirmation of the oneness of God. This affirmation is not simply a belief in the numeral unity of God, but encompasses "a general view of reality, of truth, of the world, of space and time, of human history" (Al Faruqi and al Faruqi 1986, 74). Since *tawhid* is the essence of Islam, the principles of *tawhid* are the duality of God and creation; the ability of humankind to understand reality; the basic teleology of reality; the malleability of nature for humankind; and the accountability of humankind.

From a philosophical point of view, al Faruqi's vision of Islam was far from traditional. In his elaboration of the duality of reality, al Faruqi echoes the sentiment of many an Enlightenment rationalist:

> Through *tawhid*, therefore, nature was separated from the gods and spirits of primitive religion. *Tawhid* for the first time made it possible for the religio-mythopoeic mind to outgrow itself, for the sciences of nature and civilization to develop with the blessing of a religious worldview that renounced once and for all any association of the sacred with nature. *Tawhid* is the opposite of superstition or myth, the enemies of natural science and civilization. (Al Faruqi and al Faruqi 1986, 80)

Here one can clearly see how al Faruqi restated the meaning of Islam for the twentieth century. From a theological point of view, al Faruqi's view of Islam eliminated the magical and mythical dimensions of the religion, and produced a rationalized theology. A word at this point about what al Faruqi saw as the major problem with the modernity of the West. Though he had no problem with Enlightenment rationalism, al Faruqi never tired of pointing to the West's tendency to assign ultimate value to nature and human passion. Cut off from transcendentalism, nature and human passion become the measure of all value:

> Modern western man has little tolerance for any deity as far as metaphysics is concerned. But as far as ethics and conduct are concerned, the "gods" that he

creates out of his idealization of human passions and tendencies are the real determinants of his action. (Al Faruqi and al Faruqi 1986, 86)

Al Faruqi saw major problems with nineteenth-century romanticism and historicism that would destroy the value of knowledge as truth, replacing it with subjectivism and relativism. In this regard, there is a striking affinity between him and recent critics of postmodernism. For al Faruqi, the human subject viewed as the measure of all truth is the root of all problems. Only the principles of *tawhid* affirm the capacity and ability of humankind: "The humanism of *tawhid* alone is genuine. It alone respects man as man and creature, without either deification or vilification. It alone defines the worth of man in terms of his virtues, and begins its assessment of him with a positive mark for the innate endowment God has given all men in preparation for their noble task" (al Faruqi and al Faruqi 1986, 82).

Another prominent Muslim intellectual who has written extensively about Islam in the second half of the twentieth century is Seyyed Hossein Nasr. Unlike Rahman and al Faruqi, Nasr completely rejects modernity and modernization, including the rational foundation of the Enlightenment. He reasserts the relevance of the philosophical and intellectual tradition of premodern Islam. Discussing contemporary art, Nasr attacks its propensity to see "the origin of the inward in the outward." Contemporary art "reduces sacred art with its interiorizing power to simply external, social and, in the Marxist historians, economic conditions" (Nasr 1990, 4). What is true of art is also true of modern philosophy, not to speak of the social sciences and humanities. This characterization of modernity is, to a degree, similar to al Faruqi's analysis of modernity. Nasr, however, rejects Enlightenment rationalism, which both al Faruqi and Rahman accept to a certain extent. For Nasr, the human-centered rationality of the Enlightenment is equally problematic from an Islamic perspective. He does not see the utility of the Enlightenment's practical reason and moral option that both Rahman and al Faruqi endorsed.

It seems that the search for purity and ultimacy within religion has produced various results. Like Rahman and al Faruqi, Nasr also searches for some underlying core of the tradition. For Nasr, the essence of Islam lies in its mystical dimension. Islam is the "direct call of the Absolute to man inviting him to cease his wandering in the labyrinth of the relative and to return to the Absolute and the One; it appeals to what is most permanent and immutable in man" (Nasr 1991, 148). The true purpose of Islam is not establishment of social justice (Rahman), nor establishment of Islam as a civilization (al Faruqi), but recovery of a person's true, inner, primordial nature. Nasr goes further and evaluates this inner dimension in relation to other religious traditions. Accordingly, absolute Truth is inherent in all religious traditions. Like all other religions, Islam contains both an absolute and a relative dimension. According to Nasr, Islam "contains within itself the Truth and means of attaining the Truth," but, as a historical religion, it "emphasizes a particular aspect of the Truth in conformity with the spiritual and psychological needs of the humanity for whom it is destined and to whom it is addressed" (Nasr 1994 [1966], 15). Each religious tradition "emphasizes a certain aspect of this relationship, while inwardly it contains the Truth as such in its teachings whatever the outward limitations of its forms might be" (Nasr 1994 [1966], 16). The relative dimension of religions does not pertain to practices within the religious tradition. Practices that may have been endorsed in the second century of Islam do not necessarily have to change in the twentieth century, as Rahman and al Faruqi would argue. Prayer would take different forms in Christianity and Islam, but the variations within Islam do not draw the attention of Nasr.

Within each religious tradition, Nasr insists on the efficacy of the forms of religious life as vehicles, or ultimate symbols, through which the absolute may be found and realized. The Qur'an, the *shari'a*, and practical conduct of the Prophet are all authentic means, or pure symbols, that enable one to reach inwardness. In his pursuit of inwardness, however, Nasr is not concerned with the issues of social justice and public morality with which Rahman is preoccupied.

The modernity of these attempts becomes evident when we compare Muhammad Arkoun's attempt to recover the essence of Islam in the symbolic systems that characterize Islam. But Arkoun cautions scholars about the elusiveness of modern religious mobilization:

> This notion [of an Islamic model] constitutes the triumph of a social imaginary that it terms "Islamic" but that in fact sacralizes an irreversible operation of political, economic, social and cultural secularization. Analysts have barely noticed this new role of Islam used at the collective level as an instrument of disguising behavior, institutions, and cultural and scientific activities by the very Western model that has been ideologically rejected. (Arkoun 1994, 13)

But Arkoun does not succumb to crude secularism himself. He makes a distinction between symbols in their original, mysterious quality and their subsequent elaboration and use in social life. For example, Abraham is called a *muslim* in order to "indicate an ideal religious attitude symbolized by Abraham's conduct in conformity with the pact or covenant described in the Bible and the Qur'an" (Arkoun 1994, 15). Similarly, the Qur'an as *umm al-kitab* refers to the "celestial Book, the archetype containing the inaccessible, mysterious totality of the Word of God" (Arkoun 1994, 16). In contrast to this ultimate core, Arkoun speaks of the juridical, theological, and political elaboration of symbolic systems, which, in the elaborated form, are necessarily removed from the true religious core, and must be monitored because of their propensity to masquerade as the core (Arkoun 1994, 20–21). Unlike Nasr, who, in line with his mysticism, believes in the ultimate efficacy of the received symbols of Islam, Arkoun insists that symbols are themselves subject to change. In fact, he coins new terms—symbolization and transcendentalization of social forms—that deserve study and deconstructive critique. To this end, the whole legacy of social sciences should be brought to bear on understanding this process. Arkoun's understanding of the religious core seems to be rooted in an inexplicable and inexpressible principle that is devoid of any content.

Arkoun posits the value of the inner, religious core. He echoes the sentiments of Rahman, al Faruqi, and Nasr, but does not privilege, for Islam, a set of values or symbols. Social justice, *tawhid*, and absoluteness are not the inner core values of Islam. Arkoun leaves open the possibility of the symbols and symbolic system adopting new forms under the impact of social and psychological forces.

Conclusion

This essay has suggested that the grave doubts about Islam as a coherent explanatory and interpretive category do not imply that it is of no use in understanding certain human societies and certain social agents in them. From a sociological point of view, the religious factor, taken in its broadest sense, will have to be taken into account for purposes of understanding the transformation of a society and community. Of course, this does not necessarily mean that we will get an Islamic city or social science as a counterpart to its European variant. Such discourses will always be self-reflecting mirror images for those who seek the Other in order to complete themselves. On the other hand, one cannot dissociate the meaning of Islam from social contexts and social agents. In this regard, I have illustrated the location of Islam in social change (Gellner) as well as public discourse (Salvatore). More specifically, I have shown, with the help of a small sample, how intellectuals grapple with the question of redefining the meaning of Islam. In their search for the core values of social justice, rational theology, and mysticism, they are able to reintroduce the relevance of Islam in public discourse. The substantive solutions call for further debate, but there is no mistaking the modernist formulation and subjectivist encounter. Thus, for example, the views of Rahman and Nasr on social reconstruction and development become clear in light of their understanding of premodern Islamic social forms. The former is ready to jettison the forms in favor of the fundamental principles of Islam; while the latter regards the forms as effective symbols for relating to the divine.

In spite of these differences, however, there is overwhelming agreement on the need to locate the ultimate meaning of Islam. But the search for the core meaning of Islam becomes urgent precisely as a result of the effects of modernity on traditions. Modernity does not always lead to secularization, but it does bring into question many of the functions and aspects of traditional religions. The authority of religion in the modern world is, if not completely negated, at least questioned and made doubtful (Beckford 1992; Berger 1970; Wilson 1985). The redefinition, or at least the recovery, of the core of Islam seems to me to occur under conditions determined by modernity. Gellner argues that this pattern has been a recurrent one in Islam and has no necessary link with modernity. He believes, however, that modernity and modernization favor the dominance of urban Islam. The differences between Rahman, al Faruqi, and Nasr indicate that the meaning of urban Islam is itself subject to intense debate. Their approaches to the meaning of Islam suggest that much more is happening than a simple recurrence of the early Islamic patterns. The search for the true principles, the mystical core, or the indefinable essence is part of the search for meaning in modernity. The social and political impact of modernity on Islamic society and discourse, as analyzed by Gellner and Salvatore, is matched by an intense debate among Muslim intellectuals on the true and authentic meaning of Islam.

References

Abdel-Rahim, Muddathir. 1980. "Legal Institutions." In *The Islamic City*, ed. R. B. Sergeant, 41–51. Paris: Unesco.

Arkoun, Mohammed. 1987. *Rethinking Islam Today*. Washington, DC: Center for Contemporary Arab Studies.

—1992. "Islam wa-Wahy wa-Thawrah." *Minbar al-Hiwar* 7/26: 82–96.

—1994. *Rethinking Islam: Common Questions, Uncommon Answers*. Trans. and ed. Robert D. Lee. Boulder, CO: Westview Press.

Azmeh, Aziz al-. 1993. *Islams and Modernities*. London: Verso.

Beckford, James. 1992. "Religion, Modernity and Post-Modernity." In *Religion: Contemporary Issues*, ed. Bryan Wilson, 11–23. London: Bellew Publishing.

Berger, Morroe. 1970. *Islam in Egypt Today: Social and Political Aspects of Popular Religion*. Cambridge: Cambridge University Press.

Cornell, Vincent J. 1998. *Realm of the Saint: Power and Authority in Moroccan Sufism*. Austin, TX: University of Texas Press.

Eickelman, Dale E., and James Piscatori. 1996. *Muslim Politics*. Princeton, NJ: Princeton University Press.

Faruqi, Isma'il R. al. 1974. "Islam." In *Historical Atlas of the Religions of the World*, ed. Isma'il R. al Faruqi, with David E. Sopher, map ed., 237–81. New York: Macmillan.

—1979. *Islam*. Allen, TX: Argus Communications.

—1986. *The Cultural Atlas of Islam*. New York: Macmillan.

Faruqi, Isma'il R. al, and Lois Lamya al Faruqi. 1986. *The Cultural Atlas of Islam*. New York: Macmillan.

Gellner, Ernest. 1981. *Muslim Society*. New York: Cambridge University Press.

Lapidus, Ira M. 1967. *Muslim Cities in the Later Middle Ages*. Cambridge, MA: Harvard University Press.

Nasr, Seyyed Hossein. 1990. *Islam, Art and Spirituality*. Delhi: Oxford University Press.

—1991. *Sufi Essays*. Albany, NY: State University of New York Press.

—1994 [1966]. *Ideals and Realities of Islam*. London: Harper Collins (Aquarian).

Rahman, Fazlur. 1958. *Prophecy in Islam: Philosophy and Orthodoxy*. Chicago, IL and London: University of Chicago Press.

—1965. *Islamic Methodology in History*. Karachi: Central Institute of Islamic Research.

—1982. *Islam and Modernity: Transformation of an Intellectual Tradition*. Chicago and London: University of Chicago Press.

Salvatore, Armando. 1997. *Islam and the Political Discourse of Modernity.* Reading, England: Ithaca Press.

Smith, Wilfred Cantwell. 1978. *The Meaning and End of Religion.* San Francisco: Harper & Row.

Taylor, Charles. 1989. *Sources of the Self: The Making of the Modern Identity.* Cambridge, MA: Harvard University Press.

Turner, Bryan S. 1974. *Weber and Islam: A Critical Study.* London: Routledge and Kegan Paul.

Van Leeuwen, Richard. 1995. "The Quest for the Islamic City." In *Changing Stories: Postmodernism and the Arab-Islamic World,* ed. Inge E. Boer, Annelies Moors, and Toine van Toefellen, 147–62. Amsterdam: Rodopi.

Wilson, Bryan. 1985. "Secularization: The Inherited Model." In *The Sacred in a Secular Age,* ed. P. E. Hammond, 9–20. Berkeley, CA: University of California Press.

18

ISLAM, EUROPE, THE WEST: MEANINGS-AT-STAKE AND THE WILL-TO-POWER

Mohammed Arkoun

This contribution offers an example of the strategic intervention of critical thought in the historical development of Mediterranean societies, torn as they are between religious monotheism on the one hand—in its three ritual and doctrinal forms, Judaism, Christianity, and Islam—and, on the other, a tradition of philosophical thought deriving mainly from classical Greece, but found throughout the Near East since the conquests of Alexander. The strategy here is to seek to identify the times and places of manifestation, deployment and rupture in the long history of human reason's engagement with the never-ending quest for a universally applicable meaning that will be lasting, transcendent, and able to act as a foundation for political, ethical, legal, and spiritual legitimacy. The intention to study the whole Mediterranean area may seem excessively ambitious to those who specialize in reconstructing fragmentary branches of knowledge and limited portions of history. The violent confrontations which have occurred between representatives of "Islam" and "the West" since the nineteenth century—and particularly in the last twenty years—have, however, made it necessary to call on general practitioners (to use a medical metaphor) rather than specialists. Programmes of research and teaching, at all levels and in all countries historically and politically connected with the Mediterranean, must now include the following:

i)   A critical re-reading of the history of thought, freed from the basically ideological oppositions between theology and philosophy, and from definitions concerning substance, essence, and the transcendent which have been imposed by the three religions which view the truth as something sacred, and in particular the Christian view of revealed Truth as developed from Jewish tradition and Greek logos.

ii)   History seen as a cultural anthropology of the past, enabling us to overcome the exclusion of Islamic thought from European thought, which has, since the sixteenth century, been associated with the will to extend European hegemony under the beneficial guise of modernity.

iii) A new evaluation of the meanings that are at stake, both on the side of the revealed religions and on that of the philosophical tradition inextricably linked with the supremacy of the democratic secularized state.

iv)   A critical re-reading of modernity as a philosophical process for which a back-dated justification is constantly being sought and given in order to maintain the legitimacy of hegemonic trends in what Braudel calls material civilization, which is, in turn, imposed by physical and/or symbolic violence on societies which have taken no part in its production. From this standpoint, present-day fundamentalism—rejected in the name of "Western values"—appears as a defensive reaction against aggressive forms of modernity.

v)   The historical, cultural, and spiritual reintegration of the Mediterranean would appear to be a philosophical prerequisite, both for the redefinition of European identity as the European Union takes shape, and for what I have called the "critique of Islamic reason," an inevitable project which has already begun.

vi)   All these tasks are urgent because they bear upon a new geopolitical order and new historical solidarities which will form within the matrix of the future historical environment of the European Union in about the year 2010. Of course, it will be impossible to ignore the universalizable gains in scientific, technological, and philosophical thought which have been made in Europe since the sixteenth century; but it is the methods and ways by which modernity is transferred to other societies which need to be changed, a modernity which has not been subjected to the necessary philosophical and critical control in the places where it has emerged and developed. Accordingly, the critique of Islamic, Christian, Jewish, Buddhist, Hindu, Marxist, liberal, etc. reason will take the form of an effort to identify the unthought and unthinkable, not with reference to a modernity which is conceptually one with the recurrent aspirations of European-Western hegemony, but by making the epistemological resolution to move towards an intellectual outlook based on the principles of overcoming, surpassing, and removing all constructions, all affirmations of identity, all truths deriving from or spread by violence. The utopian nature of this outlook does not signify a permanent retreat from the constraints of history, of language, of the individual and collective unconscious, of socio-politics, and of economics; this utopia means a constant mobility of thought, necessary if we are to keep the same critical eye on all sites, modalities, frameworks, and tools of a production of meaning which is in a constant state of change.

An urgent need can be felt at the present moment for reflection, with all the resources of the social sciences, on the objective historical content, geopolitical weight, paradigmatic values, and horizons of hope implied by the three words: Islam, Europe, the West. Since these three spheres of production of contemporary history have been subjected to unchecked ideological interpretation, a great deal of explanation, critical evaluation, and fresh analysis is necessary, especially with regard to the way Muslims and Occidentals see each other. As a teacher and researcher in the field of Islamic thought, I have always been concerned with the need for intellectual and cultural mediation, and by the constant confusion caused by political tensions. This has led me to publish three books in the format of questions and answers: *L'Islam, religion et société* (Arkoun 1982b), with the Italian journalist Mario Arosio; *Ouvertures sur l'Islam* (Arkoun 1992a); *Islam & de democratie* (Arkoun 1994). The questions addressed to me from different European contexts have spurred me on in differentiating the concepts of Europe and of the West, starting from two fundamental concepts which confront critical thinking about current realities: the history of what I call "Islam-as-fact" and "the societies of the Scripture-book"; and the meanings-at-stake which are connected with the will-to-power in Europe—Europe properly so-called, and Europe as belonging to what it calls the West, so as to marginalize the Mediterranean world and accentuate the ancient break between its south-east and north-west.

This means that the old debate begun by the Belgian historian Pirenne in his posthumous *Mahomet et Charlemagne* (Pirenne 1937), on the rupture engendered by a hegemonic Islam within the area unified by the *pax romana* and by Christendom, should be brought up to date and enriched by a new questioning of cultural history, or, more particularly, of the cognitive status and the psycho-socio-political functions of religion-as-fact. The reader will see that this preoccupation is present in all my responses; it even brings me to reject the immediately applicable formulaic definition the Western politician or citizen requires when faced by the "strange" behavior and beliefs of a growing number of Muslims.

The publisher of the Dutch book chose the title because European societies are above all preoccupied by the difficulties of integrating Muslim immigrants, without taking any account of the historical, legal, and cultural obligations of a law-ruled state and a civil society. For the Arabic Muslim audience, the confrontation between Islam and democracy has given rise to a populist and apologetic literature which has become so widely spread, and already so deeply rooted in the politico-religious imagination, that I feel it better to re-focus attention on the revision and restoration of perspectives which are ignored in most of what is written about the tensions, oppositions, and open conflicts between Islam, Europe, the West. I fear, though, that the Arabic Muslim reader will find it difficult to share an attitude which prefers the identification and critical analysis of the concepts at stake to the ancient notion of "just war" (*jihad*), which has been currently resuscitated in an Islam which feels dominated, threatened, and distorted by a systematically hostile West. The historical contradictions have been badly thought out, and badly translated into experience, under pressure from a modernity which has been produced without the participation of any society touched by Islam-as-fact. Material modernity is a matter of consumption, sometimes over-consumption, in the wealthiest classes, those which thereby most resemble comparable classes in the West, not the popular strata which militant Islam defends. Intellectual modernity, however, has always been limited in its diffusion and its productivity by the requirements of an ideology of combat, both in the phase of secular nationalist movements and in present-day fundamentalism. The conflict between Islam—or Christianity, Judaism, Buddhism, and so on—and democracy inevitably produces anachronisms which are fruitful from the point of view of an ideology of combat, or of religious apologetics, but which are entirely unacceptable to critical historical and anthropological thinking.

I wish, therefore, to re-examine the two great axes of research, debate, and reflection already mentioned, so as to deepen the analysis of these themes and create a new space for communication and historical action. There is no danger of exhausting the material; one is re-writing the entire history of Mediterranean thought. I have dealt with several aspects of this re-writing already in my works; what I would like to do here is draw attention to the ideas of displacement (*déplacement*) and going beyond (*dépassement*)[1] in relation to conceptual structures, categorizations, delimitations, and eliminations inherited from both Islamic and European-Western traditions. What is undeniable is that the rationality for which the social sciences are the vehicle is less widely spread in so-called Muslim societies than in Western ones, where it has always both accompanied and guided industrial, urban, political, legal, and institutional development. To identify these functional differences, to evaluate their structural effect on the historical evolution of the two worlds, means freeing ourselves from false explanations which pit an anti-scientific, anti-philosophic, anti-secular Islam against a West seen as the promoter of these values.

Islam-as-fact, and Societies of the Scripture-book

The concept of Islam-as-fact helps us out of the confusions which have accumulated around the word "Islam," especially since states, as well as movements of rebellion, that have proclaimed themselves to be Islamic, have striven by ruthless over-imitation to acquire legitimacy. This process began with the first great "dissension" (*fitna*), and has recurred ever since in the most diverse historical and social contexts. "Islam-as-fact" refers to the state appropriation of religion, already apparent with the Umayyads, richly augmented both culturally and intellectually under the Abbasids, taken up again by the Ottomans, and finally seen in the modern states with their growing determination to promote populist religion at the expense of the great theoretical and doctrinal confrontations (*munazarat*) of classical times. The administrators of the sacred (*'ulama'*) were subordinated to state power, and religious confraternities sprang up wherever the central power was weak; these are the two main characteristics of Islam-as-fact from at least the thirteenth century onwards.

This is why I have long insisted on the need to differentiate the Qur'an-as-fact from Islam-as-fact. The first stands for the historical emergence of a new phenomenon, circumscribed by time and space, which cannot however be limited to the body of texts dating from its official establishment—this requires a certain strategy of analysis and epistemological precautions (outlined in Arkoun 1991); while the second does not derive completely from the first, as the traditional view would have it, indifferent as it is to historical criticism and anxious, above all, to educate. The study of the relationship between the two demands a kind of historical, sociological, and linguistic research virtually neglected until now. Which is why millions of believers can still state today, with all the vehemence of a faith that cares nothing for the workings of historical time, that the norms of the *corpus juris* derive in an orderly and complete fashion from the Word of God as given in the Qur'an, and thus merit the name of Divine Law (*shari'a*). This most important point has been the subject of well-known investigations into the abundant *usul al-fiqh* literature, but the political urgency which it derives from present-day demands for the restoration of the *shari'a* necessitates new critical work on legal reason in Islam.

Modern Islamic discourse has accentuated the doctrinal rigidity of representations of Islam "applicable to all times and in all places" and reduced them to the socially-controlled performance of identificatory rites. Unfortunately, contemporary Islamic and political studies have added their scientific weight to the corroboration of this static and ahistorical perspective. Thus in the popular expression "Islam and the West" there is the unproblematized presentation of a static, dogmatic, essentialist, transcendentalized religious world, following the portrayal by believers who require that their "difference" should be respected, and who thus make it impossible for themselves to measure the distance that separates them from a dynamic, modern, secularized West, open to all innovations because it comprises agents who are more free, or totally detached, from traditional beliefs—although these agents too are sheltered from any scientific criticism. Believers consolidate their position by contemplating the mocking opposition—never thoroughly analysed—between the high and living spirituality of the "East" and the immoral materialism of the "West." Thus two mutually exclusive imaginary worlds are constructed out of the postulates of a hegemonic reason, proud of its technological, economic and political successes, to such an extent that it can abolish the ancient prerogatives and authority of religion, assigning it merely rudimentary and residual functions. This is the same debate that opposed Christian reason to Enlightenment reason in the eighteenth century and recurs today in explosive sociopolitical contexts, disguised as fundamentalism, integralism, and militant radicalism making use of a religious vocabulary and justification.

Not that this contributes towards a critical understanding of religion-as-fact; there is no advance beyond outward manifestations and the (often discrediting) evaluations made by all those who have adopted the religion of secularism. This formulation is not polemic; it refers to conflicts in the management of private space—abandoned to religion and public space—the exclusive business of the secular state. In France, the Ministry of the Interior is in charge of religious affairs; if religion overflows into the public space it is a matter for the police. In Belgium, the responsibility belongs to the Ministry of Justice. Compromises of greater or lesser depth, depending on the country, have replaced the sharp conflicts of the eighteenth and nineteenth centuries; the protection of goods and people has been transferred to the state; social security and the welfare state—as in Sweden, where it has become the main foundation of legitimacy—have deprived religion of essential functions it had exercised for centuries: hope in the afterlife; the source and guarantee of moral values which uphold social cohesion, providing the basis for vital solidarities; the regulation of transactions, and the invocation of legitimacy. Because Third World states did not make these substitutions when traditional codes collapsed, Islamic movements were immediately successful in restoring by, and for, religion its functions of refuge, protection, landmark and stepping-stone. The modernity of a party state like that of Boumediene or Nasser has produced a great number of losers, marginal figures who are in revolt or excluded from society; only promises of justice, brotherhood, protection, dignity, spiritual advancement, and moral purification can quieten them and mobilize them anew.

So does this mean that religion exists solely to comfort those human beings who are doomed by their fellow humans to misery, distress, and oppression—moral, intellectual, and material? Is this comfort merely a dangerous illusion, a vain hope, a belief in a hallucination, an outdated mythology that confines its victims to irremediable mental and existential backwardness?

This explanation appears directly, or by implication, in all the sociological and political literature dealing with Islam. Sometimes we are reminded that there is another Islam, that of the "High Tradition," as Olivier Carré calls it, with its majestic intellectual and cultural achievements. Thus, almost mechanically, the negative judgments which have been made upon the ideological excesses of militant Islam are refuted; in their place appear the splendors of a learned, open, tolerant Islam, associated with a brilliant civilization in its moment of greatness. These splendors are not usually considered in a chronological context, because the historical continuity or possible resurrection of this expansive and creative moment is being invoked. We are not told that the moment occurred in the Middle Ages, and that it has now been surpassed by the progress of knowledge and the alterations in *mentalité* brought about by modernity. The diffusion and assimilation of modernity have been slowed down, hindered, and in some countries brought to a standstill by an obstinate policy of constructing national identity by a process of traditionalization—the return to a fragmented, stereotyped, ritualist Islamic tradition—strongly mythologized, of course, since the historical reconstruction of the tradition is more objective and critical, and more extensive, in the works of Orientalists than in the work of Muslim researchers.

Already, in the seventies, Laroui had pointed out the importance of this "traditionalizing" process in society, especially in Morocco; and the "Islamic Revolution" in Iran extended the phenomenon to all societies experiencing Islam-as-fact. The process is a historical avatar of the transformation of Islam into a state religion, which, as has already been pointed out, began on a large scale under the Umayyads. It would be interesting to compare the way the developing tradition was integrated into society, before its official formulation in the third/ninth century, with the actions of modern states in charge of very different societies from Indonesia to Morocco, from central Asia to South Africa—the ways they have treated an Islam already subjected to many centuries of transformation and change. This is where the idea of Islam-as-fact assumes its full operative value: the appeal to an abstract Islam, a purely ideological construction, stripped of the historical and theological fullness of its Tradition (see Arkoun 1993), has above all served to distort the borrowings it has been forced to make from an explicitly rejected modernity, the product of an imperialist West, by the nationalist discourse of the recovery of personal identity. Islam-as-fact is always there, incontrovertibly; the colonialist experience has changed it into a power to select from, and eventually completely reject, modernity. Even the most positive historical contributions of modernity, its ability to integrate religion-as-fact into an extended strategy that produces and controls meaning, have been distorted to the point where the transcultural processes and the most firmly established values of Islam have become destabilized and disintegrated.

Thus we must concentrate on the interactions between Islam-as-fact and modernity, not so much in order once again to go over confrontations, rivalries, and mutual exclusions, as to better understand how Christendom and Islam—since these two religions have accompanied rival imperial processes with hegemonic intentions throughout their history—and modernity—as an alternative model for the historical formation of a society—have continuously fought with each other since the sixteenth century, and, in a sense (see Arkoun 1982a), within the Islamic context already in the fourth/tenth century. A systematic, comparative analysis of the meaning and immediate consequences—and the more remote ones too—of the most influential confrontations which have taken place in what I call the societies of the Scripture-book, would surely advance our interpretation of the issues of meaning and will-to-power in these societies.

I shall not repeat here what I have already written on this complex and essential, yet still inadequately studied, notion (see Arkoun 1992b). I intend to transfer my analysis from the theological and often polemic area of what the Qur'an calls the People of the Book (*ahl al-kitab*) to the wider, more inclusive, and specific area of historical and anthropological knowledge, and to impose a linguistic and anthropological examination of Revelation as it is understood by the three so-called "revealed" religions—with their different attitudes towards the concept of the Scripture-book as material container of God's Word—subject to all the random modifications of written transmission and of textual interpretation. Catholic theology, in particular, opposes the notion of a religion of the Book, because God's Word is incarnate in the Person of Christ and is transmitted by it. The idea of societies of the Scripture-book takes no stance on the initial pillar and transmitter of God's Word, but recalls us to the common historical datum, which cannot be denied, that in order to develop their theories of Revelation, the three communities have to pass through *book* with a small letter—the material object and mediator—in order to reach the Scripture-*Book* with a capital B— which theological speculation has surrounded with an over-determined aura of holiness. Le Goff says of the Bible in the Middle Ages what could also be said of the Qur'an:

> To speak of medieval culture is to speak first of all of the reference Book, in religion and out of it, in fidelity and rebellion, conformity and nonconformity. Whatever their level of culture or learning, mediaeval men and women found the foundations of knowledge and truth in the Bible. (Le Goff 1990: 48)

If the Middle Ages end in Europe in 1800, they rise again (with devastating fidelity) in the Islamic context, just as Europe and the West are talking about post-modernity, super-modernity, questioning received views—all the most productive characteristics of the Enlightenment. The Book, *al-Kitab*, obsesses all thinkers, recurs in all conversations, dominates all arguments, nourishes all kinds of hope, justifies the worst excesses and the most astonishing sacrifices; it is inseparable from the dislocated individual who is striving to reconstruct himself, from a disintegrating society which longs for unification, from an accelerated history which cruelly disappoints the recurrent hopes of believers. Yet the Book is now submerged, not only by books which owe nothing to it and which tend towards its elimination, but by an increasing flood of images and information which is modifying the conditions of the production and reception of meaning—a much more radical modification in the case where a civilization of the book remains firmly based on Holy Scripture.

The concept of societies of the Scripture-book also allows the re-establishment of a functional continuity, with ideological effects, between religious and modern, secular ways of producing, expanding, and controlling meaning in society: in both cases there is conflict "between the oral and the written"[2]—not between two stages of a linear progression, but between linguistic and anthropological frameworks for the articulation and cultural realization of meaning. Thus religions of the Scripture-book have struggled against paganism and its accompanying cultures; secular modernity has opposed dialects, local customs, superstitions, magic, all "popular" manifestations associated with orality—the totality of procedures suitable for the articulation of meaning in oral culture—and its procedures, which are opposed to nation construction. In the Third World, brutality and cultural destruction have accompanied rapid social change and strategies of national unification which have been taken over from the colonial pow- ers. These upheavals have entailed the most serious confusions between religion and modernity; their shared ideological function has been implemented without any critical evaluation of the different origins, functions, and aims of the two models of historical action. The benefits of nation-building in Europe, like the advances in civilization brought about by the religions of the Scripture-book, have caused recent nationalist movements to forget the price paid throughout history by peoples and cultures who were, but did not necessarily deserve to be, marginalized or eliminated. This is why both religion-as-fact and modernity require the critical re-examination of the meanings-at-stake for them both, and of the will-to-power which transforms the quest for meaning into a constant expansion of the systems of domination.

Meanings-at-stake and the Will-to-power

"Meaning" is a difficult word: it is used throughout society, by all groups in search of an identity, by all schools of thought competing to demarcate and impose the true meaning which will derive authentically from the basic Source and lead to the ultimate Signified. This was the method of classical theology and metaphysics; today all claims to meaning are turned back upon ideology, which in turn stands for the arbitrary wish to extend the "values" of one group, or even of one leader, to ever vaster social groupings. The expression "the search for meaning" is itself suspect, merely standing for a more or less disguised attempt to re-establish theological and metaphysical systems as legitimating a will-to-power.

Hence I choose the more open expression "meaning-at-stake." The stake is the amount wagered by each speaker in the great world-game of Becoming, and like any game it is a series of chance events which each player tries to master by incorporating into successive strategies. In the case of meaning, the game endlessly repeats itself and becomes ever more complicated in time and space. The players are called "social actors" by sociologists, and the game metaphor is thus enriched by that of the theatre, play-acting—"stage-power" as Balandier calls it. For each social actor, Foucault's "will to know" mingles with the aim of power. Lévi-Strauss adds another metaphor to corroborate the others on the production of meaning, that of *bricolage*, applied to the questions of *la pensée sauvage* and then extended by sociologists such as Bourricaud to ideological *bricolage*; this overcomes both political and religious reasoning, and frequently philosophical and religious reasoning too. In the long run instrumental reasoning, which cares only for immediate efficacity and is not concerned with the fragility of its results, confines critical reasoning to the examination of established facts, and discourages any anticipatory effort concerning the drift of meaning.

Thanks to linguists and literary critics, one may distinguish now between the immanent meaning of a discourse and the effects produced in its hearers. The study of the conditions of reception, especially in the case of religious statements which affect all sociocultural categories, is as necessary as (and frequently more enlightening than) the study of linguistic tools and procedures which articulate meaning. During reception, individual and collective imaginal entities are constructed which, in their turn, influence perception, judgment, and behavior. Thus the effects of meanings, which are presented as true meaning, join the ideologies which mobilize in the service of the will-to-power. All revolutions are founded on this conjuncture, which is the immediate aim of all prophets, mahdis, imams, saints, liberating heroes, and leaders, whose ability to produce effects of meaning depends on both personal charisma and historical context.

One can see the relevance of this analysis for understanding the functioning of the great foundational texts in societies of the Scripture-book, including, of course, the texts of secular religions such as communism and socialism. Social agents transform these texts into pre-texts for the operation of sacredness, mythology, and ideology disguised as appeals to truth, transcendental justice, brotherhood and so forth. The example of the Qur'an in the societies which use it is here the most striking, but one must remember that the history of every society is interwoven with similar occurrences.

It might be objected that this theory (of a meaning which is constantly back-influenced by the effects of meaning conveyed and activated by an indefinite series of social actors) cannot apply to foundational texts whose immanent meaning remains the same throughout history, in all sociocultural contexts, and resists all forms of projection and manipulation. Here we return to Plato's Ideas, to eternal reason and its product, Eternal Wisdom,[3] with their epistemological continuations in Enlightenment reasoning. The theologies of revelation in the three monotheist religions have made considerable use of Platonism and Aristotelianism in order to construct the idea of a Source-Meaning from which all human legitimacies and truths flow. Theologies, like classical metaphysics, further state that this Source-Meaning has been once and for all enclosed in the foundation-texts, and that it can be correctly grasped, transmitted and applied—in ethical-legal norms and the ritual practices codified by the doctors of the Law. One cannot overcome this opposition solely by the force of argument; there is a psycho-linguistic separation, emphasized in the case of religious reasoning by *incorporation*, which implants within the individual by ritual repetition the beliefs and non-beliefs which define each religion. Argument remains speculative until it produces political, legal, economical, social, or ritual results—one thinks of the ritual of the Republic, the conduct of trades unions, political parties, the bureaucracy, and so on and these results in turn make possible the sociocultural expansion of a new "attitude of reason." All revolutions, including those introduced by the founders of "revealed" religions, make use of this paradigm of change, yet are unable to establish irreversible situations which would make resurgence and restoration impossible—note, for example, the French Revolution, which intended to be radical; and the Arabic socialist revolution, which unintentionally produced the Islamic Revolution.

Thus one has all the more reason to talk of meanings-at-stake and the will-to-power in all types of society: all social actors—collectively and/or singly—obey effects of meaning, and produce them, in their attempts to over-imitate the transcendent, intangible, founding Source-Meaning. These reach their height when Islam—emphasizing the tension between militant Muslims' will-to-power and the West's view of it as diabolical—is promoted to the status of a world-wide "threat." Thus after a slow and complicated journey we reach the original question: how can we create a positive use of the three terms—Islam, Europe, the West—which will bring hopes for the future emancipation of mankind? At present they are more marked than ever by the struggles for hegemony which are disguised, as they were in the Middle Ages, by meanings-at-stake of an apparently transcendental nature.

Once again, we need historical details. It is the historians who have diverted the word "West" from a geographical label to a cultural and ideological one. Within Christendom, especially since the great schism of 1054, discussions of orthodoxy have led to the distinction between Eastern Orthodox and Western Catholic. East and West were engaged with even greater ideological intensity by both theologians and historians when Islam, after its first century of conquests (632–732) and later under the Ottoman empire, began to reinforce the Crusades of the Christian (and later secular) West against the heterodox, obscurantist, idle dreamers of the East. The eighteenth century made use of the East (and of Islam) in its campaign against dogmatism, intolerance, and obscurantism (represented by the Church), and in the nineteenth century romanticism added its touches of picturesqueness and poetic escapism, to the extent of inventing the belly-dance and then exporting it to its supposedly original homeland.[4]

The meaning of the West in world politics took on a new dimension when the United States imposed its presence on Europe even during the wars, when the whole Mediterranean area was inexorably—though doubtless not irremediably—demoted to the status of a satellite region, a process we shall not consider in detail here, save to say that the violent communist interregnum caused Western Europe to emphasize its Western-ness as against Eastern Europe, this time fallen away into a new—and this time purely ideological—divide. The old religious schism between Orthodoxy and Catholicism, with its underlying opposition of East and West, has risen again, especially on Yugoslav territory. One wonders how the West would have handled the conflict if the Bosnians had inflicted on Belgrade the martyrdom which the Serbs had inflicted on Sarajevo. In this tragic conflict is concentrated every meaning-at-stake and every power-strategy which, since the Middle Ages, and despite the shift from theological to secular politics, has continued to mobilize agents and legitimate "righteous wars" in this ideologically continuous but geopolitically divided area of Islam, Europe, the West.

The most recent enlargement of the West as a space for the deployment of the will to rule—of politically united but economically competing powers—occurred when Japan was added to the Group of Seven as a result of its technological, economic, and monetary strength. The primacy—and not merely the priority—of power-strategies over meanings-at-stake becomes here so obvious that it shows through all international camouflage: humanitarian action is advertised as after-sales service by weapon-dealers; the defence of human rights fails to disguise the old slogan of "our mission to civilize"; an appeal to democracy accompanies undeniable assistance rendered to governments which deny the most basic of human freedoms. An immense and painful semantic disorder is created, fostered, and increased by the conjugated efforts of states, chancelleries, bureaucracies disseminating information, banking systems, and even armies (in that they obey the politicians).

These are serious, and seriously biased, propositions; they will tend to strengthen militant Islam's radically negative and polemical image of the West and also discourage those who, in this West, seek to correct the excesses of equally negative and polemical anti-Islamic writing and thought. I repeat that my criticisms do not propose the arbitrary disqualification of an adversary to the point of denying his objective position in the history of civilization and the responsibilities which have been his since the eighteenth century, responsibilities in the genesis of human progress, and responsibilities too for ecological, political, social, cultural, and semantic disorders. Likewise my criticisms of Islamic reasoning show that I have taken my stand in that area of historical and philosophical confrontation which lies between meanings-at-stake and will-to-power, two linked and recurrent constants in human affairs.

If the European Union had not become a political and economic reality—soon to be likewise a monetary one—there would be no need to draw a distinction between this West and Europe. Fortunately, the way Europe is built has forced Europeans to concern themselves with questions of identity, although discussions are inspired more by nationalist ideologies—or resistances—than by the need to open a new space for thought and historical action; these must be able to cope with the difficulties inherited from intra-European wars, from colonial expansion, from membership in a West whose ideological divagations need the restraint and control which only the European Union can guarantee.

Seen politically and historically in its world-wide context, and from the viewpoint of Islam, this role of Europe must entail restoration of the Mediterranean area to the universe of meanings and values which first shaped European identity. I say "area" in order to open up fully all possibilities of redistribution in the matter of ownership, allegiance, values, and historical development. In this time of ideological violence, real or imagined fears, and the cultivation of ignorance, it seems unrealistic to talk of the political, economical, and especially cultural and historical reconstitution of the Mediterranean. We must also mention the priority which the European Union gives to the reintegration of Eastern Europe, with its natural connections with the liberal Christian Western world. This orientation makes clearer the distrust which is felt towards the South-East Mediterranean; an exception is made for Greece on account of the "Greek miracle"—about which all European schoolchildren learn—but the history of the Ottoman empire is still relegated to Oriental Studies departments and general works on "Islam."

Yet nearly ten million Muslims live on European soil; the peoples of Arabia, Turkey, and Iran are re-writing their history and re-interpreting their religious thought by using the inescapable methods and epistemology of critical reason; Europe, always ahead of the rest of the world, is leaving behind the outdated intellectual frameworks of her political thought and her humanism. The theologies of the three religions cannot resist much longer the repeated contradictions of history and the increasingly radical challenges of science. All these factors suggest that we may envisage, for 2010 at the latest, an overcoming of political disagreements, of ideological schism, mutual exclusion, imaginary truths, and master–servant relationships, which have characterized the Mediterranean ever since the first clashes between, on the one hand, the rising religious symbolism of monotheism, and, on the other, the analytical strength of the Greek logos, the Roman imperial order, and the flexibility of the pagan pantheon.

Unfortunately, the political classes do not cultivate historical memory as critical historians endeavor to reconstruct it; they prefer to make selections from "places of memory"[5] imposed by official historiography—images with the power to mobilize, such as noble moments and conquering heroes; these are meant to galvanize national energies and to exaggerate the qualities of each people's genius; enemies are useful for purposes of apologetics. European leaders—and, even more so, those of states/ nations/parties in the South Mediterranean—still think in terms of the old procedures for mobilizing sacred national egotism, and intellectuals are abdicating their competence- as-knowledge, while politicians and experts take over all competence-as-decision. Yet it is now that we need frequent critical interventions, not only to limit ideological— even more seriously, demagogic and electoral—divagations in debate, but also to spread as widely as possible the results of new research. A great number of institutions, conferences, and publications rich in material on the Mediterranean question remain unknown even to what we call the educated public. How different was the uproar caused by the struggles for national liberation or construction in 1959–60 (although it is true that Maoism and Soviet communism were then accepted as efficacious and unavoidable roads to definitive liberation).

I pass over the question of the intellectual's status in those Arabic, Turkish, and Iranian societies which are directly concerned with the expansion of a politico-cultural vision to respond to the expectations and explicit demands made by some considerable sectors of the European Union. An unfortunate prejudice survives from the period of independence, when, in the euphoria of ill-used victories, many valuable intellectuals joined what quickly became a bureaucratic *nomenklatura*. Algerian intellectuals are paying a high price for their solidarity with a party-state which aspires to popular democracy; some accepted this as a deliberate calculation, and others through political naïvety and lack of information. This tragic experience may help to create throughout the South-East Mediterranean that critical engagement which is still needed for a radical re-reading of these people's historical destiny; it must overcome all errors, dogmatisms, artificial values, destructive confrontations, and all the exaggerated exclusions which have stifled and delayed until now the appearance of an indestructible hope.

Notes

1. For an elaboration of these notions, see Arkoun 1995.
2. As in the title to the anthropologist Jack Goody's *The Interface Between the Oral and the Written* (Goody 1987).
3. A notion to be found throughout medieval thought, with its theory of Agent Intellect and acquired intellect, which guarantees the continuance and ontological foundation of Truth. See Arkoun 1982a.
4. Oleg Graber showed how art criticism is inseparable from the history of "Islamic" art as seen by nineteenth-century Orientalists in his lecture *"Penser l'art islamique"* at the Institut du Monde Arabe in Paris in 1995.
5. *Lieux de mémoire* is the title of an important collected volume edited by Pierre Nora, 1984–92.

References

Arkoun, Mohammed. 1982a. *Humanisme arab au IVe/Xe siècle*. 2nd ed. Paris: J. Vrin.

—1982b. *L'Islam, religion et société*. Paris: Editions du Cerf.

—1991. *Lectures du Coran*. 2nd ed. Tunis: Alif.

—1992a. *Ouvertures sur l'Islam*. Paris: J. Granchet.

—1992b. "Le concept de sociétés du Livre-livre." In *Interpréter: homage à Claude Geffré*, ed. Jean Pierre Jossua, Nicholas Sed. 211–26. Paris: Editions de Cerf.

—1993. "L'Islam actuel devant sa tradition." In idem, *Penser l'Islam aujourd'hui*. Algiers: Laphomic ENAL.

—1994. *L'Islam & de democratie*. Amsterdam: Uitgeverij Contact.

—1995. "Transgression, déplacement, dépasser." *Arabica* 41: 28-70.

Goody, Jack. 1987. *The Interface Between the Oral and the Written*. Cambridge: Cambridge University Press.

Le Goff, Jacques. 1990. *Le Moyen âge s'achève en 1800*. Paris: Société d'éditions scientifiques.

Nora, Pierre, ed. 1984–92. *Lieux de mémoire*. 7 vols. Paris: Gallimard.

Pirenne, Henri. 1937. *Mahomet et Charlemagne*. 3rd ed. Paris and Brussels: Alcan.

Part IV

Civilization

19

THE PROBLEM: UNITY IN DIVERSITY

Gustave E. von Grunebaum

I

Any study of the Islamic world as a whole will sooner or later come up against the problem of the relation between Muslim civilization and the local cultures of the areas which in the course of time have become technically Islamized. The problem of the relation between coexisting layers of a "universal" and a "provincial" civilization is by no means peculiar to the Islamic world; it is, in fact, typical of all areas culturally identified with a civilization of a supernational or "universal" outreach. The supernational civilization is characteristically but not necessarily associated with, and in its leading aspirations largely developed from, a religious message claiming universal validity, and it is in its beginnings championed by a distinct ethnic element. Hellenistic culture is perhaps the outstanding exception to the paramountcy of the religious identification in a universal civilization—the civilization of the Christian West, the most striking exception to ethnic sponsorship of the beginnings of a cultural movement. The civilization of Islam, however, conforms to this tentative typology, having grown from the original core of the message of the Arabic Prophet through amalgamation of certain cultural traditions to which it became exposed through the political successes of the Prophet's Arab adherents.

The realization of this relational problem presupposes not only the existence of a Muslim identification but also the separability, in the analysis of outlook and attitudes of a given area at a given time, of elements to which an Islamic origin may be ascribed from others whose presence cannot be connected with Islam. This assumption will sometimes be readily substantiated by the historical situation as such, which may be dominated by a clearly felt and openly discussed conflict between two cultural heritages; resolution is attempted within the framework of the universal culture whose essential tenets and values are, consciously at least, not to be compromised. At other times the conflict will not be acute, but the self-consciousness of the people themselves will have registered the heterogeneity of the ideas and of the mores to which they profess their allegiance; in actual life, however, adherence to one or the other of the insufficiently integrated traditions will depend on social stratification or on some other segmentation regulated by custom, owing to which certain activities will be governed by what is felt to be the Islamic norm while others will be conducted in accordance with the local tradition, which may be considered an awkward but unavoidable deviation from the universal ideal. It would be erroneous to suppose that it is always the upper strata of society who live out and promote the universal norm; in the Islamic area it has been, as often as not, the local elite who struggled to maintain the local cultural tradition or at least as much of it as could be upheld without eliminating its bearers from influencing the political structure and the political fate of the universal civilization. Again it is the local elite who may forsake sooner, or to a greater extent, the universal religious civilization toward which the lower orders of the local society continue to cherish a strong attachment. Present developments under Western impact in many Muslim countries will illustrate this observation.

In an encounter of disparate civilizations a subjective criterion as well as a series of objective criteria may be found in order to establish which of the two must be considered leading, that is to say, to which of them the essential cachet of the local integration is primarily due. The subjective criterion, which may on occasion conflict with the objective, analytically obtained evidence, is best described as the self-identification of the members of the particular culture community. The cohesion of the culturally Muslim-dominated area is in a large measure due to the firm conviction held by the most outlying groups that they form a part of a larger and religiously defined entity. For this unreflecting identification the problem does not arise, which in its simplest form may be stated in terms of this question: What does, say, a North African Muslim have in common with a Muslim from Java? It is taken for granted that all Muslims, whatever their "national" background, are at one in their essential beliefs and practices. That even those elementary beliefs, when scrutinized, would reveal implications and associations not altogether identical is as little suspected as are the actually rather significant variations in social and legal practice. And even were the awareness of existing differences keener than it is and has been for centuries, a community's consciousness of belonging with like-minded communities would hardly be affected. As a matter of fact, the identification in large measure creates, as it were, the affinities on which it is presumably based.

For the purpose of ascertaining at least some unequivocal objective criteria enabling us to determine the leading element(s) among coexisting and interpenetrating civilizations one may perhaps describe culture, with more than one grain of salt, "as a 'closed' system of questions and answers concerning the universe and man's behavior in it which has been accepted as authoritative by a human society. A scale of values decides the relative position and importance of the individual 'questions and answers'" (von Grunebaum 1948, 218). In the event of a conflict or even the mere coexistence of two such systems, the resultant civilization by which people actually live will be organized according to certain fundamental value judgments in which the aspirations of one of the participating cultures will be more deeply represented and by which these aspirations will be better promoted than those of the other(s).

In addition to changing the basic values of the pre-Islamic cultural system of a conquered and converted region, the new religion in its cultural unfolding will, to put it in the abstract, (a) introduce, or admit as legitimate, new questions, for which appropriate answers will be offered; and (b) suggest new answers to old questions, or legitimize answers that seem disrupting or otherwise inacceptable within the competing tradition.

From this point of view the self-identification as a Muslim of a "nationalistic" Persian of the Samanid period would appear perfectly legitimate, inasmuch as he would continue to accept the Islamic axioms of monistic theism and prophetism as well as the value judgment which dedicates the life of man to the service of God. It is only within this intellectual-emotional framework that he strives after the political independence of his people and the revival of the cultural glories of the Iranian past. Under the surface of the Muslim identification no end of changes may occur, but they will hardly ever affect the identification as such.

We can perhaps generalize in societal terms with regard to the structure of such a supernational civilization by viewing it, not as one closely knit organism, but rather as a vast number of groups which may almost be described as self-sufficient. Islam superimposes "a common veneer of general religious culture" but does not cause those groups "to lose the peculiar shade of mystical-magical feeling of their own particular life."[1] The medieval Muslim himself articulated a certain awareness of this cultural dichotomy at a fairly early time, although, as might have been expected, within an entirely different frame of reference. Thus, for example, differences in body build and intelligence are accounted for on climatic grounds by the Mu'tazilite, al-Nazzam (d. 845) (cf. Jahiz 1356–64/1938–45, V, 35–36; idem 1907, V, 12–13). His disciple, al-Jahiz (d. 869), adduces climatic considerations to explain why Zoroaster threatened his followers with eternal cold rather than with eternal fire. He goes on to argue that, since this threat would be effective only among the inhabitants of the mountainous region where Zoroaster actually began to preach his religion, this very doctrine would prove the local limitations of his mission and his message. In contrast to the merely provincial validity of Zoroastrianism, the Qur'anic hell-fire, whose terror is not based on local apprehensions—considering that the Arabs were exposed to both heat and cold—gives evidence of the universal character of Muhammad's mission and message (an interpretation which, incidentally, Jahiz finds it useful to corroborate from Revelation itself).[2] What matters in our context is, of course, not the conclusiveness of the argument but the desire to establish on whatever grounds the universal validity of Islam, within whose fold other religious and cultural systems can be observed to exist whose inherent imperfection could be described precisely in terms of the limited validity of the truths on which they are predicated.

The cultural area united by the *Gemeingefühl* of the followers of the Prophet has always harbored a multitude of local civilizations of greater or lesser completeness and of varying independence with regard to the dominant strain of Islamic civilization; and it cannot be said that this situation has changed significantly in our own day. Not only the Moroccan Berber, the Moro in Mindanao, the Hausa, only recently converted to Muhammadanism, but even the Turk of Central Asia or the Punjabi, whose allegiance to Islam is inherited from twenty or thirty generations of devout believers, will cling faithfully and often consciously to patterns of social organization and behavior, sets of beliefs and "superstitions" that are compatible with the specifically Islamic patterns not through any kinship or natural affinity but merely in terms of the actual symbiosis. The coexistence obtains *de facto* but hardly *de jure*—as the local spokesmen of the universal tradition, the *faqih* and the more educated *hajj* never tire of explaining to their moderately attentive fellows. Although in theory the acceptance of Islam would seem to imply the acceptance of a complete way of life designed to unify the faithful wherever they be by methodically unifying the rhythm of their existence, in fact a latitudinarian interpretation of the nature of an Islamic society has prevailed. The Muslim coming from the heartlands of the faith may be amazed, shocked, or moved to contempt at what he sees in the outlying provinces,[3] but he will not, in general, be inclined to contest the provincial claim to orthodoxy as long as he is satisfied of the community's determination to identify itself with the *umma Muhammadiyya*.

The essential changes which full Islamization will bring about may be inferred from the changes imposed on the pagan Arabs by the acceptance of the Prophet's message. In terms of our heuristic definition of culture, the cultural transformation imposed or induced by Islam may perhaps be described as primarily due to the introduction of three new valuations: (1) Islam sets for life an otherworldly goal. Life in this world is no longer an end in itself but rather a means to secure eternal felicity. Accordingly, the aims of heathen ambition, such as wealth, power, fame, remain acceptable aspirations only inasmuch as they are integrated in the organizational structure of the new life. (2) By making the individual responsible for his fate in the next world, the new faith completed, or at least advanced significantly, the process of legal and moral individuation. Besides, it made every moment of the believer's life supremely relevant; for the effort to gain salvation must never be relaxed. (3) By accentuating the indispensability of the community to the fulfillment of some of the basic obligations of the individual Muslim, Islam stressed the necessity of political organization. Where the pagan Arab had thought in terms of clans and tribes, the Muslim was led to think in terms of the political community coextensive with the area of the faith—and therefore ultimately destined to dominate the world. Mankind no longer divided into members of different tribes—it split into believers and unbelievers, and this cleavage was to continue beyond the grave.

The introduction of these revaluations entailed at least three new fundamental questions: how to live correctly, how to think correctly, and how to organize correctly.

Paganism had left everyday life exempt, on the whole, from religious supervision. It was only through Islam that the problem arose as to which one of the two or more possible ways of performing this or that erstwhile irrelevant routine action was more pleasing, or possibly the only one acceptable, in the eyes of the Lord. Similarly, the pagan's conclusions on transcendental problems had not affected his metaphysical standing. With Islam correctness of belief became essential, and belief involved areas of thought never touched by the pagan. Islam widened the horizon of the Arab in that it unlocked the doors of theology and metaphysics and introduced him to a new anthropology as well. The limited success of pre-Islamic attempts at state formation was due, in part at least, to the lack of any ideological purpose the proposed state was to embody or realize. The Muslim commonwealth, by contrast, was to implement the precepts of the faith, to make possible and to guarantee their punctual performance; its organization and policy had ideally to be justified by religious considerations.

But Islam not only raised questions. It also indicated novel solutions for recognized problems: it revised prevailing ideas concerning the correct education of the individual by substituting new ideal types for the human models of the pagan era; it revised the relative rating of human activities. Warfare as such is no longer deemed valuable. The fighter for the faith ranks high, but his indispensability does not bestow leadership on him. Islam turns from the aimlessness of the Bedouin to the discipline of the townsman. The ground is laid for the later precedence of the pen over the sword, the scholar over the soldier, the merchant over the peasant. The religious specialist becomes an accepted type. Only under Islam does the introvert find a place in society; only in Islam is the thinker felt to be closer to God than the doer.

So the achievement of Islam in transforming the ancestral Arab culture may be presented as the introducing of four fundamental changes: (a) a widening and refinement of human sensibilities; (b) an extension of the intellectual world and of the means of its mastery by man; (c) the creation of a morally justified and at the same time effective political organization of a locally unprecedented structure; and (d) the delineation of a new "standard" type of life, that is, a new human ideal, and a detailed pattern for its realization in a model biography extending from conception to beyond the day of judgment (cf. von Grunebaum 1948, 219–24).

The analysis of the mental world of yesterday's Arab Bedouin reveals how much of the cultural momentum of Islam has been lost again over the centuries in favor of a revival of pre-Islamic cultural attitudes, in spite of the fact that the Islamic identification has remained unquestioned. It is only on a more sophisticated level of introspection (and possibly under the impact of Western categories of cultural interpretation) that the differentiation within the spiritual heritage between a national and a religious strand could be made explicit, as was attempted, to quote only one example, by the Turkish writer Ziya Gök Alp (d. 1924).[4]

II

The civilization which the conquering Arabs brought out of the Peninsula was itself the result of a first integration of local cultural elements with elements derived from the Jewish, the Christian, and, through their mediation, the Hellenistic traditions, with the message of Islam serving at the same time as an additional constituent and as the crystallizing catalyst. This first Islamic integration imposed itself on a sizable proportion of the subject populations while it was undergoing a keen struggle with the autochthonous cultures. As a result of this *Auseinandersetzung* the philosophical and scientific potential of Islam was actualized and restated in terms acceptable to the representatives of the older traditions with which the new religious civilization had to deal. Persian administrative and political thinking, Hellenistic techniques of philosophizing and of secular science, Indian mathematics and medicine were mastered effortlessly. The linguistic Arabization of the borrowings contributed to their assimilation—the foreign viewpoint when expounded in an Islamized setting and in an Islamized terminology would be experienced as genuinely Islamic; on the other hand, the progressive expliciting of the primitive data of the faith and of their cultural implications would enlarge the basis of intercivilization receptivity. The flowering of the Abbasid Empire between AD 760 and 840 thus came to represent a second integration of Islamic civilization, in which room had been made for "local" traditions which were in part admitted in a bookish fashion but which mostly forced themselves into the new synthesis through the realities of an actual symbiosis.

This second integration was that classical Islamic civilization which competed with Byzantine civilization, which had to withstand the rise of Iranian nationalism in the ninth and tenth centuries, and which, most important of all, found itself exposed to the criticism of a competing attempt at integrating Islamic and local elements undertaken by the radical Shi'a and at times propagated by the political power of the Fatimids. With the help of the Seljuq Turks and the unwitting assistance of the Christian Crusaders, the threat of the Batinite integration was eliminated, and the emergent Sunnite orthodoxy consolidated Islam in a third ecumenical integration which was, by and large, completed by the middle of the twelfth century, and has so far remained the universally accepted self-definition of the Islamic world.

In this third integration, which is only now slowly yielding under regionally disparate reactions to the West, the piety of the popular strata was more securely anchored than it had been before the equipollence of local traditions was assured by an elastic application of the *consensus doetorum* as the verifying authority; a keener sense was shown of what elements of Hellenism are compatible with the Muslim aspiration, and an inclusive feeling about membership in the community which, notwithstanding the awareness of local variations, came to be experienced as increasingly unified in doctrine and lore, made possible the rise of a body spiritual whose hold over the faithful was well-nigh independent of the political realities of the day.

The stability which, in the consciousness of the believers, Islam as constituted in this third integration had reached in providing a balance between the claims of the universal and of the local tradition neutralized the disruptive effects of the supplanting of the multinational empire of the early Abbasid caliphs by an increasing number of rival local, and in certain cases clearly national, states. It also counteracted the disintegration potential of the local renaissances to which in the later Middle Ages Islam owed most of its significant cultural acquisitions. A limited cultural pluralism within, and under the protection of, the ideal unity of Islam—such was the solution provided by the third integration to the inescapable conflict of cultural traditions. Theology and the law, on the one hand, and the forms of conceptualization, argument, and presentation, on the other, provided the most potent means of communicating a sense of cohesion to the overextended and disorganized domain.

The medieval Muslim was himself keenly alive to the regional variations of his civilization, which he was inclined to account for in terms of national differences. Political tensions were apt to create a feeling of national distinctness accompanied by dislike or even hate of one's fellow-Muslims. In Spain, during and after the last reigns of the Umayyad dynasty (deposed in 1031), the "natural aversion," *al-nafara al-tabi'iyya*, between the Muslim Berbers from Morocco and the Andalusian Muslims was almost taken for granted.[5] The "solidarity," *'asabiyya*, of the Berbers and the opposing "solidarity" of the Andalusians were important political factors. The antagonism between the Baghdadis and the Turks in the ninth and tenth centuries, to offer but one more example, was hardly less intense. And both in Spain and in Iraq the dislike of the more highly civilized "native" population for the culturally less Islamized group is experienced and voiced in terms of ethnic or "national" hostility.

By the ninth century the interest in national characteristics had developed a generally applied technique of ethnographic description (used as much by geographers as by littérateurs) whose literary descent from Greek ethnographic technique, while obvious, still needs to be traced through the several phases of its transmission. The various nations inside and out of Islam were classified as "civilized" or "barbarous,"[6] their contributions to the sciences were inventoried, and their psychological peculiarities listed in a few striking phrases which were presumably well taken before the presentation was frozen into a number of clichés. But as a result of this semiscientific concern, the average Muslim carried in his mind a reasonably definite concept of what his "foreign" coreligionists were like as compared with himself.

Ibn Ghalib (eleventh century) describes the Andalusian Muslims as Arabs by genealogy and feeling for independence, by the loftiness of their thoughts, the eloquence of their language, and their inability to suffer oppression; as Hindus in respect to their extreme love for the sciences; as Baghdadis because of their polished ways, the refinement of their manners, and the subtlety of their minds; as Greeks for their excellence in agriculture.[7] Only rarely does the analysis transcend the limitations of the ethnographic notebook, as when al-Jahiz, possibly for propagandistic reasons, devotes a lengthy essay to a study of the Turks in which he offers a certain number of comprehensive characterizations.

> The Turks know not how to flatter or coax, they know not how to practice hypocrisy or back-biting, pretense or slander, dishonesty or haughtiness on their acquaintance, or mischief on those that associate with them. They are strangers to heresy, *bid'a,* and not spoiled by [intellectual] caprice, *ahwa';* and they do not make property lawful by quibbles. Their fault which makes them most unpopular is their love of land and love of moving freely up and down the country and propensity for raiding and preoccupation with plunder, and the intensity of their attachment to it, besides their custom of dwelling on the experienced joy of successive victory, on the delight and frequency of their plunder, and their exploits in such deserts, and their return again and again to the same prairies; and the fact that the excellence of their prowess does not become dulled from long continued idleness, and that their courage is not exhausted by the course of time ... love of the homeland, *mahabbat al-watan,* is common to all nations and prevails over all mankind. But it is peculiarly strong among the Turks, and counts for more among them owing to their mutual similarity and homogeneity of idiosyncrasy.[8]

In general, the characterization remains confined to the aphoristic quip or at any rate to concise and usually undocumented observations that are as often as not elicited by nationalistic rivalries within Islam.[9]

Awareness extended beyond the distinctive traits to such (extra-religious) elements as would reflect and perpetuate the regional peculiarities within Islam. Thus Ibn Khaldun (d. 1406) observes that throughout the Islamic domain the children are taught the Qur'an. The Holy Book provides the basis of instruction. However, "the methods of instructing the children in the Qur'an differ in accordance with the attitudes, *malakat,* which are to result from this instruction" (Ibn Khaldun 1858, III, 260). The Moroccan children are strictly confined to the study of the Qur'an; they are instructed in the spelling of the text, certain variant readings, and the like, but neither *hadith* nor jurisprudence, nor again Arabic grammar and poetry, are taken up during elementary education. In Spain, on the other hand, reading and writing are taught first. Since the Qur'an is the foundation of all instruction and the source of religion and all the sciences, the Spaniards will take it as the basis of their teaching. They will not, however, make it the sole object of their instruction. On the contrary, the Spanish teachers will at an early stage introduce their pupils to poetry and make them memorize the rules of Arabic grammar; a great deal of attention is also given to calligraphy. In Ifriqiya (Tunisia) instruction in the *hadith* and the principles of the religious sciences is added to instruction in the Qur'an, with some considerable emphasis reserved for calligraphy. Ibn Khaldun observes[10] that the educational program of Tunis is close to that of al-Andalus, owing to the influence of eastern Spanish *émigré* scholars who had settled in Tunis because of the Christian advance southward. In the Muslim east the Qur'an is taken as the point of departure, but instruction in various sciences is not neglected; calligraphy, however, does not form part of general education but has to be acquired as a special skill from a separate master. Ibn Khaldun indorses the proposal which the judge Abu Bakr b. al-'Arabi (d. 1148) directed to the eastern Muslims to the effect that the "Orientals" should adopt the Spanish system and begin the curriculum with the study of the Arabic language and poetry. Next, there should be given a cursus in arithmetic, and only then should the study of the Qur'an be undertaken, which would be greatly facilitated by the preliminary training the pupil would have received. From the Qur'an instruction should proceed to the *usul al-din*, "the Principles of Theology," and the *usul al-fiqh*, "the Principles of Jurisprudence," and finally reach the sciences of Tradition (Ibn Khaldun 1858, III, 263–64).

The different civilizational outlook of the Muslim elites in Spain, Morocco, and Tunis (and to some extent of the east) is clearly grasped in its molding effect on prevailing ideas of education. But at the same time it is obvious that Ibn Khaldun, in accordance with the Islamic erudites of all times, views the different systems of instruction but as relatively insignificant variants of one and the same universally accepted education which mirrors the ideal unity of the *dar al-Islam*. This idea of unity was not to be impaired by nationalistic pride, as it had developed with particular strength and aggressiveness on both sides of the Arabic heartlands—in Persia as well as in Spain.[11] Almost to the present time the overriding concern of the Islamic elites (and perhaps even of most of the Muslim populations in the Near East and North Africa) has been for the integrity of the *dar al-Islam* as a whole rather than for the integrity of any particular component state.

The beautiful and moving passage with which Ibn al-Athir (d. 1234) introduces, *sub anno* 617/1220, his account of the first Mongol invasion of Muslim lands is informed by an intense feeling for the oneness of all the faithful, and it betrays an intense sensitivity to any event affecting Islam in any part of the world. The misery of the Persian Muslims is experienced as a calamity that has befallen all mankind but more particularly all Muslims.[12] A comparable feeling of oneness transcending regional differentiation, but this time founded specifically on the realization of the unity of Islam as a civilization rather than solely as a religion or a sociopolitical community, was on several occasions voiced by al-Biruni (d. 1048). At the beginning of his book on India, Biruni sets forth the difficulties he has had to contend with in its preparation. "The barriers which separate Muslims and Hindus rest on different causes." It is always the cultural unit of Islam which is confronted with the cultural unit of Hindu India. Neither the oneness nor the identifiability in civilizational terms of Islam is ever questioned. Biruni goes on to point out some of the essential differences: "... they totally differ from us in religion, as we believe in nothing in which they believe, and vice versa ... in all manners and usages they differ from us to such a degree as to frighten their children with us, with our dress, and our ways and customs, and as to declare us the devil's breed, and our doings the very opposite of all that is good and proper." Biruni adds that among the Muslims as among all nations a similar disparagement of foreigners can be found.[13] Here, again, it is the world of Islam, not any particular country or tradition, with which the individual feels identified.

III

Conflict, coexistence, and interaction of the Islamic and the local culture patterns can be experienced and described in different ways depending on which aspect of the phenomenon is felt or perceived most vividly.

1. The patterns may be maintained in the relation of the great to the little tradition.[14] This is to say that one of the two patterns is recognized as the more advanced; it is assumed to make authority; it is almost exclusively represented in the writings as well as the public actions of the elite; social prestige is dependent on its adoption. In the *dar al-Islam* the Islamic pattern is in general in the position of the great tradition. In contrast, the little tradition is the catchment of the popular undercurrent; its effectiveness is still felt by the intelligentsia, but "officially" it will be denied or deprecated. Where the hypotheses of the great tradition are considered beliefs, the hypotheses of the little tradition will be considered superstitions. In fact, the social position of a person may depend on which of the two traditions he determines to live by.

The actual accommodation of the two traditions in such areas of the life of the community as are judged important may be effected through various methods of adjustment.

a) The great tradition admits the little tradition as the religion of the ignorant.[15]

b) The great tradition develops a "latitudinarian" attitude toward the practice of the little tradition. This approach can be exemplified by the custom prevailing, e.g., in Turkey and in Syria which permits Muslims to resort to the invocation of Christian saints and vice versa. Such devotion to the saints of a religion not one's own will not arouse any suspicion that the individual concerned intends to leave his native religious community.[16]

c) An integration of the two traditions may be tried:

(1) A Christian saint may, for example, be identified with a Muslim saint; or he may be considered to have been a crypto-Muslim.[17]

(2) The local cult tradition will be tied in with, and accounted for, in terms of the "genuine" great tradition. The Prophet himself set the precedent for this procedure by giving an Islamic meaning to the heathen pilgrimage rites which he welded into the Muslim *hajj* to Mecca, 'Arafa, and Mina. By the same token, the Islamic pilgrimages to the Temple area in Jerusalem or to the tombs of the patriarchs in Hebron are but the Islamization of practices familiar from Old and New Testament times (cf. Matthews

1949, xxiv). The practices were sanctioned by the local clergy when their ineradicability had been evidenced over a sufficiently long period. Great care is given in such cases to establishing the legitimacy of the practice in terms of the great tradition, whose more self-conscious or more learned representatives are apt to preserve a certain uneasiness about the admissibility of the successful intruder. The extreme attention bestowed by the mystical orders on the *silsila* which is to provide the great tradition's authorization for their practices, which are more than a little affected by folkways, is a case in point.

(3) The little tradition may be taken into the great tradition by means of an appropriate theological or philosophical explanation. In Islam one of the most characteristic examples of this tendency is the justification within the framework of orthodoxy of the cult of the saints. The saint is interpreted as the possessor of Gnostic knowledge; he is closer to God than are his fellow-Muslims, and his miracles are accounted for by the grace of Allah, who uses His elect as an instrument in furthering His mysterious ends and, according to some, even as His agent in the actual government of the universe. Qur'anic evidence is found to prove the existence of familiars of the Lord, and the theosophy of Ibn al-'Arabi (d. 1240) reconciles the saint of the little tradition with the prophet of the great tradition by arguing that "all prophets are also saints but that the saintly aspect of each prophet is higher than the prophetic aspect." Besides, all prophets and saints are but "manifestations of the Spirit or Reality of Muhammad."[18]

2. The relationships of the two cultural strains may be interpreted as that of *sunna*, the legitimate tradition of the Prophet, and *bid'a*, unauthorized innovation. Local custom appears to the guardians of the universal culture as an illicit deviation of a kind allegedly envisaged by Muhammad himself. It is then their duty to combat such customs or at least to confine the practices to the local circles already dedicated to them. The *faqih* from the Maghrib who is brought face to face with the mores of his Egyptian or Syrian coreligionists is apt to feel outraged by their unwarrantable "innovations," which will appear to him as relaxations and corruptions of the strictness of the *sunna*.[19]

3. Canon law and customary law, canon law and executive law, may coexist as an expression of divergent approaches to the social realization of the ideal Muslim community. The legal system sidestepping the *shari'a* may owe its origin to administrative exigencies; it may reflect the superimposition of an alien though Islamized ruling class on the generality of local Muslims; or it may openly constitute a systematization of regional usage with only the slightest admixture of the legal system of Islam.

4. Cultural divergencies may crystallize in sectarian developments. The success of the Kharijites among the Berbers, like that of the Shi'ite extremists in the mountainous areas of Syria and southeastern Asia Minor, is to a large extent due to the sectarian movement catching up, as it were, religious and cultural motifs that had been important

to the local people before Islam and which the (sometimes but nominally) Muslim sect was able to reintegrate.

5. Variations of local sentiment will support the proliferation of experiential and organizational variants within a movement sanctioned by the universal orthodoxy. The history of the legal rites, and even more so that of the mystical *tariqa*s with their emphasis on different aspects of the supreme experience of the *tawhid* or on different social-technical means to attain to it, can to a considerable extent be accounted for through an investigation of their relations to local cultural traditions.

6. The precepts of the universal and of the local traditions may knowingly be contrasted as norm and practice. In this situation the several areas of social life will be unevenly resistant to the Islamic pattern which in theory has been accepted as the pervasive norm; the perseverance of the social strata will differ when it comes to maintaining the traditional against the inroads of the "true" order of things; the society of women may continue an attachment that has been abandoned by the men in their extradomestic relations, and the like. The passage is well known in which Ibn Battuta (d. 1377) describes his failure, when a judge in the Maldive Islands, to induce the local women to adopt a manner of dress consonant with the Muslim custom. It would seem from his account that, with all his zeal in carrying out the prescriptions of the canon law, he did not even attempt to uproot the peculiar type of temporary marriage which was then widely practiced in those islands. At the same time, he emphasizes the piety of the inhabitants and their attachment to Islam (Ibn Battuta 1853–58, IV, 114, 123, and 151–52).

The traditions will, on occasion, conflict not so much on the fundamental religious level as on a cultural level more narrowly defined. The bilingual culture of modern Egypt and of certain Berber areas, on the one hand, and that of the Iranian elite from the ninth through the eleventh centuries, on the other, is not the result of opposing religious attitudes toward an interpretation of the universal faith of Islam but rather of an unwillingness to sacrifice a cultural aspiration which, while not rooted in the prophetic norm, is yet valued as an adequate means of collective self-expression. It would seem that the submergence or survival of a local culture that has been overrun by another culture of geographically (and spiritually) wider outreach depends in large measure on the continued identification with the ancestral tradition of the local ruling classes who buttress their self-respect and justify their self-perpetuation by upholding the tradition within which alone their position is truly meaningful. More or less fictional attempts to integrate this tradition in the historical mythology of the conquerors are often pragmatically successful, although they may not find credence among the authoritative guardians of the Islamic tradition. The Islamization of the Persian *dihqan* and, on a lower cultural level, that of the Berber chieftain, who both on the whole maintained their social role, are cases in point. The evolution of a vernacular tradition in Egypt is of course to be explained in a different manner.

IV

The universal culture of Islam disposes of several means to further the adjustment to the local cultures. Of those, the most characteristically Islamic is the *ijma'*. The *consensus omnium*, narrowed down to a *consensus prudentium*, is authorized to rule on the legitimacy of any individual belief or practice which the community may have adopted. Its verifying verdict includes its object among the normative elements of the Muslim tradition.[20] There is no appeal against the *ijma'* except to a later *ijma'*. It has often been shown how significant elements of local and popular piety were allowed to enter the orthodox norm. A typical progress leads from appraisal of a phenomenon as *bid'a sayyi'a* to that as *bid'a hasana* and thence to fissureless integration in the teachings of the doctors of the faith. The existence of a merely local *ijma'* is recognized. But while the *ijma'* of the *Haramayn* (Mecca and Medina) may count for more than that of an outlying area, and while attempts may be made to bring the local *ijma'* in line with that of more holy or more advanced places, yet even the local *ijma'* will serve to ward off from the native Muslims the suspicion of heresy; it will serve also to prevent the cleavage between universal norm and traditional practice from rendering an "Islamic" life impossible.

Genealogical theories or fictions, the sacred language, literature in the *Hochsprache* (principally Arabic, but in certain regions Persian), and, in general, the content of education as dispensed by all but the most modernist (which may imply, nationalistic) institutions, effectively assist in the adjustment of the conflicting cultural traditions. In Islam, as elsewhere, historiography plays a special part in shaping the identification of a community. The specifically Muslim elaboration of the concept of unilinear history, leading from creation to resurrection, provides a firm if elastic frame in which the fate of the individual Muslim nations can be rendered meaningful through their function in originating and spreading ultimate truth. This is not to suggest that local traditions have failed to influence local historiography. On the contrary, every type of historical writing shows in some way the peculiar outlook of its country of origin. The Arab-Muslim biography is rich in personal facts and colorful anecdote, while its Persian-Muslim counterpart is less concerned with the personal elements but more generous in offering the reader quotations from the works of the biographee. The little tradition, too, develops a historiography representative of its aspirations. The *'Antar Novel* goes back as far as the eighth century AD.[21] Local histories need not but often will represent a local cultural outlook. Yet, seen in its entirety, historiography has proved itself an exceptionally powerful instrument of universalization.

A common style of argumentation and formulation, most clearly visible in the peculiar cachet of the *hadith*[22] and the unmistakable atmosphere which its use conveys to practically all literary manifestations of the Islamic tradition, effectively promotes the impression of cultural uniformity. The local tradition, which has to assert itself through formal means recognizably borrowed from its competitor, is by this very fact put at a disadvantage. The formal unity of Muslim theological and scientific writing has done almost as much to make possible its international distribution as the international acceptance of the Arabic language.

But the factor which is in the last analysis most influential in adjusting the relations of the civilization of Islam and the traditional civilizations of the Muslim lands is the voluntary and deliberate identification of the individual believer. He may actually lead his life by ethnically or nationally inherited practices, but at the same time he recognizes his behavior as a forgivable shortcoming for which he is able to adduce numbers of reasons; besides, and this is the decisive point, his day-by-day behavior appears irrelevant to him when he views himself and his society in relation to his Creator and to the rest of mankind. For in this universal context his insignificant person appears among the followers of the Prophet, and it is from this association that he derives his dignity in this, and his invulnerability in the next, world.

Notes

1. Gibb and Bowen 1950, 211, n. 6, citing A. D. A. de Kat Angelino, *Colonial Policy* (The Hague, 1931), I, 67–8.
2. Jahiz 1356–64/1938–45, V, 66–71; idem 1907, V, 24–25. The same Jahiz quotes the Muʿtazilite, Thumama b. Ashras (d. 828), for use of the grain-snatching cocks of Marw as proof that the avarice of its human inhabitants is due to the influence of their land and its water: Jahiz 1900, 19; idem Cairo 1338/1939, I, 46; idem 1948, 14; idem 1951, 26). The geographer, Ibn al-Faqih (*fl.* after AD 902), insists that inspection reveals the untruth of Thumama's statement concerning the behavior of the cocks of Marw: Ibn al-Faqih 1885, 316–17. In this connection the passage in Yaqut (d. 1229) 1866–73, III, 630^{ult}–31^7, may be referred to in which the author co-ordinates the excellencies of the Iraqis with the virtues of the climate of Iraq.
3. Cf., as one example for many, the shock which the Moroccan traveler, Ibn Battuta, receives when he sees the visitors to the public bath in the Egyptian township of Munyat Ibn Khasib refreshing themselves in complete nakedness; cf. Ibn Battuta 1853–58, I, 100.
4. Cf., e.g., in the poetical volume *Qyzyl Elma* (Istanbul, 1330) the poem "'Uthman Ghazi qurultay-da" with its characteristic line: *Türklük-le Islamlaq qardash olajaq* (101; trans. E. Pritsch, *Festschrift F. Giese*, ed. G. Jäschke [Berlin, 1941], 122: "Zum Türkentum wird del' Islam sich gesellen"), and also in "'Asker du'asy" (88) the verse: *ana-myz watan, baba-myz millet.* For Ziya Gök Alp's ideology, see Heyd 1950, 84ff. For the attitude, cf. also Saʿid Halim Pasha (d. 1921) 1928.
5. Cf. Pérès 1937, 9; cf. also 13. Yaqut 1866–73, I, 541^{19}–42^4, 542^{18}–43^8, who quotes a number of unfavorable judgments on the Berbers.
6. Cf., e.g., Saʿid al-Andalusi (d. 1070) 1912, 7–8; idem 1935, 35, who bases his classification of the nations on their active interest in the sciences, *'ulum.* On the political level, too, three to six Great Kings are set apart from the other kings of the world. This division follows a literary tradition which has been traced back to the China of AD 240–50; it occurs in Arabic literature for the first time in AD 851; Ferrand 1930–32, 329–39. The same technique of ethnographic description is to be met with in the *Letter of Tansar*, where the author vaunts the Persian nation as uniting the *suwari* of the Turks and the *ziraki* of the Hind with the

khubkari and the *sina'at* of the Rum. In addition, all the sciences of the world have fallen to the Persians' lot: *wa-'ilm-ha-yi jumla ru-yi zamin ba-ma ruzi gardanid* (ed. and trans. J. Darmesteter, *Journal asiatique* [9th series] 1894, 241–44, esp. 242 and 243; 546–49, esp. 547).

In Jahiz 1356–64/1938–45, VI, 14–15; idem 1907, VI, 5–6, Jahiz lists the principal problems which an anthropology would have to take up: the distinction between male and female, the different life-expectancies of people, *a'mar*, their different sizes and intellectual abilities, *maqadir al-'uqul*, the different valuations of their crafts, *tafadul al-sina'at* (and the arguments brought forward in establishing their rating), and the position of man above the jinn but below the angels.

7. Abridged from Pérès' translation, Pérès 1937, 18–19; for a similar pattern of description, cf. Pérès 1937, 116, Bakri's characterization of al-Andalus.

8. Jahiz 1903, 39–41; Cairo ed. 38–39; trans. 678–79; cf. also the somewhat idealized portrayal of the Arab, idem 1903, 44–45; Cairo ed. 42–43, trans. 683–84.

9. Cf., e.g., the interesting remarks on Greeks, Indians, Arabs, etc., of Tawhidi (d. 1023) 1939–44, I, 212–13.

10. Ibn Khaldun 1858, III, 262. In 1540–41 Nicolas Clenard observes grammar to form part of elementary education in Fez; the concentration on the Qur'an as the starting point and basis of all instruction is as intense as it was in Ibn Khaldun's time; and Tunis is still ahead of Fez in the cultivation of learning outside of the sciences of the Qur'an and grammar; besides, the study of grammar does not seem to have been effective with many of the Fasis of Clenard's day; cf. Le Tourneau 1953, 19–20 of reprint.

11. For nationalism in Spain, cf. Pérès 1937, 52–53, 54. Pines 1952, 32–34, describes the "nationalism" of eastern Iran in the tenth and eleventh centuries. The Spaniard Ibn Jubayr (d. 1217) 1907, 78–79; idem 1952, 73–74, insists that only the Maghrib has the true Islam; Ibn Battuta 1853–58, IV, 334–37, vaunts the Maghrib above Egypt and Syria on various grounds. Ibn Khallikan (d. 1282) 1843–71, I, 120, quotes Tha'alibi (d. 1038) for the statement that Ibn Darraj al-Andalusi (d. 1030) "was for the country of Andalus, that which al-Mutanabbi (d. 965) was for Syria, a poet of the highest order, and equally elegant in what he said and wrote." Long before these authors, Ya'qubi (d. 897) 1891, 236–37; idem 1937, 7–8, had characterized the several regions of the caliphal empire such as Syria, Ifriqiya, and Egypt, and compared them to their disadvantage with Iraq, making his bias for Mesopotamia rather obvious; five hundred years later, Qalqashandu (d. 1418) 1913–19, III, 286, thought it worth his while to rebut Ya'qubi's verdict (cf. Ya'qubi 1937, 8, n. 1). In Egypt a distinctly national, not to say nationalistic, feeling antedates the Muslim conquest; *ca.* AD 492 Horapollon refers to his country as "our fatherland, *patris*," and the use of *patrios* in the sense of "national" as opposed to "Greek-imported" is frequent throughout the fifth century. In a derogatory sense Anastasios Sinaita (writing *ca.* AD 622) speaks of *hoi aigyptiazontes ton noun*, "intellects of an Egyptian type"; cf. Maspero 1923, 24; Bardy 1948, 52. The conflict between possible religious and ethnic alignments comes out well in the account given by Yaqut 1866–73, III, 534–35, of the princeling, *ra'is*, of Turaithith (in Khurasan, not far from Nishapur) who *ca.* AD 1136 tries to ally himself to the Turks against the Isma'ilis but finds himself compelled, owing to the aggressiveness of his *soi-disant* friends, to reverse his loyalties; he does so quite successfully but with a bit of a bad conscience.

12. Ibn al-Athir 1851–76, XII, 233–35; trans. in Gabrieli 1951, 232–34. Cf. also Yaqut 1866–73, IV, 859[4-5], qualifying the conquest of Nishapur by the Mongols in 1221 as "an unparalleled calamity for Islam."

13. Al-Biruni 1887, 9–10; idem 1888, I, 17–20; cf. also the passage in Biruni 1937, 27, in which Biruni aligns Muslim civilization with Greek, contrasting it again with that of India. Contrast with Biruni the naïve statement of Jahiz 1356–64/1938–45, VII, 29 (idem 1907, VII, 12): "The Hind are agreed with the Arabs in every respect except for the circumcision of men and women."

14. To use R. Redfield's terminology; cf. Redfield 1952/53, 224–28, esp. the last paragraph of the paper.

15. Cf., e.g., Jabarti (d. 1822) 1888–96, VI, 92. The contrast between the popular and the learned tradition comes out well in Yaqut's presentation of the legend of Bait Lihya, Yaqut 1866–73, I, 780$^{4-9}$.

16. For sanctuaries shared by Muslim and Christian devotion, cf., e.g., Sauvaget 1933–50, I, 84 and n. 3. The ambiguous attitude of the Muslim populace toward objects of Christian worship comes out well when Saladin sends a cross to Baghdad: the relic is first despised but ends by being held in reverence; cf. Levy 1929, 237–38.

17. Cf., e.g., Hasluck 1929, 58–59. A Biblical figure may become the goal of a pilgrimage even though he plays no part in the specifically Muslim ideas of prophetic history. Thus the Damascenes are fond of visiting the exact spot where Abel was killed on Mount Qasiyun; cf. Ibn Battuta 1853–58, I, 231–33.

18. Arberry 1950, 101. In this context the angelology and demonology of the theologians may be compared with popular ideas on the subject of jinn, *mala'ika*, and the like. Jahiz, 1356–64/1938–45, VI, 158–281 (with digressions; idem 1907, VI, 48–90), devotes what amounts to a monograph to the demonological notions of the Arabs; his material may be conveniently contrasted with, say, Ghazali's ideas as presented by Wensinck 1940, 168–75. In general, it may be said that the consolidation of orthodoxy which took place in the eleventh and twelfth centuries was brought about to some extent by the admission (or readmission) of beliefs appertaining to the little tradition into the great tradition, where, to the outside observer, they sometimes cut a peculiar figure. Cf., e.g., the rules recorded by Ghazali on the proper behavior in the lavatory, where behind every regulation there lurks a "superstitious" motivation: Ghazali 1358/1934, 6–7; trans. Watt 1953, 92–93; or the admonitions tendered by Zarnuji (*fl.* 1203) to the student, 1947, 67–69, where the opinions of the vulgar are provided with the rationale of (debased) science. Consider also the acceptance by Ghazali of the efficacy, in speeding a difficult delivery, of magic squares placed under the feet of a woman in labor—1939, 157–58; trans. Watt 1953, 79–80. In this connection the reading of Bukhari's (d. 870) *Sahih* as a measure to fortify Islam and to ward off a present danger should be mentioned. It was widely practiced in the Ottoman Empire; thus in Rajab, 1202/ April–May, 1788, the Sultan ordered the *shaykh*s of al-Azhar to read Bukhari as a protection against an impending public calamity; again on 20 Dhu 'l-hijja, 1220/12 March, 1806, the *shaykh*s unite to read Bukhari, with a view to staving off the dangers of an attack by the English (Jabarti 1888–96, V, 27–28, and VIII, 51). In 1228/1813, Bukhari is read to keep the plague away. Jabarti observes at this point: "People gathered at al-Azhar [for those readings] during three days; then proceedings were stopped because of laziness" (Jabarti 1888–96, IX, 9). The reading was again ordered when victory against the Wahhabis was in doubt during September/October, 1817 (Jabarti 1888–96, 250–51). Cf. further the last three instances recorded by Jabarti for March, 1818 (Jabarti 1888–96, 266–67), September, 1818 (Jabarti 1888–96, 270), and January, 1821 (Jabarti 1888–96, 329). Muhammad Rashid Rida (d. 1935) 1927–34, IV, 119, and XII, 246, still finds it necessary to ridicule the official readings of Bukhari; cf., further, Jomier 1954, 257.

19. Cf., e.g., Ibn al-Hajj (d. 1336) 1348/1929; and ʿAli b. Maimun al-Maghribi (d. 917/1511–12), whose work was analyzed by Goldziher 1874, 293–330. It is worthy of note that already Ibn Hawqal 1873, 70 (idem 1938–39, 98–99), in AD 977 speaks of the moral and religious superiority of the Islamic west over the Islamic east. His contemporary, al-Muqaddasi, writing in AD 985, 1906, 440[21–22], remarks on regional differences in funerary customs. For conflicting reactions to what in the eyes of an author from a different region will appear as deviations from accepted or canonical practice, compare Ibn Battuta's adverse reaction to the mourning ceremonies which he observes in Idhaj (Khuzistan), Ibn Battuta 1853–58, II, 35–36, with his approval of the manner in which the people of Damascus celebrate the Day of ʿArafat, Ibn Battuta 1853–58, I, 243–44.

20. The invocation of the name of Allah will often suffice to convince the conscience of the believer that his practices are in keeping with Islamic precept. It is by this device that the use of magic is legitimized in many parts of the Muslim world. By the same means the Kazak-Kirghiz, whose Islam is, however, far from recent, justify the continuation of shamanism; cf. Eliade 1951, 200–201. Winstedt 1925 contains a great number of illuminating examples of the naturalization on diverse levels of Islamic ideas in the mental world of the Muslims of the Malay Peninsula. The several possibilities of amalgamation or adjustment of two (or more) cultural strands are clearly instanced in Winstedt's material, which was collected primarily to illustrate the evolution of Malay magic. Of special interest are cases of (sunken) learned tradition, as, for instance, the following passage from the *Garden of Kings* (written in AD 1638 by an Indian missionary of Islam in Acheen, Sumatra): "Jan, the father of all jinn, was originally an angel, called firstly Aristotle but later ʿAzazil" (33). Cf. also the Islamized invocation of a Malay shaman, Winstedt 1925, 62–63.

21. Cf. Rosenthal 1952, 164–70, where under the heading "The Historical Novel" a great deal of pertinent material has been assembled.

22. On the mode of presentation typical of the *hadith*, cf. von Grunebaum 1950, 24, n. 2 (French ed. 14, n. 6). Reprinted, with modification, in von Grunebaum 1955.

References

Arberry, A. J. 1950. *Sufism: An Account of the Mystics of Islam*. London: Allen and Unwin.

Bardy, G. 1948. *La Question des langues dans l'église ancienne*. Paris: Beauchesne.

Biruni, al-. 1887. *Alberuni's India*. Ed. E. Sachau. London: Trubner.

—1888. *Alberuni's India*. Trans. E. Sachau. London: Trubner.

—1937. *Kitab al-saydana*. Trans. M. Meyerhof. In *Islamic Culture* 11: 17–29.

Eliade, M. 1951. *Le Chamanisme et les techniques archaïques de l'extase*. Paris: Payot.

Ferrand, G. 1930–32. "Les grands rois du monde." *Bulletin of the School of Oriental and African Studies* 6: 329–39.

Gabrieli, F. 1951. *Storia della letteratura araba*. Milan: Academia.

Ghazali, al-. 1358/1934. *Bidayat al-hidaya*. Cairo.

—1939. *al-Munqidh min al-dalal*. Damascus.

Gibb, H. A. R., and Bowen, H. 1950. *Islamic Society and the West*. London: Oxford University Press.

Goldziher, I. 1874. "Ali b. Mejmun al-Magribi und sein Sittenspiegel des Östlichen Islam." *Zeitschrift der deutschen morgenländischen Gesellschaft* 28: 293–330.

Hasluck, F. W. 1929. *Christianity and Islam under the Sultans.* Oxford: Clarendon Press.

Heyd, U. 1950. *Foundations of Turkish Nationalism.* London: Luzac.

Ibn al-Athir. 1851–76. *Kamil.* Ed. C. J. Tornberg. Leiden: E. J. Brill.

Ibn Battuta. 1853–58. *Rihla.* Ed. and trans. C. Defremery and B. R. Sanguinetti. Paris: Imprimerie Impériale.

Ibn al-Faqih. 1885. *Mukhtasar kitab al-buldan.* Ed. M. J. de Goeje. Leiden: E. J. Brill.

Ibn al-Hajj. 1348/1929. *al-Mudkhal.* Cairo: al-Matbaʿa al-Misriya.

Ibn Hawqal. 1873. *Bibliotheca Geographorum Arabicorum.* Ed. M. J. de Goeje. Leiden: E. J. Brill.

—1938–39. *Bibliotheca Geographorum Arabicorum.* 2nd ed. Ed. J. H. Kramers. Leiden: E. J. Brill.

Ibn Jubayr. 1907. *Travels.* 2nd ed. Ed. W. Wright and M. J. de Goeje. Leiden and London: E. J. Brill.

—1952. *Travels.* Trans. R. J. C. Broadhurst. London: Jonathan Cape.

Ibn Khaldun. 1858. *Prolegomena.* Ed. E. Quatremère. Paris.

Ibn Khallikan. 1843–71. *Wafayat al-aʿyan.* Trans. W. MacGuckin de Slane. Paris: Oriental Translation Fund.

Jabarti. 1888–96. *Merveilles biographiques et historiques.* Cairo: Imprimerie nationale.

Jahiz, al-. 1338/1939. *Kitab al-bukhala'.* Ed. A. al-ʿAwamiri and ʿAli Jarim. Cairo: Dar al-Kutub al-Misriya.

—1356–64/1938–45. *Kitab al-hayawan.* 2nd ed. Cairo: Halabi.

—1900. *Kitab al-bukhala'.* Ed. G. Van Vloten. Leiden: E. J. Brill.

—1903. *Tria opuscula.* Ed. G. Van Vloten. Leiden: E. J. Brill (another edition: Cairo 1324/1906; trans. C. T. Harley Walker, *Journal of the Royal Asiatic Society*, 1915).

—1907. *Kitab al-hayawan.* Cairo: Matbaʿat al-Saʿada.

—1948. *Kitab al-bukhala'.* Ed. T. al-Hajiri. Cairo: Dar al-Maʿarif.

—1951. *Kitab al-bukhala'.* Trans. C. Pellat. Beirut and Paris: C. P. Maisonneuve.

Jomier, J. 1954. *Le Commentaire coranique du Manar.* Paris: C. P. Maisonneuve.

Le Tourneau, R. 1953. "Un humaniste à Fès au XVIᵉ siècle." *Revue de la Méditerranée.* 54–55.

Levy, R. 1929. *A Baghdad Chronicle.* Cambridge: Cambridge University Press.

Maspero, J. 1923. *Histoire des patriarches d'Alexandrie.* Paris: E. Champion.

Matthews, C. D. 1949. *Palestine-Muhammadan Holy Land.* New Haven: Yale University Press.

Muqaddasi, al-. 1906. *Descriptio Imperii Moslemici.* Ed. M. J. de Goeje. Leiden: E. J. Brill.

Pérès, H. 1937. *La Poésie andalouse en arabe classique au XIᵉ siecle.* Paris: Adrien-Maisonneuve.

Pines, S. 1952. "La 'Philosophie orientale' d'Avicenne et sa polémique contre les bagdadiens." *Archives d'histoire doctrinale et littéraire du moyen âge* 19: 5–37.

Qalqashandu. 1913–19. *Subht al-aʿsha.* Cairo.

Redfield, R. 1952/53. "The Natural History of the Folk Society." *Social Forces* 31: 224–8.

Rida, Muhammad Rashid. 1927–34. *Tafsir al-Manar.* Cairo: Dar al-Manar.

Rosenthal, F. 1952. *A History of Muslim Historiography.* Leiden: E. J. Brill.

Saʿid al-Andalusi. 1912. *Kitab tabaqat al-umam.* Ed. L. Cheikho. Beirut: al-Matbaʿa al-Kathulikiya,

—1935. *Kitab tabaqat al-umam.* Trans. R. Blachère. Paris: Larose.

Saʿid Halim Pasha. 1928. *Islamlashmaq.* Ed. A. Fischer. Leipzig.

Sauvaget, J. 1933–50. *Matériaux pour servir à l'histoire de la ville d'Alep.* Beirut: Institut français de Damas.

Tawhidi, al-. 1939–44. *Kitab al-imta' wa'l-mu'anasa.* Ed. A. Amin and A. al-Zayn. Cairo: Lajnat al-Ta'lif wa'l-Tarjama wa'l-Nashr.

von Grunebaum, G. E. 1948. "Transformation of Culture as Illustrated by the Rise of Islam." In *Conflict of Power in Modern Culture: Proceedings of the Seventh Conference on Science, Philosophy, and Religion*. Ed. Lyman Bryson, Louis Finkelstein, and R. M. MacIver, 218–24. New York: Harper.

—1950. "Islam and Hellenism." *Scientia* 44: 21–27.

—1955. *Islam: Essays on the Nature and Growth of a Cultural Tradition*. American Anthropological Association Memoirs 81. Chicago, IL: University of Chicago Press.

Watt, W. M. 1953. *The Faith and Practice of al-Ghazali*. London: George Allen and Unwin.

Wensinck, A. J. 1940. *La Pensée de Ghazzali*. Paris: Adrien-Maisonneuve.

Winstedt, R. O. 1925. *Shaman, Saiva, and Sufi*. London: Constable.

Ya'qubi, al. 1891. *Kitab al-buldan*. Ed. M. J. de Goeje. Leiden: E. J. Brill.

—1937. *Ya'kubi, Les pays*. Trans. G. Wiet. Cairo: Institut français d'archéologie orientale du Caire.

Yaqut. 1866–73. *Mu'jam al-buldan*. Ed. F. Wüstenfeld. Leipzig and St. Petersburg: F. A. Brockhaus.

Zarnuji, al-. 1947. *Ta'lim al-muta'allim*. Trans. G. E. von Grunebaum and T. M. Abel. New York: Iranian Institute and School of Asiatic Studies.

20

The Dialectic of a Cultural Tradition

Marshall G. S. Hodgson

What has been felt as Islam, however, considered historically, in all its ramifi
cations and even in its most central implications, has of course varied enormously. The very comprehensiveness of the vision of *islam* as it is unfolded has
insured that it can never be quite the same from one place or one time to another.[1]
Empirically, any particular formulation of what the fundamental consequences of the
act of *islam* must indispensably include, would find serious Muslims to reject it—as
would a corresponding attempt with regard to any other religious tradition. Still more
would this be the case for the culture generally. For historically, Islam and its associated
lifeways form a cultural tradition, or a complex of cultural traditions; and a cultural
tradition by its nature grows and changes; the more so, the broader its scope.

Tradition can cease to be living, can degenerate to mere transmission. A recipe for
a holiday pastry may be "traditional" in the sense merely that it is transmitted unaltered
from mother to daughter for untold generations. If it is merely transmissive, a sheer
habit, then any change of circumstances may lead to its abandonment, at least once the
mother is gone. But if it is vital, meeting a real need, then the tradition will be
readjusted or grow as required by circumstances. A living cultural tradition, in fact,
is always in course of development. Even if a pattern of activity remains formally
identical in a changed context, its meaning can take on new implications; it can be
gradually, even imperceptibly, reconceived. A pastry first made when all foods were
prepared at home inevitably becomes something very different when it alone is home-
made, though exactly the recipe be used. To cling to the recipe then requires, or

perhaps produces, a new point of view toward the pastry. But even without so drastic a change in circumstances, the recipe and its use will prove to have a history. Even in primitive life, over the millennia or even only the centuries, fuel differed, or water, or the quality of the utensils. Eventually, if the tradition was genuinely alive, some cook found that the recipe itself could be improved on in the changed conditions. As she did so, she was not abandoning the tradition but rather keeping it alive by letting it grow and develop.

Living societies seem never to have been actually static. With the advent of citied and lettered life, this dynamic aspect of cultural tradition was intensified; or, rather, the living tradition-process was speeded up and became more visible, so that generation by generation within each tradition there was a conscious individual cultural initiative in response to the ever-new needs or opportunities of the time. It is in what is called "high culture," in relatively widely shared cultural forms at the literate, urban level, that social tradition has unmistakably shown itself as a process of change. Yet even in "folk culture," the culture of peasants or even of non-lettered peoples, cultural traditions share substantially the same dynamic force which is more visible in high culture.[2]

In general, then, but especially in the high culture of pre-Modern citied societies, which has been the primary milieu of Islam, we may describe the process of cultural tradition as a movement composed of three moments: a creative action, group commitment thereto, and cumulative interaction within the group. A tradition originates in a creative action, an occasion of inventive or revelatory, even charismatic, encounter: for instance, the discovery of a new aesthetic value; the launching of a new technique of craftsmanship; a rise to a new level of social expectation, one man of another; the assertion of a new ruling stock or even the working out of new patterns of governing; or, in the case of religion, an occasion of fresh awareness of something ultimate in the relation between ourselves and the cosmos—that is, an occasion of spiritual revelation, bringing a new vision. In accepting the Qur'an and its challenge, Muhammad and his followers opened themselves to vast new considerations of what life might mean, which relegated their former concerns to frivolity; their act of acceptance was thus intensely creative.

Such occasions are creative partly through the quality of the objective event itself, in which there must be something which genuinely answers to universally latent human potentialities. The human impact of the Qur'an as a sheer piece of writing is undeniable. At the same time, the occasions are creative equally through the particular receptivity of their public, of those who take up the creative event and what it has produced and assign it value, finding in it something which answers to their particular needs or interests, material or imaginative, so that it becomes normative for them. The Qur'an spoke not only in the language of but to the personal and social needs of a particular group of Arabians, of Meccans and Medinese, with particular social and moral problems. By their responses, positive and negative, they built concrete meaning into what might otherwise have remained on the verbal level as general exhortations and observations. Without such response, which indeed is presupposed in the later portions of the Qur'an itself, it could at most have become a striking but otherwise inconsequential piece of literature. This double aspect of the creative action is nowhere more crucial than in the religious life, where revelatory possibilities are doubtless latent in many an event that passes almost unnoticed; but revelatory experience occurs only when enough persons are ready to receive the impact of a given event and allow it to open their eyes.

The second moment of a cultural tradition is group commitment arising out of the creative action: the immediate public of the event is in some way institutionalized and perpetuated; that is, the creative action becomes a point of departure for a continuing body of people who share a common awareness of its importance and must take it into account in whatever they do next, whether in pursuance of its implications or in rebellion against them. Such was long the case of Occidental artists vis-à-vis Italian Renaissance painting, for instance. In a tradition of liberal education built around an agreed-on core of classics, the commitment becomes even more binding, still more so in a tradition of law. At its most effective the commitment becomes an allegiance. Thus Islam could be defined as commitment to the venture to which Muhammad's vision was leading; which meant, concretely, allegiance to Muhammad and his Book and then to the continuing community of Muhammad, or at least (later) to a supposed faithful remnant of that community. The allegiance came to be marked by such symbolic gestures as utterance of the *shahada*, the formula of Muslim belief, or performing worship toward the *qibla*, that is, toward Mecca; which acts have been sufficient to establish a person as committed to the social and juridical consequences of being a Muslim whatever the extent of his inward *islam*.

This group commitment retains its vitality through cumulative interaction among those sharing the commitment; above all, through debate and dialogue, people work out the implications and potentialities latent in the creative event to which they are bound. In the arts, the solution of one problem—itself arising from within the artistic tradition—is witnessed by other artists, who may adopt it or respond to it with alternative solutions; and these solutions open up new opportunities and new artistic problems in their turn. In philosophy and in science, the transmission of what has been done and found, especially in the case of the great initiators like Plato or Ptolemy, is but the preliminary essential to the continuing cumulative dialogue, the response and counter-response, which is the purpose of such transmission and without which the transmission itself will gradually cease. The like is true of the inventive and elaborative development of an economic order; and above all of political life, built of the thrust and parry of contrasting interests, each party striving to turn the accumulated heritage of a major state formation to its own advantage, and in doing so shifting the pattern of the heritage which the next special interest will work through.

The implications of an initial event may be relatively particular and functional— may have reference to the development of historical circumstances as the community faces them. Once the early Muslims had conquered the region from the Mediterranean through Iran, a common corpus of law and custom was required if the community was to hold together and maintain its position: some sort of *shari'a* law was needed. And if this was to be worked out in harmony with the experience that had brought the Muslims together and assured them of their highest ideals, building a *shari'a* could require, in turn, the discovery of *hadith* reports, of reports about the earliest Muslims, which could relate the Qur'anic challenge to the practical needs of the subsequent empire. Gradually, over centuries, pious Muslims building one on another's work found such *hadith*s and created such a *shari'a*. Much of their work meant coming to terms at least as much with their own society as with the Qur'anic challenge.

Or else the implications of the creative event may be relatively universal and logical—may stem, that is, from the very nature of the event, from its inherent potential for enlarging the resources of any human beings seeking truth in their lives. Thus whatever may have led a man to commit himself initially to Muhammad's community (and it was likely to have been much less than a total apprehension of Muhammad's own vision), this public commitment necessarily led him further in the direction of that *islam* which is the private affair of the soul; and of seeking an articulate conception of prophecy and of God, such as would make intelligible the *islam* he found himself being led towards. It was in dialogue, in an exchange of insights and of objections with others in a like situation, that he came to realize what sense of himself and of the universe would serve and what would not. In such searching, he might be confronting something in Islam, and perhaps something in the human spiritual condition, more or less relevant under any circumstances.

Relatively circumstantial and functional or relatively inherent and logical, in either case the implications of the initial commitment could be worked out fully only as the initially creative vision was confronted ever afresh from a new perspective in the course of cumulative interaction and dialogue among those to whom the initial events were meaningful.

But not only does a developing interaction arise out of an initial point of creativity; that interaction, that dialogue, itself is made up of a sequence of creative actions and of commitments stemming from them—secondary actions, secondary commitments, up to a point, but genuine actions, encounters and discoveries, all the same. Rather than being an ideally fixed pattern which might almost be deduced from the initial creative event, supplying a determinant body of ideas and practices, a cultural heritage forms a relatively passive setting for action. Within that setting, any given juncture may bring a fresh turn of orientation; or at least its outcome will be relatively unpredictable, for the same setting will allow for varying sorts of actions according as circumstances, temperaments, and problems vary.

Thus, within the dialogue launched by the advent of Islam, almost from the start there came to be conflicting sets of presuppositions about what Islam should involve, each producing its own commitment and its own dialogue. Around the charismatic figure of 'Ali, companion of Muhammad and the fighting man's hero, the common soldier's sense of Islamic justice crystallized, even in the first generation, against what were felt to be the backslidings of a wealthy clique which had got control of the

Muslims' conquests for its own benefit. This sentiment, sealed in the blood of rebellion, issued in a deep loyalty to 'Ali and later to his house. The resulting movement was called Shi'ism. The bulk of the Muslims were felt to have gone astray in rejecting 'Ali's leadership, only a faithful remnant holding to the original vision. Generation by generation, the widest possible implications of such a loyalty in such a remnant were worked out among the Shi'i Muslims, implications for social justice not merely in the soldiers' cause but in all fields, and (since life is whole) implications also for the personal devotional life, for metaphysics, and for the whole range of Islamic concerns. At the same time, the stirring and demanding experience of forging an effective unity among the Muslim community, despite such partisan pressures as that of the Shi'is, was yielding a contrasting loyalty, called Sunnism: a loyalty to the Muslim community as it had come historically to be constituted, despite all its faults. This loyalty likewise had its pervasive implications, gradually worked out in a long dialogue among the Sunni Muslims.

Thus arose within the Islamic setting two differing sub-traditions, sub-settings for dialogue, within which the implications of the original advent of Islam were being worked out in contrasting ways. And each secondary dialogue, like Islam itself, began with a point of creativity: within each, it was duly noted that there was something divinely guided or even revelatory—though of course not in the same degree as in the Qur'an itself—in the position of 'Ali, the hero, or in that of the *umma*, the general community, respectively. As may be seen from the map of the distribution of Shi'is, the two contrasting traditions have endured to the present. (In our day more than a quarter, perhaps a third, of the Muslims in the central lands of "old Islam" from Nile to Oxus are Shi'is. The rest there—as well as most Muslims in the more outlying lands—are chiefly Sunnis, who therefore form nine-tenths of the Muslims in the world at large.)

The Diversity of Islam in the Nexus of General History

As the Islamic tradition developed within its own terms, it was likewise interacting with other cultural traditions which were already present among the populations in which Islam was adopted. No tradition is isolable from others present in the same social context. (A culture, indeed, may be defined as a complex of interdependent traditions.) A creative event in any sphere of life is likely to have consequences in many fields; in any case, the interaction and dialogue in religious or artistic or political or scholarly settings overlap and merge because the important problems that arise are rarely so technical that only one sort of tradition proves relevant. The sub-traditions into which Islam seemed to divide, even when mutually hostile as were those of the Shi'is and Sunnis, were not in fact exclusive; it was common for an individual Muslim, almost from the start, to share to some degree in both of these. Still less did people cease to take part, when they became Muslims, in the other ongoing traditions which molded their lives, except in the few cases where the commitment involved was explicitly incompatible with the Muslim commitment: as in some, but not all, aspects of other religious traditions. For the rest, Islam found itself in a vital and multiple cultural environment. It was only as it entered into these other dialogues, in fact, that it could become significant for cultural life at large.

The artistic traditions of which Muslims found themselves at first patrons and later also practitioners had been launched in pre-Islamic times. Only as Muslims (rather gradually) found special viewpoints toward elements in these traditions—viewpoints suggested as readily by their particular social situation as by any more strictly Islamic inspiration—did the continuing development of those traditions introduce any features that might be called Islamic. The same is true of scientific and philosophical traditions, of traditions of commerce and of crafts and of public administration, even of pious legend and of ascetic practice. Always the presence of Islam made itself felt only gradually as Muslims discovered points at which it would be relevant within the settings provided by the various other traditions.

Such a difference as that, often noted, between Islam in a majority-Muslim environment (such as the Arab lands) and Islam in a minority-Muslim environment (such as India) is not, then, a matter of the degree to which Muslims are Muslims. It cannot be reduced to the difference between stale custom and enforced alertness, as an Indian Muslim might suggest; or between inbred mastery and latter-day imitation, as some Arab Muslims might feel. It will also be the difference between two equally genuine responses to the overall spiritual challenge carried in the Islamic dialogue in the midst of two different cultural environments. Indian Muslims, for instance, would read at least some books by other Indian Muslims, being stimulated by the special Indian problems those writers were contending with; and would respond positively or negatively to the creative experiences to which the writers bore witness. Arab Muslims likewise had their own subordinate dialogue with its own special Arab problems and encounters.

When we look at Islam historically, then, the integral unity of life it seemed to display when we looked at it as a working out of the act of *islam* almost vanishes. In such ever-renewed dialogues, among settings formed apart from Islam at all, is not anything possible provided only it possess a certain general human validity? We can no longer say that Islam eternally teaches a given thing, or that another thing is necessarily a corruption of Islam. Such judgments a believer may feel himself able to make, but not a historian as such. At a given time, in a limited milieu, perhaps, Islam may form a relatively delimited and inviolable pattern. But over time, and especially on a world scale, any particular formulation of thought or practice is to be seen as the result of how the ever-changing setting formed by the Islamic tradition is reflected in particular circumstances and in relation to all the other cultural traditions present.[3]

Even the persistent pressure which has existed toward some sort of unity or uniformity among Muslims everywhere is not to be seen as an inevitable attribute of Islam as such. Rather, it arose out of the relationships which held, at various times, between the ongoing Islamic tradition and the other cultural traditions among which it was developing. In the time of the first Arab conquests, the sense that the Qur'anic vision demanded some sort of unity among the war bands of the faithful was sufficiently expressed in a demand for a single supreme authority among them, a caliph who would lead their worship and their wars. The notion of a caliph was never abandoned, but later—when most Muslims were merchants or craftsmen or peasants—it became merged in the ancient notion of the disinterested royal arbiter among the several classes of a settled society; eventually Muslims could admit several caliphs at once. Muslims by then, however, represented numerous differing cultural traditions; those who were concerned to fulfill the Qur'anic vision, accordingly, found it necessary to demand a new sort of unity: a unity in the customs of social intercourse, on which could be built in common a just society. Still later, under the disruptive impact of Modern times, a third sort of demand for unity seemed required. Tendencies toward what has been called "pan-Islamic" sentiment have represented a hope that the various peoples of Islamic faith, having found themselves in a common subjugation to the Modern West, would co-operate politically in their common interests, however diverse they remained culturally.

What then is Islam? Can we study it as a meaningful whole? Is it more than the name for a hope, and a few common symbols? Clearly, yes: but only in the way that any cultural tradition, whatever its internal contradictions, is a whole. However diversely it develops, or however rapidly, a tradition does not lend itself indifferently to every possible opinion or practice. It imposes limits which are none the less enduringly effective for being impossible to formulate in advance. Dialogue within a group, indeed any dialogue, is scarcely possible if everything is put in question at once. If a new insight is to come at one point, it can be clarified only against a background of received insights, held for the moment as if they were constant, or at most shifted only in perspective. The same is true of any sort of interaction: an innovation at one point is feasible only if it can be assumed that at least some other points will remain fixed. At any given time a minimal cultural integrality can be assured at least by those features of the cultural setting which even those men take for granted who think they are out to change everything. Over the generations, innovations may indeed appear at any point. Yet so long as there is a common commitment to an initial point of departure which all acknowledge, and to the continuing body of persons which shares that acknowledgement, the dialogue will retain common features, even though these are not necessarily those most visible at any given time. For to the extent that the dialogue is cumulative, every later comer having to reckon both with the point of departure and with the later debate, there will needs be a common vocabulary of ideas (or of art forms or institutional principles or whatever) which will include somehow all generations concerned. It is this integrality of dialogue that can provide an intelligible framework for historical study.

The Unity of Islam as a Religious Tradition, and its Limits

We can distinguish two levels on which there has been effective continuity in such dialogue among Muslims over the centuries: that of religion and that of civilization. Throughout this work, we will be dealing with a religious tradition and with a civilization; we must clarify briefly here what we mean by religion and what by a civilization; and what sort of relations can exist between them. Cultural continuity among the Muslims is most visible on the level of what we call "religion." The Islamic religious tradition, for all its diversity, has retained a certain integrality; distinctly more so than, say, Christianity or Buddhism. But we will find that this religious unity among Muslims is but one expression of a wider cultural unity. This wider cultural unity is historically, doubtless, the more fundamental.

The religious unity must be recognized first; and among Muslims it already carries with it much—but by no means all—of the realms of culture that in some other contexts might not be considered religious at all. At the very least, all Muslims must come to terms with the Qur'an; and in doing so they must not only talk in part a common language, but must find themselves faced with at least partly common challenges. Hence the whole range of what appears under the Islamic name can be relevant to seeing the full implications, positive and negative, of a personal commitment to its founding events and their latent challenges. But because even the most diverse Muslims have sometimes read not only the Qur'an but each other's subsequent books, the tradition has had, in fact, more integrality than this minimum. Consequently, any serious questions about that commitment, its implications, and even its historical development will prove interdependent; the tradition must, then, be studied as a whole.

As we have seen, this religious commitment and dialogue carried far. It concerned not merely a corner of people's lives, reserved for moments of special exaltation or of special despair. It reached pervasively into daily living. How far it reached, we must see. For we cannot arbitrarily set off the sphere of "religion" in general in advance, even if we give it a broad mandate; we cannot assume that such-and-such a type of activity must be "religious" and other types of activity not. Indeed, so variable is the sphere of "religion" in different cultures that a common term for all that we call "religious" is really justifiable only by invoking a series of extended meanings.

In a person's life, we can call "religious" in the most restricted sense (in the sense of "spiritual"), his ultimate cosmic orientation and commitments and the ways in which he pays attention to them, privately or with others. Properly, we use the term "religious" for an ultimate orientation (rather than "philosophical" or "ideological"), so far as the orientation is personally committing and is meaningful in terms of a cosmos, without further precision of what this may come to. In an Islamic context, this has meant, in effect, a sense of cosmic transcendence, and we may apply the word, more concretely, to efforts, practical or symbolical, to transcend the limits of the natural order of foreseeable life—that is, efforts based on hope from or struggle toward some sort of "supernatural" realm.[4] Then we may call "religious" (extending the term a bit) those cultural traditions that have focused on such cosmic commitments: cumulative traditions of personal responses to presumed possibilities of transcending the natural order. Such traditions take off from events people have found to be revelatory of such possibilities. But in common usage the term is extended still further. A person's actual "religious" life does not necessarily consist in creative cosmic commitment; it consists in his participation in religious traditions as given to him—in any aspect of them, whether he personally cares much for the initial spiritual impulse, or carries on only those aspects of the tradition that were secondary to and supportive of the primary spiritual commitment. For historical purposes, it is not very feasible or even desirable to separate out these different extended usages.

Accordingly, though what we call the "religious" traditions have been centered on such ultimate commitments, they have not—as actual historical traditions—been reducible to them. Whatever its central concern, Islam has come to imply much else besides, not necessarily deducible from its concern with transcendence; and as a historical tradition, Islam must be seen integrally in its own terms, constituted by all these diverse things. It is not because Islam embraces a certain cultural sphere but because, in the spheres it does embrace, it happens to put central an effort toward transcendence, or toward cosmic meaning, that we call the Islamic tradition "religious," and participation in it "religious behaviour." Even narrowly conceived as cult and creed, Islam contains far more than—and also less than—what we might suppose was necessarily implied in an effort toward transcendence: in, for instance, the direct personal act of *islam*. It can be religious behaviour, for instance, to extol one's own religious heritage—in this case Islam—and to denigrate other people's; but this need not indicate a very lively sense of personal submission before the God who created all. Indeed, Islam may be highly cultivated, for social or intellectual reasons, by persons who have had little such religious experience of their own. (We must also, of course, be ready to recognize on their own merits the norms of all the sub-traditions that diversely developed Islam—all the contrasting positions that were "Islam" to one or another group of Muslims.)

The reader will find that Islam, rather more than Christianity, tended to call forth a total social pattern in the name of religion itself. None of the great religious traditions of this type has been content with occasional acts of worship in consecrated buildings—all have hoped to form men and women's daily attitudes and conduct. In principle, any religious allegiance might make demands on every aspect of life to such a degree that a religious body could constitute a complete society, its way of life a self-sufficient culture. But Islam especially has tended to make this kind of total demand on life. In many spheres, not only public worship but such spheres as civil law, historical teaching, or social etiquette, Muslims succeeded quite early in establishing distinctive patterns identifiable with Islam as religion.

But even Islam could not be total. Even in these preferred spheres, specifically Islamic patterns rarely prevailed exclusively; and in many other spheres, such as trade or poetry, the articulated religion had to be content to lay down limits which the merchant or poet should not overstep. Otherwise, these aspects of culture were cultivated, in substantial autonomy from any particular religious allegiance. What was religion and, in particular, what was Islam, was always, if diversely, kept consciously distinct from the total culture of Muslim society. In even the most pious man's life there was much that he could not call religious.

The wider cultural life of Muslims, their civilization, had its own historical integrality, which was not simply an extension of the specifically religious unity of Muslims. Indeed, this wider cultural complex included the Islamic religious life as but one facet, albeit a central one. For around the actual Islamic religious tradition was formed, historically, an overall culture not restricted to what was "religious," even granting the wide sphere claimed for Islam as religion. It was not only the Qur'anic challenge and its consequences that Muslims confronted together, but also a whole series of historical events and problems in every sphere of life. In Islamic times, to an important degree the arts and sciences (for instance) of Muslim Turks and Persians, of Muslims of Egypt and of India, were interdependent; moreover, they were clearly distinct from those of lands outside the Muslim sphere even when they defied the religious convictions of most pious Muslims. Further, since the cultural traditions which together made up the civilization associated with Muslims often depended little, directly, on the Islamic tradition as such, they were by no means restricted to Muslims. Many non-Muslims—Christians, Jews, Hindus, etc.—must be recognized not only as living socially within the sphere of the Muslim culture; they must be recognized as integral and contributory participants in it, engaging actively in many of its cultural dialogues. At the same time, some groups ardently Muslim in religion (for instance, in China) were only limitedly influenced culturally by this cultural complex. The scope of the historical civilization, then, was not only distinct from the religion as to field of activity; it was not even coextensive with it in time and space, and as to the populations involved. Here we have, then, a second, more inclusive level on which cultural traditions carried by Muslims form an interrelated whole to be studied as such.

This wider level of integrality, however, has been profoundly influenced by the religious level, especially among Muslims, not because it is an extension of it but because of the strategic position in which the carriers of the religious vision have found themselves within the civilization, notably in the high culture which gives definition to a civilization in the most meaningful sense of that term.

A Civilization as Expression of Formative Ideals

In this work we shall speak more of masterpieces of art, and dynastic policies, of religious geniuses, and scientific discoveries, than of everyday life on the farm and in the kitchen. Hence we will include in our scope those peoples among whom a few privileged men shared such masterpieces and discoveries, however much those peoples differed among themselves in farmwork or in homemaking. This may seem like arbitrary preference for the spectacular. I believe it answers to a legitimate human need to understand ourselves. In any case, we must be clear as to what we are doing, and its consequences.

The wider culture associated with Islam has been as highly differentiated and heterogeneous as any; has been, in fact, the sum of many cultures, or at least of aspects of them. The peoples concerned, flourishing from the time of Muhammad in the seventh century to the present, have extended in space over half of the Eastern hemisphere of our globe. They have been correspondingly diverse in language, climate, historical situation, and national culture patterns. It is such a compound culture that we call "a civilization": that is, a relatively extensive grouping of interrelated cultures, insofar as they have shared in cumulative traditions in the form of high culture on the urban, literate level; a culture, that is, such as that of historical India or Europe taken as cultural wholes. Such groups of peoples have varied greatly among themselves and yet have shared broadly cultural and historical experiences differing decisively from those of more distant peoples. Thus the diverse peoples of India cherished in common the Sanskritic traditions, and those of Europe the Greco-Latin. In the field of pre-Modern Afro-Eurasian history a number of such broader cultural complexes have existed, not necessarily covering without remainder the whole field of citied and lettered life, yet by and large dominating the more local cultures.

There are many ways of grouping into "civilizations" what is in fact an endless chain of interrelated local cultural life. We must know why we make the selection we do. Often one may make alternative combinations according to what questions one is concerned with. Thus the civilization that united the lands from Nile to Oxus in the Islamic period could be regarded, for some purposes, as no independent cultural body but simply the latest phase in a long-term Irano-Semitic civilization continuous from the time of the ancient Sumerians. The cultural traditions associated with Islam in India, then, would be regarded as forming part of an equally continuous Indic civilization, complicating it and relating it to the lands from Nile to Oxus, yet still regionally bound. This makes obvious sense on the level of everyday life. Even on the level of high culture, Islamic faith, for instance, is part of a longer tradition. In particular, the creative events at the founding of Islam were themselves part of an ongoing monotheistic tradition. They took place within the setting formed by the dialogue that was working through the implications of the ancient Hebrew prophetic discoveries; they formed a response to challenges presented historically in that dialogue at the point when Muhammad was drawn into it. In the Islamic dialogue, the same basic monotheistic commitment persisted, though the particular allegiance was new. The like was true of many other facets of high culture even though new languages were used.

If one is concerned primarily with socio-economic institutional evolution, conscious or unconscious, especially with that of the more local social units, such regional groupings may provide the most intelligible fields of study. (Grouping by region, itself, would offer a number of alternatives: for instance, instead of distinguishing between Europe on the one hand and the "Middle East" from Nile to Oxus on the other, one might, especially in some periods, distinguish a Mediterranean region from a region centred round the Iranian plateau.) But if one is concerned primarily with the more conscious commitments of human beings and with their public actions in the light of those commitments, as historians traditionally have been, a grouping by traditions of high culture will be more relevant than one by socio-economic regions.

When we speak of a great civilization, we mean above all a consciously cultivated human heritage—and only secondarily a collection of folkways or of sociological raw data. In the study of any culture, of course, intellectual, economic, artistic, social, political aspects all have their role; ruling classes, peasant villagers, city artisans, bands of vagrants, all must be taken into account in interpreting it. But in studying a given civilization our first interest is in those aspects of culture that have been most distinctive of it; that have been most interesting and humanly significant in their variation within its own sphere of space and time as well as in their diverging from other forms of culture. During much of history, at least, this has meant the artistic, philosophic, scientific life, the religious and political institutions, in general all the more imaginative activities among the more cultivated of the population. It is in terms of these aspects of culture that we do commonly distinguish the great civilizations from one another. And in the long run, these aspects can be decisive even for the common people who are scarcely aware of them.

This fact is especially relevant among the Muslims. Wherever it went, Islam entered into the local cultural complexes carried by local ethnic groups, as one tradition among the complex of interdependent traditions which go to make up a local culture. But these local cultures might have nothing else in common. It is not on this level that the wider culture (religious and non-religious) associated specifically with Muslims was articulated. Such a wider culture was carried primarily on the level of "high culture," rather than folk culture: that is, on the urban, literate level and more particularly on the level of the cultivated circles who were direct or indirect beneficiaries of the land revenues and who participated in the large-scale institutions that imposed a social order wider than that of family or village unit.[5] It is this culture—including, of course, its religious components—that we are to study in this work. A civilization in this sense will normally be defined by a continuity of lettered traditions: that is, of literature in the widest sense of the word, including (for instance) religious or scientific literature. Hence our field, in studying the civilization associated with the Muslims, will be delimited not by geography—as, for instance, the culture of the "Middle East" in one or another acceptance of that term—but rather by the lines of development of the high cultural traditions, wherever they lead us.[6]

Such a definition of our field can have subtle consequences. It makes for a special way of viewing religion, for instance. In the historical developments that mark a civilization so defined, religion almost inevitably plays a key role; but not necessarily so much because of the inertia of folk habits as because of its place in the consciences of a concerned minority. For the ideals of a minority can be specially seminal on the level of high culture.

Any civilization, as a delimitable complex of cultural traditions, has been constituted by standards of cultural valuation, basic expectations, and norms of legitimation, embodied in its traditions. In the high culture, these are carried partly in lettered traditions directly, and partly in other traditions, such as social and artistic ones, associated with the lettered traditions. It is the more far-reaching standards of legitimation that have served as the most dependably persistent cultural traits, endowing a civilization with such cultural integrality, such distinctive style, as it has had. What sets off most clearly one civilization in our sense, from another, then, is not so much any general stock of cultural ideas and practices—easily borrowed from one people to the next—as these formative ideals. Such a cultural heritage has been carried not only by all of the upper, educated classes, but even, to a lesser degree, by still wider sections which have absorbed something of its outlook, down to the ordinary peasants. But within this mass, a much smaller group has played a special role: those who have taken the more articulate and far-reaching ideals of the heritage as a personal responsibility, which they must themselves realize. This concerned minority for whom cultural or spiritual ideals are a major driving force are not usually the men of immediate power. But at every crossroads, they are the men of cultural initiative—it is within the framework they have clarified that new cultural choices must commonly be made.

At least in pre-Modern times, the most important focus of persistent cultural ideals has often tended to be in religion. In religion, the impact of the creative, revelatory events has tended to stand out most strongly from the continuing dialogue in which their implications were being worked out; hence religion could provide unusual continuity in the dialogue itself. Moreover, even more than in the aesthetic or the political spheres, the circle of responsive confrontation that spreads out from religion tends to be comprehensive of all life. A new aesthetic impulse may affect science in some degree, or have economic repercussions as fashions change. A new political impulse can reach further, can carry in its train economic decisions, aesthetic ideals, or the very tone, sometimes, of private life caught up in the pride of a new allegiance. A fresh sense of impact from whatever it may be in the cosmic presence that is seen as transcending the natural order may be felt strongly by only the concerned minority. But if these take it seriously, it can touch every point in the natural order of human affairs: it can reorient people's aesthetic sense, their political norms, their whole moral life, and with these everything else that can be seen to matter. A religious commitment, by its nature, tends to be more total than any other. Perhaps especially among Muslims, religious vision has often proved decisive at just the points that are historically most interesting. Moreover, that vision proved sufficiently potent to ensure that Muslims formed a single great civilization of their own.

Among Christian or Buddhist peoples, religion has indeed been very central also. But it has informed the culture of Christian Occidentals and of Christian Abyssinians, for instance, almost entirely in isolation from each other, so that there is no single civilization associated with Christianity. Nor is there one civilization associated with Buddhism. But—despite the vaster areas covered—those who participated in the tradition of Islamic faith, so far as they developed any culture of their own at all, never lost contact with each other: their cultural dialogues were always intermeshed. The bonds of Islamic faith, indeed especially the irrepressible transcendent ideals implied in the root meaning of *islam*, with their insistent demand for a godly transformation of all life, have been so telling in certain crucial aspects of the high culture of almost all Muslim peoples that we find ourselves grouping these peoples together across all their different regions, even apart from considering other facets of high culture. Islam offered creative impulses that ramified widely throughout the culture as a whole, even where it was least religious. It is largely around the central Islamic tradition that the concerned and the creative built and transmitted a common set of social and, above all, literary traditions; these were carried in many languages but looked largely to the same great classics, not only religious but secular, and especially to the norms which they express, applicable to all aspects of life. Thus Islam helped to knit together peoples who otherwise might have remained remote, or have drifted apart if they were close to begin with. Through the greatest diversity of forms (as the chart on pp. 302–3 giving an overview of the history may suggest), these traditions (religious and otherwise) have maintained a decisive continuity. Hence in studying these peoples there is special urgency for studying as a body, and hence primarily on the level of the high culture, the civilization given definition by the lettered traditions in which Islam held a central place.[7]

In studying the history of Muslims, obviously, we need distinct terms for the religious tradition on the one hand and for the more inclusive civilization on the other. Unfortunately, we have not had such terms in the past. The terms "Islam" and "Islamic" have often been used in both senses. But these two terms are clearly appropriate only to the realm of religion. If we speak in this work of "Islamic" art or literature, then, we will be referring to religious art or literature within the traditions of Islamic faith, in the same sense as we refer to "Christian" art or literature. We will require a different term for the cultural traditions of the civilization at large, when we are not restricting our reference to religion. The various peoples among whom Islam has been predominant and which have shared in the cultural traditions distinctively associated with it may be called collectively "Islamdom," as forming a vast interrelated social nexus. The distinctive civilization of Islamdom, then, may be called "Islamicate."

The civilization could have been given some other name than one derived from Islam; in fact it has, in some contexts, been referred to appropriately as the "Perso-Arabic" civilization, after the two chief languages in which it has been carried. But because of the pre-eminent role played in it by Islam and by Muslims, it has most commonly been called the "Islamic" civilization. It will be convenient to retain such a usage here, only adding the double ending (*-icate*) to avoid an ambiguity that has proved all too common. In some cases, the distinction is unimportant, and the choice between the terms "Islamic" and "Islamicate" may be a matter of emphasis. But on occasion it is essential to point up the distinction between those traditions associated relatively closely with the act of *islam* and its spiritual implications, and those traditions that were associated with Islam more indirectly, through forming a part of the overall civilization in which Muslims were leaders. The form "Islamicate" has the advantage of being almost self-defining: if it appears in a context where it is contrasted to "Islamic," it is clearly not just the same as "Islamic" but does relate somehow to what is Islamic. This is approximately the effect intended.[8]

Islamicate Civilization as Human Heritage

The Islamicate culture of the past has, of course, been very important in influencing the present condition of mankind. It is naturally the major influence from the past among the widespread Muslim peoples of our time; moreover, it has had notable effects, for good and for ill, in still wider areas, such as much of India and of Europe, where Muslims once ruled. The civilization remained actively creative within its own terms until the moment when a transformed Modern Occident put all pre-Modern heritages in question. Until that time the Muslims and their society played a pivotal role in world history as a whole, both negatively and positively; hence in almost every part of the Old World—and in the New World cultures derived therefrom— even where Islam never prevailed, at least some elements of the local culture have been traceable to Islamicate sources. Through its manifold influence on the Medieval Occident, particularly in the realms of science and technical skills, the older Islamicate culture had a significant share even in the far-reaching cultural transformations which the Modern Occident has introduced to our present world.

* * *

Late Sasani and Primitive Caliphal periods, *c.* 485–692

The intrusion of Islam into Irano-Semitic society and the genesis of a new social order. In Iran, in the Fertile Crescent, in Arabia, the way was being prepared, as it turned out, for the new order. First came the shaking up of the old Sasani political order; but the central event of the period was the advent of Muhammad and his followers' rise to power from Nile to Oxus and even beyond.

High Caliphal Period, *c.* 692–945

The first period of Islamicate civilization proper: *A classical civilization under the Marwani and earlier 'Abbasi caliphates.* Islamicate society formed a single vast state, the caliphate, with an increasingly dominant single language of science and culture, Arabic. The Islamic religion was being given its classical formulation; Muslims, Christians, Jews, and Mazdeans were renovating and weaving together the lettered traditions of several pre-Islamic backgrounds into a creative multiple flowering.

Earlier Middle Islamic Period, *c.* 945–1258

Establishment of an international civilization spreading beyond the Irano-Semitic areas. The great expansion of Islamicate society was based on a decentralization of power and culture, in many courts and in two major languages, Persian and Arabic. Unity was maintained through self-perpetuating social institutions which outgrew the caliphate and encouraged high-cultural sophistication and a synthesis of the lettered traditions that had been developed in the High Caliphal Period.

Later Middle Islamic Period, *c.* 1258–1503

The age of Mongol prestige: crisis and renewal in the Islamicate institutions and heritage. Despite devastation and conquest of the central Islamicate lands by a vigorous pagan movement, the Islamic norms reimposed themselves and hemisphere-wide expansion continued. The Mongol challenge launched a new political tradition and new horizons in high culture in the central areas, forming a Persianate culture from the Balkans to Bengal and influential even more widely.

Period of Gunpowder Empires, *c.* 1503–1789

Flowering of Persianate culture under major regional empires. The political and cultural impetus of the Mongol age was developed in regional empires with relatively regional cultures, especially in three: one primarily European, one centered in the old Islamic lands, one Indic. It was the height of Islamic material world power. The aesthetic and intellectual creativity and prosperity faded, however, before the new Occident in the course of a basic transformation.

Modern Technical Age, *c.* 1789–present

The Islamic heritage caught up in the Modern technicalistic world. Under the impact of a new world order carried by the Modern West, the world-historical conditions of the Islamicate civilization have disappeared. Instead of a continuing comprehensive society, we have a heritage which several peoples share within a wider social order where Muslims form a minority, a minority disadvantaged by just those events which, creating the new order, brought prosperity to the new West.

* * *

Important as it has been for its effects on the course of history, Islamicate civilization may be still more important for us as illustrating the evolution of a civilization as such. As we follow the traditions of that civilization in their many forms and many spheres of activity, from a time before there could be said to have been an Islamicate civilization at all, we are presented with an instructive instance of a major civilization as an evolving, historical phenomenon. Every degree of integration and disintegration, of freshness, maturity, decadence, and revival is illustrated in the most varied historical patterns. Moreover, the roots of Islamicate civilization are largely the same as those of Occidental civilization: the urban commercial tradition of the ancient Fertile Crescent, the Hebrew religious challenge, the classical Greek philosophical and scientific culture. Hence for Westerners (and for all who at least partly share now in the Occidental heritage), the Islamicate forms a sister civilization, like yet very different; acquaintance with it can throw a special light, by way of comparisons and contrasts, on Occidental civilization in particular as well as on the nature of civilizations as such.

Comparisons between the Islamicate culture and the Occidental are inevitable and very worthwhile. But one caution must be kept in mind. It is not ordinarily legitimate to compare pre-Modern Islamicate institutions and cultural patterns with those of the Modern West, and to treat that comparison as if it were primarily one between different *peoples*. Such a comparison is more likely to be one between *ages*. In recent centuries, enormous changes have supervened in the Occident; changes which produced their counter-effects almost immediately, and are now having their analogues elsewhere, in the Muslim and in other non-Western countries. Serious comparisons between the Muslim peoples and the West should be made with this fact in mind. Pre-Modern Islamicate ways can be compared with those of the pre-Modern Occident; and those aspects of society in Islamdom in which the Modern changes have taken positive effect can be compared, within measure, with the Modern West. But it is illegitimate to regard as "Western"—in contrast to "Islamic"—such traits as clock sense among workers, or democratic social expectations, or even subtler characteristics often cited; for these traits were mostly as absent in the pre-Modern Occident as in pre-Modern Islamdom, and may in the future prove as congenial to Muslim peoples as they now seem to be to Western.

But from a more deeply human point of view, perhaps neither the far-reaching historical effects of Islamicate civilization, nor its value as illustrating the nature of civilization in general, is so important as is the inherent marvel of what it built, and even of what it dared try to build. Our fundamental purpose must be an understanding of the human achievements of the civilization in their own terms. It is with this intention that our field of study has been delimited here, and the place of everything in it assessed. The place of the civilization in the world-historical chain of events, and its usefulness as an example of what culture can be, come out naturally and necessarily as we try to understand what is special to the human endeavors that have been tied together by the presence of the Islamic vision. In studying Islamicate civilization, we will be concerned with society and culture as the context in which concerned individuals have worked, especially Muslim individuals, and as the handiwork which exhibits in varying ways the intended and unintended results of their work and of their vision.[9]

Even in terms of evident relevance for current personal life among Modern humans, the Islamicate heritage is rich. Its visual arts, for instance, include surely the greatest ever known in which the element of sheer visual design could be given priority over all other considerations. Its literatures, richly unmatched in their most distinctive genres, are perhaps unparalleled in—among other things—their mastery of the esoteric as a dimension of human experience. Its philosophical and scientific and religious thought has not merely made a lasting contribution to subsequent knowledge; much of it presents continuing points of enduring challenge. As we watch the unfolding of the civilization as a whole we will gain, at the same time, essential background for appreciating the monuments of Islamicate culture which can still enrich our understanding and our life. For it is only in their total context, in the setting of the developing cultural institutions which formed them, and of the hopes and fears they embodied, that the monuments can come fully alive for us: works of architecture and painting, literary masterpieces, philosophical systems, expressions of religious insight, and, above all, living religious and social institutions among millions of mankind. Perhaps the latter sort is the most important of all the monuments of Islamicate civilization, if only because the Islamicate society represents, in part, one of the most thoroughgoing attempts in history to build a world-wide human community as if from scratch on the basis of an explicitly worked-out ideal.

But important as is the heritage of Islamdom to us as presenting resources for our current cultural ventures, the great human venture which Islam has been is even more important, for Modern mankind, as a venture: as it was in itself then. If the Modern Technical Age is to remain human, it cannot overlook the trust that our ancestors have left with us. Our past cannot be mere matter for a more or less curious utilitarianism, like iron deposits, say, on the moon. Islamicate culture is supremely important because it represents the highest creative aspirations and achievements of millions of people. Whoever we are, the hopes, the triumphs, and the failures too of any human beings are properly of concern to us; in the moral economy of mankind they are also our own hopes and failures. In studying and sharing in them we know ourselves better, understand better who we truly have been and are, we human beings.

Notes

1. Smith 1966 has pointed out that the very notion of "*a religion,*" as an integral *system* of belief and practice held to be either true or false, is relatively recent as compared with the notion of "religion" as an aspect of any one person's life, which may be more or less true as that person is more or less sincere or successful. Even in the Irano-Semitic sphere, where "religions" were earliest and most sharply set off as self-contained total communities, the notion of "a religion" as a *system* was slow to prevail and has become dominant only in quite

modern times. He suggests that what we generally have to deal with are cumulative traditions through which religious faith has been expressed. I am indebted to him for sharpening my awareness here.

2. Throughout this chapter, I have tried to take advantage of the increasing sophistication of anthropologists about cultural processes; but since I am dealing, as a historian, primarily not with folk culture but with high culture, I have had to develop my own theoretical framework here.

3. Not every scholar, and certainly not every Muslim, will be happy with so strong a limitation as I put on the existence of any eternal "true" Islam. It is conventional, in fact, for scholars to distinguish more and less "true" or "genuine" Islam among the various forms which Islamic consciousness has taken; they often label some forms "orthodox" and use other categories, implicit and explicit, which presuppose such distinctions. There is a certain validity in such usages, but only, I think, when very carefully circumscribed. Partly, of course, it is a matter of definitions. I have used "Islam" in the way which, it seems to me, most genuinely answers to its prevailing usage in ordinary contexts. Here there can be more practical accord than on the level of global theory. Perhaps my usage should always tacitly presuppose some such adjective as "historical," as against "ideal" or "metaphysical."

4. For some purposes, one can apply the term "religious" wherever an experience of the numinous or a notion of the transcendent (commonly linked thereto) becomes life-orientational. But in different life-orientational traditions, and even within the same tradition, the numinous-transcendent can play very different roles, or be absent even in primary moments. Hence, for the purpose of classifying the traditions (if one must), a more general definition will help: one can apply the term "religious" to any life-orientational experience or behavior in the degree to which it is relatively most focused on the role of a *person in an environment felt as cosmos*. Any developed life-orientational outlook, however much oriented to culture or history to the exclusion of concern with natural cosmos, deals with personal life and has some interpretation of the cosmic whole; but the term "religious" would not be applied to the central experience and behavior of, e.g., Marxism, since, in contrast, say, to "atheistic" Buddhism, the relation person-cosmos plays a relatively slight role there.

5. Shils 1965 suggests how much the high culture (his "central value system") rests on the charisma attributed to it because it represents an inclusive social order felt to be just.

6. What the civilization is that we associate with Muslims, and what its position is in world history, have been discussed from many viewpoints; but rarely in an adequately comprehensive world-historical perspective or with sufficiently flexible categories. Among the best discussions have been three which form a sequence. Becker 1924, Part I, "Zur Einleitung," brought out, among other things, that the pre-Modern Christian and Muslim societies lived by largely common cultural resources. This point was developed in a new direction by G. E. von Grunebaum (1946) who stressed the parallelism of their world views. Kraemer 1959 has recently reviewed the questions suggestively, attempting to balance the "Hellenic" character of the culture with other elements. Unfortunately he, like most scholars, still presupposes untenable notions about a fictitious "Orient," which lead much of his argument astray. He fails to see that the data he cites to support the "Oriental" character of Islamicate culture illustrate instead the indivisibility of the Afro-Eurasian historical complex as a whole, which included the Occident.

   For further development of my own thoughts on defining civilizations, see the section on historical method in the Introduction, especially the subsection on civilizations.

7. The student will find that differences in scholars' notions of what it was they were studying have left a profound impress upon the works which anyone must read if he is to pursue even casually any given line of interest in the Islamics field. In the paragraphs on the history of Islamics studies in the Introduction is a brief sketch of the major orientations and biases which the reader should learn to be aware of and, if necessary, discount.
8. For an explanation of my choice of the terms "Islamdom" and "Islamicate," see the section on usage in Islamics studies in the Introduction.
9. For a fuller presentation of the historical viewpoint which I have used in this work, see the section on historical method in the Introduction, especially the subsection on historical humanism.

References

Becker, Carl H. 1924. *Vom Werden und Wesen der islamischen Welt: Islamstudien,* Vol. I. Leipzig.

Kraemer, Jörg. 1959. *Das Problem der islamischen Kulturgeschichte.* Tübingen: M. Niemeyer.

Shils, Edward. 1965. "Charisma, Order, and Status." *American Sociological Review* 30 (April): 199–213.

Smith, Wilfred C. 1966. *The Meaning and End of Religion.* New York: New English Library.

Von Grunebaum, G. E. 1946 [2nd ed. 1953]. *Medieval Islam.* Chicago, IL: University of Chicago Press.

21

Conscience in the Construction of Religion:
A Critique of Marshall G. S. Hodgson's *The Venture of Islam*

Bryan S. Turner

Introduction

While Marshall G. S. Hodgson, who died in 1968, was influential in the United States as professor in charge of the history of Islamic civilization course at the University of Chicago and as author of a series of scholarly articles on Islamic history, art and religion,[1] Hodgson has been aptly described as "a lesser-known giant among better-known scholars" (Hodgson 1974, I, ix). Although this is unfortunate, the appreciation of the true stature of Hodgson may well be corrected by the appearance of his three-volume, posthumous work *The Venture of Islam*. This study is certainly worthy of close scrutiny since its intention is to criticize and transcend the presuppositions of traditional "Islamics"—to use Hodgson's terminology—which rest on Arabism and philology. By "Arabism" Hodgson meant the tendency to treat pre-Islamic Arabian culture as somehow native to Islam so that Bedouin culture is regarded as "lost" if it is not carried into the Islam of the Fertile Crescent. By contrast, Arabism regards Persian, Syriac and Greek cultural components as "foreign" to the genuine Arabian core of Islam. In order to counteract such assumptions, Hodgson attempted to give what he regarded as an appropriate weight to more central Islamicate regions and cultures. By the philological bias, Hodgson pointed to the exaggerated emphasis given high culture, to the neglect of more local or lower-class social conditions; and within high culture, to be preoccupied with religious, literary, and political themes, which are most accessible to a philological approach. (Hodgson 1974, I, 41)

In *The Venture of Islam*, Hodgson attempts to overcome traditional philological approaches to Islam by giving full consideration to the variety of ways in which Islam was determined or influenced by sociological, economic and geographical factors. While these intentions may be laudable, Hodgson's approach still fails to extricate itself fully from the a-sociological pitfalls of traditional orientalism. The sub-title of Hodgson's study is "Conscience and History in a World of Civilization." Islam as a religion and social system is treated as an adventure of the inner, personal conscience which creates an external, impersonal civilization. The conscience is treated as a creative, irreducible activity in history of private individuals for whom social, political and economic factors ("ecological circumstances") operate "[m]erely [to] set the limits of what is possible" (Hodgson 1974, I, 26). The consequence of such an approach is to provide, so to speak, a religious niche or hiding-place within which "faith" can remain sociologically immune. My criticism of Hodgson's treatment of Islam will consist in providing a causal account of "conscience" as a sociologically explicable phenomenon.

There is an additional reason for paying close attention to the arguments put forward in *The Venture of Islam*. In order to buttress his orientation to the problem of understanding Islam, Hodgson deploys a variety of relatively established traditions within Islamic studies and more generally within the sociology of religion. For example, his distinction between Islam as personal faith (*islam*) and Islam as a social system (*nizam*) depends explicitly on Wilfred Cantwell Smith's "special case" theory of Islam (Smith 1964). Hodgson's treatment of the problem of the commitments of the researcher and the relationship between "spiritual interests" and "material interests" follows implicitly the philosophy of social science of Max Weber. My criticism of Hodgson's approach to Islamics will consequently have much wider implications for the attempt to replace the philology of Islam for a sociology of Islam.

Conscience and Religion

In *The Venture of Islam*, Hodgson introduces a number of new terms for defining various dimensions or regions of Islam. This discussion of terminology is not simply contingent to his main purpose since it pinpoints the fundamental structure of his approach. Thus, "Islamdom" is used as a direct analogy with "Christendom" to denote a complex of social relations within which Muslims and their religion were dominant politically and culturally. Within Islamdom, of course, a range of other cultures may be present just as Jews and their institutions were part of European Christendom.

Islamdom does not refer to a specific culture; it is, rather, the channel which bears a culture for which Hodgson provides the term "Islamicate." Islamicate culture may be shared by both Muslims and non-Muslims in so far as the latter are at all integrated within the institutional nexus of Islamdom. "Islam" refers specifically to the religion of the Muslims. By "religion" is meant "any *life-orientational* experience or behaviour in the degree to which it is focussed on the role of a *person in an environment felt as cosmos*" (Hodgson 1974, I, 362). Such a focus will contain some element of experience of the numinous or transcendental on a cosmic level. Furthermore, such religious responses to the numinous may take three modes. In the "paradigm-tracing" mode, the ultimate is sought in "enduring cosmic patterns" through myth and symbol, particularly in the enduring pattern of nature. In the kerygmatic mode, ultimacy is located in the "irrevocable datable events" of history. Finally, in the mystical mode, the faithful have looked for ultimate reality in "subjective inward awareness," in transformed selfhood. These life-orientational schemes are, however, not, as it were, the rock on which Islamicate culture and Islamdom ultimately rest. Personal piety ("a person's spiritual devotion") is a person's "manner of response to the divine" whereas "religion" includes "the diverse ramifications of those traditions that are focussed on such responses" (Hodgson 1974, I, 360). Religion is the complex of institutions and practices which embody or focus personal responses to the divine; religion is the social cult which encases piety.

This encasement is partial and variable. Hodgson argues that the piety of the agents who happen to belong to religious communities may vary considerably. Similarly, piety cannot be reduced to ethics or to "zealous acceptance of myth and ritual." Piety, the individual conscience, the personal response to God—these are in "some ways but a small part of religion (as a set of institutions and orientations). Yet it is the core of it" (Hodgson 1974, I, 360). Piety is thus treated as the ultimately irreducible and creative core of religion. Religion is the sociologically explicable outer husk of which piety or conscience is the interior, sociologically inexplicable kernel.

The implication of this scheme is that the closer one draws to the inner circle of faith, the further one withdraws from sociological forces. The inner religion of faith is independent of society as an irreducible "pious fact"—to give a twist to Durkheim's notion of "social facts." Hodgson accepts the fact that religion is channeled into social traditions which are supported by "group interests" reflecting "ecological circumstances in general." These sociologically determined channels and contexts, however, provide merely the location within which piety can play an historically crucial and creative role, a charisma operating within "the interstices of routine patterns" (Hodgson 1974, I, 25). The creative acts of history must, to some extent, satisfy latent group interests otherwise they would have no social and historical effect. Yet, these creative acts of the conscience "do not merely fit into an existent pattern of interests as it stands; they lead back not to the ecology as such but to some thrust of autonomous integration within an individual" (Hodgson 1974, III, 6). Sociological factors are written into this account of the nature of religion as merely limitations on piety.

It is possible to obtain a more comprehensive view of Hodgson's treatment of piety by considering the analogy he draws between styles of art and styles of piety. Traditions in art, fashions in aesthetic appreciation and schools can be seen as analogous to the institutional and cultural network of religion, while personal piety is analogous to individual, artistic genius or creativity. Just as the existence and transformations of schools of art might be sociologically explained by reference to patronage, for example, so changes in religious institutions might be explained by reference to the decline of the feudal mode of production, but religious piety and artistic genius are not reducible to "ecological circumstances." At most, we could see the impact of traditions on personal creativity, as cramping the creative expression of the individual. Within the broad limits set by style and tradition, an enormous range of sociologically undetermined creativity is possible.

In conclusion, Hodgson's treatment of piety/religion results in the sociological immunity of faith. This immunization could be located within an implicitly Kantian view of human affairs in which men inhabit ar phenomenal world where the laws of Newtonian causality operate and a noumenal world where the private conscience is free to operate. While the outer, phenomenal world of religious institutions may be causally determined by ecological laws, the inner world of noumenal conscience knows only "the thrust of autonomous integration" of the private individual. Hodgson's most direct statement of this position is contained in the following: "Ultimately all faith is private .... We are primarily human beings and only secondarily participants in this or that tradition" (Hodgson 1974, I, 28). Islamdom, Islamicate culture and even Islam as a religion are public and can be sociologically explained; piety, faith and conscience are private, having an integrity uncontaminated by sociological factors.

Comparative Religion

Comparative religion has been riddled by problems of neutrality. As Hodgson notes, it has been all too easy for scholars with a Christian commitment to regard Islam as a "truncated" version of Christianity. Muslim scholars, by contrast, are likely to view Christianity as a perverted form of Islam. A scholar with no overt religious predilection cannot easily ignore the truth-claims of either religion.[2] If Hodgson is committed to the view that piety is the irreducible locus of religion, this does raise difficulties for anyone attempting to understand *islam* from outside. This problem is compounded by the fact that Hodgson himself was a committed Christian—a point I shall return to in detail at a later stage. Hodgson's final answer to the issue of "understanding alien-belief systems"[3] seems unsatisfactory because it is inconclusive, but has the merits of being honest and unsentimental.

Hodgson rejects any attempt to pick out of Christianity and Islam certain isolated elements which could be regarded as equal and comparable. For example, the idea that moral behavior should be based on divine revelation could be held to be common to both religions. Yet behind these superficially common elements lie profound differences in theology, relating to the moral challenge of the Qur'an and the redemptive nature of Christianity as a sacramental community. Any attempt at syncretism or any notion that ultimately all religions are the same since they rest on a common human response to the divine is rejected by Hodgson. Christianity and Islam should be treated as independent, and to some extent irreconcilable, structures which give different emphases to a range of religious elements within them. Comparative research would explore what elements within independent religious structures get subordinated or emphasized. By this method, the two religions can be seen to be in a state of tension, of productive dialogue. Persons with or without religious commitments can join in this form of analysis provided they maintain "a sensitive human awareness of what can be humanly at stake" (Hodgson 1974, I, 30). It appears that with this sort of structural approach religious commitments on the part of the researcher can be regarded as irrelevant, or at least inconsequential, but it is well known that religious and other commitments have played a major role in the work of many of the great scholars of Islam (cf. Waardenburg 1963). Hodgson recommends that the scholar should attempt to avoid the pitfalls of idiosyncratic commitments while also learning "to profit by the concern and insight they permit" (Hodgson 1974, I, 27). Furthermore, since "all faith is private," committed scholars in Christianity might be able to communicate far more easily with "congenial temperaments" in Islam than with colleagues in their own culture. The role and importance of religious commitments in scholarly research remains unsettled and ambiguous. Hodgson recommends that these commitments on the part of researchers should be explicitly and deliberately examined in order to specify what is possible within the limitations set by these commitments. One minor criticism of Hodgson which has far wider implications for the concluding sections of this paper is that he does not face his own commitments squarely and systematically. On the contrary, he informs us in one footnote that he is "a convinced Christian, of the Quaker persuasion," but goes on to assert that his viewpoint on modern religious studies owes far more to Rudolf Otto and Mircea Eliade than to his private religious commitments. One contention could be that Hodgson's whole view of conscience is a specifically Quaker interpretation.

Supporting Traditions

The primary distinction between the inner creative faith and the outward social system of religion depends heavily on the approach of Wilfred Cantwell Smith's *The Meaning and End of Religion*.[4] For Smith, the notion of religion as a social system develops relatively late in human history, whereas the idea of a personal faith was established long before the rise of religious systems. Thus, he contrasts the terms *din*, *daena*, and *islam* with Islam and *nizam*. Islam is a "special case" in the sense that it emerged in a social setting where the ideas of religion as a social system were already developed and established. Muhammad set out to create Islam as a systematic religion in a manner that differentiates him clearly from Jesus or Buddha. Islam has a special awareness of itself as a religion and in particular as a religion named by God as Islam. Nevertheless, the notion of Islam as a personal submission to God was originally more significant and central than outward submission to rituals, beliefs and customs. In the Qur'an, for example, the terms *aslama* (to submit), *iman* (faith), and *din* (piety) are far more prevalent than Islam and *nizam*. The Qur'an refers to *islamukum* as a personal Islam, as your *islam*, and Smith notes that there are passages which attack the idea of exclusive religious boundaries in favor of "a direct and uninstitutionalized moralist piety" (Smith 1964, 103). The notion of an uninstitutionalized faith directly corresponds to Hodgson's own emphasis on the pious kernel, partially encapsulated within the cultic husk. This orientation to the problem of "What is religion?" is combined, on the one hand, with Otto's theory of the numinous and, on the other hand, the treatment of religion as a public system as elaborated by the incorporation of the sociology of Emile Durkheim and Clifford Geertz.[5]

Hodgson's indebtedness to the sociology of Max Weber is far more implicit and diffuse. For one thing, Hodgson comments that it is unfortunate that Weber "said so little about Islam" (Hodgson 1974, I, 133). It is possible to identify at least three major areas in which Hodgson's approach depends fundamentally on theoretical and methodology positions elaborated by Weber. The first relates to Weber's sociology of power in terms of charisma, tradition and rationality. Hodgson's argument that piety is creative, working within the "interstices of routine patterns," parallels Weber's view of charisma as a creative force, a threat to the stability of social relations based on tradition and rationality; charismatic devotion and enthusiasm cannot be reduced to merely economic forces. By extension, Weber's distinction between virtuoso religion based on pure charisma and mass religion based on mere custom and routine parallels Hodgson's view of the pious as a holy hard-core within the tepid religiosity of mere cultic allegiance. Similarly, Weber spoke of himself as "religiously unmusical," thereby implying an analogy between charismatic gifts in music and religion. The virtuosi of religion and music stand in constant opposition to the mass routinization of public practice and taste. Unlike Hodgson, however, Weber regarded Islam as a religion in which the exterior commitment to routine practices predominated over the possibility of interior piety. Weber spoke of Islam's distinctively feudal characteristics in which one finds "essentially ritualistic character of religious obligation ... the great simplicity of religious requirements and the even greater simplicity of the modest ethical requirements" (Weber 1965, 264). Clearly, Hodgson's account of the piety which lay inside these ritualistic obligations is a direct challenge to Weber's whole position. Secondly, Hodgson's view of the independence of religious (pious) interests from group interests, specifically socio-economic features (the ecological context) depends on Weber's attempt to show the relative autonomy of political, ideological, legal and religious factors from the economic base of society. Weber's emphasis on the moral challenge of monotheistic/salvation religions in shaping human institutions and attitudes is precisely Hodgson's view of conscience as a causally significant factor in history. The basic methodology of *The Venture of Islam* could be summarized in Weber's words, namely "Not ideas, but material and ideal interests directly govern men's conduct" (Gerth and Mills 1961, 280). Finally, Hodgson's treatment of the problem of scholarly commitments closely relates to Weber's treatment of the issues of value relevance, neutrality and objectivity. For Weber, a scholar's values determine the object of his research and the range of problems that are to be identified. A social scientist, however, must exercise ethical neutrality by not taking advantage of his social prestige to make value judgments about empirical evidence. As a neo-Kantanian, Weber accepted a radical divorce between facts and values, between the phenomental and noumenal worlds. Knowledge about the real world did not entitle the sociologist to make authoritative ethical pronouncements about the quality of that world. The use of value-interpretation of the meaning of social actions was crucial if the meaning of social behaviour was to be adequately conveyed, but this method should not be confused with the general requirements of scientific objectivity. Once a sociologist had declared his values and selected his object of research, the usual criteria of objectivity in the selection and evaluation of data applied automatically. In this way, it was possible to claim that sociology was both value-relevant and value-free.[6] Hodgson's notion that the values of the scholar, while contributing as it were to the "richness" of historical understanding, sets limits within which he can delve deeply into his selected topic of research. Similarly, for Weber, since "causality is infinite," the value-commitments of the researcher are in fact crucial, not only for selecting the object of research, but for the researcher's total orientation to his subject matter. Values are not so much embarrassing obstacles, not a painful encumbrance, but a positive asset in the full appreciation of the meaning of religious and other human activities.[7] From this point of view, Hodgson's Quaker commitment would set limits to his understanding while enriching his perspective at a deeper level.

Critical Assessment

(i) Extra ecclesiam nulla salus

One problem with the Weber-Hodgson position on values is that it is by definition impossible to choose between ultimate values which are thereby rendered wholly irrational.[8] Values are sharply divorced from facts in terms of the Kantian is/ought dichotomy. No empirical evidence can ever guide, let alone dictate, moral positions. It follows that no objections can be raised against a scholar who declares that he will interpret Islam within the limitations of Quaker Christianity, but it also follows that no objections could be mounted against the interpretation of Islam from the point of view of fascism, racialism, utilitarianism, Taoism or any other belief system. Hodgson, of course, wants to deny that his Quaker convictions are central to his theoretical comprehension of Islam. As we have seen, he explicitly claims that his orientation is derived from Eliade and Otto. It is difficult, however, not to read *The Venture of Islam* without an awareness of the prominence of Quaker theology dominating certain key issues.

It could be argued that the view that religion is merely the husk of an inner, private faith is a specifically Protestant, nineteenth-century view of the relationship between ritual and faith. For Hodgson, piety is quite literally the inner light that animates the outward forms of religion. At the end of volume three, Hodgson writes that in a society dominated by "technicalist specialization" it is very difficult for individual values to find an effective expression, but small groups of inspired individuals may yet shape critical areas of social change. He refers specifically to the social impact of "the tiny Quaker society" (Hodgson 1974, III, 434). This minor comment in fact characterizes Hodgson's whole interpretation of the relationship between faith and religion, individual and society. Hodgson writes in terms of piety/individual *versus* religion/society. For example, Hodgson consistently treats the *shari'a* as "essentially oppositional," as an expression of the autonomy of society against political absolutism (Hodgson 1964, 234). The effect of the *shari'a* was "to stress the rights of the individual as such" (Hodgson 1974, I, 344). Just as the Quaker acted as a gadfly within Christianity, so the pious of Islam constantly threatened the routinization of religion by forming an oppositional group in the midst of the cultic community.[9] In short, Hodgson's emphasis on the autonomy of the individual, the centrality of conscience, the secondary quality of religious ritual and of religion itself, the oppositional nature of piety—all of these elements playing a central role within his orientation to Islam—bear decisive marks of a Quaker commitment.[10]

The problem with the Weber-Hodgson approach to the role of value-commitments, as we have noted, is that in one sense it is closed to critical inspection. For example, one might adduce evidence to the effect that Islamic ethics as expressed in the *shari'a* were not oppositional at all, not specifically conservative and ineffectual as a point of criticism of political control (cf. Lewis 1972). Hodgson could, however, easily counter such an objection by arguing that, while it is true that his value-commitments lead him to a particular position, the same can be said of all value-commitments. Every researcher has a value-position; *ergo*, all research has limitations. The price of this value-relativity is, however, inflationary in that it would ultimately silence all debate. Hodgson could have no objection to an entirely contrasted interpretation of religion, namely a Catholic viewpoint. It could be argued that ritual is not an optional extra that can somehow be tacked onto the conscience. Without ritual, sacrament, myth, community, and an objective religious law, the isolated, individual piety would not only fade away, it could not exist at all. It is religion that nurtures piety, not vice versa. Once it is conceded that there is no way of arbitrating between ultimate scholarly commitments, there is total impasse. The two positions are equally valid and equally incompatible.

Behind Hodgson's phenomenological approach to piety as the irreducible inner core of religion is, one suspects, a fairly common assumption that to give a causal account of religion is to "explain it away," thereby leaving the scholar of religion without a subject matter. If religion is not entirely explained away by sociology, then it is felt that a sociological explanation of religion in some way casts doubt upon the truth-claims of religion. To these notions is added a sense of methodological injustice in that, while the science of politics leaves politics as a phenomenon intact, a science of religion would demolish its own subject matter.[11] These three anxieties may to some extent explain the popularity of hermeneutics and phenomenology of religion amongst sociologists of religion who are "religiously musical." Hermeneutics provides a method which is congenial because it does justice to religion in its own terms (cf. Royster 1972). At least on one score, these anxieties seem paranoid in that the causal explanation of a set of beliefs has no bearing on the truth or falsity of those beliefs. That allegiance to certain minority sects by American poor whites might be explained by the theory of relative deprivation does not prove that sectarian beliefs are false. Causal explanations are appropriate in the case of true and false beliefs indiscriminately.[12] What I want to show is that a sociological explanation of "conscience" can indeed be provided. The point of this exercise is to demonstrate that one cannot distinguish between piety and religion on the grounds that there can be no sociological explanation of the former. Such an historical/sociological treatment of "conscience" does not, however, in some way call into question the validity of "conscience."

(ii) Sociological Notes on "Conscience"

To my knowledge there is no existing sociological analysis of the concept of "conscience" as it has been developed within Islam. In default of such a study, doubts can be raised against Hodgson's view of the irreducibility and universality of conscience in Islam by briefly commenting on studies of Christendom. These studies raise a number of general theoretical problems for any Islamicist wishing to take up Hodgson's general orientation to the sociology of Islamic piety. Since Hodgson does not define or discuss "conscience" in any depth or with any precision apart from general statements to the effect that piety is the human response to the divine presence, the implication is that piety is common-sensically obvious, uniform and trans-cultural. No attempt is made to spell out the difference between the Christian and Islamic notions of "conscience"—such an omission is distinctively odd, given the centrality of the concept to his scheme of analysis. "Conscience" is in fact a highly complex, if not ambiguous concept, implying "private thoughts," "self-accusation," "self-awareness" and also knowledge or consciousness. While "unconscientious" means not regulated by moral principles, the "unconscious" may mean simply something forgotten (unaware) or an actual terrain within the psychic structure. Paul Tillich comments that the Roman language

> following popular Greek usage, unites the theoretical and practical emphasis in the word *conscientia*, while philosophers like Cicero and Seneca admit it to the ethical sphere and interpret it as the trial of one's self, in accusation as well as in defence. In modern languages the theoretical and practical side are usually expressed by different words. English distinguishes *consciousness* from *conscience*, German *Bewusstsein* from *Gewissen*, French *connaissance* from *conscience*. (Tillich 1951, 153).

Aquinas distinguished between *synderesis* (habitual knowledge) and *conscientia* (application of moral rules). In Christianity, "conscience" had a juridical quality about it ("trial of the self ") which found a specific expression in the idea of a "Court of Conscience." If "conscience" can be taken as a human response to the divine, then it appears to have been a typically guilty response. This sense of guilt seems to play little part in Hodgson's interpretation of conscience and piety. Hodgson treats "conscience" as oppositional, whereas, in pre-Reformation Christianity in particular, the guilty conscience was an element of ecclesiastical control of the faithful. Conscience acted within a culture of guilt in which the task of religious confessors was "to represent law in the forum of penance and make conformity to the regulations of the hierarchy a strict matter of conscience" (Tentler 1974, 117). In Christianity, conscience was institutionalized within the sacrament of penance, controlled and monopolized by an ecclesiastical elite. As Michael Gilsenan has observed, confession (*i'tiraf*) is uncommon in Islam and where it does occur it remains distinguishable from Christian penance in having no associated act of absolution or forgiveness (Gilsenan 1973, 107). In short, Hodgson ignores the whole problem of the relativity of the concept of "conscience."

This omission leads to much more serious difficulties. "Conscience" in Christianity not only has a clear history, but its origins and development have clear sociological, or more generally "ecological," causes. Father Chenu has shown that the twelfth century prepared the way for a radically new psychology of man in which the importance of subjective intention began to replace the more traditional emphasis on exterior, objective morality (Chenu 1969). The major figure in this transformation of moral philosophy was Pierre Abelard (1079–1142). One consequence of Abelard's treatment of moral intention was to shift the whole emphasis within the confessional away from the external, ecclesiastical absolution towards the subjective, individual contrition. Chenu argues that these changes within theology were also exemplified in the emergence of platonic affection for women as persons rather than sex objects within "courtly love." The main sites of these new themes concerning the centrality of "conscience" were the guilds, the universities and urban communities. "Conscience" arose once the commercial market created new social conditions which were incompatible with feudalism. The new psychology was the product of market relations which required freedom from feudal restrictions of travel and exchange—"there is freedom in town air." The market produced "the individual" who found an interior self not present under feudalism. Chenu's argument can be supported by, for example, comparing the Irish penitentials of the feudal period with the *summas* of later theologians (cf. Bieler 1963). It is also supported by the research of Rosenwein and Little (1974) on mendicant spirituality. One might also note Goldmann's argument that the growth of an exchange economy produced characteristically a belief system based on the notions of individualism, freedom of contact and contract (Goldmann 1973). There is a sense, however, in which my objections to Hodgson would stand even if these causal accounts of the rise of "conscience" under market, urban conditions were proved inadequate or false. The point is that causal explanations of "conscience" are neither improper nor implausible; there is no *prima facie* reason for regarding "conscience" as immune from sociological investigation.

It is somewhat odd to note that Hodgson himself seems fleetingly aware of the possibility of a causal account of the rise of "conscience" in Islam. He suggests one himself which parallels the theses of Chenu, Goldmann and others. Hodgson notes that in the Axial Age (800–200 BC) new markets for inter-continental trade began to emerge alongside the development of a citied culture in which merchants arose as significant social classes. As a result, "the Cuneiform literatures of the time reflect a growing sense of personal individuality which most probably catered to the tastes of the market more than to either temple or court" (Hodgson 1974, I, 11). The problem of the relationship between the private individual and the social order, argues Hodgson, increasingly came to exercise the religious speculations of the prophets of the Axial Age, particularly Zarathushtra and the Hebrew prophets. While one might accept this assertion as at least the beginnings of a sociology of the conscience, it is incompatible with the main thrust of Hodgson's position that piety is the uncaused origin of religion, that social groups might be explained sociologically while the individual faith remains entirely independent, that piety is private while religion is public and dependent on social factors. Hodgson almost unwittingly acknowledges that both piety and religion can be explained sociologically, while explicitly maintaining that the conscience belongs to noumena not phenomena.

(iii) Virtuoso and Mass Religion

Hodgson's treatment of piety is, furthermore, ambiguous in one crucial respect. The general impression of volume one of *The Venture of Islam* is that everyone has an inward conscience, a personal piety, by virtue of being an individual. The quality of piety is also extremely variable: "Devotional response is inevitably a highly personal thing. As in the case of aesthetic appreciation, every individual has his own bent" (Hodgson 1974, I, 361). However, Hodgson also recognizes that the quantity, so to speak, of piety also varies from one individual to another in the obvious sense that some are more pious than others. The result of these variations in the quality and quantity of personal, devotional life is to produce a definite religious stratification between the mass and the virtuosi. Hodgson recognizes that the Sufis, for example, developed a clear stratification system which separated the mass from the *pir*. One could think of Sufism as a religious pyramid linking dead saints, *pirs*, disciples, novices and the mass. Hodgson's view of the relationship between "material interests" (ecology) and inward conscience commits him to the notion that the hierarchy of charismatic qualities varies independently of the secular status order. This relationship, involving the autonomy of charisma, was precisely what Weber had in mind when he wrote about the differences between mass and "heroic" religiosity.

Thus, since charisma is in great demand but in short supply,

> all intensive religiosity has a tendency towards a sort of *status* stratification, in accordance with differences in the charismatic qualifications ... By "mass" understand those who are religiously "unmusical"; we do not, of course, mean those who occupy an inferior position in the secular status order. (Weber 1965, 287)

In Hodgson's treatment of religious "talent," this means that charisma, breaking out of established routines, cannot be explained "away" by sociology, because the "proper" object of sociological scrutiny is public routine not private virtue.

There are difficulties with such an interpretation which can be illustrated by developing the analogy between musical talent and religious piety ("individual bent"). Even if we grant that there is, as it were, a pool of talent in any population, this talent (whether it is religious or musical) has to be trained, developed and practiced. It follows that any person who wishes to develop a talent must be withdrawn in some fashion from direct, productive labor. Religious charisma, on these grounds, would be more common among widows, retired men, young people or the ruling class. Where charisma appears among those actively engaged in labor, they are likely to retire from productive tasks or they must become in some way supported by their disciples. Charisma must be paid for by offering, tribute, rewards or direct cash. Those without charisma (the religiously unmusical) must be brought to support the small elite, so that charismatic services (healing, magic, divination, prophecy) are exchanged for various payments which support the elite in office. For this reason, the religious stratification system is closely connected with the secular status system. On the one hand, there is a tendency for the religious elite to be over-recruited from the secular elite. For example, between the sixth and twelfth centuries over ninety percent of Christian saints were recruited from the ruling class (George and George 1955). On the other hand, religious virtuosi who "retire" from labor in order to cultivate their talents form an unproductive class in the same way that, in Marx's terms, the ruling class is unproductive because it creates no surplus value. This difficulty in relation to Hodgson's attempt to preserve the autonomy of piety from sociological explanation is directly connected with his version of Weber's separation of "material" and "spiritual" interests.

(iv) Social Determination

We have already commented on the consequences of believing that value-commitments are totally independent of empirical facts; it leaves one with no criteria for selecting between competing interpretations. I have attempted to undermine part of that position by claiming that all social beliefs, indeed all beliefs as such, are determined. There is no residual category of beliefs which are not causally determined, but the causal determination of beliefs should not be confused with questions of rationality, truth and authenticity. That is only one aspect of the issue. The idea that politics, religion, law and all other social institutions are partly autonomous from economic forces very easily slides into the platitude that "everything influences everything else" (for this criticism cf. Turner 1974). This attempt by sociologists or Islamicists (like Weber and Hodgson) to adopt this theoretical and methodological approach is ultimately connected with the rejection of Marx, but the rejection involves a particularly crude "economist" and/or "technicalist" interpretation of Marx. This is not the place to launch into the debate about the relationship between Marx and Weber. Suffice it to say that for Marx, the economic (the mode of production) determines which of the major institutional orders (political, ideological, state, educational "instances") is dominant within any given social formation. Thus,

> that the mode of production of material life dominates the development of social, political and intellectual life generally is very true for our own time, in which material interests preponderate, but not for the middle ages, in which Catholicism, nor for Athens and Rome, where politics, reigned supreme. (Marx 1970, I a, 82)

The appearance of the dominance of "spiritual interests" should not be confused with the determination of religion by the particular stage of the development of a mode of production. In this way, Hodgson falls into the trap implied by Marx's fundamental question about Islamdom, "Why does the history of the east appear as a history of religions?" (Marx and Engels 1963, XXVIII, 251). In *The Venture of Islam*, we are presented with a history of Islamicate societies determined by the inner history of personal piety. The institutionalized husk of law, economics, political organization is thereby secondary to the sociologically unfettered dynamics of man's response to God. Because Hodgson wants to protect piety in this way and because he wants to treat the main articulation of piety as art, poetry and philosophy, Hodgson is in fact forced into the arms of philology and Orientalism from which he wants to extricate the study of Islam. Social science cannot be held at arm's length by forcing it to analyze the merely external, the circumstantial. In particular, sociology is not simply a science of "ecological circumstances in general." Such a treatment of social science leaves Orientalism to reign supreme or, as Hodgson himself admits, it is to abandon the study of Islamdom to "the 'pre-historic' period of scholarship" (Hodgson 1974, I, 47).

Notes

1. Hodgson's main publications include Hodgson 1955a, 1955b, 1959–60, 1960, 1964.
2. Cf. Turner 1973 on Maxime Rodinson in this connection.
3. Hodgson's position here bears much in common with the approach defended by Winch 1963.
4. Hodgson notes his indebtedness to Smith on page 79 of volume I.
5. In particular, Durkheim 1947 and Geertz 1966.
6. For a critical assessment, cf. Gouldner 1962.
7. On the importance of values in sociological research, cf. Dawe 1971.
8. Cf. Marcuse 1971 on the place of irrationality in Weber's sociology.
9. For one example of Quakers as a political dissident group, cf. Smith 1973.
10. One could also trace out connections with Kant's absolute Ego, Otto's Unconditioned God and Weber's decisionist ethics.
11. This is, for example, part of the general tone of Martin 1969.
12. On this point I am in disagreement with MacIntyre's view that true beliefs require no causal explanation, MacIntyre 1971.

References

Bieler, Ludwig, ed. 1963. *The Irish Penintentials*. Dublin: Dublin Institute for Advanced Studies.

Chenu, M. D. 1969. *L'Eveil de la conscience dans la civilisation medievale*. Montreal: Institute of Medieval Studies.

Dawe, Alan. 1971. "The Relevance of Values." In *Max Weber and Modern Sociology*, ed. A. Sahay, 37–66. London: Routledge and Kegan Paul.

Durkheim, Emile. 1947. *The Elementary Forms of Religious Life*. Glencoe IL: Free Press.

Geertz, Clifford. 1966. "Religion as a Cultural System." In *Anthropological Approaches to the Study of Religion*, ed. M. Banton. London: Tavistock.

George, K., and George, C. H. 1955. "Roman Catholic Sainthood and Social Status." *Journal of Religion* 35: 85–98.

Gerth, H. H., and Mills, C. Wright. 1961. *From Max Weber*. London: Routledge and Kegan Paul.

Gilsenan, Michael. 1973. *Saint and Sufi in Modern Egypt*. Oxford: Clarendon Press.

Goldmann, Lucian. 1973. *The Philosophy of the Enlightenment*. London: Routledge and Kegan Paul.

Gouldner, Alvin. 1962. "Anti-Minotaur: The Myth of a Value-free Sociology." *Social Problems* 9/3: 199–213.

Hodgson, Marshall G. S. 1955a. *The Order of Assassins*. The Hague: Mouton.

—1955b. "How Did the Early Shi'a Become Sectarian?" *Journal of the American Oriental Society* 75: 1–13.

—1959–60. "The Unity of Later Islamic History." *Journal of World History* 5: 879–914.

—1960. "A Comparison of Islam and Christianity as Framework for Religious Life." *Diogenes* 32: 49–74.

— 1964. "Islam and Image." *History of Religions* 3: 220–60.

— 1974. *The Venture of Islam, Conscience and History in a World Civilization.* Chicago, IL and London: University of Chicago Press.

Lewis, Bernard. 1972. "Islamic Concepts of Revolution." In *Revolution in the Middle East*, ed. P. J. Vatikiotis, 30–40. London: George Allen and Unwin.

MacIntyre, Alisdair. 1971. *Against the Self-Images of the Age.* London: Duckworth.

Marcuse, Herbert. 1971. "Industrialization and Capitalism." In *Max Weber and Sociology Today*, ed. Otto Stammer, 133–86. Oxford: Basil Blackwell.

Martin, D. 1969. *The Religious and the Secular.* London: Routledge and Kegan Paul.

Marx, Karl. 1970. *Capital.* London: Lawrence and Wishart.

Marx, Karl, and Frederick Engels. 1963. *Werke.* Berlin: Dietz.

Rosenwein, Barbara H., and Little, Lester K. 1974. "Social Meaning in the Monastic and Mendicant Spiritualities." *Past & Present* 63: 4–32.

Royster, James E. 1972. "The Study of Muhammad: A Survey of Approaches from the Perspective of the History and Phenomenology of Religion." *Muslim World* 62: 49–70.

Smith, George L. 1973. *Religion and Trade in New Netherland.* Ithaca, NY and London: Cornell University Press.

Smith, Wilfred Cantwell. 1964. *The Meaning and End of Religion.* New York: Mentor Books.

Tentler, Thomas N. 1974. "The Summa for Confessors as an Instrument of Social Control." In *The Pursuit of Holiness in Late Medieval and Renaissance Religion*, ed. Charles Trinkaus and Heiko A. Oberman, 103–26. Leiden: E. J. Brill.

Tillich, Paul. 1951. *The Protestant Era.* London: Nisbet.

Turner, Bryan S. 1973. "A Note on Rodinson's Mohammed." *Religion: A Journal of Religion and Religions* 3: 79–82.

—1974. *Weber and Islam.* London: Routledge and Kegan Paul.

Waardenburg, Jean-Jacques. 1963. *L'Islam dans le miroir de l'Occident.* The Hague: Mouton.

Weber, Max. 1965. *The Sociology of Religion.* London: Methuen.

Winch, Peter. 1963. *The Idea of a Social Science.* London: Routledge and Kegan Paul.

22

Conversion as a Social Process

Richard Bulliet

Conversion to Islam in the Middle Ages was somewhat different from conversion to other religions. There was, for example, no rite involved comparable to baptism.[1] The verb *aslama*, meaning "he submitted [to God]," is used to describe the procedure of becoming a Muslim, but where the verb occurs, there is no elaboration to indicate the real content of the act. Religious treatises speak of the simple utterance of the confession of faith, the *shahada*, as the defining characteristic of adherence to Islam; but there is disagreement as to the precise nature of this utterance, whether it must be made with the heart or by the lips only. Nevertheless, since we lack any concrete statement to the contrary, it may be hazarded that the formal process of conversion to Islam consisted primarily of speaking eight words. More certain is the fact that conversion did not depend upon a priestly individual. For one thing, Islam did not have priestly individuals in an institutionalized fashion; for another, there is frequent mention of people who converted at the hands of Muslims who had no noteworthy position of any kind as well as at the hands of those who held governmental but not religious office.

For present purposes, therefore, formal conversion, in the sense of utterance of the confession of faith, is not as significant as what might be termed social conversion, that is, conversion involving movement from one religiously defined social community to another. It is reported, for example, that various North African Berber tribes converted to Islam and subsequently fell away. This type of conversion, although the words of the confession of faith might actually have been mouthed by the tribesmen, would not qualify as social conversion. The tribesmen were not leaving their non-Muslim tribe to join a different, Muslim tribe. Apostasy probably had little significance because formal conversion alone meant very little in any social sense. The same could be said at a later period for the conversion of various Turkish tribes and possibly for nontribal groups as well, some of which are reported to have apostatized several times as groups.

What is implied by the term social conversion is individual rather than communal action. Having performed the act of conversion, the convert henceforth saw his identity in terms of the new religious community of which he had become a member. This possibility, in turn, implies or presupposes a society in which social identity was normally defined in religious terms as opposed, say, to tribal or national terms. Such a society prevailed over much of the area that converted to Islam in the Middle Ages, but it was the product of relatively recent historical development and was by no means universal.

One of the most important social changes of imperial Roman times was the gradual development of religion as the focus of social identity. Why this development occurred is not altogether clear, although it unquestionably was related to the changes in religious orientation associated with the rise of Christianity and to the vitiation of the meaning of citizenship within the context of the universal Roman Empire.[2] Yet if the origin of this broad social change remains cloudy, its practical dimensions are easier to delineate. Different religious groups were organized somewhat differently, and organization changed over time; but the following features are of common occurrence:

1. A formal authority structure, often hierarchical. Within the various sects of Christianity the priestly hierarchy is well known. Sassanid Zoroastrianism was likewise structured in a hierarchical fashion, as was Manichaeism.[3] With Judaism the situation is more complex since the destruction of the second temple left the religion without a center, but authoritative bodies still were recognized in Babylonia (Iraq) and Jerusalem (Goitein 1971, 5–40).

2. Some degree of legal autonomy. With Christianity and Judaism the jurisdiction of religious courts grew steadily under the late Roman Empire, and bodies of religious law were compiled and written down. The areas in which the church had the greatest legal autonomy were those of religion and personal status, but some administrative and taxation functions fell to the religious authorities as well (Pigulevskaya 1963, 106–11). The Zoroastrian legal system is little known, but what is known suggests a closer identification of church and state than was the case with the other religions (Pigulevskaya 1963, 102–11). Nevertheless, Zoroastrian legal decisions continued to be rendered after the Sassanid Empire had fallen to the Arabs (De Menasce 1967, 220–30; Anklesaria 1969).

3. Fusion of language with religion. Although some religions, such as Manichaeism, utilized whatever languages were encountered, the more common pattern was for a given religion to utilize as a religious language the ancestral tongue of the

bulk of its adherents. For Egyptian Monophysitism this meant Coptic; for Syrian Monophysitism and Nestorianism, Syriac; for Zoroastrianism, Avestan; and for Judaism, Hebrew. For purposes of instruction or exegesis, of course, vernacular languages were used wherever and whenever the liturgical language had fallen out of common use.

4. Recognition of religious authorities as spokesmen for the religious community and as exemplars of religious life. Here the role of the religious authority as the successor of the civic official is quite marked (Runciman 1956, 89–91; Frye 1963, 209–11). Christian bishops and Zoroastrian priests sometimes appear as the primary authorities of sizable communities.

Given the preeminence of religiously defined social identification in the immediately pre-Islamic period in the Middle East, the notion of social conversion is both significant and quite specific. It may be proposed as an axiom of religious conversion that the convert's expectations of his new religion will parallel his expectations of his old religion. In the case of an ecstatic convert, the old religion may have failed to satisfy spiritual expectations which seem to have greater promise of fulfillment in the new religion. Such a convert might appear as a religious malcontent before conversion and very likely as a zealot or spiritual athlete after conversion. Most converts are nonecstatic, however. People who are more or less satisfied with their previous religious life and who convert more for mundane than for spiritual reasons find life in the new religion more attractive the closer it approximates life in the old. In other words, a socially stodgy and conservative Zoroastrian would be more likely to become, upon conversion, a socially stodgy and conservative Muslim than a wild-eyed fanatic; and the attraction of Islam would be related to his perception of it as a religion that had room for stodgy conservatism.[4]

Naturally, no hard and fast determination of the individual reasons for and reactions to conversion can be derived from such an axiom, but the overall implication of the axiom is that as conversion progresses, the new religion becomes, in its social dimension, increasingly like the old. This is not to say that different religious doctrines or institutions inevitably have continuities or even close parallels, but simply that the social functions that were served by the previous religion are likely to be served by the new religion to an increasing degree as the membership of the new religion becomes dominated by converts.

Since for Middle Eastern society in the pre-Islamic period, as has already been remarked, religion prevailed as the source of the individual's social identity, conversion to Islam normally resulted in a major change in the convert's social identification; but in the long run, conversion gave rise to strong pressures that affected the course of development of the new religion. For the individual, conversion meant that he was no longer a part of his old community. He may actually have been regarded as legally dead in the eyes of his former coreligionists (De Menasce 1967, 224–5).[5] Consequently, for defining his social life he looked to new exemplars to replace the bishop or rabbi or *mobad* (Zoroastrian priest) who had previously filled that role. He came to think of a new language, Arabic, as a sacred language, and he normally gave his children names from the Arabic onomasticon. If there were too few Muslims in his home community for him to feel that he could live a good Muslim life—a concept that was inevitably affected by how he had conceived a good Christian, Jewish, or Zoroastrian life—he was likely to emigrate to a community with a larger Muslim population. This last tendency might well be enhanced by economics insofar as a convert might find himself frozen out of his customary participation in the economic life of his erstwhile coreligionists and consequently seek out a large Muslim community in whose economic life he could participate more or less in his accustomed fashion (Anklesaria 1969; De Menasce 1967).[6] Together these changes constituted what has been termed social conversion.

A given individual could obviously utter the profession of faith and go through none of these social changes, but such an individual would scarcely be noticeable as a member of the Muslim community. What built the Muslim community as a distinct and historically visible social entity was social conversion. It was also social rather than formal conversion that created pressures for change which affected the course of Islamic religious development.

In the earliest stages of Islam, when the Muslim community was still confined to the Arabian peninsula, social conversion was as yet an uncommon phenomenon. It is not that the bedouin, of whose conversion the Qur'an speaks disparagingly, were merely mouthing words without understanding or appreciating their meaning; it is rather that the religious expectations of the bedouin were colored by their pre-Islamic religious experience. Outside of Mecca and the Yemen, religion in tribal Arabia impinged only slightly upon the social lives of the Arabs (Fares 1932, chap. 4). Even among nominally Christian Arabs religion appears to have had scant social impact. Sacred shrines and mantic seers known as *kahins* played only an occasional part in tribal life. The rules governing the normal turning points in personal life—birth, puberty, marriage, death—were determined by tribal custom more than by religious doctrine and required no supervision by priestly persons (Fares 1932).

As a consequence of this tangential relationship of religion to Arab tribal life, the religious development of Islam was affected primarily by the original Meccan community where religion meant more than it did elsewhere in the peninsula. The impact of the conversion of the Arab tribesmen was most of all a steady dilution of the early sense of Islam as a social community. An Islam dominated numerically by converts of tribal nomadic origin was an Islam threatened with relegation to a subordinate social role. The Umayyads did not deliberately promote an Arab kingdom at the expense of an Islamic caliphate; the tribal preponderance of the Muslim population dictated a course to be followed which they could not ignore and still continue in power.

In part, indeed in large part, Islam survived this threat through efforts made in Mecca, Medina, Kufa, and Basra during its first century and a half by an Arab Muslim society that was tribal to a steadily decreasing degree and not nomadic at all. The pious circles of these cities raised and debated religious questions that were of little concern to most Muslims of that time. But socially speaking, the Muslim societies of these four cities were still dominated by Arab tribal identity to a strong degree (Hinds 1971, 346–67; Shaban 1971). The questions that were raised and debated were more concerned with the relation of the individual believer to God than the relation of the individual Muslim to his fellows.

The socialization of Islamic thought was largely the product of pressures brought by non-Arab converts from the Christian, Jewish, or Zoroastrian communities. Insofar as Islamic social life was oriented toward Arab tribes to which all Muslims belonged by birth, or by fictive adoption in the case of converts, Islam did not provide the social structure afforded by the religions whence converts were to be made. This lack was a barrier to conversion which could be broken down only by developing such a social structure on the basis of the Qur'an and the experience of the early community in Mecca and Medina. Certainly there was no conscious effort to create a society that would "compete" with the various non-Muslim societies in attractiveness. Yet it is hardly surprising that the interests of converts frequently centered around social questions as they searched in their new religion for the social structure they had abandoned by converting and that in their search they adumbrated the shape of such a structure.

Looking back at the four characteristics mentioned earlier as hallmarks of pre-Islamic religious social structure, the first of them, a formal authority structure, was most strongly promoted in Islam by converts. Ibn al-Muqaffa', a convert from Zoroastrianism, is the best known early advocate of caesaropapism as a model for the caliphate, and the development of the centralized judicial system in early Abbasid times was a concrete step in that direction (Ibn al-Muqaffa' 1966, 345–61; Tyan 1960–2005, IV, 373–4). There may also be something of the same impulse in the attraction of many converts to Shi'ism, with its rigid authority structure based upon the theory of the Imamate. The truest expression of this drive, however, was the later emergence of the Muslim religious scholars, the *'ulama'*, as a quasi-priestly class.

The second point, legal autonomy, is exemplified in the development of Muslim religious law, the *shari'a*. Although civil law has always existed in Islam alongside religious law, it has been comparatively insignificant. Yet Islamic religious law, for all its importance, did not take shape until some two centuries after the origin of the religion. During the Umayyad period, when Arabs constituted the vast majority of all Muslims, the ideal of judgment was the sage determination of the caliph acting more as a tribal arbitrator than as a religious figure. The numerous stories of the *hilm* or judicial forbearance of Mu'awiya bespeak this ideal (Lammens 1908, 66–108). Only when the convert population began to become numerically significant did religion come to the fore in the legal field.

The third point, fusion of language with religion, needs some comment. Obviously, Arabic was as important when the Arabs were numerically predominant as it was after the convert population began to make itself felt. Formal study of the Arabic language for purposes of elucidating religious texts was a later development, however: only then did Arabic begin to become a sacred tongue of the type familiar in the other religious communities. It is noteworthy that many of the pioneering grammarians of the Arabic language were themselves non-Arabs.

The fourth point is possibly the most important. It deals with the recognition of religious authorities as the spokesmen for religious communities. Since medieval Islam did not develop a clerical hierarchy or, indeed, a formal priestly office of any kind, no direct parallel to the bishop, rabbi, or mobad can be put forward. The converts to Islam did desire guidance, however, in how to live a good Muslim life. Since the role of exemplar was not filled by a formally invested religious functionary, certain obviously pious individuals came to be informally recognized as exemplars. Recognition might derive from membership in or association with the Prophet's family or the families of other saintly early figures, but more often it went to individuals who simply appeared to be good Muslims, notably to those who were studious and ascetic. Indeed, to some extent the Muslim population of convert origin probably recognized as exemplars of good Muslim life individuals whom they judged to be so qualified not by still-uncertain Islamic social standards but by standards they were accustomed to associate with formally defined religious leaders in the non-Islamic communities. The Muslim ascetic or *zahid*, for example, may have taken the place in the minds of converts from Christianity previously filled by the monk.

Not only did the pious, the ascetic, and the studious achieve notice in this fashion, but they had the role of spokesman thrust upon them. The convert population used them as their life models as well as their communal voices in the way Muslim Arab tribesmen had previously used their tribal shaykhs.[7] Lacking a formally constituted priesthood, the community looked to them as surrogate priests. Ultimately, the product of this evolution was the accumulation of power and authority in the hands of this unappointed clergy.

In this entire process, it must be realized, the role of the Muslim population of non-Arab convert origin was primarily that of applying pressure for social-religious development and providing a receptive audience. The convert population was proportionately still small when this pressure began to be felt, and the individuals who responded were more often than not Arabs, at least up to the tenth century when the convert population began to overwhelm the Arab population numerically. To be sure, specific non-Arabs made significant contributions as the pressure began to bring responses, but they were much more visible on a local level as social exemplars or proto-*'ulama'* than they were at the top level of intellectual achievement. This was undoubtedly owing to much of the convert population's feeling that the lifestyle of someone of their own linguistic and social background provided a more meaningful model than that provided by an Arab who was ethnically and linguistically a foreigner.

How the fuller accomplishment of the conversion process affected this situation must be left for a later discussion, however.

What is necessary at this point is to introduce a second axiom of conversion, which states that leaving aside ecstatic converts, no one willingly converts from one religion to another if by virtue of conversion he markedly lowers his social status. More starkly put, if an emperor converts to a religion of slaves, he does not become a slave: the religion becomes a religion of emperors.

The import of this axiom for the history of Islamic conversion in the medieval Middle East is great indeed. The conquests of Islam are just as properly viewed as the conquests of the Arabs. Being an Arab and being a Muslim were so much the same thing that people in the conquered territories were sometimes unaware of the specific religious character of the invaders. This identity of Arab and Muslim continued to be the predominant view for over a century. As already mentioned, non-Arabs who converted to Islam were obliged to become *mawali*, that is, fictive members of Arab tribes.[8] Only thus could they obtain any social identity as Muslims. Yet being a *mawla* of an Arab tribe was fraught with disadvantages. *Mawali* were regarded as racially inferior by many Arabs because they did not truly share the pure blood lineage that was the focus of tribal honor and loyalty. They were discriminated against in marriage, denied inclusion on the military payroll, and made to suffer revilement and social slights.[9]

Applying the second axiom of conversion, one must conclude that those who converted to Islam during the period when the *mawali* were so heavily stigmatized must have been people for whom being second-class Arabs was superior to any other options. In effect, for the Umayyad period, this statement implies that the major sources of non-Arab converts were two: prisoners of war who might seek through conversion to escape slavery and people, such as poor farm laborers, from the very lowest classes. Civil servants working for the new Arab rulers were not obliged to convert to keep their jobs. Certain others who felt economic pressure under the new regime preferred to convert to Christianity and become clerics, thus evading taxation, rather than convert to Islam and become lackeys of the Arabs (Morony 1976, 54).

This highly discriminatory situation eventually changed, but while it obtained it shaped the character of the first several generations of converts. The product was a mixture of a relatively few upper-class converts, largely former prisoners of war, and a larger number of riffraff. The former found a better reception in the new religious community than the latter, who were on occasion herded about like cattle; but all suffered from their subordinate status. It is scarcely surprising that some Arabs, such as Ibn Qutayba, formed the opinion that non-Arab converts to Islam were, in general, the dregs of society (Lecomte 1965, 345). It was this mixed group, however, that initially, by their very existence, posed questions about the social character of Islam which had such far-reaching results in later centuries.[10]

Notes

1. Circumcision was unquestionably performed in at least some instances, but it is rarely mentioned. For evidence of it see De Menasce 1967, 225. For Zoroastrians the act of conversion to Islam would include removal of the sacred thread worn on the body, but this was naturally of little interest to Muslim chroniclers.
2. A good survey of social and religious change in the Hellenistic period is to be found in Peters 1970.
3. The *perfecti* of Manichaeism constituted an elite group of religiously pure individuals. For the Zoroastrian ecclesiastical structure see, for example, Frye 1963, 17.
4. The notion that new converts to a religion are usually zealots arises from the practice of studying only the early stages of a conversion process. More conservative later converts pass into the new religion without giving much evidence of fanaticism or zealous observance.
5. De Menasce gives a Zoroastrian legal text confirming that the property of a convert to Islam could legally be seized by other Zoroastrians.
6. Anklesaria 1969. Zoroastrians were constrained by their law from purchasing goods in Muslim markets (Anklesaria 1969, 137–38) and from consorting with non-Zoroastrians in caravanserais (129). They could sell livestock to Muslims only if there was no other way of earning a living (De Menasce 1967, 223). Constraints of this sort must eventually have broken down as the Zoroastrian community became a minority, but initially they must have amounted to economic ostracism for many converts to Islam.
7. In one surprising instance in the mid-ninth century, a group of ascetics forming a brotherhood (*ikhwan*) may actually have used the word monk (*rahib*) to describe themselves; Abu Nu'aym 1931–4: II, 54, 57, 140.
8. The term *mawla* is used here in its generally accepted sense. Recently completed, Ph.D. dissertations by Patricia Crone (Oxford University, 1974) and Daniel Pipes (Harvard University, 1978) indicate that the actual meaning of the word during the period in question is much more complex, although it does carry the sense of "convert fictively linked to an Arab tribe" in many instances. The retention of the older understanding of the word is not intended to deny the newly revealed nuances but rather to indicate in shorthand fashion that body of early converts who were subject to discriminatory actions on the part of Arab Muslims.
9. A striking example of Arab derision of *mawali* is provided by al-Jahiz 1955, 87, where a poem likens miscegenation of Arab and non-Arab to Arab women fornicating with donkeys and mules.
10. Editor's note: the original text of this chapter continues, "To examine stage by stage how this process occurred, we must return to a consideration of Iran and make use of the curve of conversion derived in the last chapter."

References

Abu Nu'aym. 1931–4. *Kitab dhikr akhbar Isbahan*, ed. S. Dedering. Leiden: Brill.
Anklesaria, Behramgore Tahmuras. 1969. *The Pahlavi Rivayat of Aturfarnbag and Farnbag-sroš*. 2 vols. Bombay: Industrial Press.

De Menasce, Jean. 1967. "Problèmes des Mazdeens dans l'Iran musulman." In *Festschrift für Wilhelm Eilers: Ein Dokument der Internationalen Forschung zum 27. September 1966*, ed. G. Wiessner. Wiesbaden: Harrassowitz.

Fares, Edouard. 1932. *L'honneur chez les arabes avant l'Islam*. Paris: Adrien-Maisonneuve.

Frye, Richard N. 1963. *The Heritage of Persia*. Cleveland: World.

—1975. *The Golden Age of Persia*. New York: Barnes & Noble.

Goitein, S. D. 1971. *A Mediterranean Society. II. The Community*. Berkeley, CA: University of California Press.

Hinds, Martin. 1971. "Kufan Political Alignments and their Background in the Mid-Seventh Century A.D." *International Journal of Middle East Studies* 2: 346–67.

Ibn al-Muqaffa'. 1966. "Ar-Risala fi'l-sahaba." In *Athar Ibn al-Muqaffa'*. Beirut: al-Hayat.

Jahiz, al-. 1955. *Kitab al-qawl fi'l-bighal*. Ed. C. Pellat. Cairo: Mustafa al-Babi al-Halabi.

Lammens, Henri. 1908. *Etudes sur le règne du calife omaiyade Mo'awia Ier*. Paris: Paul Geuthner.

Lecomte, Gérard. 1965. *Ibn Qutayba (mort en 276/889), l'homme, son oeuvre, ses idées*. Damascus: Institut français de Damas.

Morony, Michael G. 1976. "The Effects of the Muslim Conquest on the Persian Population of Iraq." *Iran* 14: 41-55.

Peters, Francis E. 1970. *The Harvest of Hellenism*. New York: Simon and Schuster.

Pigulevskaya, N. 1963. *Les villes de l'état iranien aux époques parthe et sassanide*. Paris: Mouton.

Runciman, Steven. 1956. *Byzantine Civilization*. Cleveland: World.

Shaban, M. A. 1971. *Islamic History, A.D. 600–750 (A.H. 132)*. Cambridge: Cambridge University Press.

Tyan, E. 1960–2005. "Kadi." In *Encyclopaedia of Islam*. 2nd ed., IV, 373–74. Leiden: E. J. Brill.

PART V

THE MEDIA

23

Islam and the West

Edward Said

In order to make a point about alternative energy sources for Americans, Consolidated Edison of New York (Con Ed) ran a striking television advertisement in the summer of 1980. Film clips of various immediately recognizable OPEC [Organization of the Petroleum Exporting Countries] personalities—Yamani, Qaddafi, lesser-known robed Arab figures—alternated with stills as well as clips of other people associated with oil and Islam: Khomeini, Arafat, Hafez al-Assad. None of these figures was mentioned by name, but we were told ominously that "these men" control America's sources of oil. The solemn voice-over in the background made no reference to who "these men" actually are or where they come from, leaving it to be felt that this all-male cast of villains has placed Americans in the grip of an unrestrained sadism. It was enough for "these men" to appear as they have appeared in newspapers and on television for American viewers to feel a combination of anger, resentment, and fear. And it is this combination of feelings that Con Ed instantly aroused and exploited for domestic commercial reasons, just as a year earlier Stuart Eizenstat, President Carter's domestic policy adviser, had urged the president that "with strong steps we [should] mobilize the nation around a real crisis and with a clear enemy—OPEC."

There are two things about the Con Ed commercial that, taken together, form the subject of this book [*Covering Islam: How the Media and the Experts Determine How We See the Rest of the World*]. One, of course, is Islam, or rather the image of Islam in the West generally and in the United States in particular. The other is the use of that image in the West and especially in the United States. As we shall see, these are connected in ways that ultimately reveal as much about the West and the United States as they do, in a far less concrete and interesting way, about Islam. But let us first consider the history of relationships between Islam and the Christian West before we go on to examine the current phase.

From at least the end of the eighteenth century until our own day, modern Occidental reactions to Islam have been dominated by a radically simplified type of thinking that may still be called Orientalist. The general basis of Orientalist thought is an imaginative and yet drastically polarized geography dividing the world into two unequal parts: the larger, "different" one called the Orient; the other, also known as "our" world, called the Occident or the West (Said 1978, 49–73). Such divisions always come about when one society or culture thinks about another one, different from it; but it is interesting that even when the Orient has uniformly been considered an inferior part of the world, it has always been endowed both with greater size and with a greater potential for power (usually destructive) than the West. Insofar as Islam has always been seen as belonging to the Orient, its particular fate within the general structure of Orientalism has been to be looked at first of all as if it were one monolithic thing, and then with a very special hostility and fear. There are, of course, many religious, psychological, and political reasons for this, but all of these reasons derive from a sense that so far as the West is concerned, Islam represents not only a formidable competitor but also a latecoming challenge to Christianity.

For most of the Middle Ages and during the early part of the Renaissance in Europe, Islam was believed to be a demonic religion of apostasy, blasphemy, and obscurity.[1] It did not seem to matter that Muslims considered Muhammad a prophet and not a god; what mattered to Christians was that Muhammad was a false prophet, a sower of discord, a sensualist, a hypocrite, an agent of the devil. Nor was this view of Muhammad strictly a doctrinal one. Real events in the real world made of Islam a considerable political force. For hundreds of years great Islamic armies and navies threatened Europe, destroyed its outposts, colonized its domains. It was as if a younger, more virile and energetic version of Christianity had arisen in the East, equipped itself with the learning of the ancient Greeks, invigorated itself with a simple, fearless, and warlike creed, and set about destroying Christianity. Even when the world of Islam entered a period of decline and Europe a period of ascendancy, fear of "Mohammedanism" persisted. Closer to Europe than any of the other non-Christian religions, the Islamic world by its very adjacency evoked memories of its encroachments on Europe, and always, of its latent power again and again to disturb the West. Other great civilizations of the East—India and China among them—could be thought of as defeated and distant and hence not a constant worry. Only Islam seemed never to have submitted completely to the West; and when, after the dramatic oil-price rises of the early 1970s, the Muslim world seemed once more on the verge of repeating its early conquests, the whole West seemed to shudder.

Then in 1978 Iran occupied center stage, causing Americans to feel increasing anxiety and passion. Few nations so distant and different from the United States have so intensely engaged Americans. Never have Americans seemed so paralyzed, so seemingly powerless to stop one dramatic event after another from happening. And never in all this could they put Iran out of mind, since on so many levels the country impinged on their lives with a defiant obtrusiveness. Iran was a major oil supplier during a period of energy scarcity. It lies in a region of the world that is commonly regarded as volatile and strategically vital. An important ally, it lost its imperial regime, its army, its value in American global calculations during a year of tumultuous revolutionary upheaval virtually unprecedented on so huge a scale since October 1917. A new order which called itself Islamic, and appeared to be popular and anti-imperialist, was struggling to be born. Ayatollah Khomeini's image and presence took over the media, which failed to make much of him except that he was obdurate, powerful, and deeply angry at the United States. Finally, as a result of the ex-shah's entry into the United States on October 22, 1979, the United States Embassy in Teheran was captured by a group of students on November 4; many American hostages were held. This crisis nears its end as I write.

Reactions to what took place in Iran did not occur in a vacuum. Further back in the public's subliminal cultural consciousness, there was the longstanding attitude to Islam, the Arabs, and the Orient in general that I have been calling Orientalism. For whether one looked at such recent, critically acclaimed fiction as V. S. Naipaul's *A Bend in the River* and John Updike's *The Coup*, or at grade-school history textbooks, comic strips, television serials, films, and cartoons, the iconography of Islam was uniform, was uniformly ubiquitous, and drew its material from the same time-honored view of Islam: hence the frequent caricatures of Muslims as oil suppliers, as terrorists, and more recently, as bloodthirsty mobs. Conversely, there has been very little place either in the culture generally or in discourse about non-Westerners in particular to speak or even to think about, much less to portray, Islam or anything Islamic sympathetically. Most people, if asked to name a *modern* Islamic writer, would probably be able to pick only Khalil Gibran (who wasn't Islamic). The academic experts whose specialty is Islam have generally treated the religion and its various cultures within an invented or culturally determined ideological framework filled with passion, defensive prejudice, sometimes even revulsion; because of this framework, *understanding* of Islam has been a very difficult thing to achieve. And to judge from the various in-depth media studies and interviews on the Iranian revolution during the spring of 1979, there has been little inclination to accept the revolution itself as much more than a defeat for the United States (which in a very specific sense, of course, it was), or a victory of dark over light.

V. S. Naipaul's role in helping to clarify this general hostility towards Islam is an interesting one. In a recent interview published in *Newsweek International* (August 18, 1980) he spoke about a book he was writing on "Islam," and then volunteered that "Muslim fundamentalism has no intellectual substance to it, therefore it must collapse." What Muslim fundamentalism he was referring to specifically, and what sort of intellectual substance he had in mind, he did not say: Iran was undoubtedly meant, but

337

so too—in equally vague terms—was the whole postwar wave of Islamic anti-imperialism in the Third World, for which Naipaul has developed a particularly intense antipathy. In *Guerrillas* and *A Bend in the River*, Naipaul's last two novels, Islam is in question, and it is part of Naipaul' s general (and with liberal Western readers, popular) indictment of the Third World that he lumps together the corrupt viciousness of a few grotesque rulers, the end of European colonialism, and postcolonial efforts at rebuilding native societies as instances of an overall intellectual failure in Africa and Asia. "Islam" plays a major part according to Naipaul, whether it is in the use of Islamic surnames by pathetic West Indian guerrillas, or in the vestiges of the African slave trade. For Naipaul and his readers, "Islam" somehow is made to cover everything that one most disapproves of from the standpoint of civilized, and Western, rationality.[2]

It is as if discriminations between religious passion, a struggle for a just cause, ordinary human weakness, political competition, and the history of men, women, and societies seen *as* the history of men, women, and societies cannot be made when "Islam," or the Islam now at work in Iran and in other parts of the Muslim world, is dealt with by novelists, reporters, policy-makers, "experts." "Islam" seems to engulf all aspects of the diverse Muslim world, reducing them all to a special malevolent and unthinking essence. Instead of analysis and understanding as a result, there can be for the most part only the crudest form of us-versus-them. Whatever Iranians or Muslims say about their sense of justice, their history of oppression, their vision of their own societies, seems irrelevant; what counts for the United States instead is what the "Islamic revolution" is doing right now, how many people have been executed by the Komitehs, how many bizarre outrages the Ayatollah, in the name of Islam, has ordered. Of course no one has equated the Jonestown massacre or the destructive frenzy produced at the Who concert in Cincinnati or the devastation of Indochina with Christianity, or with Western or American culture at large; that sort of equation has been reserved for "Islam."

Why is it that a whole range of political, cultural, social, and even economic events has often seemed reducible in so Pavlovian a way to "Islam"? What is it about "Islam" that provokes so quick and unrestrained a response? In what way do "Islam" and the Islamic world differ for Westerners from, say, the rest of the Third World and from the Soviet Union? These are far from simple questions, and they must therefore be answered piecemeal, with many qualifications and much differentiation.

Labels purporting to name very large and complex realities are notoriously vague and at the same time unavoidable. If it is true that "Islam" is an imprecise and ideologically loaded label, it is also true that "the West" and "Christianity" are just as problematic. Yet there is no easy way of avoiding these labels, since Muslims speak of Islam, Christians of Christianity, Westerners of the West, and all of them about all the others in ways that seem to be both convincing and exact. Instead of trying to propose ways of going around the labels, I think it is more immediately useful to admit at the outset that they exist and have long been in use as an integral part of cultural history rather than as objective classifications: a little later in this chapter I shall speak about them as interpretations produced for and by what I shall call communities of interpretation. We must therefore remember that "Islam," "the West," and even "Christianity" function in at least two different ways, and produce at least two meanings, each time they are used. First, they perform a simple identifying function, as when we say Khomeini is a Muslim, or Pope John Paul II is a Christian. Such statements tell us as a bare minimum what something is, as opposed to all other things. On this level we can distinguish between an orange and an apple (as we might distinguish between a Muslim and a Christian) only to the extent that we know they are different fruits, growing on different trees, and so forth.

The second function of these several labels is to produce a much more complex meaning. To speak of "Islam" in the West today is to mean a lot of the unpleasant things I have been mentioning. Moreover, "Islam" is unlikely to mean anything one knows either directly or objectively. The same is true of our use of "the West." How many people who use the labels angrily or assertively have a solid grip on all aspects of the Western tradition, or on Islamic jurisprudence, or on the actual languages of the Islamic world? Very few, obviously, but this does not prevent people from confidently characterizing "Islam" and "the West," or from believing they know exactly what it is they are talking about.

For that reason, we must take the labels seriously. To a Muslim who talks about "the West" or to an American who talks about "Islam," these enormous generalizations have behind them a whole history, enabling and disabling at the same time. Ideological and shot through with powerful emotions, the labels have survived many experiences and have been capable of adapting to new events, information, and realities. At present, "Islam" and "the West" have taken on a powerful new urgency everywhere. And we must note immediately that it is always the West, and not Christianity, that seems pitted against Islam. Why? Because the assumption is that whereas "the West" is greater than and has surpassed the stage of Christianity, its principal religion, the world of Islam—its varied societies, histories, and languages notwithstanding—is still mired in religion, primitivity, and backwardness. Therefore, the West is modern, greater than the sum of its parts, full of enriching contradictions and yet always "Western" in its cultural identity; the world of Islam, on the other hand, is no more than "Islam," reducible to a small number of unchanging characteristics despite the appearance of contradictions and experiences of variety that seem on the surface to be as plentiful as those of the West.

A recent example of what I mean is to be found in an article for the "News of the Week in Review" section of the Sunday *New York Times*, September 14, 1980. The piece in question is by John Kifner, the able *Times* correspondent in Beirut, and its subject is the extent of Soviet penetration of the Muslim world. Kifner's notion is evident enough from his article's title ("Marx and Mosque are Less Compatible than Ever"), but what is noteworthy is his use of Islam to make what in any other instance would be an unacceptably direct and unqualified connection between an abstraction and a vastly complex reality. Even if it is allowed that, unlike all other religions,

Islam is totalistic and makes no separation between church and state or between religion and everyday life, there is something uniquely—and perhaps deliberately—uninformed and uninforming, albeit conventional enough, about such statements as the following:

> The reason for Moscow's receding influence is disarmingly simple: Marx and mosque are incompatible. [Are we to assume, then, that Marx and church, or Marx and temple, are more compatible?]

For the Western mind [this is the point, obviously enough], conditioned since the Reformation to historical and intellectual developments which have steadily diminished the role of religion, it is difficult to grasp the power exerted by Islam [which, presumably, has been conditioned neither by history nor by intellect]. Yet, for centuries it has been the central force in the life of this region and, for the moment at least, its power seems on the upsurge.

> In Islam, there is no separation between church and state. It is a total system not only of belief but of action, with fixed rules for everyday life and a messianic drive to combat or convert the infidel. To the deeply religious, particularly to the scholars and clergy but also to the masses [in other words, no one is excluded], Marxism, with its purely secular view of man, is not only alien but heretical.

Not only does Kifner simply ignore history and such complications as the admittedly limited but interesting series of parallels between Marxism and Islam (studied by Maxime Rodinson in a book that attempts to explain why Marxism seems to have made some inroads in Islamic societies over the years [Rodinson 1979; Hodgkin 1980]) but he also rests his argument on a hidden comparison between "Islam" and the West, so much more various and uncharacterizable than simple, monolithic, totalitarian Islam. The interesting thing is that Kifner can say what he says without any danger of appearing either wrong or absurd.

Islam versus the West: this is the ground basis for a staggeringly fertile set of variations. Europe versus Islam, no less than America versus Islam, is a thesis that it subsumes.[3] But quite different concrete experiences with the West as a whole play a significant role too. For there is an extremely important distinction to be made between American and European awareness of Islam. France and England, for example, until very recently possessed large Muslim empires; in both countries, and to a lesser degree in Italy and Holland, both of which had Muslim colonies too, there is a long tradition of direct experience with the Islamic world (Rodinson 1980). This is reflected in a distinguished European academic discipline of Orientalism, which of course existed in those countries with colonies as well as in those (Germany, Spain, prerevolutionary Russia) that either wanted them, or were close to Muslim territories, or were once Muslim states. Today the Soviet Union has a Muslim population of about 50 million, and since the last days of 1979 has been in military occupation of Muslim Afghanistan. None of these things is comparably true of the United States, even though never before have so many Americans written, thought, or spoken about Islam.

The absence in America either of a colonial past or of a longstanding cultural attention to Islam makes the current obsession all the more peculiar, more abstract, more secondhand. Very few Americans, comparatively speaking, have actually had much to do with real Muslims; by comparison, in France the country's second religion in point of numbers is Islam, which may not be more popular as a result, but is certainly more known. The modern European burst of interest in Islam was part of what was called "the Oriental renaissance," a period in the late eighteenth and early nineteenth centuries when French and British scholars discovered "the East" anew— India, China, Japan, Egypt, Mesopotamia, the Holy Land. Islam was seen, for better or for worse, as part of the East, sharing in its mystery, exoticism, corruption, and latent power. True, Islam had been a direct military threat to Europe for centuries before; and true also that during the Middle Ages and early Renaissance, Islam was a problem for Christian thinkers, who continued for hundreds of years to see it and its prophet Muhammad as the rankest variety of apostasy. But at least Islam existed for many Europeans as a kind of standing religiocultural challenge, which did not prevent European imperialism from building its institutions on Islamic territory. And however much hostility there was between Europe and Islam, there was also direct experience, and in the case of poets, novelists, and scholars like Goethe, Gérard de Nerval, Richard Burton, Flaubert, and Louis Massignon, there was imagination and refinement.

Yet in spite of these figures and others like them, Islam has never been welcome in Europe. Most of the great philosophers of history from Hegel to Spengler have regarded Islam without much enthusiasm. In a dispassionately lucid essay, "Islam and the Philosophy of History," Albert Hourani has discussed this strikingly constant derogation of Islam as a system of faith (Hourani 1980). Apart from some occasional interest in the odd Sufi writer or saint, European vogues for "the wisdom of the East" rarely included Islamic sages or poets. Omar Khayyam, Harun al-Rashid, Sindbad, Aladdin, Hajji Baba, Scheherazade, Saladin, more or less make up the entire list of Islamic figures known to modern educated Europeans. Not even Carlyle could make the Prophet widely acceptable, and as for the substance of the faith Mohammed propagated, this has long seemed to Europeans basically unacceptable on Christian grounds, although precisely for that reason not uninteresting. Towards the end of the nineteenth century, as Islamic nationalism in Asia and Africa increased, there was a widely shared view that Muslim colonies were meant to remain under European tutelage, as much because they were profitable as because they were underdeveloped and in need of Western discipline.[4] Be that as it may, and despite the frequent racism and aggression directed at the Muslim world, Europeans *did* express a fairly energetic sense of what Islam meant to them. Hence the representations of Islam—in scholarship, art, literature, music, and public discourse—all across European culture, from the end of the eighteenth century until our own day.

Little of this concreteness is to be found in America's experience of Islam. Nineteenth-century American contacts with Islam were very restricted; one thinks of occasional travelers like Mark Twain and Herman Melville, or of missionaries here and there, or of short-lived military expeditions to North Africa. Culturally there was no distinct place in America for Islam before World War II. Academic experts did their work on Islam usually in quiet corners of schools of divinity, not in the glamorous limelight of Orientalism nor in the pages of leading journals. For about a century there has existed a fascinating although quiet symbiosis between American missionary families to Islamic countries and cadres of the foreign service and the oil companies; periodically this has surfaced in the form of hostile comments about State Department and oil company "Arabists," who are considered to harbor an especially virulent and anti-Semitic form of philo-Islamism. On the other hand, all the great figures known in the United States as important academic experts on Islam have been foreign-born: Lebanese Philip Hitti at Princeton, Austrian Gustave von Grunebaum at Chicago and UCLA, British H. A. R. Gibb at Harvard, German Joseph Schacht at Columbia. Yet none of these men has had the relative cultural prestige enjoyed by Jacques Berque in France and Albert Hourani in England.

But even men like Hitti, Gibb, von Grunebaum, and Schacht have disappeared from the American scene, as indeed it is unlikely that scholars such as Berque and Hourani will have successors in France and England. No one today has their breadth of culture, nor anything like their range of authority. Academic experts on Islam in the West today tend to know about jurisprudential schools in tenth-century Baghdad or nineteenth-century Moroccan urban patterns, but never (or almost never) about the whole civilization of Islam—literature, law, politics, history, sociology, and so on. This has not prevented experts from generalizing from time to time about the "Islamic mind-set" or the "Shi'a penchant for martyrdom," but such pronouncements have been confined to popular journals or to the media, which solicited these opinions in the first place. More significantly, the occasions for public discussions of Islam, by experts or by nonexperts, have almost always been provided by political crises. It is extremely rare to see informative articles on Islamic culture in the *New York Review of Books*, say, or in *Harper's*. Only when the stability of Saudi Arabia or Iran has been in question has "Islam" seemed worthy of general comment.

Consider therefore that Islam has entered the consciousness of most Americans— even of academic and general intellectuals who know a great deal about Europe and Latin America—principally if not exclusively because it has been connected to newsworthy issues like oil, Iran and Afghanistan, or terrorism.[5] And all of this by the middle of 1979 had come to be called either the Islamic revolution, or "the crescent of crisis," or "the arc of instability," or "the return of Islam." A particularly telling example was the Atlantic Council's Special Working Group on the Middle East (which included Brent Scowcroft, George Ball, Richard Helms, Lyman Lemnitzer, Walter Levy, Eugene Rostow, Kermit Roosevelt, and Joseph Sisco, among others): when this group issued its report in the fall of 1979 the title given it was "Oil and

Turmoil: Western Choices in the Middle East."[6] When *Time* magazine devoted its major story to Islam on April 16, 1979, the cover was adorned with a Gerome painting of a bearded muezzin standing in a minaret, calmly summoning the faithful to prayer; it was as florid and overstated a nineteenth-century period piece of Orientalist art as one could imagine. Anachronistically, however, this quiet scene was emblazoned with a caption that had nothing to do with it: "The Militant Revival." There could be no better way of symbolizing the difference between Europe and America on the subject of Islam. A placid and decorative painting done almost routinely in Europe as an aspect of one's general culture had been transformed by three words into a general American obsession.

But surely I am exaggerating? Wasn't *Time*'s cover story on Islam simply a piece of vulgarization, catering to a supposed taste for the sensational? Does it *really* reveal anything more serious than that? And since when have the media mattered a great deal on questions of substance, or of policy, or of culture? Besides, was it *not* the case that Islam had indeed thrust itself upon the world's attention? And what had happened to the experts on Islam, and why were their contributions either bypassed entirely or submerged in the "Islam" discussed and diffused by the media?

A few simple explanations are in order first. As I said above, there has never been any American expert on the Islamic world whose audience was a wide one; moreover, with the exception of the late Marshall Hodgson's three-volume *The Venture of Islam*, posthumously published in 1974, no general work on Islam has ever been put squarely before the literate reading public.[7] Either the experts were so specialized that they only addressed other specialists, or their work was not distinguished enough intellectually to command the kind of audience that came to books on Japan, Western Europe, or India. But these things work both ways. While it is true that one could not name an American "Orientalist" with a reputation outside Orientalism, as compared with Berque or Rodinson in France, it is also true that the study of Islam is neither truly encouraged in the American university nor sustained in the culture at large by personalities whose fame and intrinsic merit might make their experiences of Islam important on their own.[8] Who are the American equivalents of Rebecca West, Freya Stark, T. E. Lawrence, Wilfred Thesiger, Gertrude Bell, P. H. Newby, or more recently, Jonathan Raban? At best, they might be former CIA people like Miles Copeland or Kermit Roosevelt, very rarely writers or thinkers of any cultural distinction.

A second reason for the critical absence of expert opinion on Islam is the experts' marginality to what seemed to be happening in the world of Islam when it became "news" in the mid-1970s. The brutally impressive facts are, of course, that the Gulf oil-producing states suddenly appeared to be very powerful; there was an extraordinarily ferocious and seemingly unending civil war in Lebanon; Ethiopia and Somalia were involved in a long war; the Kurdish problem unexpectedly became pivotal and then, after 1975, just as unexpectedly subsided; Iran deposed its monarch in the wake of a massive, wholly surprising "Islamic" revolution; Afghanistan was gripped by a Marxist coup in 1978, then invaded by Soviet troops in late 1979; Algeria and Morocco were drawn into protracted conflict over the Southern Sahara issue; a Pakistani president was executed and a new military dictatorship set up. There were other things taking place too, most recently a war between Iran and Iraq, but let us be satisfied with these. On the whole I think it is fair to say that few of these happenings might have been illuminated by expert writing on Islam in the West; for not only had the experts not predicted them nor prepared their readers for them, they had instead provided a mass of literature that seemed, when compared with what was happening, to be about an impossibly distant region of the world, one that bore practically no relation to the turbulent and threatening confusion erupting before one's eyes in the media.

This is a central matter, which has scarcely begun to be discussed rationally even now, and so we should proceed carefully. Academic experts whose province was Islam before the seventeenth century worked in an essentially antiquarian field; moreover, like that of specialists in other fields, their work was very compartmentalized. They neither wanted nor tried in a responsible way to concern themselves with the modern consequences of Islamic history. To some extent their work was tied to notions of a "classical" Islam, or to supposedly unchanging patterns of Islamic life, or to archaic philological questions. In any event, there was no way of using it to understand the modern Islamic world, which to all intents and purposes, and depending on what part of it was of interest, had been developing along very different lines from those adumbrated in Islam's earliest centuries (that is, from the seventh to the ninth century).

The experts whose field was modern Islam—or to be more precise, whose field was made up of societies, people, and institutions within the Islamic world since the eighteenth century—worked within an agreed-upon framework for research formed according to notions decidedly *not* set in the Islamic world. This fact, in all its complexity and variety, cannot be overestimated. There is no denying that a scholar sitting in Oxford or Boston writes and researches principally, though not exclusively, according to standards, conventions, and expectations shaped by his or her peers, not by the Muslims being studied. This is a truism, perhaps, but it needs emphasis just the same. Modern Islamic studies in the academy belong to "area programs" generally—Western Europe, the Soviet Union, Southeast Asia, and so on. They are therefore affiliated to the mechanism by which national policy is set. This is not a matter of choice for the individual scholar. If someone at Princeton happened to be studying contemporary Afghan religious schools, it would be obvious (especially during times like these) that such a study *could* have "policy implications," and whether or not the scholar wanted it he or she would be drawn into the network of government, corporate, and foreign-policy associations; funding would be affected, the kind of people met would also be affected, and in general, certain rewards and types of interaction would be offered. Willy-nilly, the scholar would be transmuted into an "area expert."

For scholars whose interests are directly connected to policy issues (political scientists, principally, but also modern historians, economists, sociologists, and anthropologists), there are sensitive, not to say dangerous, questions to be addressed. For example, how is one's status as a scholar reconciled with the demands made on one by governments? Iran is a perfect case in point. During the shah's regime, there were funds available to Iranologists from the Pahlevi Foundation, and of course from American institutions. These funds were disbursed for studies that took as their point of departure the status quo (in this case, the presence of a Pahlevi regime tied militarily and economically to the United States), which in a sense became the research paradigm for students of the country. Late in the crisis a House Permanent Select Committee on Intelligence staff study said that the United States' assessments of the regime were influenced by existing policy "not directly, through the conscious suppression of unfavorable news, but indirectly ... policymakers were not asking whether the Shah's autocracy would survive indefinitely; policy was premised on that assumption."[9] This in turn produced only a tiny handful of studies seriously assessing the shah's regime and identifying the sources of popular opposition to him. To my knowledge only one scholar, Hamid Algar of Berkeley, was correct in estimating the contemporary political force of Iranian religious feelings, and only Algar went so far as to predict that Ayatollah Khomeini was likely to bring down the regime. Other scholars—Richard Cottam and Ervand Abrahamian among them—also departed from the status quo in what they wrote, but they were a small band indeed (Algar 1972; Abrahamian 1968, 1978, 1979, 1980; Cottam 1979). (In fairness we must note that European scholars on the left, who were less sanguine about the shah's survival, did not do very well either in identifying the religious sources of Iranian opposition.[10])

Even if we leave aside Iran, there were plenty of no less important intellectual failures elsewhere, all of them the result of relying uncritically on what a combination of government policy and cliché dictated. Here, the Lebanese and Palestinian cases are instructive. For years Lebanon had been regarded as a model of what a pluralistic or mosaic culture was supposed to be. Yet so reified and static had the models been which were used for the study of Lebanon that no inkling was possible of the ferocity and violence of the civil war (which ran from 1975 to 1980 at least). Expert eyes seem in the past to have been extraordinarily transfixed by images of Lebanese "stability": traditional leaders, elites, parties, national character, and successful modernization were what was studied.

Even when Lebanon's polity was described as precarious, or when its insufficient "civility" was analyzed, there was a uniform assumption that its problems were on the whole manageable and far from being radically disruptive.[11] During the sixties, Lebanon was portrayed as "stable" because, one expert tells us, the "inter-Arab" situation was stable; so long as that equation was kept up, he argued, Lebanon would be secure (Kerr 1966, 209). It was never even supposed that there could be inter-Arab stability and Lebanese *instability*, mainly because—as with most subjects in this consensus-ridden field—the conventional wisdom assigned perpetual "pluralism" and harmonious continuity to Lebanon, its internal cleavages and its Arab neighbors' irrelevance notwithstanding. Any trouble for Lebanon therefore had to come from the surrounding *Arab* environment, never from Israel or from the United States, both of which had specific but never-analyzed designs on Lebanon.[12] Then too, there was the Lebanon that embodied the modernization myth. Reading a classic of this sort of ostrich-wisdom today, one is struck by how serenely the fable could be advanced as recently as 1973, when the civil war had in fact begun. Lebanon might undergo revolutionary change, we were told, but that was a "remote" likelihood; what was much more likely was "future modernization involving the public [a sadly ironic euphemism for what was to be the bloodiest civil war in recent Arab history] within the prevailing political structure" (Salem 1972, 144).[13]] Or as a distinguished anthropologist put it, "The Lebanese 'nice piece of mosaic' remains intact. Indeed ... Lebanon has continued to be the most effective in containing its deep primordial cleavages" (Geertz 1973, 296).

As a result, in Lebanon and in other places, experts failed to understand that much of what truly mattered about postcolonial states could not easily be herded under the rubric of "stability." In Lebanon it was precisely those devastatingly mobile forces the experts had never documented or had consistently underestimated—social dislocations; demographic shifts, confessional loyalties, ideological currents—that tore the country apart so savagely.[14] Similarly, it has been conventional wisdom for years to regard the Palestinians merely as resettlable refugees, not as a political force having estimable consequences for any reasonably accurate assessment of the Near East. Yet by the mid-seventies the Palestinians were one of the major acknowledged problems for United States policy, and still they had not received the scholarly and intellectual attention their importance deserved (I have discussed this in Said 1979, 3–53 and *passim*); instead, the persisting attitude was to treat them as adjuncts to United States policy toward Egypt and Israel and quite literally to ignore them in the Lebanese conflagration. There has been no important *scholarly* or expert counterweight to this policy, and the results for American national interests are likely to be disastrous, especially since the Iran-Iraq war seems, once again, to have caught the intelligence community offguard and very wrong in estimates of both countries' military capacities.

Add to this conformity between a docilely plodding scholarship and unfocused government interests the sorry truth that too many expert writers on the Islamic world did not command the relevant languages and hence had to depend on the press or other Western writers for their information. This reinforced dependence on the official or the conventional picture of things was a trap into which, in their overall performance on prerevolutionary Iran, the media fell. There was a tendency to study and restudy, to focus resolutely on the same things: elites, modernization programs, the role of the military, greatly visible leaders, geopolitical strategy (from the American point of view), communist inroads.[15] Those things may at the time have seemed interesting to the United States as a nation, yet the fact is that in Iran they were all literally swept away by the revolution in a matter of days. The whole imperial court crumbled; the army, into which billions of dollars had been poured, disintegrated; the so-called elites either disappeared or found their way into the new state of affairs, though in neither case could it be asserted, as it had been, that they determined Iranian political behavior. One of the experts given credit for predicting what the "crisis of '78" might lead to, James Bill of the University of Texas, nevertheless recommended to American policy-makers as late as December 1978 that the United States government should encourage "the shah ... to open the system up" (Bill 1978–79, 341). In other words, even a supposedly dissenting expert voice was still committed to maintaining a regime against which, at the very moment he spoke, literally millions of its people had risen in one of the most massive insurrections in modern history.

Yet Bill made important points about general United States ignorance on Iran. He was right to say that media coverage was superficial, that official information had been geared to what the Pahlevis wanted, and that the United States made no effort either to get to know the country in depth or to make contact with the opposition. Although Bill did not go on to say it, these failures were and are symptomatic of the general United States and European attitude toward the Islamic world and, as we shall see, toward most of the Third World; indeed, the fact that Bill did not connect what he was justly saying about Iran to the rest of the Islamic world was part of the attitude too. There has been no responsible grappling first of all with the central methodological question, namely, What is the value (if any) of speaking about "Islam" and the Islamic resurgence? What, secondly, is or ought to be the relationship between government policy and scholarly research? Is the expert supposed to be above politics or a political adjunct to governments? Bill and William Beeman of Brown University argued on separate occasions that a major cause of the United States-Iran crisis in 1979 was the failure to consult those academic experts who had been given expensive educations precisely to learn to know the Islamic world (Beeman 1980; Bill 1980). Yet what went unexamined by Bill and Beeman was the possibility that it was *because* scholars sought out such a role, at the same time calling themselves scholars, that they seemed ambiguous and hence not credible figures to the government as well as to the intellectual community.[16]

Besides, is there any way for an independent intellectual (which is, after all, what an academic scholar is meant to be) to maintain his or her independence and also to work directly for the state? What is the connection between frank political partisanship and good insight? Does one preclude the other, or is that true only in some cases? Why was it that the whole (but admittedly small) cadre of Islamic scholars in the country could not get a larger hearing? Why was this the case at a time when the United States seemed to be most in need of instruction? All of these questions, of course, can be answered only within the actual and largely political framework governing relationships historically between the West and the Islamic world. Let us look at this framework and see what role there is in it for the expert.

I have not been able to discover any period in European or American history since the Middle Ages in which Islam was generally discussed or thought about *outside* a framework created by passion, prejudice, and political interests. This may not seem a surprising discovery, but included in it is the entire gamut of scholarly and scientific disciplines which, since the early nineteenth century, have either called themselves collectively the discipline of Orientalism or have tried systematically to deal with the Orient. No one would disagree with the statement that early commentators on Islam like Peter the Venerable and Barthélemy d'Herbelot were passionate Christian polemicists in what they said. But it has been an unexamined assumption that since Europe and the West advanced into the modern scientific age and freed themselves of superstition and ignorance, the march must have included Orientalism. Wasn't it true that Silvestre de Sacy, Edward Lane, Ernest Renan, Hamilton Gibb, and Louis Massignon were learned, objective scholars, and isn't it true that following upon all sorts of advances in twentieth-century sociology, anthropology, linguistics, and history, American scholars who teach the Middle East and Islam in places like Princeton, Harvard, and Chicago are therefore unbiased and free of special pleading in what they do? The answer is no. Not that Orientalism is more biased than other social and humanistic sciences; it is simply as ideological and as contaminated by the world as other disciplines. The main difference is that Orientalist scholars have tended to use their standing as experts to deny—and sometimes even to cover—their deep-seated feelings about Islam with a language of authority whose purpose is to certify their "objectivity" and "scientific impartiality."

That is one point. The other distinguishes a historical pattern in what would otherwise be an undifferentiated characterization of Orientalism. Whenever in modern times an acutely political tension has been felt between the Occident and *its* Orient (or between the West and *its* Islam), there has been a tendency in the West to resort not to direct violence but first to the cool, relatively detached instruments of scientific, quasi-objective representation. In this way "Islam" is made more clear, the "true nature" of its threat appears, an implicit course of action against it is proposed. In such a context both science and direct violence come to be viewed by many Muslims, living in widely varied circumstances, as forms of aggression against Islam.

Two strikingly similar examples illustrate my thesis. We can now see retrospectively that during the nineteenth century both France and England preceded their occupations of portions of the Islamic East with a period in which the various scholarly means of characterizing and understanding the Orient underwent remarkable technical modernization and development (see Said 1978, 123–66). The French occupation of Algeria in 1830 followed a period of about two decades during which French scholars literally transformed the study of the Orient from an antiquarian into a rational discipline. Of course, there had been Napoleon Bonaparte's occupation of Egypt in 1798, and of course one should remark the fact that he had prepared for his expedition by marshaling a sophisticated group of scientists to make his enterprise more efficient. My point, however, is that Napoleon's short-lived occupation of Egypt closed a chapter. A new one began with the long period during which, under Silvestre de Sacy's stewardship at French institutions of Oriental study, France became the world leader in Orientalism; this chapter climaxed a little later when French armies occupied Algiers in 1830.

I do not at all want to suggest a causal relationship between one thing and the other, nor to adopt the anti-intellectual view that all scientific learning necessarily leads to violence and suffering. All I want to say is that empires are not born instantaneously, nor during the modern period have they been run by improvisation. If the development of learning involves the redefinition and reconstitution of fields of human experience by scientists who stand above the material they study, it is not impertinent to see the same development occurring among politicians whose realm of authority is redefined to include "inferior" regions of the world where new "national" interests can be discovered—and later seen to be in need of close supervision.[17] I very much doubt that England would have occupied Egypt in so long and massively institutionalized a way had it not been for the durable investment in Oriental learning first cultivated by scholars like Edward William Lane and William Jones. Familiarity, accessibility, representability: these were what Orientalists demonstrated about the Orient. The Orient could be seen, it could be studied, it could be managed. It need not remain a distant, marvelous, incomprehensible, and yet very rich place. It could be brought home—or more simply, Europe could make itself at home there, as it subsequently did.

My second example is a contemporary one. The Islamic Orient today is clearly important for its resources or for its geopolitical location. Neither of these, however, is interchangeable with the interests, needs, or aspirations of the native Orientals. Ever since the end of World War II, the United States has been taking positions of dominance and hegemony once held in the Islamic world by Britain and France. With this replacement of one imperial system by another have gone two things: first, the moderate burgeoning of crisis-oriented academic and expert interest in Islam, and second, an extraordinary revolution in the techniques available to the largely private-sector press and electronic journalism industries. Never before has an international trouble spot like Iran been covered so instantaneously and so regularly as it has by the media: Iran has therefore seemed to be *in* American lives, and yet deeply alien from them, with an unprecedented intensity. Together these two phenomena—the second much more than the first—by which a sizable apparatus of university, government, and business experts study Islam and the Middle East and by which Islam has become a subject familiar to every consumer of news in the West, have almost entirely domesticated the Islamic world, or at least those aspects of it that are considered newsworthy. Not only has that world become the subject of the most profound cultural and economic Western saturation in history—for no non-Western realm has been so dominated by the United States as the Arabic-Islamic world is today—but the interchange between Islam and the West, in this case the United States, is profoundly one-sided and, so far as other, less newsworthy parts of the Islamic world are concerned, profoundly skewed.

It is only a slight overstatement to say that Muslims and Arabs are essentially covered, discussed, apprehended, either as oil suppliers or as potential terrorists. Very little of the detail, the human density, the passion of Arab-Muslim life has entered the awareness of even those people whose profession it is to report the Islamic world. What we have instead is a limited series of crude, essentialized caricatures of the Islamic world presented in such a way as, among other things, to make that world vulnerable to military aggression (see Ghareeb 1977; for the British counterpart see Nasir 1979, 140–72). I do not think it is an accident that recent talk of United States military intervention in the Arabian Gulf, or the Carter Doctrine, or discussions of Rapid Deployment Forces, has been preceded by a period of "Islam's" rational presentation through the cool medium of television and through "objective" Orientalist study (which, paradoxically, either in its "irrelevance" to modern actualities or in its propagandistic "objective" variety, has a uniformly alienating effect): in many ways our actual situation today bears a chilling resemblance to the nineteenth-century British and French examples cited previously.

There are other political and cultural reasons for this. After World War II, when the United States took over the imperial role played by France and Britain, a set of policies was devised for dealing with the world that suited the peculiarities and the problems of each region that affected (and was affected by) United States interests. Europe was designated for postwar recovery, for which the Marshall Plan, among other similar American policies, was suited. The Soviet Union of course emerged as the United States' most formidable competitor, and, as no one needs to be told, the cold war produced policies, studies, even a mentality, which still dominate relationships between one superpower and the other. That left what has come to be called the Third World, an arena of competition not only between the United States and the Soviet Union but also between the United States and various native powers only recently in possession of their independence from European colonizers.

Almost without exception, the Third World seemed to American policy-makers to be "underdeveloped," in the grip of unnecessarily archaic and static "traditional" modes of life, dangerously prone to communist subversion and internal stagnation. For the Third World "modernization" became the order of the day, so far as the United States was concerned. And, as has been suggested by James Peck, "modernization theory was the ideological answer to a world of increasing revolutionary upheaval and continued reaction among traditional political elites" (Peck 1975, 71; see also Gendzier 1978). Huge sums were poured into Africa and Asia with the aim of stopping communism, promoting United States trade, and above all, developing a cadre of native allies whose express *raison d'être* seemed to be the transformation of backward countries into mini-Americas. In time the initial investments required additional sums and increased military support to keep them going. And this in turn produced the interventions all over Asia and Latin America which regularly pitted the United States against almost every brand of native nationalism.

The history of United States efforts on behalf of modernization and development in the Third World can never be completely understood unless it is also noted how the policy itself produced a style of thought and a habit of seeing the Third World which increased the political, emotional, and strategic investment in the very idea of modernization. Vietnam is a perfect instance of this. Once it was decided that the country was to be saved from communism and indeed from itself, a whole science of modernization for Vietnam (whose latest and most costly phase came to be known as "Vietnamization") came into being. Not only government specialists but university experts were involved. In time, the survival of pro-American and anticommunist regimes in Saigon dominated everything, even when it became clear that a huge majority of the population viewed those regimes as alien and oppressive, and even when the cost of fighting unsuccessful wars on behalf of those regimes had devastated the whole region and cost Lyndon Johnson the presidency. Still, a very great amount of writing on the virtues of modernizing traditional society had acquired an almost unquestioned social, and certainly cultural, authority in the United States, at the same time that in many parts of the Third World "modernization" was connected in the popular mind with foolish spending, unnecessary gadgetry and armaments, corrupt rulers, and brutal United States intervention in the affairs of small, weak countries.

Among the many illusions that persisted in modernization theory was one that seemed to have a special pertinence to the Islamic world: namely, that before the advent of the United States, Islam existed in a kind of timeless childhood, shielded from true development by an archaic set of superstitions, prevented by its strange priests and scribes from moving out of the Middle Ages into the modern world. At this point, Orientalism and modernization theory dovetail nicely. If, as Orientalist scholarship had traditionally taught, Muslims were no more than fatalistic children tyrannized by their mind-set, their *'ulama'*, and their wild-eyed political leaders into resisting the West and progress, could not every political scientist, anthropologist, and sociologist worthy of trust show that, given a reasonable chance, something resembling the American way of life might be introduced into Islam via consumer goods, anticommunist propaganda, and "good" leaders? The main difficulty with Islam, however, was that unlike India and China, it had never really been pacified or defeated. For reasons which seemed always to defy the understanding of scholars, Islam (or some version of it) continued its sway over its adherents, who, it came regularly to be argued, were unwilling to accept reality, or at least that part of reality in which the West's superiority was demonstrable.

Efforts at modernization persisted all through the two decades that followed World War II. Iran became in effect the modernization success story and its ruler the "modernized" leader *par excellence.* As for the rest of the Islamic world, whether it was Arab nationalists, Egypt's Gamal Abdel Nasser, Indonesia's Sukarno, the Palestinian nationalists, Iranian opposition groups, or thousands of unknown Islamic teachers, brotherhoods, and orders, it was all either opposed or not covered by Western scholars with a heavy investment in modernization theory and American strategic and economic interests in the Islamic world.

During the explosive decade of the seventies, Islam gave further proof of its fundamental intransigence. There was, for example, the Iranian revolution: neither procommunist nor promodernization, the people who overthrew the shah were simply not explainable according to the canons of behavior presupposed by modernization theory. They did not seem grateful for the quotidian benefits of modernization (cars, an enormous military and security apparatus, a stable regime) and appeared indifferent to the blandishments of "Western" ideas altogether.[18] What was especially troubling about their attitude—Khomeini's in particular—was their fierce unwillingness to accept any style of politics (or, for that matter, of rationality) that was not deliberately their own. Above all, it was their attachment to Islam that seemed especially defiant. Ironically, only a few commentators on "Islamic" atavism and medieval modes of logic in the West noted that a few miles to the west of Iran, in Begin's Israel, there was a regime fully willing to mandate its actions by religious authority and by a very backward-looking theological doctrine.[19] An even smaller number of commentators decrying the apparent upsurge in Islamic religiosity connected it to the upsurge in the United States of television religions numbering many millions of adherents, or to the fact that two of the three major presidential candidates in 1980 were enthusiastic born-again Christians.

Religious intensity was thus ascribed solely to Islam even when religious feeling was spreading remarkably everywhere: one need only remember the effusive treatment by the liberal press of patently illiberal religious figures like Solzhenitsyn or Pope John Paul II to see how one-sidedly hostile the attitude to Islam was.[20] A retreat into religion became the way most Islamic states could be explained, from Saudi Arabia—which, with what was supposed to be a peculiarly Islamic logic, refused to ratify the Camp David Accords—to Pakistan, Afghanistan, and Algeria. In this way, we can see how the Islamic world was differentiated, in the Western mind generally, in the United States' in particular, from regions of the world to which a cold-war analysis could be applied. There seemed to be no way, for example, in which one could speak of Saudi Arabia and Kuwait as parts of "the free world"; even Iran during the shah's regime, despite its overwhelming anti-Soviet commitment, never really belonged to "our" side the way France and Britain do. Nevertheless policy-makers in the United States persisted in speaking of the "loss" of Iran as, during the past three decades, they spoke of the "loss" of China, Vietnam, and Angola. Moreover it has been the singularly unhappy lot of the Persian Gulf's Islamic states to be considered by American crisis managers as places ready for American military occupation. Thus George Ball in the *New York Times Magazine* of June 28, 1970, warned that "the tragedy of Vietnam" might lead to "pacifism and isolation" at home, whereas United States interests in the Middle East were so great that the president ought to "educate" Americans about the possibility of military intervention there (see the excellent and exhaustive study, Buheiry 1980).

One more thing needs mention here: the role of Israel in mediating Western and particularly American views of the Islamic world since World War II. In the first place, Israel's avowedly religious character is rarely mentioned in the Western press: only recently have there been overt references to Israeli religious fanaticism, and all of these have been to the zealots of Gush Emunim, whose principal activity has been the violent setting up of illegal settlements on the West Bank. Yet most accounts of Gush Emunim in the West simply leave out the inconvenient fact that it was "secular" labor governments that first instituted illegal settlements in occupied Arab territory, not just the religious fanatics now stirring things up. This kind of one-sided reporting is, I think, an indication of how Israel—the Middle East's "only democracy" and "our staunch ally"—has been used as a foil for Islam.[21] Thus Israel has appeared as a bastion of Western civilization hewn (with much approbation and self-congratulation) out of the Islamic wilderness. Secondly, Israel's security in American eyes has become conveniently interchangeable with fending off Islam, perpetuating Western hegemony, and demonstrating the virtues of modernization. In these ways, three sets of illusions economically buttress and reproduce one another in the interests of shoring up the Western self-image and promoting Western power over the Orient: the view of Islam, the ideology of modernization, and the affirmations of Israel's general value to the West.

In addition, and to make "our" attitudes to Islam very clear, a whole information and policy-making apparatus in the United States depends on these illusions and diffuses them widely. Large segments of the intelligentsia allied to the community of geopolitical strategists together deliver themselves of expansive ideas about Islam, oil, the future of Western civilization, and the fight for democracy against turmoil and terrorism. For reasons that I have already discussed, the Islamic specialists feed into this great stream, despite the undeniable fact that only a relative fraction of what goes on in academic Islamic studies is directly infected with the cultural and political visions to be found in geopolitics and cold-war ideology. A little lower down come the mass media, which take from the other two units of the apparatus what is most easily compressed into images: hence the caricatures, the frightening mobs, the concentration on "Islamic" punishment, and so on. All of this is presided over by the great power establishments—the oil companies, the mammoth corporations and multi-nationals, the defense and intelligence communities, the executive branch of the government. When President Carter spent his first New Year in office with the shah in 1978, and said that Iran was "an island of stability," he was speaking with the mobilized force of this formidable apparatus, representing United States interests and covering Islam at the same time.

Notes

1. See Daniel 1975; also his earlier and very useful Daniel 1960. There is a first-rate survey of this matter, set in the political context of the 1956 Suez War: Childers 1962, 25–61.
2. I have discussed Naipaul in Said 1980, 522–25.
3. There is an elegant account of this theme, done by a contemporary Tunisian intellectual: see Djaït 1979. A brilliant psychoanalytic/structuralist reading of one "Islamic" motif in European literature—the seraglio—is to be found in Grosrichard 1979.

4. As an instance, see the penetrating study Alatas 1977.
5. Not that this has always meant poor writing and scholarship: as an informative general account which answers principally to political exigencies and not mainly to the need for new knowledge about Islam, there is Kramer 1980. This was written for the Center for Strategic and International Studies, Georgetown University, and therefore belongs to the category of policy, not of "objective," knowledge. Another instance is in the January 1980 (vol. 78, no. 453) special issue on "The Middle East, 1980" of *Current History*.
6. Atlantic Council's Special Working Group on the Middle East, "Oil and Turmoil: Western Choices in the Middle East," *Atlantic Community Quarterly* 17, no. 3 (Fall 1979): 291–305, 377–78.
7. See the important review of this by Albert Hourani, *Journal of Near Eastern Studies* 37, no. 1 (January 1978): 53–62.
8. One index of this is the report "Middle Eastern and African Studies: Developments and Needs" commissioned by the U.S. Department of Health, Education and Welfare in 1967, written by Professor Morroe Berger of Princeton, also president of the Middle East Studies Association (MESA). In this report Berger asserts that the Middle East "is not a center of great cultural achievement ... and therefore does not constitute its own reward so far as modern culture is concerned .... [It] has been receding in immediate political importance to the U.S." For a discussion of this extraordinary document and the context that produced it, see Said 1978, 287–93.
9. Quoted in Michael A. Ledeen and William H. Lewis, "Carter and the Fall of the Shah: The Inside Story," *Washington Quarterly* 3, no. 2 (Spring 1980): 11–12. Ledeen and Lewis are supplemented (and supported to a degree) by Sullivan 1980; Sullivan was United States ambassador to Iran before and during the revolution. See also the six-part series by Scott Armstrong, "The Fall of the Shah," *Washington Post*, October 25, 26, 27, 28, 29, 30, 1980.
10. This is especially true of Halliday 1979 which is nevertheless one of the two or three best studies of Iran done since World War II. Rodinson 1979 has nearly nothing to say about the Muslim religious opposition. Only Algar 1972 seems to have been right on this point—a remarkable achievement.
11. This is the argument put forward in Shils 1966.
12. See the extraordinarily rich material found in Sharett 1979; Rokach 1980. See also the revelations about the CIA role in Lebanon by former CIA advisor Wilbur Crane Eveland (Eveland 1980).
13. Elie Adib Salem is also the author of "Form and Substance: A Critical Examination of the Arabic Language," *Middle East Forum* 33 (July 1958): 17–19. The title indicates the approach.
14. For an interesting description of "expert" illusions about Lebanon on the eve of the civil war, see Starr and Starr 1977.
15. For a brilliant account of this collective delusion see Jandaghi (pseud.) 1973; see also Schaar 1979.
16. As opposed to scholars during the Vietnam War who made a stronger case for themselves as "scientists" willingly serving the state: here it would be good to know why Vietnam specialists were consulted (with no less disastrous results) and Iran experts not. See Chomsky 1969, 23–158.
17. On the connection between scholarship and politics as it has affected the colonial world, see Moniot 1976. On the way in which "fields" of study coincide with national interests see "Special Supplement: Modern China Studies," *Bulletin of Concerned Asia Scholars* 3, nos. 3–4 (Summer–Fall, 1971): 91–168.

18. An account of the Pahlevi regime's "modernization" is to be found in Graham 1979; see also Brun 1978; Rouleau 1978. Also Briere and Blanchet 1979; this book has an interview with Michel Foucault appended to it.
19. There has been an extraordinary reluctance on the part of the press to say anything about the explicitly *religious* formulation of positions and policies inside Israel, especially when these are directed at non-Jews. There would be interesting material found in the Gush Emunim literature, or the pronouncements of the various rabbinic authorities, and so on.
20. See Garry Wills, "The Greatest Story Ever Told," subtitled "Blissed out by the pope's U.S. visit—'unique,' 'historic,' 'transcendent'—the breathless press produced a load of papal bull," *Columbia Journalism Review* 17, no. 5 (January–February 1980): 25–33.
21. This is a peculiarly American syndrome. In Europe, the situation *is* considerably more fair, at least as far as journalism on the whole *is* concerned.

References

Abrahamian, Ervand. 1968. "The Crowd in Iranian Politics, 1905–1953." *Past and Present* 41 (December): 184–210.

—1978. "Factionalism in Iran: Political Groups in the 14th Parliament (1944–46)." *Middle Eastern Studies* 14, no. 1 (January): 22–25.

—1979. "The Causes of the Constitutional Revolution in Iran." *International Journal of Middle East Studies* 10, no. 3 (August): 381–414.

—1980. "Structural Causes of the Iranian Revolution." *MERIP Reports* 87 (May): 21–26.

Alatas, Syed Hussein. 1977. *The Myth of the Lazy Native: A Study of the Image of the Malays, Filipinos, and Javanese from the 16th to the 20th Century and in the Ideology of Colonial Capitalism.* London: Frank Cass & Co.

Algar, Hamid. 1972. "The Oppositional Role of the Ulama in Twentieth Century Iran." In *Scholars, Saints, and Sufis: Muslim Religious Institutions Since 1500*, ed. Nikki R. Keddie, 231–55. Berkeley, Los Angeles and London: University of California Press.

Beeman, William O. 1980. "Devaluing Experts on Iran." *New York Times.* April 11.

Bill, James A. 1978–79. "Iran and the Crisis of '78." *Foreign Affairs* 57, no. 2 (Winter): 341.

—1980. "Iran Experts: Proven Right But Not Consulted." *Christian Science Monitor.* May 6.

Briere, Claire, and Blanchet, Pierre. 1979. *Iran: La Revolution au nom de Dieu.* Paris: Editions du Seuil.

Brun, Thierry-A. 1978. "The Failures of Western-Style Development Add to the Regime's Problems." In *Iran Erupts*, ed. Ali-Reza Nobari. Stanford, CA: Iran-America Documentation Group.

Buheiry, Marwan R. 1980. *U.S. Threats Against Arab Oil: 1973–1979*, IPS Papers 4. Beirut: Institute for Palestine Studies.

Childers, Erskine B. 1962. *The Road to Suez: A Study of Western-Arab Relations.* London: MacGibbon & Kee.

Chomsky, Noam. 1969. "Objectivity and Liberal Scholarship." In his *American Power and the New Mandarins: Historical and Political Essays*, 23–158. New York: Pantheon Books.

Cottam, Richard W. 1979. *Nationalism in Iran.* Pittsburgh, PA: University of Pittsburgh Press.

Daniel, Norman. 1960. *Islam and the West: The Making of an Image.* Edinburgh: Edinburgh University Press.

—1975. *The Arabs and Medieval Europe*. London: Longmans, Green & Co.

Djaït, Hichem. 1979. *L'Europe et l'Islam*. Paris: Editions du Seuil.

Eveland, Wilbur Crane. 1980. *Ropes of Sand: America's Failure in the Middle East*. New York: W. W. Norton & Co.

Geertz, Clifford. 1973. "The Integrative Revolution: Primordial Sentiments and Civil Politics in the New States." In his *The Interpretation of Cultures*. New York: Basic Books.

Gendzier, Irene L. 1978. "Notes Toward a Reading of *The Passing of Traditional Society*." *Review of Middle East Studies* 3: 32–47.

Ghareeb, Edmund, ed. 1977. *Split Vision: Arab Portrayal in the American Media*. Washington, DC: Institute of Middle Eastern and North African Affairs.

Graham, Robert. 1979. *Iran: The Illusion of Power*. New York: St. Martin's Press.

Grosrichard, Alain. 1979. *Structure du sérail: La fiction du despotisme asiatique dans l'Occident classique*. Paris: Editions du Seuil.

Halliday, Fred. 1979. *Iran: Dictatorship and Development*. New York: Penguin Books.

Hodgkin, Thomas. 1980. "The Revolutionary Tradition in Islam." *Race and Class* 21, no. 3 (Winter): 221–37.

Hodgson, Marshall G. S. 1974. *The Venture of Islam*. 3 vols. Chicago, IL and London: University of Chicago Press.

Hourani, Albert. 1980. "Islam and the Philosophy of History." In his *Europe and the Middle East*, 19–73. London: Macmillan & Co.

Jandaghi, Ali (pseud.). 1973. "The Present Situation in Iran." *Monthly Review* (November): 34–47.

Kerr, Malcolm. 1966. "Political Decision Making in a Confessional Democracy." In *Politics in Lebanon*, ed. Leonard Binder. New York: John Wiley and Sons.

Kramer, Martin. 1980. *Political Islam*. Washington, DC: Sage Publications.

Moniot, H., ed. 1976. *Le Mal de voir: Ethnologie et orientalisme: politique et epistémologie, critique et autocritique*. Cahiers Jussieu no. 2. Paris: Collections 10/18.

Nasir, Sari. 1979. *The Arabs and the English*. London: Longmans, Green & Co.

Peck, James. 1975. "Revolution Versus Modernization and Revisionism: A Two-Front Struggle." In *China's Uninterrupted Revolution: From 1840 to the Present*, ed. Victor G. Nee and James Peck. New York: Pantheon Books.

Rodinson, Maxime. 1979. *Marxism and the Modern World*. Trans. Michael Pallis. London: Zed Press.

—1980. *La fascination de l'Islam*. Paris: Maspéro.

Rokach, Livia. 1980. *Israel's Sacred Terrorism: A Study Based on Moshe Sharett's Personal Diary and Other Documents*. Intro. Noam Chomsky. Belmont, MA: Association of Arab-American University Graduates.

Rouleau, Eric. 1978. "Oil Riches Underwrite Ominous Militarization in a Repressive Society." In *Iran Erupts*, ed. Ali-Reza Nobari. Stanford, CA: Iran-America Documentation Group.

Said, Edward W. 1978. *Orientalism*. New York: Pantheon Books.

—1979. *The Question of Palestine*. New York: Times Books.

—1980. "Bitter Dispatches from the Third World." *The Nation* (May 3): 522–25.

Salem, Elie Adib. 1972. *Modernization without Revolution: Lebanon's Experience*. Bloomington and London: Indiana University Press.

Schaar, Stuart. 1979. "Orientalism at the Service of Imperialism." *Race and Class* 21, no. 1 (Summer): 67–80.

Sharett, Moshe. 1979. *Personal Diary*. Tel Aviv: Ma'ariv.

Shils, Edward. 1966. "The Prospect for Lebanese Civility." In *Politics in Lebanon*, ed. Leonard Binder. New York: John Wiley and Sons.

Starr, Paul, and Susan Starr. 1977. "Blindness in Lebanon." *Human Behavior* 6 (January): 56–61.

Sullivan, William H. 1980. "Dateline Iran: The Road Not Taken." *Foreign Policy* 40 (Fall): 175–86.

24

Islam and the Western Journalist

Edward Mortimer

"An expert is someone who did the story yesterday." I have often thought of that old Reuter's adage since the day, in the spring of 1973, when the then editor of the London *Times*, William Rees-Mogg, summoned me into his office and said, "Edward, would you do the Middle East?" I had recently joined the London staff of the paper as a leader-writer (what Americans call a member of the editorial board) with until then a rather ill-defined area of "expertise" in European affairs. Britain had just joined the European community, and my previous experience had been as a correspondent in the paper's Paris office. In that capacity I had covered one or two stories in the Maghrib, but to the Middle East proper I had never been.

I pointed this out to Mr. Rees-Mogg. "Well, of course you must go," he replied, and I went on a three-week tour of Israel, Jordan, Egypt and Lebanon. But even before I departed on this quasi-presidential "swing," I had written, and *The Times* had published, two leading articles on events in the Middle East. (Leading articles, or leaders for short, are unsigned editorials, supposedly reflecting the accumulated collective wisdom of a newspaper that had by then existed for 190 years, and had been known for a century as the "Jupiter," of whose thunder all British statesmen lived in fear.) Once I had got back to London and published my impressions of the Palestinian problem in three signed articles, my accreditation as an "expert" was complete. I could be interviewed by the BBC World Service for elucidation of an attempted coup in Iraq, or asked to lecture on "the Arab-Israeli dispute" at the Royal Staff College, Camberley.

If this sounds like boasting, it is not meant as such. My own role in this overnight "making of an expert" process was an almost passive one, and I am at least half ashamed of it, or anyway sheepish about it. I recount it only as an example of how journalism works. Journalism could be defined, I think, as "the production of general knowledge." A journalist is someone who has to sift the particular knowledge and experience of individuals or groups of people, and to extract from it a message which larger groups are able to understand and willing to hear. His true expertise is not in any subject matter but in the *rapid* assimilation and communication of facts and ideas.

I emphasize "rapid." The journalist does not have time to be an expert or specialist in the academic sense. He is a generalist, and his reports are always interim reports. His most essential qualification, without which he will never make a living in his chosen profession, has little to do with the substance of what he says or writes: it is the ability to produce the right amount of "copy" (that is, the right number of words), or in television the right "footage," at the right time. Next in importance comes the ability to say something intelligible, and preferably interesting, to the reader or audience. Only when those conditions are satisfied can a journalist begin to be judged by the relationship between what he says and "objective" reality, or truth.

The illusion persists, both outside journalism and to a lesser extent inside it, that reality is out there somewhere, ready-made, waiting to be found, like the treasure in a treasure-hunt, and that the journalist's task is simply to find it and bring it back undamaged to his public. Of course no one who has ever taken an elementary course in philosophy, no one who has even half understood the meaning of the word "epistemology," should succumb to this illusion. But most people either never did take such a course, or have long since forgotten it.

It does not occur to them that the "reality" which journalists are expected to report is essentially a reality of human experience, and that human experience is by definition subjective; that an "event" such as, let us say, a bombing raid in Lebanon or a demonstration in Tehran, is a composite of thousands of individual experiences, no two of which will be quite identical; and that none of those experiences will be shared by the reader or listener or watcher in America however technically perfect the process by which the "event" is transmitted to him. What you receive in America (or in Greenwich Village when the event is in the South Bronx, or vice versa) is, either literally or metaphorically, a picture in a frame. The composition of the picture is determined by the subjective outlook of the journalist(s) transmitting it, and *there is no way that that can be avoided.*

Most journalists become aware of this in the course of their work, even if they were not when they started, because of the frequency with which their honest efforts to report the truth as they see it are indignantly repudiated by people directly involved. At first the experience of repudiation is very hurtful to one's professional pride, and one is inclined to suspect the complainant's good faith. But after a bit one comes to realize that his experience is necessarily different from one's own, and that the experience of the reader or viewer or listener is necessarily different again. That realization is very dangerous. It is the moment when many journalists turn cynical. Since you *cannot* convey reality precisely, since in the last resort there is no precise reality to convey, why worry? All that's expected of you is a good story, so let them have it. Truth? What is truth?

The answer is that truth is *your* experience, *your* opinion, honestly arrived at and as intelligibly as possible conveyed. The public should not expect you to become someone else, still less to make *them* someone else. They do expect, and have a right to expect, that you yourself will make every effort to understand what is happening, to find the terms and concepts among your own mental furniture which best correspond to it, and to describe it using terms and concepts which you believe pave the same significative value for your public.

In other words, you must send them the picture which seems *to you* to convey the reality of the event most accurately. But you have to be aware that your perception of reality will be shaped by your own personality, preconceptions and values. You are almost bound to have some preconceptions about any subject you are reporting on, and your image of yourself—which includes, of course, your image of any group, such as a class, a profession, a race, a gender, a nation or a civilization, that you identify yourself with.

These observations may seem tiresomely general, if not self-evident.[1] They are certainly not peculiar to journalism in the Middle East, or to journalistic coverage of Islam. But they are still highly relevant to any consideration of those subjects. For if there is a general weakness in the treatment of the Islamic world by Western journalists, it is precisely that we tend a little too much to treat it as a special case. I think this is the hard core of Edward Said's complaint in his angry, rather confusing book, *Covering Islam*. He feels that the journalists have let themselves be towed along in the wake of the orientalists whom he castigated in his earlier book *Orientalism* for arbitrarily consigning millions of their fellow human beings to an artificial category (the Orient) in which the ordinary laws of human nature are thought to be superseded by special laws of oriental nature, many of them embodied in a mysterious, menacing entity called "Islam." Rather than applying their common sense to understanding events in the Islamic world, Said says in substance, journalists have tried to explain them in terms of the peculiarities of Islam as a religion, or of Islamic languages and cultures such as Arabic and Persian, which are supposed to predetermine the course of Muslim thought.

The result is that the Western public, instead of beginning to understand and sympathize with the various Muslim peoples, is confirmed in its view that they are inscrutable, irrational savages whose behavior is governed by an arcane but primitive moral code, and who are incapable of feeling normal human emotions. When they express resentment at the behavior of Western powers in their countries or regions, it is assumed that that resentment is not meaningfully related to actual Western behavior but proceeds from a deep-seated, irrational xenophobia. It is therefore thought to be futile for Western powers to take seriously any criticisms of their behavior emanating from the Muslim world; and any moral scruples about basing policy in that region purely on national self-interest, and relations with its peoples purely on coercion, are thereby banished. Thus orientalism, vulgarized through the news media, fulfills what Said sees as its traditional function: providing the ideological and psychological justification for Western violence against "Oriental" peoples.

Unhappily I think that this picture, even if somewhat overdrawn as I have summarized it, contains an element of truth. Said is, in my view, a little too prone to tar all journalists and all orientalists with the same brush. He grudgingly admits that in both professions there are honorable exceptions to his general thesis but brushes these aside as insufficient and insignificant. This judgment is of course no less subjective, and perhaps hardly less "reductive," than the judgments about the Islamic world which he is attacking. But the phenomenon he is describing does exist. There is, certainly, a connection between perceptions of national interest and the way that foreigners are portrayed in news media.

This is often particularly obvious in political cartoons, perhaps because the cartoonist usually has no direct contact with the foreigners he is depicting. He is dependent for his view of them entirely on other journalists, and the question of how they see themselves (let alone how they see his own country) is less likely to occur to him. Hence the innumerable cartoons which show racially stereotyped Arab shaykhs holding the world to ransom out of sheer greed or gratuitous malice. These were a staple of the American and British popular press throughout the middle and late 1970s, but in the summer of 1979 a particularly unpleasant one by Gerald Scarfe appeared even in the supposedly left-wing British weekly, *The New Statesman*. A further rich crop, on Islamic and related themes, sprang from the Iranian revolution and especially, of course, the taking of American hostages. To take an example more or less at random, here are two which appeared together in the *Washington Post* of January 3, 1981: one, by MacNelly from the *Richmond News Leader*, shows Iran as a concrete bunker against which "reason," used by Uncle Sam and others as a battering ram, is crumbling to smithereens; the other, by Auth from the *Philadelphia Inquirer*, shows an *ayatullah* with an evil grin who has just completed carving on stone tablets a new set of commandments such as "hate thy neighbor," "war on earth," "ill will toward men," etc.

Some Americans (and some Middle Easterners) believe that the European press is much better than the American press in this respect. Said himself encourages this by contrasting the record of *Le Monde*'s Eric Rouleau and the *Guardian*'s David Hirst— Middle East "experts" of at least fifteen or twenty years' standing—with the *New York Times*'s practice of changing its correspondents in the Middle East every two or three years. (The London *Times*, perhaps mercifully, is not mentioned!) But, whatever the case of the "quality" press, the popular press (at least in Britain) has nothing to envy its American counterparts in rabid anti-Arab and anti-Muslim prejudice.

One morning in September 1979 I was on my way to a seminar in London on "The Image of the Arab in the Western Mass Media," financed by the government of the

United Arab Emirates. I was just thinking that all this fuss about "image" was rather overdone, and that the Arabs ought to concentrate on putting up a better political and economic performance rather than whine about their image in the Western press, when the front page of that day's *Daily Express* caught my eye. "Arabs grab British girl," it said. This titillating headline turned out to be based on the disappearance, in Egyptian airspace, of a private plane carrying a Saudi millionaire and his entourage, which happened to include a British secretary. The only evidence that anyone had "grabbed" anyone was speculation that the plane might have been forced down by the Libyan airforce (how? where?) in order to disrupt an arms sale to Syria (why?) in which the millionaire was allegedly involved.

The sources quoted for this speculation were Lord Chalfont (a British journalist who once served in a Labour government but is now best known for his admiration of such anti-Soviet Third World "statesmen" as the late Shah of Iran) and Israeli intelligence. How many of those who saw the headline, I wondered, would actually read the story underneath, and how many who read the story would stop to think about its obvious weaknesses, rather than allow it to reinforce their assumption that "Arabs," in general, were a band of lustful villains from whom no British virgin was safe? Luckily Britain no longer has the military power to invade Arab countries, but if she did I fear that British public opinion would not be a serious obstacle, any more today than it was in the past.

Said is surely right, too, to pinpoint the relations between academia and journalism as a danger area. Journalists posing, or treating each other, as "experts" on matters they have no qualifications to discuss is one aspect of the problem. Academics acting as journalists is another. Academics, it seems to me, are in general even more aware than journalists are of the difference between the two professions and the different meanings they assign to the word "expert." There is a certain mutual contempt between the two. Journalists often despise academics for their inability to write to a deadline or to a precise length, for the obscurity of their language, for their unwillingness to give a straight, simple answer to a complex question. Yet many journalists also envy academics the time they have to pursue detail for its own sake, and to think, the space they have in which to hedge their bets and nuance their judgments, even the freedom they have to be dull when there is nothing sensational to report. If it were not so, would so many journalists accept one-year fellowships at universities, or at institutions like the Carnegie Endowment?

Academics often despise journalists for giving priority to speed over precision—which often seems like a cavalier disregard for accuracy, for their tendency to sensationalize, trivialize and oversimplify, for their impatience with qualifications or objections to a crude but striking generalization. But many academics also envy journalists the boldness with which they stick their necks out and make sweeping judgments, their involvement in the drama of events, and the size of the audience which they can address directly. If it were not so, would so many academics agree to be interviewed on television or be quoted in newspapers; indeed, would they contribute so many articles to newspapers and magazines themselves?

The trouble is that some academics have so low a notion of "journalistic" standards that when they stoop to journalism themselves they take liberties which a journalist would hardly get away with. Take, for instance, an article by Professor Walter Laqueur in *The New Republic* of October 11, 1980, welcoming the previous month's military coup in Turkey. Professor Laqueur accepts General Evren's own statement that the aim of the coup was "to prevent the followers of fascist and communist ideologies, as well as religious fanatics from destroying the Turkish Republic." It is "pointless," he says "now to demand the 'speedy restoration of democracy' in Turkey, since democracy, as we understand it, no longer existed even before the coup." Those are perfectly tenable opinions, but Laqueur goes on to support them with arguments which, at best, wildly oversimplify recent Turkish history. Referring to the terrorism of the last few years, he writes: "it seemed to be a contest of strength between the 'Marxist' extreme left and the Islamic far right. Why should there be so much hostility between the camp hoisting the red flags and quoting Lenin and the right-wingers displaying green banners invoking the Koran? ... On most questions there seems to be agreement. Both left and right are violently anti-Greek, anti-Israeli, and of course anti-Western, and both want to leave NATO."

What has happened here, as any of Professor Laqueur's research students working on Turkish politics could have told him, is that he has confused and for the purposes of argument amalgamated into a single "Islamic far right" two quite distinct political groups with different and largely opposing ideologies. The National Salvation Party (NSP) is indeed Islamic, anti-Israeli and anti-Western. But the National Action Party (NAP), correctly described by Laqueur later in the article as "para-fascist" (though the "para" is probably superfluous), is not anti-Western or anti-NATO at all, nor in any convincing way Islamic: it took to emphasizing Islam only in the last few years, partly because the NSP's electoral success suggested there were votes in it, and partly because, as the NAP leader, Colonel Alpaslan Türkeś, had put it to me earlier in 1980, "if you live empty [of religious faith] so communist ideology infiltrates very easily." It was the NAP and its "Idealist" youth movement that had made all the running in right-wing terrorism during the 1970s. Laqueur seems to be aware of this awkward gap in his argument, for he later writes, "the extreme right (or 'Idealists' as they prefer to be called) has espoused Panturanism and Moslem revivalism. While there is no more ideological unanimity on the extreme right than on the left, most of its factions seem to feel comfortable, broadly speaking, with some form of clerico-fascism such as recently appeared in other parts of the Middle East." He omits to mention that "Idealism" is linked specifically to the NAP, some sections of which are attracted by Panturanian ideas, whereas it is the NSP that expresses admiration for the Islamic revival and in particular the Iranian revolution.

There is no parallel in any Turkish party to the theocratic pretensions of the Iranian *'ulama'*—presumably what Laqueur means by "clerico-fascism." I don't believe

Professor Laqueur would try to get away with such sloppy and inexact arguments when writing in an academic journal. But in journalism, he seems to think, anything goes.

The same issue of *The New Republic* contained a piece by the New Zealand historian J. B. Kelly, at that time Wilson Guest Scholar at the Woodrow Wilson International Center for Scholars, whose theme is perfectly conveyed by its title: "Islam's Revenge—War Against the West." This includes the assertion that "the West"—an entity Kelly does not bother to define—"had been present in the Middle East in one form or another since long before the advent of Islam. Thereafter the role it played in the area more often than not was that of an adversary of Islam." Kelly argues the case for "Islam's" fundamental and unalterable hostility to the West with such verve that one is rather surprised, in the article's tenth column, to come across the admission that "Islam, for all the wordy pronouncements to the contrary, is a very tenuous bond among those who profess its tenets." But this statement is introduced only to refute the suggestion that the West should put any faith in affirmations of Islamic solidarity with the invaded Afghans. It does not, apparently, invalidate the view that *all* Muslims, beneath the skin, are incorrigibly anti-Western and untrustworthy and will stab the West in the back whenever they get the chance. Unfortunately, in Kelly's view, Western weakness and gullibility have been giving them the chance all too often of late. "Through their vacillation and willful self-delusion over the past decade, the Western nations have left themselves no alternative but to project their military power into the Gulf region."

J. B. Kelly, I am told, is a perfectly reputable academic historian. He was also once adviser on something-or-other to the Amir of Abu Dhabi. This makes him a "distinguished British Arabist" (he lives in London and used to teach at the School of Oriental and African Studies there) and thus a valuable supporter for the anti-Arab views favored by *The New Republic*. (The previous issue of the same magazine had carried an ecstatic review by Edward Luttwak of Kelly's book *Arabia, the Gulf and the West* whose jingoistic conclusion, urging modern Western powers to emulate "the captains-general of Portugal long ago" by having "the boldness to grasp" Oman while it is "still within their reach," is rightly characterized by Said in *Covering Islam* as "a little quaint.") All I am saying is that, like Laqueur, Kelly is setting a bad example to us journalists. Can we journalistic pseudo-experts be blamed for giving an over-simplified, schematic, alarmist picture of "Islam" when this is the kind of steer we get from the academics who should be the real experts? Is it surprising in these circumstances that Joseph Kraft reacts to the attempt on the Pope's life with a column devoted to "The Dark Side of Islam" containing so many manifest absurdities that he actually has to apologize for it in print the following week? Kraft, a mere journalist, does not get away with it. Laqueur and Kelly, as academic experts, apparently do. No apologies have yet been heard from them.

In point of fact, journalists were very slow to respond to academic promptings and take up "Islam" as a political theme. It was in January 1976 that Professor Bernard

Lewis's famous article, "The Return of Islam," appeared in *Commentary*. In this article Lewis complained of the unwillingness of correspondents for the *New York Times* and "other lesser newspapers" to face up to the importance of religion in the Lebanese conflict and, generally, in "the current affairs of the Muslim world." I do not presume to judge Professor Lewis as a scholar but I will say, having read two of his books and several of his articles, that he is a much better journalist than either Laqueur or Kelly, in the sense that he is much more careful about what he writes. I certainly was much impressed by the *Commentary* article when it came out. I learned from it, in particular, that national and confessional loyalties are much more closely related, not to say entangled, in the Middle East than in most Western countries (Northern Ireland being the obvious exception), and I have tried since then to allow for this in my own writing.

I was not fully convinced, however, by his statement that the use of "the language of left-wing and right-wing, progressive and conservative, and the rest of the Western terminology ... in explaining Muslim political phenomena is about as accurate and as enlightening as an account of a cricket match by a baseball correspondent." Against that I think one has to set the opinion of another orientalist, whose reputation as a scholar is not less than that of Professor Lewis, Maxime Rodinson, who wrote in 1972: "One should always look behind the words and ask the real questions: how is the social product redistributed? Who takes the investment decisions?" (1979, 213)

Not that these are the only "real questions"—Rodinson was referring specifically to models of economic development—but they are questions which are pertinent in any society, and the terminology that relates to them is not of exclusively Western application. I still think it is not unreasonable to refer to one side in the Lebanese conflict of 1975–76 as "the left," because it was seeking a redistribution of power and wealth in the country and the other side as "the right" because it was opposing that. It is true that most of those who believed they would benefit from such a redistribution were Muslims, and that many of them saw the conflict in sectarian terms. It is also true that virtually all those who fought on the other side were Christians, and that most of them did so because they believed that their community collectively had something to lose.

Obviously no simple formula can sum up all that was at stake. Perhaps "Christian Lebanese nationalist" would be a fair description for one side, and "an alliance of Muslim and secular radicals and Arab nationalists, supported by the Palestinians" for the other. But in journalism some sort of shorthand is necessary. Most of us fell back on "Muslim-leftist" and "right-wing Christian." If we had depicted it as a war between Islam and Christianity, as Professor Lewis seemed to hint we should, that would, I believe, have been more seriously misleading.

However that may be, the fact is that Professor Lewis's warning that we should take Islam more seriously as a political phenomenon went largely unheeded by the journalistic profession until the autumn of 1978, when we belatedly grasped the fact that what had seemed the strongest as well as the most pro-Western regime in the

Muslim world was being brought to its knees by crowds of people shouting "*Allahu akbar*." Up to that point, journalistic writing on Muslim countries paid very little attention to Islam as such.

Where we did allude to Islam it was generally in terms which suggested that it was virtually interchangeable with other religions, and particularly with Christianity, the religion with which most Western journalists are most familiar. (The fact that there is actually "incomparably larger common ground" between Islam and Judaism, as the late Professor Uriel Heyd pointed out [1968, 7], remains, so far as I know, completely unexplored by journalists.) Muslim countries, like other countries of the Third World, are assumed to be following along behind the West on a linear route of "modernization," which included secularization. Islam was assumed to be organized in some kind of church which would have to accept separation from the state and relegation to the area of private life. Where it intruded on public life its role was assumed to be reactionary.

It was Iran that jolted us out of that view—partially and temporarily at least; and yet, from today's perspective, it seems that in some ways that view was less out of place in Iran than in some other countries. If any form of Islam resembles Christianity then surely it is Iranian Shi'ism, with its Holy Family, its passion plays, its apostolic succession of imams, its emphasis on suffering, its ambivalent attitude towards temporal power and political involvement, its *mujtahids* acting as interpreters of God's Word for the faithful and forming a powerful, self-conscious institution largely independent from the state. That is the traditional "catholic" Shi'ism, so to speak, and then there is the new "protestant" Shi'ism of Ali Shari'ati, warning that the Imam may be living among us without being recognized; asserting that an uneducated person who reads the Qur'an and the life of Muhammad can be a better Muslim than a learned jurist or philosopher; proposing a "theology of liberation" which makes Imam Husayn the champion of the poor and the oppressed. Perhaps our mistake was not that we assumed a parallel between Islam and Christianity but that we failed to pursue the parallel far enough. Perhaps we had forgotten our own history. Was not the ideology of all the "progressive" movements of medieval and early modern Europe, including the one that created English-speaking America, expressed in religious terms?

Our linear view of Iran's development may have been facile, but one person who turns out to have shared it is Ayatollah Khomeini. Only he wanted to reverse the engine and pull Iran back up the line instead of further along it. The Western press was perhaps too prone to accept the Shah's view of himself as a modernizing leader, and to treat the various changes occurring in Iran—growing dictatorship, industrialization, urbanization, Westernization, agrarian reform, female emancipation— as a package. But Khomeini seems to have been more firmly convinced of this than most Western journalists, and even more certain that the package was to be rejected *en bloc* than they were that on balance it was worth having. The only aspects of the Shah's policies which he has allowed to continue are the suppression of dissent and the violations of human rights. The intervention of Iran's "clergy" in public life has indeed proved to be reactionary, by any known definition of that term.

366

The main difference in our perception today is that whereas we never dreamed such a thing could happen in Iran we are now constantly on the lookout for it in every Muslim country. Where before Islam was largely ignored, now it is seen everywhere, even where it has no particular relevance. The procedures of Iran's revolutionary courts, for instance, have been described as "Islamic" though as far as is known they are not based on any Islamic precedent. Since 1978 Professor Lewis must have read more about Islam, in the *New York Times* and "lesser" newspapers, than he ever bargained for or wished to. He and other orientalists have been quoted and interviewed to their heart's delight, and no doubt beyond. Is Islam essentially anti-Western, or essentially anti-communist, or both? Is it compatible with democracy, with human rights, with minority rights, with women's rights? Is it reactionary or revolutionary? Is it incurably violent, intolerant, despotic, anti-rational? These and others like them were the questions with which experts were constantly bombarded during 1979 and 1980.

In America such questions were usually asked in the expectation of an unpleasant answer. In Europe there was slightly greater interest in the idea that Islam might turn out to be a Good Thing. The above-mentioned Mr. Rees-Mogg, editor of the London *Times*, a Conservative and a Catholic, was on the whole encouraged by the "Islamic revival." Firmly convinced that the key to Britain's recovery lay in a revival of faith and of national tradition, he saw it as natural and good that Muslim societies were moving that way. He was, I think, the first journalist to express interest in its implications for the Muslim peoples of the Soviet Union. That type of interest increased enormously, of course, after the Soviet invasion of Afghanistan, when the idea that "Islam" and the West should combine to resist the Soviet tide became a major element of British foreign policy. Zbigniew Brzezinski also showed interest in that idea, but it was not followed up with the same eagerness by the American media. Both the hostage crisis and America's commitment to support Israel made an alliance with "Islam" rather difficult for Americans to imagine. The J. B. Kelly version of Islam was more saleable on the American market.

Either way, the Western media did come for a time[2] to accept the notion of Islam as a central factor in the life of all Muslim countries, linking them closely together and imposing a uniform pattern on their thought and behavior. This was encouraged not so much by academic experts, most of whom soon felt the thing was being wildly exaggerated, as by editors who liked a good, strong, simple, sensational idea (the idea of a series on "upsurge in Islam" virtually imposed itself after the Mecca siege and accompanying events in the first days of the year 1400 AH) and also by a number of Muslims. Many Muslims do, after all, passionately want to believe that Islam is the dominant force molding the society in which they live, and that the Islamic world is a single *umma* which will soon be restored to its historic unity and strength. Many Muslims quite sincerely believe that Islam is a complete social and economic system in its own right, distinct from both capitalism and socialism and needing to borrow nothing from either because it already contains the solution to every problem. Many believe that if only the *shari'a* were correctly understood and applied, injustice and crime could be abolished and an ideal society brought into existence.

Such people are often called "fundamentalists" but it is not clear what that means in the context of Islam. If it means believing that every word in the Qur'an and the *hadith* is literally true and requires no interpretation, then very few Muslims are fundamentalists, since virtually all Muslim schools of thought recognize the need for scholarship and set a high premium on it. If on the other hand it means an effort to define the fundamentals of one's religion and a refusal to budge from them once defined, then anyone with serious religious beliefs of any sort must be a fundamentalist. I think the French word *integrisme* better conveys the attitude of the Muslims I am talking about: I take it to mean the belief that Islam is a total system affecting all areas of human activity. Within that broad category, of course, there is room for many different interpretations. The alert journalist will soon notice this, and will therefore be cautious about accepting any one interpretation as "true Islam." But journalists should not be too harshly censured for taking seriously a view of Islam to which many Muslims are deeply committed.

What it does seem reasonable to ask of journalists is that they try not to start from the assumption that Muslims are different and that their behavior can *only* be explained in terms of Islam—or for that matter in terms of a particular Muslim culture. Of course one should not ignore Islam. For some time yet one will find it difficult to do that even if one wants to. No doubt cultural patterns and traditions do affect human behavior. After all what Edward Said himself is writing about is in large part the way that certain cultural patterns affect Western journalistic behavior. He would hardly deny that the same exercise could be valid for Iranian *'ulama'* or Palestinian *fida'iyin* or, for that matter, himself. But it seems reasonable to assume that when a major social change occurs, involving large masses of people, then cultural patterns are likely to explain the form rather than the substance of the change. The form will be interesting, perhaps picturesque, certainly worth describing; a journalist is not sent to a foreign country to ignore everything that makes it different from his own. But a good journalist will not let the form obscure the substance. He will be wise to adopt, at least as a working hypothesis, the assumption that behavior can be *explained* in terms of human needs and emotions which are recognizable to his audience or public.

Here is a small example. At a certain point in the later stages of the hostage negotiations it was announced in Tehran that the mutual fulfillment of the conditions of the agreement by Iran and the United States would be the subject of a *tahod* by the Algerian government. Different translations of this Persian word were given. Some said it meant the Algerians had agreed to guarantee the fulfillment of the agreement, which would in effect have broken the deadlock. Others said they had only promised their "best endeavors," which would have meant very little. John Kifner, who had the very difficult job of reporting the negotiations for the *New York Times*, was naturally exasperated by this lack of precision, and blamed it on the "elusive quality of the Persian language," which, he said, was "more suitable for poetry than for politics."

He might have asked himself in which known language there is no word that can mean different things in different contexts. As it happens, the English word "undertake" contains precisely the same ambiguity: if you undertake to do something, you may be promising to do it, or you may be simply trying. The Iranian prime minister, in using the word *tahod*, may have been accidentally or deliberately ambiguous. In either case he would not be the first politician, nor a peculiarly Iranian one, to confuse his audience. Funnily enough, at that very time the American press was full of caustic comments about the imprecise use of the language by the Secretary of State designate, General Alexander Haig.

Similar questions should be asked before one describes the political importance of personal relationships as a peculiarly Saudi phenomenon, or the overlapping of religion and politics as a peculiarly Muslim one. Did Iran's grievances against the United States arise from some primitive Islamic code of justice, or was Iran not accusing Americans of violating the code of international relations to which they themselves claim to subscribe? And so on.

Once again, this problem is not peculiar to the Muslim world. It affects any attempt to report on one culture for another culture. One must give due weight to the specifics of the other culture. But one must also try to avoid using cultural differences as a screen to conceal from oneself, and from one's public, social, political and economic aspirations which are in fact perfectly intelligible in terms of one's own culture. The fact that some Muslims *want* Islam to be treated as a special case is not an excuse. Of course one must show respect for their beliefs. But showing respect does not mean refusing to judge them by one's own standards. If one has standards worth the name one must believe that they are valid for everybody. If we refrain from analyzing Muslim societies in the light of our own values we are in fact showing not respect but condescension.

Notes

1. I believe they are self-evident, in the sense that few people will deny them once they understand them. Yet all of us constantly speak and write as though they were not true.
2. The fashion may already have passed. Islam was barely mentioned, for instance, in *Newsweek*'s July 1981 cover story on Qadhdhafi.

References

Heyd, Uriel. 1968. *Revival of Islam in Modern Turkey*. Jerusalem: Magnes Press.

Rodinson, Maxime. 1979. *Marxism and the Muslim World*. London: Zed Press (French original, 1972).

Said, Edward. 1978. *Orientalism*. New York: Pantheon Books.

—1981. *Covering Islam*. New York: Pantheon Books.

GLOSSARY

adat (Ar. *'ada*)	customary practice or law
'ahd	covenant
'alim (pl. *'ulama'*)	learned person
Allahu a'lam	God knows best
amir	commander
'aqa'id	beliefs, creeds
ashraf (sing. *sharif*)	descendants of Muhammad
ayat	verses (of the Qur'an)
baraka	blessing
batin	hidden, interior
bida'	innovation
dakwah	preach, proselytizing, religious
dar al-Islam	House of Islam
datu	title of royalty, tribal chieftain
al-da'wa ila 'l-tawhid	the call to profess the unity of God
da'wa	summons to Islam
dhikr	recollection, repetition, Sufi ritual

dihqan	member of a lesser feudal nobility
din	religion
dini	religious
faqih	jurist
fara'id	laws
fatawa/fatwa	legal ruling of a *mufti*
fatiha	first chapter for the Qur'an
fiqh	law
fitra	natural disposition of humans towards Islam
furu'	articles of law
hadith	traditions from or about Muhammad
hajj	pilgrimage to Mecca
halal	permitted by law (often for food)
haram	forbidden by law
hijri	Muslim calendar reckoning
ibadat	laws covering ritual activities
'id al-adha	festival in the pilgrimage
'id al-fitr	festival at the end of Ramadan
ijma'	legal consensus
ijtihad	independent reasoning
'ilm al-bayan	understanding, explication
iman	faith
isnad	chain of transmitters of a *hadith* report
jahili/jahiliyya	(belonging to) the age of ignorance
jihad	striving for God; holy war
jinn	genie
juma'	Friday noon prayer
kafir	unbeliever
kalima	the "word", that being the *shahada*, the witness to faith
khalifa	caliph
khatib	person delivering the sermon in the Friday noon prayer
khutba	sermon in Friday noon prayer
la ilah illa Allah	there is no god but God

Mahdi	foretold messiah-like person
majaz	figurative language
mashaikh (*mashayikh*)	elder(s)
mawlid al-nabi	celebration of the birthday of Muhammad
Muhammad rasul Allah	Muhammad is the messenger of God
Murji'a	early theological group
mutashabihat	the unclear verses of the Qur'an
muwahhidun	those who believe in the oneness of God
pir	Sufi saint
qadi	judge
qanun	land taxes, code of regulations of the state
Ramadan	month of fasting
salat	prayer
sawah	irrigated crops
shahada	witness to faith
shari'a	legal path of Islam
sharif (pl. *ashraf*)	descendant of Muhammad
shaykh/sheikh	elder, respected person
shirk	polytheism, unbelief
silsila	spiritual chain of descent
siyasa	politics and political policy
sunna	Muhammad's example
sunna of God	the nature way things happen in creation
surau	prayer house/mosque
tabi'a	successor generation after the companions of Muhammad
taluqdar	a great landholder
tariqa (pl. *turuq*)	Sufi group or order
tawba	fear of God
tawhid	unity of God
turuq (sing. *tariqa*)	Sufi groups or orders
'ulama' (sing *'alim*)	learned people
umm al-kitab	mother of the book
'ushr	tithe, tax on land owned by Muslims or on commercial goods

ustaz	professor, learned person
usul	sources
zahir	apparent or obvious meaning
zakat	charity
zamindar	landowner, collector of land revenue

Index of Authors

Index of Subjects